The Hub

A PLACE FOR READING AND WRITING

Dear Instructor,

Over the last ten years, developmental writing and reading courses at colleges across the country have undergone immense changes: corequisite models such as the Accelerated Learning Program (ALP) are spreading quickly, reading and writing are being integrated, faculty are implementing active learning approaches, and instructors are more frequently choosing to address the challenges students face in balancing school, work, and life issues. These seismic changes in the way we teach developmental writing and reading are the primary reasons for the creation of *The Hub: A Place for Reading and Writing*.

Photo courtesy of Donna Crivello

As faculty members at the Community College of Baltimore County, we pioneered ALP to meet the needs of our students. Our model took shape through many brainstorming sessions, conferences by active learning specialists, and continuous research around our students' outcomes and our courses. It emerged as the best model we could create to support our students, and better still, as further research by our faculty and others confirmed, it works.

Based on my experience developing ALP, and on my thirty-six years of experience teaching writing, I developed *The Hub: A Place for Reading and Writing* to bring students and instructors all of the materials and support they need to succeed in the composition classroom. I have designed *The Hub* around a series of carefully scaffolded multipart reading and writing projects that offer abundant opportunities for students to develop rhetorical knowledge, genre awareness, and critical reading and writing skills. At the same time, *The Hub* provides ideas, topics, activities, and other resources to support underprepared students and help accelerate their development into confident and successful college readers and writers.

The Hub is the result of all of the research and classroom work I've spent my career doing. The inquiry-based, active learning pedagogy you'll find in *The Hub* is thoroughly classroom-tested. The advice for instructors is based on the best practices for corequisite composition courses, as validated by outcomes research. I firmly believe it will help your students learn and succeed, just as it helped mine. So, welcome to *The Hub*! I hope you'll find it the place—your place—for reading and writing.

—*Peter*

The Hub

A PLACE FOR READING AND WRITING

SECOND EDITION

B
Balancing School,
Work, and Life

P
Reading/Writing
Projects

D
Research and
Documentation

W
Writing

R
Reading

for North Central Texas College

Peter Adams

Community College of Baltimore County, Emeritus

bedford/st.martin's
Macmillan Learning

Boston | New York

For Bedford/St. Martin's

Vice President, Humanities: Leasa Burton
Program Director: Laura Arcari
Senior Program Manager: Nancy Tran
Director of Content Development: Jane Knetzger
Senior Development Editor: Leah Strauss
Executive Development Editor: Jane Carter
Associate Media Editor: Paola Garcia-Muniz
Editorial Assistant: Kalinda Collins
Director of Media Editorial: Adam Whitehurst
Senior Media Editor: Sarah Gatenby
Executive Marketing Manager: Joy Fisher Williams
Senior Market Development Manager: Azelie Fortier
Senior Director, Content Management Enhancement: Tracey Kuehn
Senior Managing Editor: Michael Granger
Senior Digital Content Project Manager: Ryan Sullivan
Senior Workflow Project Manager: Lisa McDowell
Production Supervisor: Jose Olivera
Director of Design, Content Management: Diana Blume
Interior Design: Diana Blume, Claire Seng-Niemoeller
Cover Design: William Boardman
Director of Rights and Permissions: Hilary Newman
Text Permissions Editor: Allison Ziebka-Viering
Text Permissions Researcher: Elaine Kosta, Lumina Datamatics, Inc.
Photo Researcher: Cheryl Du Bois, Lumina Datamatics, Inc.
Director of Digital Production: Keri deManigold
Associate Media Project Manager: Sophie Good
Copyeditor: Nancy Benjamin, Lumina Datamatics, Inc.
Composition: Lumina Datamatics, Inc.
Printing and Binding: King Printing Co., Inc.

Library of Congress Control Number: 2022949593
ISBN 978-1-319-49356-1

Printed in the United States of America.

1 2 3 4 5 6   28 27 26 25 24 23

Acknowledgments

Text acknowledgments and copyrights appear at the back of the book on pages 698–700, which constitute an extension of the copyright page. Art acknowledgments and copyrights appear on the same page as the art selections they cover.

At the time of publication all internet URLs published in this text were found to accurately link to their intended websites. If you do find a broken link, please forward the information to TheHub@macmillan.com so that it can be corrected for the next printing.

For information, write: Bedford/St. Martin's, 75 Arlington Street, Boston, MA 02116

Preface for North Central Texas College

NCTC's First-Year Composition Curriculum: An Overview

Welcome to English Composition at North Central Texas College! You've signed up for Integrated Reading and Writing (INRW 0305), Composition I (ENGL 1301), or Composition II (ENGL 1302). We are excited that you've enrolled in the course and that you're here at NCTC.

We've designed this course in keeping with the college's mission and values statement:

> **NCTC Mission:** North Central Texas College is dedicated to student success through institutional excellence.

> **NCTC Values Statement:** North Central Texas College is accountable to its students, colleagues, and the community and holds the following values to be fundamental: an affordable, quality education; stimulating learning environments; integrity; innovation; cohesive relationships; and encouragement.

This course is part of a year-long study of a common theme that centers around students' writing and reading interests. This custom rhetoric textbook is bundled with our year-long common reads and an access code to *Achieve* for additional resources and support. At the end of this semester, we encourage you to sign up for the next course in your communication core and continue to use these texts in the following semesters. Completing your First-Year Composition (FYC) courses within an academic year will save you money on books, and research shows that students are more successful if they take FYC courses in succession and early in their academic careers. (So, be sure to keep your access code.)

This bundle consists of a custom writing textbook, the common reads, and access to the online course materials. We also created specific courses in Canvas designed to meet your needs with this bundle. Our goal is to align our multiple campuses, dual credit sites, online courses, and developmental courses to provide you with an academically rigorous and meaningful experience. As an added benefit, proceeds from the textbook sales will be used to bring the authors to campus.

This custom textbook is specific to NCTC and is composed of two parts:

> The first part, the preface, includes a description of the course outcomes, required writing assignments, and assessment rubrics. The assignments facilitate alignment between the composition courses and provide consistent experiences that scaffold from one semester to the next. Your instructors have collaborated on course design and assessment best practices for our diverse students, and we have designed this custom preface so that the assignments are open-ended. The rubrics are also holistic and complement your class's interests, your instructor's expertise, and the department's goals for consistency, transparency, and rigor.

> The second part is a writing and rhetoric textbook, *The Hub*. We've carefully selected the chapters that we believe are relevant to our students for this custom textbook. Because INRW 0305 students use the exact text as students in ENGL 1301 and ENGL 1302, we hope that all students moving through the communications core feel more confident with the course readings and course design.

The common reads are books related to the year's selected theme. Each spring semester, the college will invite your texts' authors to campus.

We hope that our year-long theme and common reads encourage you to develop a "community of scholars" with each other—adding energy, excitement, and urgency to your writing courses. Your English faculty members at NCTC are committed to your success. We all want the best *from* you and the best *for* you, and we're excited to explore this topic together in a series of invitational, rigorous courses that inspire your curiosity.

> We are not here to drill pupils in spelling, punctuation, and grammar, but to bestow upon them the potentiality of service of thousands and perhaps millions of their [people]—to develop in them the power to move humanity to noble deeds by the communication of the truth. If there is in the teaching profession a higher or a more stimulating function than that, I do not know what it is. —Fred Newton Scott

First-Year Composition Focus 2022–2023

You probably have never heard of Mike Rose, but in a very real way, he is responsible for you reading this introduction to this textbook. Mike Rose, who died in 2021, believed all people, no matter where they start or what obstacles they do or do not have stacked against them, possess the ability to succeed. In the introduction to his book, *The Mind at Work,* Rose writes,

> I grew up a witness to the intelligence of the waitress in motion, the reflective welder, the strategy of the guy on the assembly line. This, then, is something I know: the thought it takes to do physical work. Such work put food on our table, gave shape to stories of affliction and ability, framed how I saw the world.
>
> Measures of intellectual ability and assumptions about it are woven throughout this history. So I've been thinking about this business of intelligence for a long time: the way we decide who's smart and who isn't, the way the work someone does feeds into that judgment, and the effect such judgment has on our sense of who we are and what we can do.

During this course, you'll have an opportunity to read and hear Rose's views on the work of learning and how often society underestimates learners. Rose and teachers like him are the inspiration for the first-year writing program here at NCTC.

In an essay posted to his blog in 2016, Rose shares several tips on writing and thinking. These tips are as relevant to you, a first-year writing student at a Texas community college, as they are to the UCLA graduate students Rose was writing to. In his first tip, Rose tells us to "pay attention" to our writing. This seems natural enough, coming from a writing teacher, but Rose does not see writing as only something we do while in school. Writing is "invaluable," he explains, and "an exceptionally potent tool … as you see things that trouble you and you want to give voice to or—something we don't do enough—when you see things that need to be celebrated."

Rose implores us to view writing as a skill worth practicing and improving because it is a skill that empowers the writer as a thinker and as an achiever. Some of you (a lot of you?) may be rolling your eyes right now.

Fair enough.

But let's consider bell hooks, one of the most influential thinkers, writers, and educators of the late 20th and early 21st centuries. Like Mike Rose, bell hooks died in 2021, and as with Rose, thinkers, writers, former students, and readers shared essay after essay and remembrance after remembrance of the effect hooks had on them through her writing and her emphasis on speaking out and talking back.

In a memorial essay in *The New Yorker,* Hua Hsu reminds us that bell hooks began as Gloria Watkins, born in highly segregated Kentucky in 1952. Her father was a janitor, and her mother was a maid. The schools that hooks attended were segregated. In her autobiographical writings, hooks explain that as a Black girl growing up in 1950s America, "to make yourself heard … was to invite punishment, the back-hand lick, the slap across the face that would catch you unaware" (5). These silencings had the desired effect, for although in intimate spaces of women, between sisters, mothers and daughters, and friends, women spoke with "pleasure" and "joy" along with "loud talk" and "angry words" within the community (whether the household kitchen or the national forum), "the voices of black women … could be tuned out, could become a kind of background music, audible but not acknowledged as significant speech" (hooks 6). It was significant, though, and hooks understood that it needed to be recorded, held onto, and considered: to be written.

For hooks and for you, writing may be "not solely an expression of creative power" but also "an act of resistance" (8). Let's consider two other of Mike Rose's "Tips on Thinking and Writing": "Investigate the things that trouble you" and "Whatever it is you're interested in or become interested in … learn its history." In the common read for INRW and ENGL 1301, *The Address Book*, Deirdre Mask writes that her book, which explores *What Addresses Reveal about Identity, Race, Wealth, and Power*, began with a simple act, mailing a birthday card from Ireland to her father in North Carolina, and a question, how do letters, bills, tax forms, and other important documents find us? This simple question about the process led to a deep exploration of how an address can determine much about a person's financial, political, and career potential. Throughout *The Address Book*, Mask demonstrates Rose's argument that through careful investigation, "you will have a better understanding of what you [see], a deeper grasp of the dynamics and background factors of what [troubles] you—which puts you in a better position to critique…in a substantial and principled way" ("Tips on Thinking and Writing"). Mask argues that our home addresses "are about identity, wealth, and … race. But most of all they are about power—the power to name, the power to shape history, the power to decide who counts, who doesn't, and why" (13). She can make that argument because she investigated what troubled her and learned it deeply. Like Rose, Mask understands that studying the history of an idea or situation—where it began and how it developed—equips us to recognize and act on opportunities for change.

Recognition is not a matter of instinct, however, and we must move beyond feeling or even belief. In ENGL 1302, you will be reading and writing with a book called *Factfulness*, which represents the life-long work of Hans Rosling, a physician and researcher on issues of health on a global scale. Rosling's ideas and arguments have been shared on stage in front of the most influential people in the world. Yet, in his work, Rosling follows two final tips from Mike Rose's simple list for students: seek out multiple types of evidence (e.g., qualitative and quantitative—that is, stories and numbers) and remember that human behavior is complex while individual perspectives are limited ("Tips on Thinking and Writing"). Rosling's book shows us those limits and challenges us to face our wrongness about the world. *Factfulness* is honest and full of all the statistics and facts that show us where the world is, where we started, and how far we have come. Although each chapter is filled with infographics to show the data, each also shares stories that reveal the common humanity within the numbers: the fears, hopes, and progress. Through *Factfulness*, Rosling hopes to "awaken [readers] curiosity about what is possible, which is different from what they believe, and from what they see in the news every day" (16). His aim, like Rose's and like your composition teachers', is to equip you with knowledge and tools for writing and thinking so that when you do find an idea worth grasping or a problem worth investigating, you'll be prepared.

> This past teaching year, a student confronted me in class with the question of what I expected from them ... I told him and the class that I thought the most important learning experience that could happen in our classroom was that students would learn to think critically and analytically, not just about the required books, but about the world they live in. (hooks, 102)

Strategies for Success: Writing in First-Year Composition

First-Year Composition courses have several goals: to prepare you for the demands of writing in your classes throughout your academic career, to help you understand and deconstruct writing situations so you can write effectively in the workplace, and to help you develop an appreciation and love of language that sparks your curiosity and brings you joy.

These are grand ambitions. Your instructors are committed to helping you achieve these goals. Still, you also have to do your part to succeed in this course. Here are some tips to help you be a successful student:

Consider your audience. As you write your papers, think about your audience's expectations. Specifically, academic readers favor logic over emotion, demand evidence for claims that are made (often even for what might appear to be minor claims), define "interesting" as the originality of thought and potential for intellectual stimulation, favor directness and clarity over inference when they read academic papers, define "creative" more in terms of originality of ideas than in stylistic flourish, and read carefully, actively, and methodically.

Take responsibility for your learning. You can't be a passive observer in your classes and expect to learn. Active learning requires engagement, participation, focus, and time. Your instructor will create optimal conditions for your success; however, you still have to work.

Come to class and participate. Research shows that students who regularly come to class are more successful in their courses. So come to class consistently, on time, and arrive prepared with your book, notebook, assignments, and readings. Take notes, highlight and annotate your texts, ask questions, and avoid distractions. When in class, you'll have opportunities to get additional feedback from your instructor and peers, so ask questions, and seek clarification. Take advantage of those opportunities to be an active participant and not merely a passive observer. Avoid the temptation to "check out" if the conversation steers into unfamiliar or uninteresting territory to you. Be fully present and engaged in class discussion to get as much out of the experience as possible. Find ways to communicate in the classroom. If you're not comfortable sharing in front of everyone, find a different way to engage with the conversation.

Get to know your classmates. Coming to class helps you learn from your classmates and support each other. It's essential to "collaborate to graduate." After all, the first word in "community college" is "community." Four thousand other students are enrolled in INRW 0305, ENGL 1301, and ENGL 1302 at NCTC, so don't be afraid to talk to your peers in class or in other courses.

Be curious. You will take courses that do not appear to dovetail perfectly with your interests throughout your college career. Nonetheless, in every college course, you have the chance to explore the materials deeply and in a manner that sustains your attention and enriches your understanding. You will be encouraged to narrow the focus of consideration and discussion in each course. Seize this opportunity to find ways to make the reading and writing compelling and relevant to you. However, to achieve this, you must be willing to look beyond obvious answers, interpretations, and viewpoints. Follow up with your instructor and classmates if you're stuck and don't know how to proceed with a topic. Above all, don't be afraid to ask questions.

Take risks. Move beyond apparent observations and tired arguments. Look for opportunities to challenge the status quo, explore new ideas, and be inspired. You can challenge an idea or belief and come out on the other side okay. Be open to new ideas and respectfully question everything in the spirit of exploration.

Plan ahead. Effective academic writing takes time, reflection, and revision. Waiting until the last minute does not provide the time and space to produce your best work. Students often think that they write their best work under pressure, but really, students do their best writing when they have time to revisit their ideas, seek feedback, and work toward greater clarity.

Visit with your instructors. All NCTC instructors keep office hours at designated times—at least two hours each week for each course—to meet with students and provide additional feedback and support. Check your syllabus for your instructor's hours, and make a point to stop by to ask questions and get clarification on assignments or ideas. Don't give up if you can't meet with your instructor during posted office hours. Ask to schedule some time to chat before or after class, on the phone, or via Webex. Email your instructor to schedule an appointment.

Don't cheat. Remember that your first-year composition courses are designed to prepare you for the demands of writing in your future classes and your profession. If you cheat or plagiarize, you are only hurting yourself in the long run. Ultimately, you are responsible for your education and experience, and you will suffer consequences immediately and in the future.

Pay attention to the details. Read the assignment directions in this book and your instructor's specific directions, follow the minimum requirements, and review the evaluation criteria. Part of paying attention to the details is planning, so you have enough time to make minor changes and revise your drafts to meet the requirements for the assignment.

Use your resources. You have access to the NCTC library and campus writing centers. Further, you also have access to books, academic journals, films, newspapers, and study rooms. If the NCTC libraries don't have a source you need, the librarians will locate the source at another library and have it shipped to NCTC for you to pick up. In the writing centers, tutors can help you with all stages of the writing process: brainstorming, locating research, drafting, and revising. Online tutoring is also available. Successful students find and take advantage of support and resources to help them to be successful.

Strategies for Success: Reading in Academic Contexts

John Locke writes, "Reading furnishes our mind only with materials of knowledge; it is thinking [that] makes what we read ours." Reading to think and reading to write can be challenging, but they are essential skills to practice. Being a stronger writer means you are also working on being a stronger reader. In college and your career, you will be expected to read, understand, and use information from textbooks, articles, reports, manuals, charts, case studies, poetry, nonfiction, editorials, fiction, brochures, and proposals. Furthermore, you will be expected to figure out what each text means to you personally and not simply what it generally means.

Active reading skills are vital as you progress through your courses and beyond. Active reading differs from passive reading because active reading means you do something (e.g., take notes, highlight, or annotate) while you read. Instructors will not assign reading as busywork. Your instructors choose readings for a reason, and you need to know what the reason is. Before you read, ask yourself (and, if needed, your instructor) the following questions:

- Are you preparing to write a summary, response, analysis, or research paper?

- Are you preparing for class discussion?

- Are you reading to prepare for a lecture or a test?

Knowing your purpose determines your approach and engagement with the text.

Your instructor will discuss many suggestions and strategies for success when reading academic texts. Here are a few to help get you started:

Read strategically. Not everything you read in college will be enjoyable. The assigned texts may be dense, have an unknown vocabulary, and be boring. Give yourself time to read, re-read, and comprehend the materials.

Preview the text and adjust your reading speed. Challenging assignments will take longer to read, so allow for that time. Consider what you already know about the topic and skim the text to understand the organization and structure.

Annotate. Taking notes forces you to read carefully, and understanding your purpose will help determine what you should annotate. Use a pen or a highlighter. If reading online, have a notepad in front of you to write down significant points or comments. But don't overuse it. Easy annotations to start with are questions about the text.

Consider the rhetorical situation. Note any words that indicate the author's stance or tone. Think about the audience and mark anything that illustrates how the author addresses the audience's needs.

Read your textbooks. Divide your reading into manageable pieces. If the passage is not making sense, take a break. Your brain may be tired and need a rest. Another strategy is to read the assigned material aloud. Doing so may help you process the material in a new way.

Talk back to the text. Write comments, questions, or interesting observations in your book or a notebook, especially if you know there will be a class discussion or lecture over the material. If you cannot write in the book, use a notebook or post-it notes to keep track of the main ideas, questions, and comments.

Strategies for Success: Understanding Arguments

When thinking about arguments, it's helpful to start with a basic definition:

> An argument is a disputable claim supported by facts or reasons.

Notice that the claim has to be disputable. For example, the claim that regular tobacco use can be harmful is not an argument because most people would agree.

It's also helpful to recognize different types of arguments that people make. Though people may seem to be making many different types of arguments, in many cases, their claims boil down to one of two types.

- Fact-based claims (Is it true?)
- Value-based claims (Is it good?)

Since these two types are the most common, we'll focus on them in this section. We'll also discuss some common logical fallacies or types of deceptive or misleading arguments.

Fact-Based Arguments

Students are sometimes confused by the term "fact-based argument"; if something is a fact, they ask, how can someone argue about it? Fact-based claims occur whenever people disagree about the truth of some claim. For example, although most people would agree that regular tobacco use can be harmful, there is disagreement (even among experts) about whether moderate consumption of diet sodas is harmful.

Factual claims rely on proof that something is true or not true and rely on facts to challenge or change people's beliefs. Factual arguments rely on extensive research to support claims (e.g., scientific studies, encyclopedia entries, and textbooks).

Fact-based arguments are inductive arguments that rely on logos. In other words, the truth of a claim is based on the amount and quality of the evidence presented. When writing a fact-based argument, it is important to allow plenty of time and energy to locate, identify, interpret, and relay the research.

There are different types of factual arguments:

- **Existence** claims argue that something does or doesn't exist.

- **Occurrence** claims argue that something did or didn't happen.

- **Causal** claims argue that one action did or didn't lead to another. Causal arguments identify causes or possible effects. For example, a student's paper that argues that fast food advertising contributes to the obesity epidemic presents a **causal** argument.

Value-Based Arguments

Value claims rely on the author demonstrating that something is or isn't moral (e.g., good, right, fair, just). Such arguments rely on abstract concepts such as good, right, duty, obligation, virtue, honor, and choice. For example, a newspaper editorial that argues that torture is never justified because torture is wrong is presenting an **ethical** argument.

Value claims are deductive arguments: the truth of the claim is based on connecting it to a generally accepted moral value or an ordinary human moral intuition.

Value-based arguments can rely on ethos, logos, and pathos for proof. To prove a value-based argument, writers might rely on the ethical arguments made by other writers.

Composite Arguments

Composite arguments combine factual- and value-based claims. The most common type of composite argument is a proposal argument. **Proposal** arguments suggest a solution to a problem to convince people that a problem exists and that the solution is both practical and worthwhile. For example, a research paper that argues that more psychological resources should be available to gastric bypass patients is a **proposal** argument. This argument combines an implied factual claim (i.e., psychological resources can benefit gastric bypass patients) and an ethical claim (i.e., society has a moral obligation to improve the mental health of its citizens).

Evaluation-Based Arguments

Evaluative or interpretative claims express an opinion about the quality of an item, product, service, performance, program, or work of literature or art. An example of an evaluation argument might be a film review that argues that *Citizen Kane* is the most important film in cinematic history. Another evaluative argument might argue that standardized tests are poor measures of student learning. Other examples include literary analyses and legal arguments.

Logical Fallacies

Logical fallacies are common errors in reasoning. Understanding the most common logical fallacies is important because, once you understand them, you'll be a more critical thinker and mindful of how they influence audiences.

Anecdotal

This fallacy relies on personal experience and observation to prove a claim. While personal stories can be compelling, they are insufficient proof for proving a fact-based claim because they may not represent the most common situation. For fact-based claims, the quality and the amount of evidence matters. One research study is better proof than an anecdote from a friend, but multiple research studies would be even better proof. Below are examples of anecdotal fallacies:

> "I use social media, and I've never been bullied. Therefore, cyberbullying is not an issue."

> "I took an herbal supplement, and my headache went away. Therefore, herbal supplements are useful for treating headaches."

One person's experience with cyberbullying or herbal supplements is insufficient evidence to make a fact-based claim.

Faulty Analogy

The fallacy of false analogy arises when one attempts to prove or disprove a claim using an analogy that is not suitable for the situation. One makes wrong assumptions about a situation based on observations from another situation. Below are examples of faulty analogy arguments:

> "To say humans are immortal is like saying a car can run forever."

> "Making people register their guns is like the Nazis making the Jews register with their government."

> "People who buy stocks are no different from people who bet on horse racing. They both risk their money with little chance of making a big profit." ("Faulty Analogy")

False Dilemma

This fallacy simplifies an argument's premise by suggesting a limited number of options, such as an either/or proposition or that an issue is either "black or white." There may be many options; however, a false dilemma dishonestly oversimplifies the argument. False dilemmas are much like playing a game of "would you rather?" Below are examples of false dilemma arguments:

> "Facebook: Love it or leave it."

> "You can use social media or live in isolation."

> "Would you rather have free speech online or live in a totalitarian state?"

Non-Sequitur

The conclusions drawn from non-sequitur arguments "do not follow" the reasoning or rationale provided. Non-sequiturs do not follow logic and introduce arguments that are beside the point, are often untrue, rely on absurd reasoning, or jump to conclusions. Below are examples of non-sequitur arguments:

"If drinking and driving are dangerous, then so is social media."

"Young people are not politically engaged because they spend too much time on social media."

"Social media is democratic because everyone has access to it."

Post-Hoc

This fallacy means "after this therefore because of this." Post-hoc arguments suggest false causes: something happened entirely because of something else. Superstitions are based on post-hoc arguments: While a football player might have won a game while wearing striped socks, it doesn't mean that the team won because of the socks. A counterargument to a post-hoc argument is that "correlation doesn't equal causation," meaning that something occurred near or after the first occurrence doesn't mean that one thing caused the other. Below are examples of post-hoc arguments:

"More children are receiving the MMR vaccine, and more children are diagnosed with autism; therefore, the MMR vaccine causes autism."

"More young people are on social media, and there is more gun violence; therefore, social media causes gun violence."

Straw Man

This is a common fallacy used in political debates or when arguing controversial topics. Straw man fallacies present distorted interpretations, leave out important information, take information out of context, "cherry-pick" certain facts, or exaggerate claims. Straw man arguments are meant to distract audiences from the actual issue and misrepresent someone's argument to make it easier to attack. When we misrepresent someone else's argument, we falsely present our own as more reasonable, undermining honest, rational debate. Below are examples of straw man arguments:

Speaker A: "We shouldn't allocate more funds to cyber security."
Speaker B: "You want to weaken our country's defenses and leave it vulnerable to invasion?"

Speaker A: "I believe that Facebook and Twitter should moderate their content."

Speaker B: "So you believe that we shouldn't have first amendment rights to free speech."

Speaker A: "I believe that people should be able to participate in online platforms without using their real names."

Speaker B: "So you want to be able to harass people online without consequences anonymously."

Speaker B's responses mischaracterize and oversimplify Speaker A's arguments in these examples.

Strategies for Success: Collaboration and Teamwork

Collaborative learning is important for building a deeper understanding of ourselves and the course readings, and learning to be a good collaborator helps us learn to resolve conflict and understand each other better.

Writers also often work together in our composition classrooms when researching, writing, and revising. Being a good collaborator is an important skill and one that takes practice. The only way to practice is to participate in opportunities for group collaboration.

The good news is that we have plenty of online resources and tools to help us become better collaborators, including *Google Docs*, *Google Forms*, *Google Slides*, *Facetime*, text messaging, *Webex*, *Microsoft Open Office*, *Zoom*, *Pinterest*, *Twitter*.

Still, most students frequently comment that they do not like group projects. Students have had negative experiences and are afraid that their partners will let them down and that they'll be left "holding the bag" for the class assignment.

But, learning to work with people is one of the most essential skills students can develop. Our jobs often require working and collaborating with others. Students often think: "I don't want to work with a team because my grade is on the line." However, we'll work with teams in the workforce when our jobs are on the line. Also, learning to be a good team player is an essential skill because if we're not good teammates, we can get fired.

Second, with all of the technological resources we have available, there's also no reason we can't do group projects in the course. Much of the work that writers and scholars do in publishing and research is completed with collaborators who are on the other side of the country. They, too, work just like students do in various jobs with different work schedules, and they use *Google Docs*, *Facetime*, *Zoom*, and text messaging to make it work. At the end of the semester, most students enjoy meeting other students in the class.

Finally, the state of Texas Higher Education Coordinating Board mandates that students complete collaborative group projects in our Communication courses under the umbrella of teaching "teamwork."

So, here are some suggestions for how you might work together:

- Consider assigning a team leader. This person is responsible for reaching out to classmates, making sure the project is progressing and letting the instructor know if any students aren't participating, following up on project deadlines, checking in and reporting progress, and making final decisions when there needs to be someone who says, "This is what we're going to do." The team lead might also make any final decisions when there needs to be someone who says, "This is what we're going to do."

- Allocate sections of the project to specific team members.

- Identify how you will communicate with each other and include contact information: *Canvas Inbox*? Email? Text? *Zoom? Facetime? Facebook? Twitter?*

- Use *Google Docs* to write one document with each student participating. Authors use *Google Docs* to write together from around the country. If you're working in *Google Docs*, you'll be able to see each others' progress on the sections. Then come together at, say, Sunday at 4:00 in time for revisions to proof, edit, and turn in.

- Use *Zoom/WebEx/FaceTime/Skype* to meet with each other in real-time. While your classmates might be all across the state (and country), you can still work together and communicate using online tools without sitting in the same room.

- Create a schedule and set deadlines for parts to be completed. Creating a schedule is easier if you work backward with the due date in mind. For example, identify specific dates and deadlines in the writing process.
  - Final project due date
  - Final revision completed
  - Deadline for each member's completed contribution
  - Deadline for each member's rough draft
  - Deadline for each member to complete research/interview
  - Deadline for introduction
  - Deadline to select a topic and assign sections

- Finally, have faith and trust your teammates to do their parts. By the inverse: Don't let your teammates down. You may be reporting on your classmates' participation each week. If you're not participating, your grade may be negatively impacted. Your team may remove you from the group, and you'd have to complete an alternative collaborative project independently.

Work together. Conflict doesn't always mean dysfunction. Communicate. Be nice.

Strategies for Success: Revision

Revision is one of the most exciting parts of your writing process; however, we often only think of revision as adding a few commas and correcting a couple of spelling errors. Correcting typographical errors is proofreading; it is not revision. In his book, *Several Short Sentences About Writing*, Verlyn Klinkenborg says, "Revision is thinking applied to language, an opening and reopening of discovery, a search for the sentence that says the thing you had no idea you could say hidden inside the sentence you're making." It is also as personal as your writing process. So, practice revising in different places and postures and find out what works best.

In college, revision is a collaborative effort that works best through open-ended questions and reflective responses to feedback. Effective revision requires us to think critically and read our work carefully, exploring new ways to speak clearly and write with power and passion. It requires that we make substantial and meaningful changes to our text, and revision takes time, practice, and planning. All of those changes cannot happen simultaneously. Like your writing process, your revision style will grow and change as you practice it.

Do not overwhelm yourself by trying to fix every issue that arises in your essay. To revise like a writer, you will have to make multiple passes through, writing and rewriting with a specific goal each time. Revision is not a single action done in the writing process. It is an attitude that you develop when you engage with your text. When practiced as an art, revising helps your best work become realized.

Here are some tips and suggestions for successful revision.

- Before you begin revising:
  - Read back through your essay and think about why you created each sentence. What does each sentence say, not say, or imply?
  - Take time to reflect on your instructor's feedback. Do you agree with the observations? In what ways? Do you disagree? How so?
  - Paraphrase your instructor's feedback. What is the main point that he/she/they made regarding your text? What feedback back did your instructor give you in class? On the final submission?
  - Practice humility and remember that no draft is perfect from its inception. We can all grow as writers.

- During the revision process:
  - Don't be self-deprecating. The more time you spend thinking and talking about how bad your writing is, the less time you will spend making it better. All writing can be revised.
  - Start with a single goal in mind. For example, the first time you read through your work, make sure each sentence conveys a clear and concise idea. Clarity is a great starting point for your revision process. Once you're done with that round, choose another aspect of your essay, maybe one that your instructor pointed out, to work on.
  - Ask questions. When you ask questions, be specific. Don't merely ask: "How do I improve this paper?" Or, "What can I do to make a better grade?" Instead, consider what you understand the comment to mean and then identify the point it breaks down for you. If you are confused by your instructor's comments or need further clarification, visit with your instructor and clarify anything that you did not comprehend.
  - Solicit feedback. Make an appointment with your instructor during office hours and bring in revised versions of your assignments to get additional feedback. Visit your on-campus writing center and work with a writing tutor to improve your writing. Make friends with your classmates and start your writing community. Share your drafts and ask for suggestions recommendations. Collaborate to graduate!

Strategies for Success: Marketable Skills

It is essential as a future college graduate that you can convey the knowledge and skills you've acquired in your writing courses in your new profession. We want you to leave this course able to articulate your marketable skills.

Marketable skills are the abilities, knowledge, attitudes, and beliefs that equip you for a fruitful career and productive life. These marketable skills—also called transferable skills, portable skills, or employability skills—are acquired through formal education, like your writing courses, and informal experiences, such as extracurricular activities, student organizations, hobbies, and volunteer/community service work.

There are two large bodies of skills that employers are seeking: hard skills and soft skills.

- **Hard skills** include the specific knowledge required for a job, such as coding or carpentry. Hard skills are teachable abilities that your instructor might grade or assess. Generally, students learn hard skills through education, apprenticeships, certification programs, and on-the-job training. These skills are usually listed on job postings. Hard skills are usually included in resumés and applications, and applicants that possess the minimum skills required will be hired. Students are usually good at highlighting these skill sets.

- **Soft skills** differ from hard skills in that they are more closely aligned with personality traits, behaviors, and attitudes rather than technical knowledge. Soft skills are generally not job-specific and include critical thinking and communication skills. Soft skills are also the traits that make a good team member, such as showing up on time, being able to "read" others' emotional cues, and getting along with other people. Soft skills also are learned and developed with practice and experience. Specific soft skills may or may not be listed in job descriptions, but they are increasingly important in getting an interview and advancing a career. Students generally have a more difficult time highlighting these skills because they may not be required for a particular job, even though they may be as important as the hard skills.

Employers value job candidates with both sets of these marketable skills, hard and soft. Therefore, we'll continue to work on both in your writing courses. While it would be impossible to list all the skills, specific skills are often most important to employers:

- Communication
- Critical Thinking
- Problem Solving

- Creative Thinking
- Teamwork
- Leadership

- Positive Attitude
- Strong Work Ethic
- Adaptability

INRW 0305 and ENGL 1301

Introduction to INRW 0305

According to the college's catalog, INRW 0305: Integrated Reading and Writing is a "performance-based course designed to develop students' critical reading and academic writing skills. The focus of the course will be on applying critical reading skills for organizing, analyzing, and retaining the material and developing written work appropriate to the audience, purpose, situation, and length of the assignment." The work you do in this course prepares you for the demands of writing in other academic contexts.

Perhaps you struggled with reading dense texts in the past. Maybe you struggled with coming up with ideas or writing grammatically correct sentences. Suppose you have anxiety coming into this course based on those experiences. It would help if you understood that this course creates a physical/virtual space for you to develop as a reader and writer. As writing scholar Susan Naomi Bernstein states, this course "provides opportunities for students to discover the kinds of writing that they will encounter throughout college and in the workplace." Moreover, this course offers time to practice writing "intensively and extensively." Therefore, the readings and writing assignments that you do in this course will directly correlate to the kinds of reading and writing assignments you'll do in English 1301 and 1302.

Remember that your talents and skills inform your appropriation of academic writing conventions. Many times, those who are successful rely on a network of resources. For instance, in "A Framework for Understanding Latino/a Cultural Wealth," researchers Vijay Kanagala, Laura Rendon, and Amaury Nora researched minority Latino students at the University of Texas at San Antonio. Kanagala, Rendon, and Nora argue that minority students, for instance, must often navigate complex discursive spaces (i.e., home community, cultural communities, academia) as well as external conflicts (i.e., financial, childrearing) when attending college (18). Perhaps your experience is different from those Kanagala, Rendon, and Nora studied; however, you also bring your network of resources to this course that we invite you to draw from and lean on.

To meet those objectives, we have developed this course to align closely with the readings and writing assignments in Composition I so that, according to the ACGM, when you complete this course, you can:

- Locate explicit textual information, draw complex inferences, and describe, analyze, and evaluate the information within and across multiple texts of varying lengths.

- Comprehend and use vocabulary effectively in oral communication, reading, and writing.

- Identify and analyze the audience, purpose, and message across a variety of texts.

- Describe and apply insights gained from reading and writing a variety of texts.

- Compose a variety of texts that demonstrate reading comprehension, clear focus, logical development of ideas, and use of appropriate language that advance the writer's purpose.

- Determine and use effective approaches and rhetorical strategies for given reading and writing situations.

- Generate ideas and gather information relevant to the topic and purpose, incorporating the thoughts and words of other writers in student writing using established strategies.

- Evaluate the relevance and quality of ideas and information in recognizing, formulating, and developing a claim.

We believe that you'll meet the course outcomes through meaningful participation and by reading various texts and writing the genres that prepare you to produce the kinds of essays you'll be writing next semester in ENGL 1301: Composition I and throughout your academic career. We encourage you to participate in academic conversations and tackle relevant topics by engaging with our year-long theme. You should participate as emerging writers in the broader academic community because we need your voice and perspectives.

Introduction to ENGL 1301

According to the college's catalog, ENGL 1301: Composition I is a course designed for "intensive study of and practice in writing processes, from invention and researching to drafting, revising, and editing, both individually and collaboratively." In Composition I, we emphasize "effective rhetorical choices, including audience, purpose, arrangement, and style." We focus the assignments in the course on writing academic essays because that genre serves "as a vehicle for learning, communicating, and critical analysis."

According to the ACGM, you should, when you conclude this course, be able to:

- Demonstrate knowledge of individual and collaborative writing processes.
- Develop ideas with appropriate support and attribution.
- Write in a style appropriate to the audience and purpose.
- Read, reflect, and respond critically to a variety of texts.
- Use Edited American English in academic essays.

But what does this mean? Specifically, English 1301 is a service course designed to prepare you to write in your other classes and when you enter the workforce. It is our goal that when you conclude this course, you have the resources to write effectively and understand the importance of audience and purpose as it shapes your writing in your history, political science, humanities, literature, lab science, and art appreciation courses. We also aim to prepare you for the demands of writing on the job when you're asked to produce a cover letter and resume, reflect on a process, or problem-solve with your colleagues via email. Beyond academics and the workplace, we hope that you enjoy the challenge of reading and writing and remember the joy that each one can bring.

We also hope that this course allows you to consider, discuss, and reflect on yourself and others. How do we present ourselves in our texts? How do we read others in theirs? How does our engagement with the writing process help us develop and hone our ideas? And, how does language shape our experiences?

To help you achieve these goals, we will spend this semester engaging with and reflecting on the arguments of others. We will spend time constructing our thoughts and ideas through meaningful engagement with each other and our texts. We will continue to refine those thoughts through sustained and considerate revision that emphasizes inquiry and reflection.

INRW 0305 and ENGL 1301: Narrative of Place

"We come and go, but the land is always here. And the people who love it and understand it are the people who own it—for a little while." —Willa Cather

The places from your past have profoundly affected who you are right now—the "you" who is sitting here, reading this assignment sheet. Some places and spaces hold special importance or meaning for you. It could be your hometown, your elementary school, your grandparents' kitchen, an arcade, a specific tree you climbed, the fort you built out of bamboo behind the building that no one dared to walk through. It is somewhere that has held onto you and has never let go. It is where the people you love life—the place where you are loved back.

The impact of these places is closely tied to our memories, and our connections to these places help shape our characters. No matter our age, the spaces we inhabit help us understand truths (and untruths) about the world around us. When did you learn your first lesson about love or happiness or loss? Where were you? What room were you in when life introduced you to the joy of cooking or the pain of regret? Where were you when you figured out the person you wanted to be when you grew up? Where is the place you sought refuge or comfort? There are places in your past that helped define you, helped you figure out how to live, and taught you lesson after lesson.

For this assignment, you will revisit one of those places or spaces as realistically, specifically, detailed, and personally as you possibly can to write a Narrative of Place.

You will reach back to that place and recall where, what, why, and how it changed you and write a narrative essay in which you explore this place and discuss how it influenced you, shaped your identity, and/or modified your outlook on the world. You will show your reader how this place has helped you become the person you are by taking us back into that place in the world. For this assignment, you will write a narrative essay about an impactful moment connected to a place, not just a day in your past.

To start, think about the following ideas for your drafting process:

- Revisit this place with all six senses as best you can (the sixth being emotional feeling—not the creepy one from the movie where the little boy saw dead people).
  - What smells live inside this memory?
  - What would we hear? What are the sounds associated with this memory?
  - What would we see that was important?
  - How did you feel, and what can you say to communicate that to your reader?
  - What did you taste?
  - What could you touch and feel in that memory?
  - How/when/why did you engage with this place?

- Write a list of how the place shaped who you are today and the lessons you learned while in this environment.

- Consider these other questions to help you paint a vivid picture:
  - What sorts of life were present? Animals? Plants? Specific people?
  - What was there that was non-living? Was it indoors or outdoors?
  - What was the story behind the setting that allowed you to learn the lesson? What specific situation occurred that acted as your teacher?

Your job is quite simple: Tell us a story in the form of an essay about a place that's important to you and why. Focus on the place not the people. Fill it with details for us. We are there alongside you—learning the lessons, listening in.

Specific Requirements:

- Include a creative title.
- INRW 0305: Approximately 500 words.
- ENGL 1301: Approximately 1000 words.
- Rhetorically format/build your essay to communicate meaning: considering your narrative's development, organization, and style.
- Write in MLA or APA format (when/if appropriate).

Evaluation Criteria (Narrative of Place)

	Accomplished	Emerging	Average	Below Average	Failing
Purpose (Development)	The essay **clearly** identifies a specific place. The essay develops upon its main thesis by offering **exceptionally** specific, convincing, and concrete supporting sensory details. These details are **exceptionally** unique and insightful.	The essay **clearly** identifies a specific place. The essay **frequently** develops upon its main thesis by offering (**most often**) convincing and concrete supporting sensory details. These details are **often** unique and insightful.	The essay identifies a specific place. The essay **occasionally** develops upon the essay's main thesis by offering supporting sensory details. These details offer insights that could be insightful with more development.	The essay **hints** at a specific place. The essay **rarely** develops upon the essay's main thesis by offering supporting sensory details. These details need more development.	The essay **does not** identify a specific place. The essay **does not** develop upon the essay's main thesis by offering supporting sensory details.
Coherence (Organization)	The essay's organization and coherence are **consistently** logical.	The essay's organization and coherence are **often** logical.	The essay's organization and coherence are **occasionally** logical.	The essay's organization and coherence are **rarely** logical.	The essay's organization and coherence are **not** logical.
Convention (Mechanics)	The essay **consistently** demonstrates an ability to utilize the conventions of academic prose, including spelling, formatting, mechanical correctness.	The essay **often** demonstrates an ability to utilize the conventions of academic prose, including spelling, formatting, mechanical correctness.	The essay **occasionally** demonstrates an ability to utilize the conventions of academic prose, including spelling, formatting, mechanical correctness.	The essay **rarely** demonstrates an ability to utilize the conventions of academic prose, including spelling, formatting, mechanical correctness.	The essay **does not** demonstrate an ability to utilize the conventions of academic prose, including spelling, formatting, mechanical correctness.

ENGL 1301: *The Address Book* Collaborative Project

For this assignment, you will create a collaborative essay with peers from your class based on our common read, *The Address Book*. For this assignment, you'll need to:

First, work together in small groups to identify a common or unifying theme. You have plenty of opportunities regarding the theme to focus on a singular *location* (e.g., Denton, Flower Mound, Pilot Point) or a common *locale* (e.g., cemeteries, national parks, historic monuments, historic buildings, local haunts). Some successful projects have included a variety of topics, such as university towns, famous haunted spaces, and popular vacation spots.

Then, each group member will research a place of their choosing and write an essay (approximately 250 words) based on that place. You can refer to the chapters in *The Address Book* as models of the kind of reflection and analysis that you might do for your contribution to the project. Please include a photograph of your location or locale in your essay and document your sources in your essay.

Finally, the group will collect all of the essays (including both an introduction and conclusion) into a single document that begins with a written introduction (around 200 words) composed together, introduces the significance of the document or theme, and includes outside research. Look at the introduction to *The Address Book* as an example.

When writing, thoughtfully consider how you will organize your collaborative project: how you will introduce the issue, develop the story and relevance of your issue, and achieve an effect on your audience.

Consider how to create a uniform final product using *Google Docs* or *Microsoft Word* for your final submission. Each member should work together to revise for clarity to form one comprehensive essay that comments on the unifying theme you are exploring.

Evaluation Criteria (*The Address Book* Collaborative Project)

	Accomplished	Emerging	Average	Below Average	Failing
Purpose (Development)	The project clearly identifies the theme and offers a consistently well-developed analysis in which **all** discussions are exceptionally supported with convincing and specific supporting details.	The project clearly identifies the theme and offers an analysis in which **most** discussions are supported with convincing and specific supporting details.	The project identifies the theme and offers a cursory analysis in which **some** discussions are supported with convincing and specific supporting details.	The project identifies hints at the theme and offers a rudimentary analysis in which discussions **rarely** offer convincing and specific supporting details.	The project does not identify the theme and/ or offer ineffective analysis in which discussions **do not** offer convincing and specific supporting details.

	Accomplished	Emerging	Average	Below Average	Failing
Coherence (Organization)	The project's organization and coherence are **consistent and logical.**	The project's organization and coherence are **often** consistent and logical.	The project's organization and coherence are **occasionally** consistent and logical.	The project's organization and coherence are **rarely** consistent and logical.	The project **does not** demonstrate a consistent, logical, and coherent organization.
Convention (Style and Mechanics)	The project **consistently** demonstrates appropriate formality.	The project **often** demonstrates appropriate formality.	The project **occasionally** demonstrates appropriate formality.	The project **rarely** demonstrates appropriate formality.	The project **does not** demonstrate appropriate formality.
	The project **consistently** demonstrates an ability to utilize the conventions appropriate to the audience, including spelling, formatting, and mechanical correctness.	The project **often** demonstrates an ability to utilize the conventions appropriate to the audience, including spelling, formatting, and mechanical correctness.	The project **occasionally** demonstrates an ability to utilize the conventions appropriate to the audience, including spelling, formatting, and mechanical correctness.	The project **rarely** demonstrates an ability to utilize the conventions appropriate to the audience, including spelling, formatting, and mechanical correctness.	The project **does not** demonstrate an ability to utilize the conventions appropriate to the audience, including spelling, formatting, and mechanical correctness.
Contribution and Collaboration	The project conveys the team member's **consistent** contributions and an overwhelming commitment to collaboration.	The project conveys the team member's **frequent** contributions and a commitment to collaboration.	The project conveys the team member's **occasional** contributions and **occasionally** demonstrates a commitment to collaboration.	The project conveys the team member's **sparse** contributions and **rarely** demonstrates a commitment to collaboration.	The project **does not** convey the team member's contributions and **does not** demonstrate a commitment to collaboration.

INRW 0305 and ENGL 1301: Analysis and Critique Essay

For this final major assignment in the course, you will identify, analyze, and critique a specific location or locale of your choosing.

For this assignment, consider then:

- The location/locale that you're writing about.

- The central idea(s) or thesis that you're focusing on.

- The supporting ideas that contribute to the audiences' understanding of the thesis.

- The relevance and quality of the research that you're using to support your thesis and supporting ideas.

Assignment Requirements:

- INRW 0305: 500 words

- ENGL 1301: 1000 words

- Include a title

Strategies for Writing an Analysis and Critique Essay

Writing allows us to focus our attention through sustained reflection that furthers our understanding and improves our critical thinking abilities. Writing is essentially about understanding and developing our ideas through careful analysis. Engaging in the writing and research process is a part of that analysis and critique.

An **analysis**, then, invites us to break down or examine a topic considering the historical, personal, political, economic, social, cultural, or geographic contexts. An analysis is often more fact-driven.

A **critique** invites us to use what we have learned in our analysis and carry the conversation one step further by evaluating, hypothesizing, inferring, or drawing conclusions about a topic.

Students, though, often think that offering analysis and critique is critical. There is a difference between a critique and criticism, just as there is a difference between offering an argument and being argumentative. Criticism is often rooted in a negative observation or is often viewed as being antagonistic.

However, for students writing an analysis and critique essay, it is essential to approach the assignment from a position of openness. One way to engage in a stance of openness is to engage in rhetorical listening, or listening to understand, comprehend, or, in the Platonic sense, strive toward "Truth" with a capital T. We can't grow as students and scholars if we only listen to voices that we agree with or to people who have similar backgrounds. Krista Radcliffe explains that rhetorical listening is a "stance of *openness*" that a person may choose to assume (1). To engage in rhetorical listening means to listen not "*for* intent but *with* intent" (Ratcliff 15). Dr. Radcliffe explains that agreement is not necessarily the goal when engaging in rhetorical listening. We often disagree; however, rhetorical listening means that we recognize others' points of view as different and work toward understanding, not agreement (Ratcliff 33).

When writing your analysis and critique essay, then consider the following questions:

- Why is [this] important?
- How did we get to [this]?
- Who is/was most impacted by [this]?
- What are the implications of [this]?
- How does [this] impact us today?

Need some ideas? Consider the following questions as illustrative examples and look closely at the model essay. The questions will help you get started, and the model provides an idea of how your essay should be organized.

- What can we learn about the harsh conditions of pioneer life, segregation, or settler/Native American conflicts from our local cemeteries?
- What can we learn about a community based on access to the arts, museums, libraries?
- What do we know about German immigration from towns like Muenster during the turn of the century? Or Czech immigration in West, Texas? Or how cities such as Houston are considered one of the most ethnically diverse in the country?
- What was the historical significance of the confederate monument in Denton, Texas? What should readers know or understand regarding the efforts to remove it?
- What is the historical significance of Quakertown in Denton, Texas, near Texas Woman's University? What should readers know or understand regarding efforts to preserve its history?
- How did the Trinity River in Dallas or I-35 in Austin preserve segregation efforts? How do those efforts impact the areas today?
- Why do so many courthouses in Texas resemble Victorian architecture with a limestone facade? What is significant about the downtowns' layout?
- What is the significance of public memorials like the one in Oklahoma City? What function do memorials serve to the community?
- What can we learn about a community's history and economy from feed silos or cattle stockyards (e.g., Valley View, Saginaw, Fort Worth)? How does that economy manifest itself in the communities' population?

Evaluation Criteria (Analysis and Critique Essay)

	Accomplished	**Emerging**	**Average**	**Below Average**	**Failing**
Purpose (Development)	The essay **thoroughly** identifies and **summarily** analyzes the topic.	The essay **consistently** identifies and analyzes the topic.	The essay **often** identifies and analyzes the topic.	The essay **rarely** identifies and analyzes the topic.	The essay **does not** identify and analyze the topic.
	The writer offers a **thoroughly** convincing critique of the issue.	The writer offers a **mostly** convincing critique of the issue.	The writer offers a **basic** critique of the issue.	The writer offers an **inadequate** critique of the issue.	The writer **does not** offer a critique of the issue.
	The writer **thoroughly** develops all of the points with examples from research.	The writer **mostly** develops the points with examples from research.	The writer develops the points with **some** examples from research.	The writer develops the points with **few** examples from research.	The writer **does not** develop the points with examples from research.
Insight (Development)	The essay **consistently** draws insightful observations from research specific and relevant to the essay's purpose.	The essay **often** draws insightful observations from research specific and relevant to the essay's purpose.	The essay **occasionally** draws insightful observations from research specific and relevant to the essay's purpose.	The essay **rarely** draws insightful observations from research specific and relevant to the essay's purpose.	The essay **does not** draw insightful observations from research specific and relevant to the essay's purpose.

	Accomplished	Emerging	Average	Below Average	Failing
Coherence (Organization)	The essay's organization and coherence are **overwhelmingly** consistent and logical.	The essay's organization and coherence are **often** consistent and logical.	The essay's organization and coherence are **occasionally** consistent and logical.	The essay's organization and coherence are **rarely** consistent and logical.	The essay **does not** demonstrate a consistent, logical, and coherent organization.
	The essay **consistently** demonstrates conventions of academic writing (e.g., **thoroughly** developed introduction, discussion sections, conclusion).	The essay **often** demonstrates conventions of academic writing (e.g., **well-developed** introduction, discussion sections, conclusion).	The essay **occasionally** demonstrates conventions of academic writing (e.g., **occasionally** developed introduction, discussion sections, conclusion).	The essay **rarely** demonstrates conventions of academic writing (e.g., **rarely** developed introduction, discussion sections, conclusion).	The essay **does not** demonstrate conventions of academic writing (e.g., **no** introduction, discussion sections, conclusion).
Convention (Style and Mechanics)	The essay **consistently** demonstrates appropriate formality.	The essay **often** demonstrates appropriate formality.	The essay **occasionally** demonstrates appropriate formality.	The essay **rarely** demonstrates appropriate formality.	The essay **does not** demonstrate appropriate formality.
	The essay **consistently** utilizes the conventions of academic prose, which include spelling, formatting, mechanical correctness, and citation practices.	The essay **often** utilizes the conventions of academic prose, which include spelling, formatting, mechanical correctness, and citation practices.	The essay **occasionally** utilizes the conventions of academic prose, which include spelling, formatting, mechanical correctness, and citation practices.	The essay **rarely** utilizes the conventions of academic prose, which include spelling, formatting, mechanical correctness, and citation practices.	The essay **does not** utilize the conventions of academic prose, which include spelling, formatting, mechanical correctness, and citation practices.

Sample Analysis Critique

Samantha Humphries
Professor Smart
English 1301
30 June 2022

Allen High School: Community at Heart

Students from Allen High School probably struggle to fathom how their elders graduated with 14 people in their class since they attend the largest school in Texas. After all, everything is bigger in Texas, especially Allen High School. According to Jeff Andrews in an article about the history and growth of the high school, 6,664 students attended the 880,000 square feet school in 2017 (Vox). That number has continued to grow.

Just as Texas boasts about its size, it also loves its football. Eagle Stadium, home to only one team, is the largest of any high school football stadium in the country. Allen's 57-game winning streak from 2012 to 2015 and three straight state titles have put Friday night lights in Texas on the national stage (Andrews). No one goes to a bigger school in Texas, and no one seems to have a more dominant football team than Allen High School. However, to understand the school's history and reputation, one must consider how it rose to its dominance, perceive its size as advantageous, and analyze the dramatic amount of stress and attention the football team has to manage.

Role of Size

To begin, despite its present-day spotlight, the town of Allen was not always this massive. Beneath its impressive school, Allen started early on as a small farm town before turning into a rapidly sprawling area. Its growth is attributed to a booming Dallas area working population moving out near Allen and similar areas to seek "a short commute to work and a quiet place to raise their children," according to the same article (Andrews).

What is unique about Allen today is that its vast high school shows its attempt to retain the feeling of community and the culture of a small town that is rooted in successful football traditions. For example, in the aforementioned article, it explains that "an affluent growing suburban town with one high school is an ideal condition" for building a winning Texas high school program (Andrews).

The problem is that the condition rarely lasts. Inevitably, the town's student body outgrows the high school, and the school board will vote to open a new school to alleviate crowding, and the pool of players—and the community's allegiance—are split in two" (Andrews). The other Collin County major cities, as they were also experiencing explosive growth due to Dallas expanding outward, decided to embrace their new urban identity by building multiple schools to accommodate more students. However, the people of Allen "tried to keep its small-town feel by rallying behind its one high school, and, of course, its high school football team" by simply voting to expand its school (Andrews). This action shows that the town incorporated the single high school into the community's identity and wanted to preserve the culture it had kept for so long. Part of this culture was uniting behind a single winning football team, and Allen grew its school's building instead of splitting up the school and community in order to keep it.

As a result, this action affected the depth of the school in terms of athletics. Of course, a large, single high school will inevitably have a larger team than a district that is divided into three or more schools. On top of this fact, Allen's prestigious winning tradition attracts more student players to move to the school to be a part of the success. These factors enrage many critics because "the size of the student body gives the football team a built-in advantage in the form of a huge pool of players from which the coaches can form a team" (Andrews).

Additionally, according to Ethan Grant in an article explaining this controversy in the *Allen American*, Allen has "outrun and outgunned every opponent in their path over parts of the last three seasons, but they can't seem to escape the favorite hypothetical of every school and school district laid out in the wake of their path" (Grant). This attitude demonstrates that playing against Allen seems unfair to many, making people from all over Texas question what their school would be like if it did not split, such as Frisco ISD, who is currently building its ninth high school. Since Texas prizes high school football, it is evident that people use Allen High School's giant school and team to excuse an alarming defeat.

Not only does the school pose an extreme athletic advantage to many, but there is also a philosophical debate over whether a single high school in Allen prevents the creation of more jobs, smaller classes, and growth accommodation. In simpler terms, some question if there is enough opportunity in a crowded school (Grant). Ultimately, though, an edge in athletics and overly packed halls are unintended consequences that flew to the surface level, burying the innocent attempt to preserve a beloved sense of community.

High Stakes of Greatness

The value of football in the Allen community correspondingly brings a lot of attention and pressure to the administration and the players to maintain a certain standard that the public follows very closely. An example of the stressed importance of football and performance at the school is the team's college-size stadium, which "has been used as an example of misplaced priorities in the public education system by school advocates who believe football plays an outsized role" (Andrews). This information is significant to the ego of the school because it compels the administration to avoid the embarrassment of building a mediocre team to represent that stadium, especially because the state government has been less willing to put money into other schools' budgets.

Surely, with the high tension to maintain a winning history and positive image, Allen's administration would not accept anything less than those expectations. The person responsible for taking on all the pressure and putting the school's reputation on its back is ultimately the head football coach. Based on the information in a WFAA news article covering the team's recent change, the Allen Eagles recently hired its third new head coach in three years. Chad Morris was recruited to coach "the Allen program in the spring of 2021. He led the Eagles to an 11-3 record" (Livengood). Although he coached at multiple Division I universities before replacing the previous head coach at Allen, he led the team to its worst record since 2005 (Livengood). Evidently, the standards for the football team are outstandingly high since three losses cost the head coach his job. This insight is crucial because it shows the school's desire to have a coach that will build upon its winning tradition and success, no matter the coach's previous experience. The decision to let go of a decorated coach further demonstrates what a top-notch football team and the impressive stadium truly mean to the pride of the community and the school.

In the end, in light of critics arguing that the school is too big, the population growth will not be able to be maintained much longer. Andrews continues in his article to add that Allen only has so much land available to build new housing, so the growth rate has begun to slow (Andrews). It will be challenging to estimate how the town's population and school's student enrollment will change in the future, but the traditions and values of the city and the school have been sustained too long to say the standards will ever change. As long as there is life in the town of Allen, there will only be one Allen High School, and the Allen Eagles will be one of the best football teams in the state of Texas.

Works Cited

Andrews, Jeff. "The Friday Night Lights Effect." *Curbed*, Vox Media, 12 Dec. 2017, https://archive.curbed.com/2017/12/12/16754492/ allen-texas-high-school-football-stadium.

Grant, Ethan. "Column: The Loneliest Number? Allen's Single High School Model a Topic of Controversy, Especially in Athletics." *Allen American*, Star Local Media, 1 Oct. 2015, https://starlo-calmedia.com/allenamerican/sports/column-the-loneliest-number-allen-s-single-high-school-model-a-topic-of-controversy-especially/ article_4ecc411a-6790-11e5-bf91-53e4c50a2217.html.

Livengood, Paul. "Allen Eagles head coach Chad Morris is stepping down after one season - Morris joined the Allen Eagles football program in the Spring of 2021, and he led the team to an 11-3 record." *NewsBank: Access World News,* ABC - 8 WFAA (Dallas, TX), 13 May 2022, https://infoweb.newsbank.com/apps/news/ document-view?p=AWNB&docref=news/189FC2DD1F84A250.

ENGL 1302

According to the college catalog, ENGL 1302: Composition II is a course designed for the "intensive study of and practice in the strategies and techniques for developing research-based expository and persuasive texts. Emphasis on effective and ethical rhetorical inquiry, including primary and secondary research methods; critical reading of verbal, visual, and multimedia texts; systematic evaluation, synthesis, and documentation of information sources; and critical thinking about evidence and conclusions."

As the second half of your communication core, this course encourages you to move from the structured inquiry in Composition I toward a free inquiry of the course theme in Composition II. You'll also be invited to locate and evaluate sources beyond the course readings to help you support the claims that you'll be making.

Therefore, according to the course syllabus, on successful completion of this course, students will:

1. Demonstrate knowledge of individual and collaborative research processes.
2. Develop ideas and synthesize primary and secondary sources within focused academic arguments, including one or more research-based essays.
3. Analyze, interpret, and evaluate a variety of texts for the ethical and logical uses of evidence.
4. Write in a style that clearly communicates meaning, builds credibility, and inspires belief or action.
5. Apply the conventions of style manuals for specific academic disciplines (e.g., APA, CMS, MLA, etc.).

This course is often the last dedicated writing course that students take in their academic careers; therefore, you may not have another opportunity to participate in a class focused solely on helping you become a better writer and researcher. It is vital then that this course prepares you for the demands of writing in your academic career and in the workforce. Also, we hope that your writing courses at NCTC have helped you appreciate your power to move, inspire, challenge, or persuade others with your words.

ENGL 1302: Multimodal Digital Collaborative Project

Consider how humans have engaged in "writing" to produce "texts" throughout human history—from sketches on cave walls, handwriting on papyrus, books produced on Gutenberg's printing press, to fingers typing on home computers. Our writing technologies have evolved, and these technologies consequently shape our understanding of the world around us.

Consider, for instance, how we understand the world now through images and texts:

- Memes and dance reels on *Instagram* and *Tik Tok* offer (often through humor) commentary on socially and culturally relevant ideas.

- Graphs and charts in technical reports offer visual representations of more easily digestible ideas than walls of words.

- Photographs in newspapers and magazines illicit emotions from readers that are not as persuasive as mere descriptions alone.

- *YouTube* videos with various contributors discussing an issue in a roundtable-like manner.

For this assignment, you will work in small groups to create a multimodal digital collaborative project that examines and critically adds to one of the arguments (chapters) presented in our text. A "multimodal" digital project relies on more than one modality—in other words, images and text (written or oral) in a digital medium.

For this assignment, you can use any digital media platform where users can create online communities to share information, ideas, and/or other content: *Google Docs*, *Google Slides*, *Tumblr*, *Medium*, *Zoom*, *YouTube*. Specifically, the final product must rely on both text and images to examine one of the arguments presented in the text and provide adequate proof of the position taken by the group.

Each member of the group will be responsible for contributing to the project. When producing your collaborative project, follow these directions:

- As a group, choose a section from the text. (You can look ahead to essays that we haven't read yet as a class if you'd like. Nothing in the book is off-limits.) Every group member needs to read, annotate, and think about your chosen section.

- Create and share a *Google Doc* that will outline your group's approach to the project. You will turn this in as a project proposal to your instructor.

- Decide as a group whether you want to add to the argument(s) and prove their validity or you want to oppose the argument(s) and attempt to provide counter-arguments.

- Create a multimodal digital collaborative project that:
  - incorporates digital media and is supported by words (either written or spoken).
  - engages with the material in a meaningful and insightful way.

- Everyone must participate in the project to be successful.

- Intentionally craft your final project for submission. Think through the following questions: How will you present your argument? What will act as evidence? Is your message clear? Did you accomplish the original goal? Why did you use the specific platform for your final project?

- Every student must upload the project to Canvas.

Need some ideas? Consider the following as illustrative examples:

- Write a collaborative essay using *Google Docs* that incorporates images (e.g., charts, graphs, photographs, diagrams) to illustrate the points.
- Create a *WordPress, Tumblr,* or *Medium* article that explores and analyzes an issue and utilizes the platform's features (e.g., images, charts, graphs, hashtags).
- Create a *Google Slides* presentation with audio, images, and text.
- Host a *Zoom* conversation or YouTube Live event and invite guests to participate.

Evaluation Criteria (Multimodal Digital Collaborative Project)

	Accomplished	Emerging	Average	Below Average	Failing
Purpose (Development)	The project clearly identifies an argument and **consistently** develops it by offering **exceptionally** convincing and specific supporting details.	The project clearly identifies an argument and **frequently** develops it by offering convincing and specific supporting details.	The project introduces an argument and **occasionally** develops it by offering supporting details.	The project **hints** at an argument but **rarely** develops it by offering supporting details.	The project **does not identify** an argument and **does not** develop it by offering supporting details.
	The project is multimodal—relying **exceptionally** well on both images and texts to convey its message.	The project is multimodal—relying **frequently** on both images and texts to convey its message.	The project is multimodal—relying **occasssionally** on both images and texts to convey its message.	The project is not multimodal—it **does not** rely on both images and texts to convey its message.	The project is not multimodal—it **does not** rely on both images and texts to convey its message.

	Accomplished	**Emerging**	**Average**	**Below Average**	**Failing**
Coherence (Organization)	The project's organization and coherence are **consistently** logical.	The project's organization and coherence are **often** logical.	The project's organization and coherence are **occasionally** logical.	The project's organization and coherence are **rarely** logical.	The project's organization and coherence are **not** logical.
Convention (Style and Mechanics)	The project **consistently** demonstrates appropriate formality.	The project **often** demonstrates appropriate formality.	The project **occasionally** demonstrates appropriate formality.	The project **rarely** demonstrates appropriate formality.	The project **does not** demonstrate appropriate formality.
	The project **consistently** demonstrates an ability to utilize the conventions appropriate to the audience, including spelling, formatting, and mechanical correctness.	The project **often** demonstrates an ability to utilize the conventions appropriate to the audience, including spelling, formatting, and mechanical correctness.	The project **occasionally** demonstrates an ability to utilize the conventions appropriate to the audience, including spelling, formatting, and mechanical correctness.	The project **rarely** demonstrates an ability to utilize the conventions appropriate to the audience, including spelling, formatting, and mechanical correctness.	The project **does not** demonstrate an ability to utilize the conventions appropriate to the audience, including spelling, formatting, and mechanical correctness.
Contribution and Collaboration	The project conveys the team member's **consistent** contributions and an overwhelming commitment to collaboration.	The project conveys the team member's **frequent** contributions and a commitment to collaboration.	The project conveys the team member's **occasional** contributions and **occasionally** demonstrates a commitment to collaboration.	The project conveys the team member's **sparse** contributions and **rarely** demonstrates a commitment to collaboration.	The project **does not** convey the team member's contributions and **does not** demonstrate a commitment to collaboration.

ENGL 1302: Annotated Bibliography

For this assignment in Composition II, you will write an annotated bibliography that includes five sources you are planning to use in your research essay.

About the annotated bibliography. Completing an annotated bibliography of existing research is a fundamental component of writing an academic research essay. This assignment provides you with an important tool as you begin the research and writing phases of the argumentative essay. The annotated bibliography assignment serves several purposes:

- Locating sources and engaging in a close reading of a text help you grow as a writer. It is also helpful to see models of how other writers have approached the topic and structured their arguments.

- The annotation summarizes the article's contents to inform the reader of the relevance and quality of the sources cited. When collected, these annotations can serve as a "research log."

- The annotated bibliography allows you to evaluate the quality, breadth, and relevance of the research you've acquired. In other words, if you have five articles, each with little more than the same biographical information, then you know that you will need to do more research to find sources that offer a more in-depth and robust analysis of your issue. You'll need to revisit the databases to find more diverse scholarship.

For your annotated bibliography, you need to complete the following steps:

State your tentative thesis or research question. At this point, you should have a tentative thesis or research question for your research paper. Include a one-sentence thesis or research question at the top of the bibliography, just below the title.

Remember that refining your thesis or answering your research question is a recursive process. While your tentative thesis or research question will guide your search, you may discover new information or arguments that persuade you to modify your thesis or approach. You can then use the revised thesis or research question to guide your research. At this point in the process, nothing should be set in stone.

Locate sources. This annotated bibliography assignment aims to locate five scholarly sources that directly relate to your tentative thesis or research question. The sources can provide arguments or evidence supporting your position, or they can provide other significant positions on the topic.

Because the essays in our course readings are academic texts, you may use one of those to get your research started. The other four sources will be found using the academic research databases (e.g., Academic Search Complete, JSTOR, and Opposing Viewpoints in Context).

Write the annotations. The annotation should be written in complete sentences and should include the following information:

- A summary of the source's thesis and supporting arguments. Use active verbs.

- If the source supports your thesis or research question, an explanation of which information or arguments you will use in your essay.

- If the source provides a different or opposing position, explain how you will respond to that position.

- An analysis of what makes this source a good one, including the credentials of the author(s) and the reliability of the arguments and information. Consider what portions of your selected sources might be useful to your topic and argument. Include specific text that supports (or opposes) your argument.

Formatting the bibliography. When writing the annotated bibliography, consider the following guidelines:

- Use MLA or APA style to provide a complete citation for the article.

- MLA or APA formatting and heading.

- MLA or APA formatted citations.

Evaluation Criteria (Annotated Bibliography)

	Accomplished	Emerging	Average	Below Average	Failing
Development	Annotations **summarily overview** and identify the main argument. Annotations **consistently** describe the supporting points.	Annotations **overview** and identify the main argument. Annotations **indicate** the supporting points.	Annotations **suggest** the main argument. Annotations **occasionally** describe the supporting points.	Annotations **hint** at the main argument. Annotations **rarely** describe the supporting points.	Annotations **do not** identify the main argument. Annotations do not describe the supporting points.
	The descriptive focus **is maintained** throughout the bibliography.	The descriptive focus is **consistently** maintained throughout the bibliography.	The descriptive focus is **often** maintained throughout the bibliography.	The descriptive focus is **rarely** maintained throughout the bibliography.	The descriptive focus **is not** maintained throughout the bibliography.

Continues

	Accomplished	Emerging	Average	Below Average	Failing
Coherence	Annotations **consistently** unfold logically.	Annotations **often** unfold logically.	Annotations **occasionally** unfold logically.	Annotations **rarely** unfold logically.	Annotations **do not** unfold logically.
	Annotations **consistently** identify information or arguments relevant to the thesis statement.	Annotations **often** identify information or arguments relevant to the thesis statement.	Annotations **occasionally** identify information or arguments relevant to the thesis statement.	Annotations **rarely** identify information or arguments relevant to the thesis statement.	Annotations **do not** identify information or arguments relevant to the thesis statement.
Analysis	Annotations **consistently** demonstrate an ability to evaluate the quality of the sources.	Annotations **often** demonstrate an ability to evaluate the quality of the sources.	Annotations **occasionally** demonstrate an ability to evaluate the quality of the sources.	Annotations **rarely** demonstrate an ability to evaluate the quality of the sources.	Annotations **do not** demonstrate an ability to evaluate the quality of the sources.
Convention (Style and Mechanics)	The annotations **consistently** demonstrate appropriate formality.	The annotations **often** demonstrate appropriate formality.	The annotations **occasionally** demonstrate appropriate formality.	The annotations **rarely** demonstrate appropriate formality.	The annotations **do not** demonstrate appropriate formality.
	Annotations **consistently** demonstrate an ability to utilize academic prose conventions, including spelling, formatting, mechanical correctness, and citation practices.	Annotations **often** demonstrate an ability to utilize academic prose conventions, including spelling, formatting, mechanical correctness, and citation practices.	Annotations **occasionally** demonstrate an ability to utilize academic prose conventions, including spelling, formatting, mechanical correctness, and citation practices.	Annotations **rarely** demonstrate an ability to utilize academic prose conventions, including spelling, formatting, mechanical correctness, and citation practices.	Annotations **do not** demonstrate an ability to utilize academic prose conventions, including spelling, formatting, mechanical correctness, and citation practices.

ENGL 1302: Research Essay

Throughout Composition I and II, you have engaged in many academic conversations. The texts and research you've studied have offered new insights, findings, and perspectives that you might not otherwise know.

For this following essay, then, you'll incorporate your reading and research into an academic research-based, argumentative essay. Meaningful academic and civic discourses go beyond merely reporting research findings; instead, academic papers add to these broader conversations by reiterating what others have said (or what most already know) and adding new "voices" to the conversation. This essay is your opportunity to join the academic conversation.

Remember that an effective research essay does not provoke the audience as if the essay were a personal blog post or opinion piece in a newspaper. Nor does academic argument attempt to appeal to or replicate popular opinion. Instead, seize the chance to showcase your critical thinking about complex and diverse issues.

Your research essay should:

- Be appropriate for an audience of your peers at NCTC,

- Be unified around a research question rather than merely reporting on several different aspects of a topic,

- Be "original" in that it attempts to wrestle with a topic that has not already been rehashed again and again in print, and

- Incorporate research, which may mean textual study, library sources, historical sources, or media sources.

As for all writings this semester, this paper will be written for your peers and your instructor. Therefore, you should assume that your reader is favorable to your analysis but might be unfamiliar with your sources. Your paper will need to background and clarify the content of the articles that you cite in your text.

Assignment Requirements:

- 12-point font, Times New Roman
- Double-spaced, approximately 1750 words
- MLA or APA guidelines for submission, citation, and documentation
- Minimum of 5 cited sources

Strategies for Writing a Research Essay

To begin this assignment, you'll want to first think of a research topic. You'll want to narrow your focus to an issue addressed or explored throughout our year-long discussion. Talk to your instructor about possible topics. Your research essay might focus on ethical arguments, proposal arguments, cause/effect arguments, classification arguments, or arguments of definition.

Once you have narrowed down a research topic, you need to construct a series of questions that you will attempt to answer throughout your research. You may not know the answers to these questions, and you probably won't. That's a good thing because your research is an opportunity for you to investigate the answers.

When considering research questions, you might focus on issues specific to a particular time, place, media, or circumstance. You can transition from your research topic to your research questions by narrowing your focus and looking at what would make your research "original."

Coming up with an "original topic" might mean:

- **You frame your research topic within a particular time.** *This topic is relevant and original because I focus on recent advancements and concerns.*

- **You frame your research topic by examining particular examples.** *This topic is relevant and original because I focus on these specific examples.*

- **You go against the grain.** *This topic is relevant and original because I will present counter-arguments that are often overlooked or dismissed.*

- **You frame your research topic by examining specific locations.** *This topic is relevant and original because I'm focusing my research on North Texas.*

Construct specific research questions that avoid questions that have simple "yes" or "no" answers. Compose questions that ask "what," "how," and "why." For example, rather than begin a research report on the facts about genetically modified food, begin your research based on questions specific to time, location, utilization, or motivation. Delve into questions beyond merely summarizing a topic toward presenting an original argument. Such questions might look something like these:

- How are organic foods discussed in news articles throughout the past five years?

- Why is the news coverage of organic foods relevant?

- And how do these news stories shape public opinion and, in turn, shape public policy?

When narrowing your research topic, consider alternative research methods to explore the issue from an original or unique perspective by developing questionnaires; conducting interviews; engaging in close readings of film, television, or social media; or crafting and distributing surveys. While you'll need to include scholarly research from the NCTC library databases to locate your topic in a broader conversation and support your claims, you may also use other research methods to develop a more robust and original focus. Here is a model essay that gives you an idea of how your paper should look and sound. Notice how the works cited page is formatted. Know that your instructor may require transitions within the paragraphs rather than sub-headings.

Evaluation Criteria (Research Essay)

	Accomplished	Emerging	Average	Below Average	Failing
Purpose (Development)	The essay identifies and presents a **fully** developed argument that overviews and develops **all** of the main points.	The essay identifies a central argument and describes **most** of its points.	The essay suggests an argument and describes **some** of its main points.	The essay hints at an argument and describes a **few** main points.	The essay fails to identify an argument and does **not** describe the main points.
	The focus is **consistently** maintained on making and supporting arguments throughout the essay.	The focus is **often** maintained on making and supporting arguments throughout the essay.	Original research focus **is generally** maintained throughout the essay.	Original research focus is **rarely** maintained throughout the essay.	Original research focus is **not** maintained throughout the essay.
Insight and Evaluation (Development)	The essay identifies and draws **fully** developed and insightful observations from sources specific and relevant to the essay's purpose.	The essay **often** draws insightful observations from specific and relevant sources to the essay's purpose.	The essay **occasionally** draws insightful observations from specific and relevant sources to the essay's purpose.	The essay **rarely** draws insightful observations from specific and relevant sources to the essay's purpose.	The essay **does not** draw insightful observations from specific and relevant sources to the essay's purpose.
	The sources are **fully** attributed in the essay (e.g., speaker tags, framing, avoiding double-voicing).	The sources are **often** attributed in the essay (e.g., speaker tags, framing, avoiding double-voicing).	The essay **occasionally** uses sources to present a fair and accurate picture of the conversation (e.g., avoiding logical fallacies and engaging in rhetorical listening).	The essay relies on sources to **rarely** present a fair and accurate picture of the conversation (e.g., avoiding logical fallacies, engaging in rhetorical listening).	The essay does **not** present a fair and accurate picture of the conversation (e.g., avoiding logical fallacies, engaging in rhetorical listening).

Continues

	Accomplished	Emerging	Average	Below Average	Failing
	The essay relies on sources to **fully** present a fair and accurate picture of the conversation (e.g., avoiding logical fallacies, engaging in rhetorical listening).	The essay relies on sources to present a fair and accurate picture of the conversation (e.g., avoiding logical fallacies and engaging in rhetorical listening).			
Coherence (Organization)	The essay's organization and coherence are **consistent and logical.** The essay consistently demonstrates conventions of the academic paper (e.g., title, introduction, discussion sections, conclusion, transitions, moving from general to specific, headings, subheadings).	The essay's organization and coherence are **often** consistent and logical. The essay often demonstrates conventions of the academic paper (e.g., title, introduction, discussion sections, conclusion, transitions, moving from general to specific, headings, subheadings).	The essay's organization and coherence are **occasionally** consistent and logical. The essay occasionally demonstrates conventions of the academic paper (e.g., title, introduction, discussion sections, conclusion, transitions, moving from general to specific, headings, subheadings).	The essay's organization and coherence are **rarely** consistent and logical. The essay rarely demonstrates conventions of the academic paper (e.g., title, introduction, discussion sections, conclusion, transitions, moving from general to specific, headings, subheadings).	The essay **does not** demonstrate a consistent, logical, and coherent organization. The essay does not demonstrate conventions of the academic paper (e.g., title, introduction, discussion sections, conclusion, transitions, moving from general to specific, headings, subheadings).

	Accomplished	Emerging	Average	Below Average	Failing
Convention (Style & Mechanics)	The essay consistently demonstrates appropriate formality.	The essay often demonstrates appropriate formality.	The essay occasionally demonstrates appropriate formality.	The essay rarely demonstrates appropriate formality.	The essay does not demonstrate appropriate formality.
	The essay consistently demonstrates an ability to utilize academic prose conventions, including spelling, formatting, and mechanical correctness.	The essay often demonstrates an ability to utilize academic prose conventions, including spelling, formatting, and mechanical correctness.	The essay occasionally demonstrates an ability to utilize academic prose conventions, including spelling, formatting, and mechanical correctness.	The essay rarely demonstrates an ability to utilize academic prose conventions, including spelling, formatting, and mechanical correctness.	The essay does not demonstrate an ability to utilize academic prose conventions, including spelling, formatting, and mechanical correctness.
Documentation (Citation Practices)	The essay consistently applies the conventions of academic documentation (e.g., document formatting; MLA: in-text citations, Works Cited; APA: in-text citations, References).	The essay often applies the conventions of academic documentation (e.g., document formatting; MLA: in-text citations, Works Cited; APA: in-text citations, References).	The essay occasionally applies the conventions of academic documentation (e.g., document formatting; MLA: in-text citations, Works Cited; APA: in-text citations, References).	The essay rarely applies the conventions of academic documentation (e.g., document formatting; MLA: in-text citations, Works Cited; APA: in-text citations, References).	The essay does not apply the conventions of academic documentation (e.g., document formatting; MLA: in-text citations, Works Cited; APA: in-text citations, References).

Emily Vasquez

Professor Peña

ENGL 1302.0413

5 December 2022

Research Essay: The Blame Instinct on the

Media and Environment

The blame instinct is described as the human impulse to find a cursory reason as to why something is wrong. By blaming another individual or organization, people are able to feel like everything is done with intent and by one entity that can take fault. Without this intuition, "the world feels unpredictable, confusing, and frightening" (Rosling 207). The internet is more influential in the present digital age, meaning more information is available, but there are fewer and fewer guarantees that this information is factual. Therefore, it is important for consumers to sift through this information to find actual facts.

Reliable sources are becoming difficult to confirm, as media information and news outlets are often biased towards one side of an argument to lure in like-minded people and maintain their number of viewers. For example, Dr. Erick Elejalde, a researcher from the L3S Research Center–a notable worldwide research organization based in Germany–reviews the likelihood of a media source presenting a story in a way that would either defend or rebuke the topic depending on the political siding of the source. Elejalde states the "results show that the media has a measurable bias, and illustrates that by showing favoritism... for the ruling political parties" (17). This point addresses the problem of how society receives their information from media outlets, thus reinforcing an individual's echo chamber of like-minded opinions rather than trying to understand ideas different from their own.

The effects of the blame instinct are seen in many aspects of society, ingrained as something so familiar that it has become a trend. This is most has especially been seen in the media and how it affects the environment as a result of the Covid-19 pandemic. Scapegoating, however, is dangerous because it prevents problem-solving and blocks people from acknowledging that other factors could be accounting for the situation at hand, resulting in an extreme case of societal tunnel vision.

The Blame Instinct in the Media and Societal Impact

People around the world get their news from a variety of sources: from news outlets, online journals, or social media. Most people obtain information about the world from some sort of media outlet. All media outlets are not created equally, and many are met with bias, altered headlines, and sometimes incorrect information. This is due to whichever political party the news source lean towards. In order for these networks to stay in business, it is crucial for headlines to spark the attention of viewers that have the same mindset as the presented headlines. News outlets will utilize the blame instinct to cater information more suited to their audience demographic to retain their viewer numbers to the point of altering the subject to suit their viewpoints.

These biases allow newscasters to easily pick out what stories to broadcast because the only headlines media outlets choose are the ones that cater to the attention of their returning viewers. A clear example of news outlet bias can be seen through Fox and CNN. These two outlets continuously contradict each other by using the blame instinct to debunk each other's claims in an attempt to convince the viewer they are on the "correct" side by labeling the opposition as *fake news*.

Bruce Mutsvairo, Journalism Professor at Auburn University, discovered this connection in a 2020 study. In his study, "You Are Fake News: Political Bias in Perceptions of Fake News," Mutsvairo explores the similar beliefs of opposing political sides by exposing "evidence that both liberals and conservatives freely associate traditionally left-wing (e.g. CNN) and right-wing (e.g. Fox News) media sources with the term fake news" (Mutsvairo et. al.). Fox News and CNN use the blame instinct on one another to invalidate their claims, making their audiences more likely to ignore opposing arguments, resulting in a case of tunnel vision that prevents discussion and positive societal change. By blaming others, the sense of responsibility is shifted away from the one pointing a finger to create a false sense of innocence. However, absconding this responsibility results in no compromises being met or a solution being found. Ultimately, this does not help society.

Creating sides in important arguments divides society and makes individuals believe that there is an evil that needs to be defeated, oftentimes because people believe the perceived enemy has the power and desire to commit the problem in question. In other words, this means that the blame instinct creates the illusion of a clear conscience so consumers think that what they are listening to is the correct side and the *other* is completely wrong. Nobody wants to be in the wrong, and it's not any easier to admit that one is in the wrong either, further thickening the dividing line created by the blame instinct. Stereotyping is a major effect of the dividing line created by the blame instinct. For example, people automatically correlate certain traits about a person depending on if they watch Fox or CNN.

According to the findings of Hans Rosling, a Swedish physician from the University of Uppsala, in his book, *Factfulness*, "this instinct to find a guilty party derails our ability to develop a true, fact-based understanding of the world; it steals our focus as we obsess about someone to blame, then blocks out learning...[so] we stop looking for explanations elsewhere" (207). Humans have the natural inclination to stick with the most convenient answer they find so they can remove the blame from themselves and place it on another entity, thereby shifting the problem for others to handle. People would rather believe a villain exists in an issue, and tend to blame the entity to try and clear their conscience. This allows people to divide themselves into opposing sides and avoid communication so they can continue to point fingers. This tactic, again, does not benefit society in any way.

The Blame Instinct on the COVID-19 Pandemic and Environment

The media's utilization of the blame instinct does not just stop at dividing people from each other; it also affects people's perceptions of important shared issues. During the year 2020 and onward, coverage of the COVID-19 pandemic was considered unreliable, since multiple sources would state different facts. Factual information became harder to find because, as previously mentioned, the media was more focused on gaining viewers than spreading accurate information. Media outlets highlighted situations that blamed other demographics of people and medical professionals for not creating a timely solution to the COVID-19 pandemic. This tactic was for the purpose of causing outrage and spreading fear to gain more views rather than to spread factual information. As people were panicking in light of the unknown factors of the virus, they sought more information to better prepare themselves for any eventuality, only exacerbating the situation by seeking more unreliable information.

Bernardo Sousa-Pinto, an author and researcher from the Center for Health and Technology and Service Research in Portugal, conducted a study over five years that examines terms related to the COVID-19 pandemic. This study, "Assessment of the Impact of Media Coverage on COVID-19–Related Google Trends Data: Infodemiology Study" explains, "results indicate that COVID-19–related Google Trends data are more closely related to media coverage than to epidemic trends" (Sousa-Pinto et al.). In other words, developments in the virus were more popular when the media reported on it, not necessarily when developments were actually made by medical professionals.

People are inclined to care more about issues that will affect day-to-day life rather than the more widespread problems of the world, so they were extremely focused on the pandemic since it was both a personal and widespread issue. Changes that were reported outside of the pandemic weren't regarded with as much attention since they didn't gain any views. The blame instinct affected the world's perception of COVID-19 and was not strategic in guiding society to the many other changes that were occurring. This is important to study because the urgency of getting the information to the public was rushed and unreliable in many cases, and these actions turned people against one another rather than unifying society to navigate the problem.

The pandemic was widely covered as something to closely regard, but its urgency overshadowed many other events that affected the world, as well. As the media focused on the problems of the pandemic and how it impacted the personal lives of their viewers, the monumental impact the environment experienced as a result of society's reaction to COVID-19 was largely ignored. While the world was hyper-focused on the COVID-19 pandemic, the environment's recovery was clearly shown in the reduction of air pollution and smog around some of the world's most populated cities as people were called to stay inside and avoid social interaction.

Although air quality was improving, the pandemic did bring about another form of pollution into our environment: disposable personal protective equipment. Masks, gloves, and cleaning wipes were being used at an excessive rate and this littered the environment. Many people would hastily find partial solutions to the rapid growth of disposable pollution by using reusable masks and opting out of using latex vinyl gloves in favor of washing their hands more frequently. Since these environmental matters had no effect on daily life, media outlets did not feel the need to report on these situations, both positive and negative.

It is also important to consider the fact that the media tends to put the blame on the average individual for why the world is so contaminated and not improving, even though big corporations are continuously and furtively polluting. The media uses the blame instinct to convince the public that the general population is the main catalyst in pollution, and not the bigger system that facilitates it.

In time, research should consider the harmful effects of the COVID-19 pandemic on the environment. Han Jiatong, a researcher from Bejing Normal University, finds in her study, "Environment and COVID-19 Incidence: A Critical Review:" "research should be extended to cover both the effects of the environment on the COVID-19 pandemic and COVID-19-induced impacts on the environment." This means that future research involving the environment should consider the COVID-19 pandemic and its effects to reduce pollution worldwide.

In 2022, the effects of the COVID-19 pandemic are still prevalent in studies focused on how nature was changed as a result. The environment was able to slightly heal as society struggled to adapt to the new normal that came with lockdowns and social distancing, although with mask requirements and the influx of purchasing disposable personal protective equipment, there was a massive increase of garbage pollutants in our ecosystems. Therefore, the environment experienced both positives and negatives because of the COVID-19 pandemic.

Conclusion

The blame instinct has been used by the media for years to gain views and cause discord among the populace. News outlets have become increasingly unreliable as they divulge different interpretations of the same story. Different topics have become subjects of division in an effort to maintain viewer retention rather than present information in an unbiased way. The blame instinct is a coping mechanism that helps people feel as if there is a greater power doing bad things intentionally so they do not have to take the responsibility of the issue at hand. This is especially dangerous when the media uses it to divide their consumers rather than unite them against a common problem. A more noticeable issue that has come from the media's use of the blame instinct is stereotyping. By scapegoating an issue onto a certain population, this allows the one who is absconding the blame to not feel guilty because they no longer feel as if the issue is their fault. This further divides society and harms populations when mass amounts of people believe what is being said on television or read from their screens.

The blame instinct and the media's use of it combined with COVID-19 utilized the panic and fear that society was experiencing to keep them focused on the negativity happening rather than other important events. The environmental changes that occurred in the year 2020 and beyond were direct results of society's reactions to COVID-19, yet no major environmental stories broke in the media during that time. Future data will be affected by humanity's isolation period and subsequent reaction to being able to re-enter the world. The drop in air pollution due to lack of traveling and immediate increase in landfill pollution with the disposal of personal protective equipment and sanitary products was so dramatic that it was noted by scientists across the world, yet it was glossed over in news stories because it wasn't seen as a high priority next to the updates on the pandemic. The blame instinct has had major effects on society and the environment, proving that it is a dangerous mindset. Problem solving is not prioritized when using the blame instinct. Its usage only continues to be a weapon, while others rather use it to blame each other, as opposed to working towards a solution. Therefore, it is important to be aware of the blame instinct and combat it for future generations to come.

Works Cited

Elejalde, Erick, et al. "On the Nature of Real and Perceived Bias in the Mainstream Media." *PLoS ONE*, vol. 13, no. 3, Mar. 2018, pp. 1–28. EBSCOhost, https://doi-org.northcenttexascollegelibrary.idm.oclc. org/10.1371/journal.pone.0193765. Accessed 9 November 2022.

Han, Jiatong, et al. "Environment and COVID-19 Incidence: A Critical Review." *Journal of Environmental Sciences (China)*, vol. 124, Jan. 2023, pp. 933–51. EBSCOhost, https://doi-org.northcenttexascol-legelibrary.idm.oclc.org/10.1016/j.jes.2022.02.016. Accessed 11 Nov. 2022.

Mutsvairo, Bruce, et al. "You Are Fake News: Political Bias in Percep-tions of Fake News." *Media, Culture & Society*, vol. 42, no. 3, Apr. 2020, pp. 460–70. EBSCOhost, https://doi-org.northcenttexascol-legelibrary.idm.oclc.org/10.1177/0163443720906992. Accessed 11 Oct. 2022.

Rosling, Hans, et al. *Factfulness Ten Reasons We're Wrong About the World - and Why Things Are Better Than You Think*. Flatiron Books. 2018.

Sousa-Pinto, Bernardo, et al. "Assessment of the Impact of Media Coverage on COVID-19-Related Google Trends Data: Infodemiol-ogy Study." *Journal of Medical Internet Research*, vol. 22, no. 8, Aug. 2020, p. e19611. EBSCOhost, https://doi-org.northcenttexas-collegelibrary.idm.oclc.org/10.2196/19611. Accessed 27 Oct. 2022.

NCTC's Statement on Plagiarism and Academic Dishonesty in First-Year Composition

Over the course of this academic year, you'll learn how to locate, synthesize, paraphrase, and quote outside sources to support your points. A foundational component of academic research is learning to integrate sources to avoid "double-voicing" (when it's unclear when your voice ends and your sources begin). It is why both ENGL 1301 and 1302 include *attribution* and *documentation* in the learning outcomes.

- ENGL 1301: Develop ideas with appropriate support and attribution
- ENGL 1302: Apply the conventions of style manuals for specific academic disciplines (e.g., APA, CMS, MLA, etc.)

You must learn how to document your sources and have the time and space to practice those skills. You'll probably make mistakes, and it's our job to help you see those errors and learn from them.

However, there is a difference between incorrectly documenting your sources and intentionally trying to deceive your instructor by submitting someone else's work or thoughts and claiming them to be your own. A deliberate attempt to circumvent doing your own writing—whether it's a sentence, paragraph, or entire essay—is considering academic dishonesty or plagiarism.

For our part, we've taken several measures to create a classroom environment that discourages plagiarism:

- First, we've designed your courses so that the readings and writing assignments are specific to NCTC and our course discussions. We do this to engage you in the course activities so that you feel invested and motivated to participate fully in the course.

- Second, we customize our courses to prevent students from turning in generic, tired writing assignments about topics that have been hashed out time and time again online. The assignments in your courses are also designed so that papers cannot be easily copied from online paper mills.

For your part, we ask you to consider how you can avoid plagiarism or academic dishonesty by not engaging in the following actions:

1. Turning in someone else's ideas, opinions, theories, or work as your own;
2. Unintentionally or inadvertently turning in someone else's ideas, opinions, theories, or work as your own as the result of failing to document sources both internally and on the Works Cited page;

3. Copying words, ideas, or images from someone without giving credit and failing to put a quotation in quotations marks;

4. Giving incorrect information about the source of information, quotations, or images;

5. Changing words but copying the sentence structure of a source without giving credit; and/or

6. Giving your paper, discussion board posts, or reflections to a classmate to use as his/her/their own.

7. Copying so many words, ideas, or images from a source that it makes up the majority of the student's work, whether or not the student gives credit.

8. Using artificial intelligence (AI) products, such as Chat GPT, and submitting it as original work

In other words, according to the student handbook, academic dishonesty shall include but is not limited to cheating on a test, plagiarism, and collusion. (See *Student Handbook* "Student Rights & Responsibilities: Student Conduct [FLB-(LOCAL)]" #18.)

Please pay careful attention to the consequences of academic dishonesty:

> *Disciplinary Actions* [*Student Handbook*, #5]: "When cheating, collusion, or plagiarism has occurred beyond any reasonable doubt, the instructor may give the student or students involved an "F" on a particular assignment or in the course. [See Scholastic Dishonesty FLB (Local)] The instructor shall make a written report of the incident and the planned action to the Department Chair. The Department Chair shall report the incident and action to the appropriate instructional dean who shall review the case, notify the student and, if necessary, take further action. This may involve either probation or suspension of the student or students in question. If such disciplinary action is deemed necessary, the Dean of Student Services shall be notified, and the action shall be taken through that office."

Please be advised that your instructor and our department take plagiarism or academic dishonesty seriously. To avoid plagiarism or academic dishonesty, we encourage you to do your own work, embrace any struggles or challenges as part of the learning process, start early on your assignments, and seek out feedback or clarification from your instructor or the writing center if you're confused about whether you've appropriately documented your sources.

Works Cited

hooks, bell. *Talking Back: Thinking Feminist, Thinking Black*. 2nd ed., Routledge, 2014.

Hsu, Hua. "The Revolutionary Writing of bell hooks." *The New Yorker*, 16 Dec. 2021, www.newyorker.com/culture/postscript/the-revolutionary-writing-of-bell-hooks.

Mask, Deirdre. *The Address Book: What Street Addresses Reveal about Identity, Race, Wealth, and Power*. St. Martin's Griffin, 2021.

Rose, Mike. *The Mind at Work: Valuing the Intelligence of the American Worker*. Kindle ed., Penguin Books, 2005.

——. "Tips on Thinking and Writing." *Mike Rose's Blog*, 26 Sept. 2016, mikerosebooks.blogspot.com/2016/09/tips-on-thinking-and-writing.html.

Rosling, Hans, et al. *Factfulness: Ten Reasons We're Wrong About the World—and Why Things Are Better Than You Think*. Flatiron Books, 2020.

Contents

W6: Using Language Powerfully 70

W7: Thinking While Writing 88

W8: Revising 96

W9: Editing 115

W10: Introductions, Conclusions, and Titles 188

W11: Writing Strategies 196

Reading 241

R1: Preparing to Read 242

R2: Reading Actively 257

R3: Reading Critically 275

D Research and Documentation 293

D1: Research 294

B # Balancing School, Work, and Life 401

B2: Life Issues 405

B3: Staying the Course 412

B4: College Knowledge 415

Acknowledgments

I am grateful to my colleagues at the Conference (now, Council) on Basic Writing for their support of my early thinking about corequisites (or, as we called it then, "mainstreaming" basic writers): Suellynn Duffey, Greg Glau, Barbara Gleason, Sugie Goen-Salter, Carolyn Kirkpatrick, Bill Lalicker, Rebecca Mlynarczyk, Deborah Mutnick, and Karen Uehling. I owe equal gratitude to my colleagues at the Community College of Baltimore County: Linda De La Ysla, Susan Gabriel, Jamey Gallagher, Sarah Gearhardt, Terry Hirsch, Patrick Kelleher, Donna McKusick, Bob Miller, Anne Roberts, Jackie Scott, and Monica Walker.

The corequisite idea also received important support from Tom Bailey at the Community College Research Center, from Bruce Vandal at Complete College America, and from David Bartholomae, whose "Tidy House" presentation at the CBW conference in 1992 provided reassurance that corequisite developmental writing was not a crazy idea.

For the development of the first edition of *The Hub*, I was fortunate to have a faculty advisory board who provided insights, suggestions, corrections, and examples that greatly improved the final manuscript under extremely tight time constraints. Warm thank-yous to Paul Beehler, University of California–Riverside; Mark Blaauw-Hara, North Central Michigan College; Brian Dickson, Community College of Denver; Jacqueline Gray, St. Charles Community College; Angelique Johnston, Monroe Community College; Meridith Leo, Suffolk County Community College; Angelina Oberdan, Central Piedmont Community College; Kelli Prejean, Marshall University; Sarah Snyder, Western Arizona College; and Christina Tarabicos, Delaware Technical Community College.

I also want to thank colleagues across the country who found time to provide feedback and advice on the manuscript of *The Hub*, Second Edition: Ashlee Brand, Cuyahoga Community College–Westshore Campus; Bert Barry, PhD, St. Charles Community College; Katharine Boraz, Miracosta College; Elizabeth Burton, Hopkinsville Community College; Anthony Cavaluzzi, Adirondack Community College; Malkiel A. Choseed, PhD, Onondaga Community College; James M. Cochran, PhD, Hartwick College; Morgan Dancy, Methodist University; Caroline Davis, San Antonio College; Sarah E. DeCapua, PhD, North Central Texas College; Matt Delconte, Onondaga Community College; Marian Dillahunt, Methodist University; Anthony Edgington, University of Toledo; Christina Ethridge, Hopkinsville Community College; Deborah Ferguson, Central Piedmont Community College; Jacqueline Gray, St. Charles Community College; Rochelle Gregory, North Central Texas College; Dr. Jacob Hutchinson, Arkansas State University Mid South; Julia Laffoon-Jackson, Hopkinsville Community College; Meridith A. Leo, PhD, Suffolk County Community College Ammerman; Amy S. Lerman, Mesa Community College; Jill Lynch, Houston Community College, Central; Jeffrey Miller, St. Charles

Community College; JessiRae Morton, Central Piedmont Community College; Jayme Novara, St. Charles Community College; Anne Page, Central Piedmont Community College; Shelley Harper Palmer, Central Piedmont Community College; Leslie A. Rice, San Jose City College; Margie A. Ricks, Houston Community College, SW College; Dr. Timothy Robinson, Central Piedmont Community College; Sherry Rosenthal, College of Southern Nevada; Kristen Weinzapfel, North Central Texas College.

I especially thank Elisabeth Bass, Camden County Community College, for sharing insights from her studies of trauma-informed pedagogy; Sarah DeCapua, North Central Texas College, who provided a different perspective on the two new reading/writing projects on individual and community and immigration; and Malkiel Choseed, Onondaga Community College, who connected us with two of his talented student writers. Many thanks—and apologies, too—to Zoey Devoid for allowing us to include her essay in *The Hub*, Second Edition, and to introduce some issues into her writing in order to demonstrate to other students how to attend to them. (Her paper, "In Pursuit of Happiness," appears in W8.)

I am also grateful to students and recent graduates who participated in a focus group on *The Hub*: Julia Cheunkarndee, Kaylin Fussell, Clarah Grossman, Heather Haase, Angelica Hernandez, Amanda Nava, Autumn Oliver, Bailey Salimes, and Juliana Verrelli. Their insights allowed me to see the text from a student perspective and to make many improvements as a result.

I am particularly indebted to the expert reviewers who helped me conceptualize, develop, and revise early drafts of the new reading/writing project on disability: Suzanne Ament, Radford University; Dev Bose, The University of Arizona; Rochelle Gregory, North Central Texas College; Elizabeth Olsen, Central Connecticut State University; Annemarie Ross, National Technical Institute for the Deaf, Rochester Institute of Technology; and Patrice Wheeler, California State University Northridge.

Rochelle Gregory was particularly generous with her time and thoughtful intelligence. In addition to reviewing drafts of all the new reading/writing projects and consulting with me on the new Project 7, Disability, from conception to final draft, she also helped by conducting a keen review focusing on issues of diversity, equity, and inclusion (DEI) for material carried over from the first edition and new content developed especially for the second edition.

I would also like to thank Courtney Mauck, Ohio University, and Michael Reyes, California Polytechnic State University, for their thoughtful comments on DEI issues.

It has been a great pleasure to work with the team at Bedford/St. Martin's. Their knowledge of the fields of composition and basic writing, their experience in textbook development, their willingness to talk through complex issues, and the breadth of their expertise have meant that working on this project for seven years has been an exhilarating experience for me. I, first, want to thank my executive development editor for the first edition, Gillian Cook; her wit, expertise, and common sense are still present in much of the book. Next I'd like to thank my executive development editor and friend, Jane Carter, who, until her recent retirement, guided and inspired my work on this second edition with her expertise, intelligence, sense of humor, and patience. Her brilliance and hard work are present on every page. When Jane retired, senior development editor Leah Strauss stepped in to guide this edition through its final stages. Her ability to quickly master the intricacies and idiosyncrasies of the book were truly impressive, and her ongoing support, insight, and intelligence have meant the project continued without missing a beat. Ryan Sullivan, Senior Digital Content Project Manager, coordinated all the moving parts masterfully, and was very ably assisted by Michael Granger, Senior Managing Editor. Heartfelt thanks to Paola Garcia-Muniz, Associate Media Editor, and Kalinda Collins, Editorial Assistant, for their dedication to this project. Leasa Burton, Vice President, Editorial, Macmillan Learning Humanities, and Stacey Purviance, formerly Program Director for English, provided the kind of advice, support, and encouragement every author hopes for.

Thanks also to Joy Fisher Williams, Executive Marketing Manager, and Azelie Fortier, Senior Market Development Manager, who brilliantly organized meetings, brochures, letters, and blogs to spread the word about *The Hub*. I am also grateful to the digital experts—Adam Whitehurst, Director of Media Editorial, Humanities, and Sarah Gatenby, Senior Media Editor—for making my dream of a digital publication into a reality. My thanks also to William Boardman, Senior Design Manager, for *The Hub*'s delightful cover design.

Finally, I want to express my loving gratitude to my wife, Donna, and my mother-in-law, Rosemarie, who have provided the kind of environment that allowed me to hole up in my office for the past six years to work on this book and who were always ready with thoughtful suggestions when I needed them. I also owe thanks to my daughters, Melia and Emily, who have kept me connected to a younger generation, and to my grandchildren, Casey and Nick, who have provided the same connections to an even younger generation.

Definitions of Terms Used in *The Hub*

Academic Essay	At the end of each reading/writing project, there are three writing assignments. One of the three is a traditional academic essay.
Advice	Instructional text that discusses issues and strategies for writing, reading, and research, designed to be read in preparation for class.
Exploration	A unit designed for students to do some thinking, usually in a group, but most of these can be assigned as individual work if preferred.
Multimodal Composition	At the end of each reading/writing project, there are three writing assignments, one of which asks students to produce a multimodal composition.
Part	One of the five major divisions of *The Hub*—Part P: Reading/Writing Projects, Part W: Writing, Part R: Reading, Part D: Research and Documentation, and Part B: Balancing School, Work, and Life. Each part contains a series of chapters on major subjects relevant to the part.
Project	One of the seven reading/writing projects that constitute Part P.
Reading	A reading can be an essay, newspaper article, journal article, blog post, excerpt from a nonfiction or fiction text, chapter from a book, legal statute, set of college policies, and more. These readings are the primary material in the reading/writing projects in Part P. Students are expected to read them in preparation for class.
Real World Essay	At the end of each reading/writing project, there are three writing assignments. The "Real World Essay" asks students to write an essay that addresses an audience outside their classroom (e.g., next year's students, the community, visitors to an art museum, a career counselor, a college committee, or readers of a newspaper).
Unit	Each chapter consists of a series of units that provide instruction (advice and videos), practice (exploration), and reading and writing opportunities (readings, writing prompts, and essay assignments).
Video	A short video, almost always less than five minutes, and usually available on YouTube.
Writing	The word *Writing* is used in the titles of units to indicate the many short writing assignments. These usually call for a page or so of writing, but sometimes even less. The idea, especially in Part P, is that some of this writing may later be incorporated into the major writing projects, such as those at the end of each reading/writing project.

W Writing

W1 ▸ The Writing Process

W1 does not discuss what effective writing is; instead, it explores what you need to do to produce effective writing by examining the processes that effective writers follow.

Introduction to the Writing Process

The writing process encompasses a range of tasks, from prewriting and finding a focus to developing and organizing ideas to drafting, revising, and editing. Most effective writers move back and forth among these different steps in the process.

W1.1 Exploration
How Do *You* Write an Essay?

For this activity, you're going to do a short piece of informal writing. Your instructor will let you know whether you will write this in class or at home and when it should be turned in.

For this assignment, you will need to think back to a time when you had to write an essay, perhaps in high school, in another course, or even earlier in this course. Write a numbered list of the steps that you took to write the paper.

If it's been a while since you wrote an essay in a class and you can't remember a specific essay you had to write, you can use the following assignment. Don't write this essay. Simply make a list of the steps you would take today to write it.

Assignment

Write a letter to the editor of the *New York Times* in which you discuss an event or an issue reported in the news this week. A selection of letters written to the editor is published each day. The letters are seldom more than 250 words long. Your goal is to get your letter published in the *New York Times*.

The Writing Process

You can watch this video presentation on the writing process from Achieve with *The Hub*.

How Effective Writers Go about Writing

Good writing takes time and effort. Developing a process that you can follow and change as needed based on your rhetorical situation will improve your writing. (To learn more about the rhetorical situation, see W2.3, Components of the Rhetorical Situation, p. 287.) The chart below lists seven major activities involved in the writing process.

| Preparing to Write | Finding a Focus | Developing Ideas | Organizing Ideas | Writing | Revising | Editing |

Thoughtful writers do not simply move through the steps listed in the chart, performing each activity once and then moving on to the next in the linear fashion shown in the diagram below.

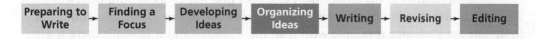

Instead, they weave back and forth among these activities as they find new information, generate new ideas, revise their thesis, reorganize their ideas, add support, revise their writing, and edit their final draft. Their process is messy and involves lots of circling back to improve parts of the paper they worked on earlier—messy, yes, but very productive.

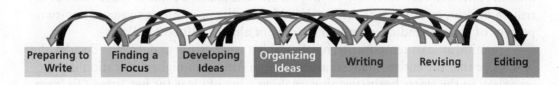

One Student's Writing Process

How Juanita Wrote Her Essay

This example shows the writing process of one student (Juanita) while she was working on an assignment for her first-year composition class. Analyzing what Juanita did can show you how recursive the writing process can be.

Juanita starts by reading the assignment from her teacher:

> Write a letter to the editor of the *New York Times* in which you discuss an event or an issue reported in the news this week. A selection of letters written to the editor is published each day. The letters are seldom more than 250 words long. Your goal is to get your letter published in the *New York Times*.

Juanita doesn't just start writing. She takes some steps to help her get ready to write. She **analyzes the assignment carefully**. Since she has never read a letter to the editor of the *New York Times* before, **she goes online to see what the letters to the editor look like.** She also gets a sense of how they sound—the tone writers use and the words they select—and the kinds of topics they are written about. (To learn more about tone and word choice, see W6, Using Language Powerfully, p. 70.)

Juanita returns to the assignment and sees that her essay should be fewer than 250 words and that her **purpose** is to get it published in the *Times*. She thinks, at first, that her **audience** is people who read the *Times*—and it is—but there is also another audience: the editors at the paper who decide which letters to publish. (To learn more about audience and purpose, see W2.4, Thinking about Audience, p. 13, and W2.6, Thinking about Purpose, p. 16.) From the letters she read online, she decides the editors at the *Times* seem to prefer letters that take a strong stand and back up their positions with thoughtful arguments.

Juanita notices an article about student debt. She is startled to learn that 43 million Americans are currently paying off student loans, a total of more than $1.6 trillion in debt, an amount that has tripled in just the past thirteen years. Sixty-two percent of college graduates owe an average of almost $30,000 dollars.

Juanita, at least temporarily, has found her topic: student debt. She decides she will argue that the entire financial aid system in American higher education is too complex. So she **starts brainstorming**, making a list of ideas for her letter. (To learn more about brainstorming, see W3.1, Using Invention Strategies to Generate Ideas, p. 21; W3.2, Brainstorming, p. 22; and W3.3, Using Invention Strategies to Select a Topic, p. 27.) Tuition has increased dramatically over the last decade, the process of applying for financial aid is unnecessarily complex, the amount of information a student must provide is burdensome. After a few minutes, Juanita discovers that her ideas about financial aid are not very original; she is just repeating the complaints she has heard from fellow students.

She then remembers that, when she went to college, her older sister, Helena, had received some scholarship money but still had to borrow more than $4,000 her first year. Even with this financial aid, she still owed several thousand dollars in tuition. When she was late with her tuition payment for her second semester, she received a notice that she would not be allowed to register for spring semester classes until her account was current. By the time she got things straightened out, she had missed the registration period for the spring and had to do late registration. As a result, several of the classes she needed to take were full and several others were only available early in the morning. None of this would have happened, Helena told Juanita, if the entire system weren't so complicated.

Juanita **next finds a website** that provides statistics on how many students default on their loans each year, how many don't even fill out the FAFSA (Free Application for Federal Student Aid) form, and how many, like her sister, are denied registration because of outstanding bills. (See D1.4–D1.9 in the section "Finding and Evaluating Sources, and Taking Notes," pp. 298–309.) She **returns to her draft** and starts writing, combining her sister's story with the statistics she has found.

At this point, Juanita pauses to read over what she has written and comes to a disappointing conclusion. There is no way she can say all she has to say in 250 words or less, so she decides to **narrow her thesis** to focus only on how her sister was denied registration because of her late tuition payment. (See W3.6, Using Invention Strategies to Arrive at a Thesis, p. 31.)

Next, Juanita **goes back online looking for more information.** She finds an article in the *New York Times* about the state university system in New York changing its approach to students who are behind on their tuition payments. Some students, she learns, have been prevented from registering for sums as low as $100, but all this will change when the new policy goes into effect.

Juanita thinks that maybe, if changes can be made in New York, they can be made in other states. She decides to write a letter to the editor about the national need for a more compassionate system of student debt collection.

She **returns to her draft** and adds a few sentences about the changes underway in New York. Next, **she reads her letter to the editor over** looking for places that might need revising. She changes the order of some of her ideas, provides more support for her assertions, and adds a few transitions to improve coherence. (See W8, Revising, p. 96.) Finally, she pours herself a fresh cup of coffee and **reads the entire paper** several times, correcting problems with spelling, grammar, punctuation, wording, and style. (See W9, Editing, p. 115.)

W1.5 Advice

How Juanita's Process Relates to You

Although every writer's process is different, and even the same writer's process is different for different writing tasks, the most effective writers carry out all seven activities in the writing process and keep circling back to do them over and over. This kind of recursive process may take more time than you are used to devoting to an essay, but it produces consistently better results.

Conducting Peer Review

W1.6 Advice

Guidelines for Peer Review

After finishing a draft of a piece of writing, many writers like to ask a friend, a classmate, a coworker, or someone else to look their writing over and give them some feedback. Because this practice—asking a reader to provide feedback—is so useful and so common in the world outside college, many instructors in college writing courses ask their students to participate in *peer review*, a process in which students take turns giving each other feedback on their writing. (A *peer* is someone who has the same standing as you, someone like one of your classmates.)

There are two ways you might participate in peer review this semester:

1. Your instructor may organize a peer review session either during class or as homework, face-to-face or online.

2. You may decide, on your own, to ask a classmate or a friend to look over a draft of your writing.

The guidelines below should be useful whether you are informally asking a friend for feedback or you are more formally getting feedback from classmates in a peer review session for class.

Giving Feedback

1. **Make sure you understand the assignment for the piece of writing.** Be sure to check whether the writer is actually doing the kind of writing the assignment asks for and whether the writer has satisfied all the requirements of the assignment.

2. **Determine where the writer is in the process of writing this paper.** If you are reviewing a very early rough draft, you will want to concentrate on the big issues. Is the main point clear, and is the evidence convincing? (To learn more about revising for thesis and support, see W8.5, Revising for Thesis and Unity, p. 102, and W8.9, Revising for Support, p. 105.) If you are reviewing a paper that is further along, you may want to focus on organization and coherence. Does the flow of ideas makes sense? Is anything missing that would make the essay hang together better? (To learn more about revising for organization or coherence, see W8.7, Revising for Organization, p. 104, or W8.11, Revising for Coherence, p. 108.)

3. **Keep in mind that receiving criticism is not exactly fun.** The writer of the paper wants to hear what can be improved but is probably also dreading hearing criticism. One way to make your comments easier for the writer to hear is to make sure you praise what you really like about the paper. Find a place where the writer has made a good point or expressed an idea in particularly powerful language. Be sure you are sincere in this praise; most writers can see right through empty compliments.

4. **Use a guide (rubric) if one has been provided.** If you're reviewing a piece of writing because your instructor has required the class to do so, you may have received a list of topics or questions to guide your review. Be sure you follow this guide.

5. **If you are not given a guide (rubric) for your review, you might want to use the following suggestions.**

   a. *Comment on the focus of the writing.* Is the main argument—the thesis of the writing—clear? Does that thesis remain the focus of the whole paper or does the writer lose track and wander into other topics in some places? Is the main idea of the paper the same at the end of the paper as it was at the beginning? If there are problems with the thesis and unity, point out exactly where the problems occur and, if possible, suggest how they might be eliminated. (You may want to take a look at W5.1, Creating Unity, p. 53.)

   b. *Comment on how well the writer provided convincing evidence to support the thesis.* Compliment the writer on evidence that really works, but also point out where the writer has made assertions without convincing support or where evidence does not support the argument. (W4.2, Types of Evidence, p. 42, and W11.4, Three Types of Appeal: *Logos*, *Ethos*, and *Pathos*, p. 198, might be useful.)

   c. *Comment on how well the writer has responded to possible opposing arguments.* Does the essay simply ignore obvious arguments that those who disagree with its thesis would raise? When acknowledging arguments that opponents would make, does the writer provide effective counterarguments? Or, when it seems necessary, does the writer concede the point and then explain why the point is of minimal importance? (For more about responding to opposing viewpoints, see W11.6, Responses to Positions Different from Yours, p. 203.)

d. *Comment on how easy it was to follow the paper's argument*. Are there places that confused you? Are there places where the paper seemed to jump from one point to the next without a clear connection between the points? If possible, suggest changes to the organization or the addition of transitions to make the argument easier to follow. (Take a look at W5, Organizing Ideas, especially W5.1, Creating Unity, p. 53; W5.5, Chunking and Ordering, p. 58; and W5.10, Strategies for Creating Coherence, p. 65.)

6. **Try to make your comments as specific as possible.** Don't just write, "You need more evidence to support your assertions." Instead, point out a specific assertion that needs more evidence and, if possible, give some suggestions about what kind of evidence might help.

7. **Write or type your comments directly in the essay, so the writer has a record.** If you are reviewing an essay that you receive as a Word or Google document, you may want to use the "Review" (Word) or "Suggesting" (Google) functions to make your comments. (The illustration below shows what these comments look like.) If not, you could use a different font and color or put your comments in brackets, so your comments are distinct from what the writer used.

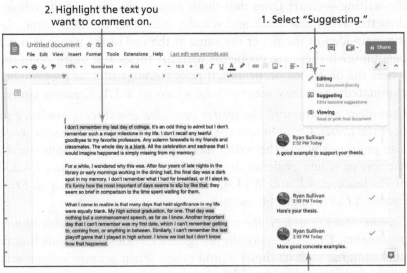

2. Highlight the text you want to comment on.

1. Select "Suggesting."

3. Type your comments in the box that appears on the right and hit "Comment."

Getting Feedback

Here are some suggestions for how to respond when someone reviews your writing.

1. **Identify your concerns.**   Ask your reviewer to address the specific things you'd like to know about your draft. (What is my thesis—is it clear? Is the evidence I provided convincing? Where do I need more evidence?)

2. **Take notes.**   If your reviewer is giving feedback orally, be sure to write down the comments, so you have a record for when you revise.

3. **Ask for specifics.**   If your reviewer's comments are vague or unclear, ask for examples.

4. **Don't get in an argument with your reviewer.**   If the reviewer offers suggestions you don't agree with, listen carefully to what is said, but feel free to find your strategy for resolving the issue. It's your paper.

W1.7 Exploration

Practicing Peer Review

Your instructor will give you instructions about working in pairs or small groups to review one another's essay drafts. Use the suggestions in W1.6, Guidelines for Peer Review (p. 6), to keep your session productive.

W2 ▸ Preparing to Write

I n W2, you'll learn about some important steps you can take before starting to write an essay, steps that will take only a few minutes but will greatly improve the effectiveness of what you write.

Reading and Analyzing the Assignment

Writing effectively starts with reading and analyzing the assignment, paying attention to the exact words used in the assignment and what exactly those words ask you to do.

W2.1 Advice

Reading an Assignment

To write effectively in a college class, it is essential that you read each assignment carefully, making sure you understand exactly what the instructor expects you to do. If possible, read the assignment when it's handed out in class and ask any questions you have about it then. When you are ready to start working on the assignment later, read it again slowly, perhaps marking it up with comments, reminders, and questions. If you do have questions, check whether your instructor is willing to discuss the assignment with you individually — in office hours or by phone, text, or email.

When reading an assignment, be particularly attentive to the verbs your instructor has used. Were you asked to *explain* something? To *define* something? To *propose* something? If you have already completed B4.2, Defining Terms for Writing Assignments (p. 416), you'll have a list of these terms and their definitions. (If not, you might consider working on B4.2 now.) Words like these provide important clues to the kind of writing your instructor expects.

Also, you need to note the specific requirements of the assignment: How long should it be? How should it be formatted? Is research required, and if so, what type of citations are required? When is the first draft due? What is the due date for the final draft?

Analyzing an Assignment

Below is a writing assignment you might receive in a college course on *grit*, defined by psychologist Angela Duckworth as "perseverance and passion for long-term goals." Working on your own or in your group, make a numbered list of everything this assignment asks you to do.

> ### Assignment
>
> For this assignment, you will write a three- to four-page essay that grows out of your reading, discussion, and thinking about grit, an essay suitable for a class in psychology, sociology, education, or even first-year composition. In this essay, you will define *grit*, present the arguments on both sides of the controversy about grit, and take a position on the significance of grit, a position you support with evidence.
>
> As you write this essay, you will want to include information from the articles you have read in this project and at least one article you find on your own by quoting, paraphrasing, or summarizing relevant passages. When you do this, be sure to provide appropriate citations and include a works cited list or list of references at the end of your essay.

Understanding the Rhetorical Situation

As long ago as classical Greece—300 BCE or so—thinkers have been aware that four important components exist for every text: the *author* of the text, the *audience* for the text, the *topic* of the text, and the *purpose* of the text. You will need to analyze these as you prepare to write.

W2.3   Advice

Components of Rhetorical Analysis

The following are the four traditional components of rhetorical analysis.

1. **Author.**   Of course, you know who the author is; it's you. But what version of *you* do you want your readers to encounter? Having done considerable research

and thinking about your topic, do you want to take on the role of an expert? Or would it be a better strategy to be up front about the fact that you are a college student and argue that being a college student gives you a valuable perspective on the topic? If you have been personally affected in some way by the topic, do you want your readers to see you as someone with personal experience of the issue?

2. **Audience.** What do you know about your audience, the people who will read what you have written? (Audience analysis is discussed more fully in W2.4, Thinking about Audience, p. 13.)

3. **Topic.** What will you be writing about? Early in the process your topic may be very broad, but before you start to write, you will need to narrow it down to something manageable. (See W3.3, Using Invention Strategies to Select a Topic, p. 27.)

4. **Purpose.** What is your purpose for writing? What do you want to have happen as a result of people reading your essay? (Read more about this in W2.6, Thinking about Purpose, p. 16.)

These four important elements are discussed from the point of view of the reader in R1.6, Previewing and Making Predictions about a Text (p. 245). There readers are urged, before diving into reading a text, to take a few minutes to analyze the rhetorical situation, as it will help them to better understand and analyze what they are reading. These same four components are also important for a *writer* to think about before and during any writing project.

In addition to the four traditional components of rhetorical analysis, before starting to write, you should also think about three additional elements that have come to be considered part of a rhetorical analysis in the modern world:

5. **Context.** *Where* does the writing you're doing fit into the world in which it will be read? Is your topic the center of a firestorm of public argument? Are you writing about a topic that has been neglected, that most people have not been thinking about? Are you breaking new ground? Are you writing about a topic that has been much discussed already, but which you are addressing from a new perspective or as a result of new evidence? Thinking about where your writing fits into the broader conversation will help you to adopt the most effective tone and style. (See W6, Using Language Powerfully, p. 77.)

6. **Genre.** What *kind* of writing are you doing? Is this going to be a memo, a formal report, an essay for publication, an application for a job, a letter to potential supporters of a project? What style and tone are expected in this genre? What length is expected? What kind of evidence? What kind of documentation of sources? Does the type of writing you're doing call for the use of a series of paragraphs, or would the use of bulleted or numbered lists be more effective?

7. **Medium.** Give some thought to what medium would be most effective for presenting your argument. Don't assume that a ten-page formal written report is your best option. Depending on the situation, your writing may be more effective if it's enriched with images, charts, and diagrams. Is a PowerPoint or web page an option? Considering your topic, purpose, and audience, what medium would be most effective?

W2.4 Advice

Thinking about Audience

Before starting any writing task, most writers find it helpful to think about who their audience will be. Who will be reading what they are about to write? This knowledge will shape the tone of their writing, the content, the examples, and the amount of detail they provide.

Identify Your Audience

This task can actually be a little more complicated than it seems. Suppose the writing assignment you are responding to asks you to write to your college or university's Committee on the Student Code of Conduct to propose a change in its policy on bringing children on campus. As with most assignments in college English classes, your essay will have two different audiences. The first is the committee, but the second is your instructor. And if that's not complicated enough, your instructor will be reading and evaluating your essay based on how well it addresses the committee as audience.

Writing tasks in the workplace can just as easily have multiple audiences. Imagine that a company you work for has discovered a flaw in a product it sells. Your boss has asked you to write a letter to customers explaining what the flaw is and what steps the company will take to correct it. Your audience is, obviously, the people who bought the product, but remember that first your letter will be read by your boss. In addition, it may be sent to others, like the head of the legal affairs office, for approval.

Analyze Your Audience

Once you know who your audience is, you will need to think about them and answer questions such as the following.

- **How much does your audience already know about the subject you are writing about?** Do you need to provide some context, such as a brief overview of events preceding a political crisis you are analyzing or the different ways people in the past have addressed a problem to which you are proposing a new solution?

- **How technical should you be with this audience?** If you are writing for a general audience, you may need to define important terms and be careful not to assume your readers know more than they do. On the other hand, if you are writing for people knowledgeable about your topic, you may be able to use more technical language and assume that they are familiar with certain basic information.

- **Are they likely to agree or disagree with what you have to say?** How you think an audience might react to your writing can help you determine how to present your position. For those who agree, you might only need to present a well-researched and supported argument. For those who hold different opinions, you might also need to acknowledge their positions, establish some common ground, and provide well-supported examples and counterarguments they will find persuasive. (See also the advice about argumentation in W11, Writing Strategies, p. 236.)

- **Are there characteristics about your audience you should take into account as you write?** Do most of them have children? Are most of them in school? Do most of them read a newspaper? Are there demographic characteristics (e.g., race, gender identity, sexual orientation, religion, economic status) you should be aware of? What style of writing is most likely to be successful with this group of readers?

Tailor Your Evidence to Your Audience

One way to make your writing more convincing is to tailor your evidence to your audience. This doesn't mean that you alter or fake your evidence. Rather, think about the following:

- What do your readers need to know in order to understand your point of view?

- What kinds of assumptions or biases might they have?

- What kinds of common ground do you share?

These questions will help you figure out what kinds of evidence and appeals your audience is likely to find convincing, what it will take to win them over to your position. (To learn more about using evidence, see W4, Providing Support for Your Thesis, p. 37, especially W4.1, Evidence and Assertions, p. 37; W4.2, Types of Evidence, p. 42; and W4.4, Connecting Evidence to Your Thesis, p. 46. To learn about different ways to appeal to your audience—through their minds, their ethics, or their emotions—see W11.4, Three Types of Appeal: *Logos*, *Ethos*, and *Pathos*, p. 198.)

W2.5 Exploration

Practice Thinking about Audience

Below is an assignment similar to one you might be asked to write about in this course. For this activity, you're not going to write the paper; you're just going to do some thinking about your audience.

On your own or in a group—your instructor will tell you which—consider who the audience will be for this writing assignment. What do you know about your readers? Is there only one audience for this assignment? If you think there is more than one, what do you know about the second audience? Who might they be?

How much does each audience know about the topic of delayed gratification? How much are they likely to agree or disagree with your point? What will be the most effective stance for you to take? Can you pull off being an expert? Or should you take on the role of a student who has experienced similar struggles? Remember, you are not being asked to actually write a paper at this time.

NOTE: *Delayed gratification* is when you put off something that you'd like to do until later in order to achieve a more important goal. For example, you want to watch a football game on TV on Sunday afternoon, but instead, you record it for later so you can finish your English assignment.

For this assignment, you will write a three- to four-page essay that grows out of your reading, discussion, and thinking about delayed gratification. Your audience for this paper is students who will be arriving at your institution next year. Your essay, if accepted by the college's New Student Orientation Committee, will be included in a packet of information new students will receive to help them understand how to be more successful in college.

Think deeply about *delayed gratification*—what it is, when it is a good strategy, how one might be successful at doing it. Support your argument with information from the selections you have read or others you locate yourself and/or with examples from your own life or from the lives of people you know.

W2.6 Advice

Thinking about Purpose

Before starting any writing task, most writers find it helpful to think about the purpose of the writing they are about to do. Knowing what they want to accomplish will shape the tone of their writing, the examples they use, the amount of detail they include, and the way they present their ideas.

Traditionally, a small number of possible purposes for writing have been identified:

1. To persuade
2. To explain
3. To express (feelings or thoughts)
4. To entertain

However, you could add more purposes for writing, like those listed below:

5. To request
6. To recommend
7. To reassure
8. To summarize

Lots of writing certainly does have one of these as its purpose, although more often a piece of writing will combine several of them.

Nonetheless, instead of thinking about purpose in terms of these very broad and general descriptions, you can think about purpose in another way: you can think more specifically and concretely about *your* purpose. To identify a specific focused purpose, think about this question: *What do you want to happen as a result of this writing?*

Realistically, most times when you write, you will have several different purposes. Consider the following example.

> One Saturday afternoon, Tanya Jennings was backing her car out of a parking space at a local mall when she heard a sickening crashing sound. She had backed into a car parked beside her. When she got out and saw the damage she had done, she was horrified. The other car's fender, taillight, and bumper were all damaged, although her own car was not even dented. She also noticed a small crowd had gathered and was watching her.
>
> Tanya was late for a doctor's appointment, so she decided to write a note to the owner of the other car and leave it under the windshield wiper.

The note she wrote had several different purposes, illustrating how complicated the purpose of a piece of writing can be:

1. To apologize to the owner of the car
2. To provide contact information so the owner of the car could reach her
3. To convince the people gathered around, who might read the note after she left, that she had really left contact information
4. To make the point that the other car was parked over the line into her parking space in case the accident ended up in court

This next example demonstrates how thinking carefully about purpose can help someone be a more effective writer.

Imagine that you've heard about a job you would really like: an evening receptionist position in a hospital that's within walking distance of your college. Perfect. You make sure your résumé is up to date, and then you go to work on a cover letter to go with the résumé.

If you don't give it a lot of thought, the purpose of the cover letter may seem almost obvious: you want to be hired for the job. However, the actual purpose for a cover letter is slightly different. Seldom do employers hire someone based simply on a résumé and cover letter. They will invite some of the applicants in for an interview and then hire one person based on the interviews, the résumé and letter, and perhaps other factors like recommendations or college transcripts.

The purpose of the cover letter is to be invited for an interview, which you hope will lead to the job. If you keep this purpose in mind, you will probably close the letter by saying something like "I would be available for an interview any day next week." But if you do not realize what the true purpose of the letter is, you might close with something like "If you hire me, I can be available to start in one week." The latter closing is inappropriate in this scenario and could lead the employer to think you are not savvy enough about the working world to be considered for the job.

W2.7 Exploration

Practice Thinking about Purpose

Working on your own or in a group—your instructor will tell you which—read the following text, and then list as many different possible purposes as you can for the letter you would write about the experience described below.

> A few weeks ago, you purchased a laptop computer at a local electronics store. When you got home and set up your computer, all that appeared on the screen was "Error Message 134," which informed you that your computer was damaged, and you would have to take it to an authorized repair shop.
>
> When you returned the computer to the store where you had purchased it, the salesperson said you must have damaged the computer while taking it home and refused to repair it for free. When you explained that you had taken it home in its factory packaging and had opened it up very carefully when you got there, he insisted that you must have done something to damage it. He argued that "Error Message 134" could only be the result of extreme carelessness. When you asked to see the manager, he informed you that he was the manager and suggested you were being unreasonably difficult.
>
> Before you completely lost your cool, you decided to leave the store. The salesperson yelled something at you as you left, but you couldn't hear what it was.
>
> When you arrived home, you decided to write a letter about your experience to the general manager of the store.

Making a Plan

Taking some time to make a plan for a writing project—*before* you start to write—is well worth it.

W2.8 Advice

Using a Calendar

If you have four weeks to complete an elaborate research project that culminates in a twelve-page research paper, you will clearly need to make a plan. Many students like to do this planning on a calendar like the one below.

Sunday	Monday	Tuesday	Wednesday	Thursday	Friday	Saturday
3	4 Read assignment. Analyze audience and purpose.	5	6 Brainstorm for a topic.	7 Browse library and online resources.	8 Select a narrowed topic. Draft thesis.	9 Conduct research focused on topic. Start bibliography.
10 Brainstorm ideas for paper.	11	12 Chunk ideas and order them.	13 Revise thesis.	14	15 Identify ideas that need more sources.	16 Conduct research for missing sources.
17 Start first draft.	18	19 Continue work on draft.	20 Draft for peer review.	21 Revise.	22	23 Create works cited list.
24 Revise.	25 Edit MLA citations and works cited list.	26	27 Do a careful edit for the little stuff.	28 Research paper due!	29	30

Working backward from the due date, put any intermediate due dates (such as the date your draft thesis is due or the date by which you need a draft for peer review) on the calendar. Some students also find it helpful to include their work schedule or due dates for other assignments, so they know what they will have to plan around.

W2.9 Advice

Creating a Scratch Plan

You don't need an elaborate plan like the one in W2.8 (p. 19) if you're writing something much shorter, but believe it or not, even if you are writing an in-class essay and have only an hour, it is still a good idea to take a minute to plan your time. A scratch outline like the one that follows will remind you when it's time to move on to the next step in the process. In fact, some students even use the alarm on their phones to alert them to when they need to move on.

> 5 mins: Read assignment and analyze audience and purpose
> 5 mins: Brainstorm & order
> 30 mins: Draft
> 10 mins: Revise
> 10 mins: Edit

NOTE: Students who find it difficult to perform under the pressure of rigid time limits may qualify for an accommodation that will grant them more time to complete the exam or in-class writing. Visit the Office for Students with Disabilities (it may be called something different on your campus) to request an authorization for accommodation and to discuss any documentation you may need to provide. (To learn more about asking for an accommodation, see B4.3, Advocating for Your Rights, p. 416.)

W3 Finding a Focus

n W3, you'll learn to use various invention strategies to develop a focus for your writing and create a draft thesis.

Generating Ideas and Narrowing a Topic

For many writers, getting started is the hardest part. In this section, you'll find many ideas and strategies to help you generate ideas and identify and narrow a topic.

W3.1 Advice

Using Invention Strategies to Generate Ideas

Sometimes when you are asked to write in college, you are given complete freedom to write about a topic of your choosing or, at least, a very wide topic area in which to carve out a specific topic. Broad assignments might sound like this:

- Write a three-page essay in which you argue for a cause you believe in.
- Write a three- to four-page essay discussing an issue involving the labor movement in America.
- Write a fifteen-page research paper on American immigration policy over the past fifty years.
- Write a three-page essay discussing one issue raised by the book you read last week for this course.

Sometimes your professors will give you more specifics about what they want you to write about:

- Based on the articles we read last week, write a three-page essay in which you identify three effects of global warming and explain their causes.
- Write a four-page essay arguing for the claim that public schools in the United States do or do not provide an equal education to all citizens.

At work, your boss might ask for writing that addresses certain situations:

- The copiers in the office are old and break down frequently. Investigate options for replacing them and have a proposal for new copiers on my desk by noon on Friday.
- Write a letter to customer X explaining why the television he ordered took three weeks to arrive and explaining what we will do to compensate him for the inconvenience.

Whether you have significant leeway in finding a topic or fairly narrow guidelines to work within, the following material offers four techniques—brainstorming, freewriting, browsing and reading, and mapping—to help you generate ideas and develop a focus.

Brainstorming

To brainstorm, you have to turn your internal censor off. Just write down every idea that comes to you. Don't worry about writing complete sentences; phrases are fine. Don't even worry about spelling. Just get every idea you can think of written down. When you run out of ideas, read over what you've written. That will often generate additional ideas. When you run out again, go get a cup of coffee or take a break. When you come back, more ideas may come to you.

Many people like to brainstorm on a blank sheet of paper; others prefer to do it in a blank document on a computer. Try both to see what works best for you, but keep in mind that the next step, organizing your list, is much easier to do on a computer, so you may want to choose that approach. (You can launch a video demonstration of brainstorming from Achieve with *The Hub*.)

Here's an example from one student—Tania—who was preparing to write an essay on disciplining her five- and seven-year-old daughters. Working on her computer, she began by typing short phrases as they popped into her head.

spanking

time out

no screen time

chores

yelling

a formal sit-down talk

setting clear rules and limits that everyone understands

talking about the rules from time to time, not just when they are broken

explaining the reasons behind the rules

---

what kinds of rules?

rules about cleaning up after making a mess

rules about teasing your sister

rules about not eating snacks between meals

rules about going to bed on time

rules about lying

rules about throwing balls in the house

do I need all these rules???

Something really interesting (and not that unusual) happened as Tania did this brainstorming. She started out thinking about how to discipline her children, but at the point where she drew the first line, her focus seems to shift. Instead of thinking about what she might do when her daughters misbehave, she starts thinking about what she might do to reduce the times when a need for discipline comes up. Below the second line, Tania's focus shifts again. She starts listing all the rules she might need to discuss, and then pauses to wonder whether she really needs all these rules.

Brainstorming, as it did for Tania, often goes in directions writers weren't even thinking about when they started. Tania ended up with some good ideas for three different topics:

1. What kind of discipline to use with her daughters
2. Steps she could take to reduce the need for discipline
3. Why does she need so many rules?

But now Tania will have to make a decision. She cannot write about three different topics, even though they are somewhat related. She'll have to settle on one of these and then generate more ideas on that topic.

Freewriting

Other writers use a system called freewriting when they are trying to find ideas. They just start writing about whatever comes to mind, and they keep writing for an extended time without worrying about whether what they are writing is coherent, whether it has unity, or whether it even makes sense. Some writers like to set themselves a goal: they will write for twenty minutes or until they have filled two pages.

The idea is to write freely, hoping to generate a few good ideas surrounded, usually, by a lot of not-so-good stuff.

When they're finished, they read over what they've written, searching for the nuggets. They may end up discarding a large percentage of what they wrote, but the effort will have been worthwhile if it produced a few good ideas.

When Karina started working on an essay for her composition class, she chose freewriting as her invention strategy.

> It's not easy deciding what kind of career I should pursue. I know I want a job in which I make enough money not to have to struggle with paying my bills or working two jobs the way my father had to for most of his life. But I also don't want to go after a career like journalism that is cutting down on jobs. I need to know I won't end up unemployed. And I don't want to stay in school running up debt for years, so a career that requires a graduate degree is out of the question.

At this point, Karina took a break. At least she had started, but she needed a cup of coffee. When she returned, she reread what she had written, and wasn't completely happy with it. So she decided to take her essay in a different direction.

> Those are very practicle consideration, but, to my way of thinking, there is something more important than practical matters. I want to be happy. I want to look forward to going to work every day. I don't want to dread Monday mornings. So, what would make me happy? I want to do something I'm good at. I get a great sense of satisfaction when I do something well. So a career that requires good math skills is out for me. What else? I'm happy when I'm around people. I like talking together, working together. I like being part of a team. I don't like working in competative, cutthroat environment. Most important, though, I want to feel I'm making a contribution, doing something that makes the world a little better place.

After her coffee, Karina moved in a new direction—more concerned with her feelings about work and less about practical issues. She may end up discarding that first paragraph, or she may decide to include both ideas and make her essay about the need for a balance between the practical and the emotional. In any case, her freewriting has given her a good start on her paper. Notice that she didn't spend time correcting typos or other errors—this is freewriting, getting some ideas down as fast as you can.

Browsing and Reading

Another great way to generate ideas to write about is through browsing and reading, either in the library or online. Using the library's online portal, start with a broad topic and then browse titles or subjects until something catches your eye. Or using Google, start a search for a broad topic and then follow links to wherever they lead. Skim articles or browse books making lots of notes of ideas that hold promise. When you finish, you'll have a long list of ideas that needs to be organized and focused.

Lani knew she wanted to write about health care and older adults. Her mother was in her late seventies, and it was clear she was not going to be able to live alone too much longer without some in-home support, so this topic was important to Lani. She first visited her college library's website, where she used the library's portal to find listings for a couple of books that looked promising. She made a note of the titles, authors, and call numbers, in case she decided to use these in her works cited list. Then she headed to the library to locate the books in the stacks.

> *The Psychology of Aging: Theory, Research, and Practice* by Janet Belsky (BF724.55.A35 B44 1984)
>
> *Learning to Be Old: Gender, Culture, and Aging* by Margaret Cruikshank (BF724.55.A35 C78 2013)

When Lani found these two books on a shelf on the second floor of the library, she took them to a table and started browsing. In the Belsky book, Chapter 6 discusses cognition and aging. Lani had worried that her mother was getting a little forgetful and sometimes seemed confused, so that chapter caught her attention. The Cruikshank book didn't have a chapter on cognition, so Lani headed back to the shelf where she'd found the first two books. She returned the second book to the shelf, and when she looked a little farther down the shelf, she was really excited. There were three more books focused specifically on cognition and aging.

> *Aging and Cognition: Research Methodologies and Empirical Advances*, edited by Hayden B. Bosworth (BF724.55.C63 A47 2009)
>
> *Everyday Cognition in Adulthood and Late Life*, edited by Leonard W. Poon, David C. Rubin, Barbara A. Wilson (BF724.55.C63 P66 1989)
>
> *Adult Cognition and Aging: Developmental Changes in Processing, Knowing and Thinking* by John M. Rybas (BF724.55.C63 R93 1986)

Armed with these four books, Lani headed over to her library's periodicals databases to use the ProQuest Nursing and Allied Health database. She typed in the words "aging and cognition" and was startled to learn 21,268 articles were available. She was greatly relieved to learn that she could narrow her search criteria so she would get a smaller, more focused list of articles, which she could print out. (To learn more about efficient searching for articles and books, see D1.5, Developing a List of Key Terms, p. 298, and D1.6, Finding Sources in the Library, p. 300.)

Lani's trip to the library was very productive. She not only focused her topic on a narrower topic—aging and cognition—but she was headed home with four books on the subject and access to lots of articles.

Mapping

Mapping is much like brainstorming, only more visual. Start by writing down a single idea in the center of a blank page and drawing an oval around it. Then add additional ideas and position them around the first idea. Draw lines to show connections among the ideas. Keep going until you run out of ideas or the page is full. At this point, you might want to select one of the more promising ideas, write it in the middle of a fresh sheet of paper, and start an entirely new map with it.

John was interested in writing about the dangers of driving. He placed "dangers of driving" at the center, and then added four boxes for what he considered the major categories of danger: other drivers, bad weather, road hazards, and driver error. For each of these categories, he added related ideas. Using this process, he came up with enough ideas that he could use any one of the four major topics as the basis for a paper.

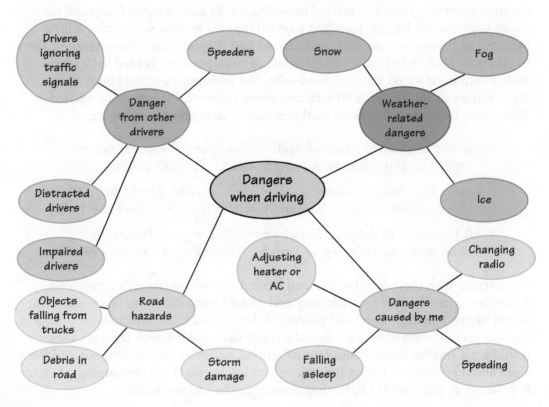

W3.2 Video

Brainstorming

You can launch this video presentation on brainstorming, a particularly useful prewriting strategy, from Achieve with *The Hub*.

W3.3 Advice

Using Invention Strategies to Select a Topic

Using invention strategies to come up with a topic to write about is often a two-stage process. In the first stage, you use one or more of the strategies described in W3.1, Using Invention Strategies to Generate Ideas (p. 21), to develop a collection of potential ideas to write about. Then you read through your list, crossing out or deleting any ideas that no longer appeal to you, that don't match the assignment, or that you don't think you have much to say about. Now you should have a handful of ideas that might work as a topic for a paper. You might try them out on other people. Get their reactions and suggestions. Or you might select one of the ideas and try writing about it. If it seems to work, you may have your topic. If it doesn't, try another one. Finally, with luck and perseverance, you will arrive at one topic that seems like it will work for your essay.

Topics at the beginning often look something like these:

- Solar energy
- What is success?
- Career planning
- Freedom of speech on campus
- Religious freedom
- Paying for college

The most common problem that students have with early topics is that they are too broad. Most of those listed above would need books — maybe in multiple volumes — to discuss them adequately. So, in the second stage, you take the broad topic you've selected and use an invention strategy to find more ideas that relate to it.

One student, Caroline, chose *career planning* as her topic and brainstormed this list:

- When to choose a career
- What exactly is a career?
- Is it possible to try out a career?
- Where to get information about careers
- How to make decisions about a career
- Should I be thinking about a career or just a job?

Following the same technique she had used to settle on a broad topic, she read through her list, deleting any ideas that no longer appealed to her, that didn't match the assignment, or that she didn't have many ideas about. Once Caroline had narrowed her choices down to just a few, it was time to make a decision: She needed to select the one topic that would allow her to write most effectively.

W3.4 Exploration
Using Brainstorming to Narrow a Topic

Use the following steps to narrow a broad topic to one you could write about in a three- to four-page paper.

1. Choose one of the broad topics listed below or one from your next essay assignment for this course and brainstorm a list of more focused topics you might write about.

   - Gender
   - Lying
   - Success
   - The environment

   - Relationships
   - Disability
   - Happiness
   - Balancing life and school

2. Go over your list to eliminate any topics that don't seem very promising, that you don't know enough about, or that you simply aren't interested in writing about. Then review the remaining topics to see if any can be combined into one topic. Finally, select the one topic you could write an essay about.

3. Complete a second round of brainstorming, using the topic you wound up with in step 2. List all the ideas you might include in a paper about that topic. If you run out of ideas, you might want to take a short break and relax for a few minutes. Then return to brainstorming to see if you can come up with some more ideas, or try one of the other invention strategies listed in W3.1, Using Invention Strategies to Generate Ideas (p. 21).

4. As you did in step 3, review your list of ideas, eliminating any that don't seem to fit under your topic, that you don't know enough to write about, or that you are not interested in writing about.

For information on how to organize the ideas you have now generated for your topic, see W5.5, Chunking and Ordering (p. 58); W5.6, Using Chunking and Ordering (p. 59); and W5.9, Outlining (p. 62).

Thesis Statements

Most successful college essays focus on a single idea or main point, referred to as the *thesis* or *thesis statement*.

W3.5 Advice
Developing a Working Thesis

Early in the process of writing an essay, you will usually find it very useful to come up with a working thesis, called *working* because it is a work in progress. As you continue to draft and revise your essay, you will modify your original thesis or even abandon it for a different one.

A well-structured thesis should include two major parts: (1) the subject or topic for the essay and (2) an assertion about that subject or topic.

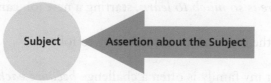

Here are some examples:

- Shopping for my family is often a challenge.
- For many college students, a job in a restaurant works out well.
- Starting a new job can be very stressful.

Notice that each of these theses (*theses* is the plural form of *thesis*) has two parts:

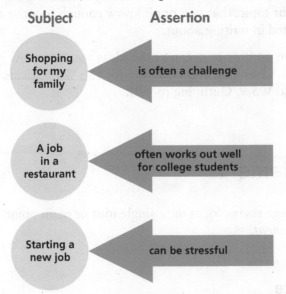

Subject   **Assertion**

- Shopping for my family — is often a challenge
- A job in a restaurant — often works out well for college students
- Starting a new job — can be stressful

A thesis statement must do these two things—identify the topic and make an assertion about that topic—but it can also do other things.

1. It can provide some background information about the topic of the paper.

   - *Given my tight schedule and budget as a college student*, shopping for my family is often a challenge.
   - *To cover the costs of attending college*, a restaurant job often works out well for college students.
   - *Because there is so much to learn*, starting a new job can be stressful.

2. It can preview the organization of the essay to follow.

   - Shopping for my family is often a challenge *because each family member has special requests.*
   - For many college students a job in a restaurant often works out well *because the hours are flexible, the pay is decent, and the colleagues are often other young people.*
   - Starting a new job can be very stressful; *not only do you have to learn how to do your job, but you also have to learn when to ask for help and how to fit in with the culture.*

In fact, you may need to add background information or preview the organization to make your thesis specific enough to develop fully and engage readers.

W3.6 Advice

Using Invention Strategies to Arrive at a Thesis

Once you have a topic, how do you turn it into a thesis? Use an invention strategy (or more than one) that works for you to come up with a variety of ideas about your topic. Working with the list of topics she came up with previously (see W3.3, Using Invention Strategies to Select a Topic, p. 27), Caroline chose *career planning* and brainstormed more specific topics:

> 1. To decide on a career requires doing a lot of research.
> 2. To decide on a career, you need to think about what you would enjoy doing, what the job availability is, and what you are good at.
> 3. To decide on a career takes years of exploration.
> 4. To decide on a career, you should see the college's career coordinator.
> 5. The most important factor in deciding on a career is salary.

Caroline then reread the assignment and examined each thesis on her brainstormed list to determine whether it met the assignment. She thought about the audience and purpose for the essay as described by her instructor, and she eliminated those theses that would not address both sufficiently. She asked several friends their opinions about the remaining theses, and she thought about how much she had to say about each. Finally, she tentatively decided she would use number 2 as her thesis. Then she did some freewriting focused on that thesis and found she had plenty of ideas. Now she was ready to start drafting her essay.

Remember: The choice of a thesis is important, but it is not irrevocable. Later in the writing process, your thesis can be modified or even replaced, based on where your reading, research, or writing takes you.

W3.7 Advice

Guidelines for Drafting a Thesis

To create an effective thesis, avoid these four common pitfalls:

The thesis states a widely accepted fact, rather than taking an arguable position

States a fact	Prescription drug prices are very high.
	College tuition has been rising for decades.
Revised: Takes an arguable position	To bring prescription drug prices down, a fair price should be established by the government.
	In an effort to compete for students, colleges have been building ever fancier gyms, student centers, and dorms—all of which have dramatically increased the cost of tuition.

The thesis focuses on more than one point

Focuses on several points	This city needs to hire more police officers, repair the highways, and pay teachers better.
Revised: Focuses on a single point	This city needs to get to work on repairing key infrastructure, especially our highways and bridges.

The thesis is expressed as an opinion

States the thesis as an opinion	In my opinion, community colleges should be tuition free.
Revised: States the thesis directly	Community colleges should be tuition free.

The thesis is expressed as an announcement

Makes an announcement	In this paper I will argue that all U.S. citizens, regardless of gender or gender identity, should have to register for the draft.
Revised: States the thesis directly	All U.S. citizens, regardless of gender or gender identity, should have to register for the draft.

W3.8 Exploration

Where Should the Thesis Be Located?

Read over the following short essays that were written to argue that the city of Baltimore should install a traffic light at the intersection of Northern Parkway and Chinquapin Parkway. These essays were intended to be sent as letters to the director of transportation for the city.

The three essays are quite similar, but they are organized in different ways. Working in groups, study them carefully, looking particularly at the location of the thesis in each. Discuss which way of organizing the essay your group thinks is most effective.

Essay 1

For the past six years, I've been living a few houses away from the intersection of Northern Parkway and Chinquapin Parkway, a busy intersection in a neighborhood where many families have children. I urge the city to install a traffic light at this intersection.

In the years I've lived here I've seen and heard far too many accidents at this intersection. In the last month, I have observed two, one of which involved serious personal injury. In the past year, I have personally witnessed twenty-one accidents. While I was out of town last summer, a terrible four-car accident occurred after which five people were admitted to the hospital. I know that two accidents at this busy intersection have resulted in loss of life. Something needs to be done.

This morning as I was leaving my house for work, I heard the squealing sound of the brakes of a large city bus trying to stop suddenly, followed by the sickening sound of that bus crashing into the side of a station wagon carrying three small children. As I ran to the station wagon, I saw that two children were scared but had been restrained by their seatbelts. The third child, unfortunately, had not been wearing her seatbelt. She flew through the windshield and landed in a forsythia bush on the opposite side of the intersection. Fortunately, the bush cushioned her impact. She was bleeding from many scratches and cuts, but did not suffer any serious injuries. We were lucky this time.

I checked with the Department of Transportation and learned that the minimum traffic requirement to trigger a new traffic light is at least 1,200 vehicles per hour on the more congested road at peak traffic periods and at least 50% of that volume on the less congested road. My neighbor and I sat near the intersection on three different work days last week. On Northern Parkway, I counted more than 1,500 vehicles per hour each day. My neighbor counted 855 vehicles per hour on Chinquapin Parkway. In addition to exceeding the minimum traffic requirements for a new traffic light, I'd like to point out that there is a large public school just a block away from this intersection, meaning that large numbers of children cross at this intersection every school day.

In light of the alarming number of accidents at this intersection and the fact that the traffic density exceeds the minimum requirements, I urge the Department of Transportation to install a traffic light at the intersection of Northern and Chinquapin Parkways.

Essay 2

This morning as I was leaving my house for work, I heard the squealing sound of the brakes of a large city bus trying to stop suddenly, followed by the sickening sound of that bus crashing into the side of a station wagon carrying three small children. As I ran to the station wagon, I saw that two children were scared but had been restrained by their seatbelts. The third child, unfortunately, had not been wearing her seatbelt. She flew through the windshield and landed in a forsythia bush on the opposite side of the intersection. Fortunately, the bush cushioned her impact. She was bleeding from many scratches and cuts, but did not suffer any serious injuries. We were lucky this time.

In the years I've lived here I've seen and heard far too many accidents at this intersection. In the last month, I have observed two, one of which involved serious personal injury. In the past year, I have personally witnessed twenty-one accidents. While I was out of town last summer, a terrible four-car accident occurred after which five people were admitted to the hospital. I know that two accidents at this busy intersection have resulted in loss of life. Something needs to be done.

For the past six years, I've been living a few houses away from the intersection of Northern Parkway and Chinquapin Parkway, a busy intersection in a neighborhood where many families have children. I urge the city to install a traffic light at this intersection.

I checked with the Department of Transportation and learned that the minimum traffic requirement to trigger a new traffic light is at least 1,200 vehicles per hour on the more congested road at peak traffic periods and at least 50% of that volume on the less congested road. My neighbor and I sat near the intersection on three different work days last week. On Northern Parkway, I counted more than 1,500 vehicles per hour each day. My neighbor counted 855 vehicles per hour on Chinquapin Parkway. In addition to exceeding the minimum traffic requirements for a new traffic light, I'd like to point out that there is a large public school just a block away from this intersection, meaning that large numbers of children cross at this intersection every school day.

As I said earlier, the Department of Transportation needs to install a traffic light at the intersection of Northern and Chinquapin Parkways.

Essay 3

This morning as I was leaving my house for work, I heard the squealing sound of the brakes of a large city bus trying to stop suddenly, followed by the sickening sound of that bus crashing into the side of a station wagon carrying three small children. As I ran to the station wagon, I saw that two children were scared but had been restrained by their seatbelts. The third child, unfortunately, had not been wearing her seatbelt. She flew through the windshield and landed in a forsythia bush on the opposite side of the intersection. Fortunately, the bush cushioned her impact. She was bleeding from many scratches and cuts, but did not suffer any serious injuries. We were lucky this time.

In the years I've lived here I've seen and heard far too many accidents at this intersection. In the last month, I have observed two, one of which involved serious personal injury. In the past year, I have personally witnessed twenty-one accidents. While I was out of town last summer, a terrible four-car accident occurred after which five people were admitted to the hospital. I know that two accidents at this busy intersection have resulted in loss of life. Something needs to be done.

I checked with the Department of Transportation and learned that the minimum traffic requirement to trigger a new traffic light is at least 1,200 vehicles per hour on the more congested road at peak traffic periods and at least 50% of that volume on the less congested road. My neighbor and I sat near the intersection on three different work days last week. On Northern Parkway, I counted more than 1,500 vehicles per hour each day. My neighbor counted 855 vehicles per hour on Chinquapin Parkway. In addition to exceeding the minimum traffic requirements for a new traffic light, I'd like to point out that there is a large public school just a block away from this intersection, meaning that large numbers of children cross at this intersection every school day.

In light of the alarming number of accidents at this intersection and the fact that the traffic density exceeds the minimum requirements, I urge the Department of Transportation to install a traffic light at the intersection of Northern and Chinquapin Parkways.

Know Your Instructor's Preferences

There is some disagreement among English teachers about *where* a thesis statement should be located in an essay. Some insist that it appear in the first paragraph; some even specify a particular location in that paragraph, like the last sentence. Others recognize that the thesis can effectively be withheld until later in the paper, even until the final paragraph. Making sure you understand your instructor's preferences about thesis placement before you start writing is always a good idea.

W4 ▶ Providing Support for Your Thesis

One of the most effective ways to make an essay stronger is to provide more "development," more support, more reasons for readers to agree with your thesis. In W4, you will learn a variety of strategies for providing support for your thesis.

Supporting Your Assertions with Evidence

The sections that follow will help you write stronger, more convincing essays by showing you how to support your assertions with evidence.

W4.1 Exploration

Evidence and Assertions

On October 15, 2022, a man left his jacket (with his wallet in his pocket) over the back of a chair in a Starbucks in Baltimore, Maryland. The employees emptied the jacket's pockets to help them figure out the owner's identity and how to contact him. The following items were found in his pockets and in his wallet.

   Working on your own or in a group, make a list of observations about the man based on the contents of his pockets.

▶

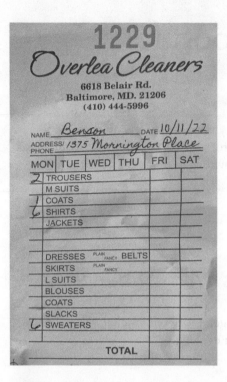

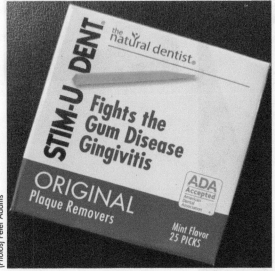

(Photos) Peter Adams

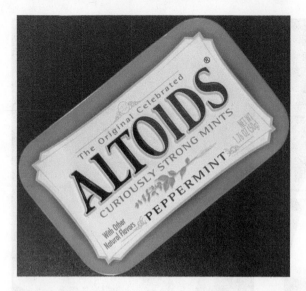

(Photos) Peter Adams

W4.2 Advice

Types of Evidence

At one time or another, you've probably been told that something you've written needs more development, more support, or more evidence. Such suggestions usually indicate that you've expressed an opinion or made an assertion that the reader finds unconvincing. Providing more development, support, or evidence—especially if it is selected with your readers in mind (see W2.4, Thinking about Audience, p. 13)—will make it more likely that your readers will be persuaded to agree with your assertion. In this discussion, these words—*development*, *support*, and *evidence*—will be used interchangeably, although sometimes people do make fine distinctions among them.

Suppose you wanted to argue that this country is not doing enough to address poverty. To support your opinion, you would need to provide evidence, which could take several different forms: facts, anecdotes and examples, statistics or numerical evidence, and expert testimony.

Facts

It was John Adams who said that "facts are stubborn things," and indeed they are. Facts are based on reality; they are known to exist or to have happened because they have been experienced or observed. They don't leave room for argument. They establish the credibility of a writer who "knows the facts," and they can be assembled into a well-structured argument. An essay on poverty would be strengthened by the inclusion of facts like these:

- Poverty among older people in the United States was dramatically reduced by two programs: Social Security and Medicare.

- The largest federal program targeting hunger is SNAP, the Supplemental Nutrition Assistance Program.

- New York City has more than 400 food pantries and over 100 soup kitchens distributing food aid across the five boroughs.

(For more discussion of facts, see R3.1, Distinguishing between Facts and Opinions, p. 275.)

Anecdotes and Examples

One of the most common and most effective ways to provide support is to present anecdotes and examples, stories and descriptions of situations that illustrate the point a writer is making. Anecdotes and examples can take several different forms, such as a single brief example, an extended example with more detail, a story, or a report of the results of an interview:

- **Brief Examples.** You might describe in a sentence or two the situation of one or more people living in poverty.

- **Extended Examples.** In an extended example, you might have to dig down to provide more detail about a particularly apt example. For example, you could describe what it's like to run out of food before the next payday, to be afraid to answer the phone because it might be a collection agency, or to worry when there's a knock at the door that it might be an eviction notice.

- **Anecdotes and Other Stories.** One of the oldest methods that human beings have used to convince an audience of a point is to tell a compelling anecdote, or story. You might tell the story of a family in which the mother was laid off from her job: You'd start by providing some background information about the family, its members, and its economic situation. Then you might describe the slowing down of work in the face of the pandemic. Next, you'd tell how the mother arrives home to announce that the expected layoff had finally occurred. Finally, you'd describe how the family came together to pick up the slack until the mother could find a new job. (See W11.14, Strategies for Writing Narratives, p. 212.)

- **Report of an Interview.** An interview with someone who has expertise or direct knowledge that supports your argument. Your report could include quotations, paraphrases, summaries, data, or examples provided by your interviewee.

At some point, though, examples and stories begin to lose their power to convince, and you need to include more broadly applicable types of evidence.

Statistics or Numerical Evidence

Statistics are a powerful form of evidence because they represent the experience of many, not just a few. Statistics as a subject is a branch of mathematics related to collecting, organizing, analyzing, and interpreting large quantities of numerical data. Statistical analysis is particularly useful for drawing general conclusions based on representative samples of people who have been asked to answer questions on specific topics. Statistical data may also be presented in a visual format—a graph, a chart, or an infographic—that can make it easy to see trends or to compare sets of information.

- **Statistics.** Add statistics that show the scale of a problem. For example, you might report how many people in the United States are living in poverty, or how many single mothers live in poverty, or how many children live in poverty.

You could also create graphics to illustrate or compare statistical information or borrow graphs and charts from published material, providing you clearly document your sources.

- **Survey Results.**   You may be able to conduct a survey and use the results to support your position. If you are arguing that a large percentage of students on your campus experience food insecurity, for example, you could conduct a survey and present the information you gather. (For more details on surveying, see D1.16, Conducting Surveys: A Checklist, p. 321.) More often, you will use the results of surveys others conduct.

- **Analysis of Trends.**   When you analyze trends, you are not just looking at statistics at one point in time. You are showing how those statistics change over time. In the essay on poverty, for instance, you could bolster your argument by demonstrating, say, that the percentage of children living in poverty decreased as a result of federal programs for COVID-19 relief, but they rebounded once those relief programs were discontinued.

Expert Testimony

On almost any topic, a little research will lead you to people who are recognized experts in their field. To determine whether individuals are experts in their fields, take note of their titles, publications, credentials, and how often other experts mention them. (For more discussion on identifying experts, see R3.1, Distinguishing between Facts and Opinions, p. 275.) Supporting your argument with testimony from a widely respected expert, such as a quotation from Peter Townsend, a sociologist at the London School of Economics who studied poverty and co-founded the Child Poverty Action Group, can make your argument more convincing.

W4.3   Exploration
Developing Strong Support for an Argument

Below is a thesis statement followed by a brainstormed list of the kinds of strong, convincing evidence that could be used to support it. Read the thesis and supporting evidence carefully. Then, using this example as a model, select one of the following five theses and list the kinds of evidence that would help provide strong support for it.

> **Thesis:** Selecting a major in college is not a decision that determines the rest of your life.
>
> - statistics on the percentage of college graduates who are working in jobs that have little to do with their majors
>
> - examples of people you know who are now in careers unrelated to their college major
>
> - statements by experts such as career counselors at your college
>
> - the story of someone you know who majored in a subject but then worked in three different jobs, none of which were related to their major
>
> - an interview with a human resources specialist who oversees hiring for a company and explains what that company considers when making hiring decisions

1. While an internet "holiday" every week may sound like torture, taking a weekly break from technology can help students focus, reflect, and practice important face-to-face social skills.
2. The world is facing a sustainability crisis, and our college needs to do more to decrease its dependence on carbon-based fuels.
3. This university needs to move on from telling students how to avoid being the victim of date rape to changing the dating culture on campus.
4. Student workers shouldn't be paid less than the minimum wage just because they work on campus.
5. This college needs to do a better job of making the campus accessible to students, faculty, and staff with mobility issues.

Connecting Support to Assertions

It's not enough for a writer to include support for an assertion; how that evidence connects to the assertion must also be made clear to the reader.

W4.4 Advice

Connecting Evidence to Your Thesis

It is usually quite clear to the *writer* of an essay why a particular piece of evidence is there and how it relates to the main point of a paragraph or essay, but sometimes this connection is not so clear to the *reader*. For example, to support the assertion that affluent children's schools receive much greater financial support than do poor children's schools, a student might provide the following sentence as evidence:

> The value of homes in affluent neighborhoods can be ten times as high as the value of those in poorer neighborhoods.

The writer knows why this support is relevant: U.S. schools are supported by local property taxes, so wealthy school districts (where property values are higher) generate more tax revenue for their schools than do poorer school districts (where property values are lower). But the writer hasn't made this connection clear to the reader. To make the connection explicit, the writer could have written this:

> Because property taxes are used to fund schools, neighborhoods with a greater proportion of wealthy families who pay higher property taxes will have schools with more and better resources than neighborhoods with predominantly poorer residents who pay less.

W4.5 Reading

"Violence Vanquished," Steven Pinker

The following essay by Steven Pinker, a professor of psychology at Harvard University, is adapted from his book *The Better Angels of Our Nature: Why Violence Has Declined* and appeared in the *Wall Street Journal*. After you've read the article, you'll be asked to identify the evidence Pinker uses to support his claims and how he connects the two. Keep this in mind as you read. (You may want to annotate the reading with this purpose in mind; if you want a refresher on annotation, see R2.2, Explaining Annotations, p. 257.)

Violence Vanquished

STEVEN PINKER

SEPTEMBER 24, 2011

1   On the day this article appears, you will read about a shocking act of violence. Somewhere in the world there will be a terrorist bombing, a senseless murder, a bloody <u>insurrection</u>. It's impossible to learn about these catastrophes without thinking, "What is the world coming to?"

2   But a better question may be, "How bad was the world in the past?"

3   Believe it or not, the world of the past was *much* worse. Violence has been in decline for thousands of years, and today we may be living in the most peaceable era in the existence of our species.

4   The decline, to be sure, has not been smooth. It has not brought violence down to zero, and it is not guaranteed to continue. But it is a persistent historical development, visible on scales from <u>millennia</u> to years, from the waging of wars to the spanking of children.

5   This claim, I know, invites skepticism, <u>incredulity</u>, and sometimes anger. We tend to estimate the probability of an event from the ease with which we can recall examples, and scenes of <u>carnage</u> are more likely to be beamed into our homes and burned into our memories than footage of people dying of old age. There will always be enough violent deaths to fill the evening news, so people's impressions of violence will be disconnected from its actual likelihood.

6   Evidence of our bloody history is not hard to find. Consider the genocides in the Old Testament and the crucifixions in the New, the gory mutilations in Shakespeare's tragedies and Grimm's fairy tales, the British monarchs who beheaded their relatives and the American founders who dueled with their rivals.

7   Today the decline in these brutal practices can be quantified. A look at the numbers shows that over the course of our history, humankind has been blessed with six major declines of violence.

8   The first was a process of pacification: the transition from the anarchy of the hunting, gathering and <u>horticultural</u> societies in which our species spent most of its evolutionary history to the first agricultural civilizations, with cities and governments, starting about 5,000 years ago.

9   For centuries, social theorists like Hobbes and Rousseau speculated from their armchairs about what life was like in a "state of nature." Nowadays we can do better. Forensic archeology—a kind of "CSI: Paleolithic"—can estimate rates of violence from the proportion of skeletons in ancient sites with bashed-in skulls, <u>decapitations</u> ▶

or arrowheads embedded in bones. And ethnographers can tally the causes of death in tribal peoples that have recently lived outside of state control.

10   These investigations show that, on average, about 15% of people in prestate eras died violently, compared to about 3% of the citizens of the earliest states. Tribal violence commonly <u>subsides</u> when a state or empire imposes control over a territory, leading to the various "<u>paxes</u>" (Romana, Islamica, Britannica and so on) that are familiar to readers of history.

11   It's not that the first kings had a <u>benevolent</u> interest in the welfare of their citizens. Just as a farmer tries to prevent his livestock from killing one another, so a ruler will try to keep his subjects from cycles of raiding and feuding. From his point of view, such squabbling is a dead loss—forgone opportunities to extract taxes, tributes, soldiers and slaves.

12   The second decline of violence was a civilizing process that is best documented in Europe. Historical records show that between the late Middle Ages and the 20th century, European countries saw a 10- to 50-fold decline in their rates of homicide.

13   The numbers are consistent with narrative histories of the brutality of life in the Middle Ages, when highwaymen made travel a risk to life and limb and dinners were commonly enlivened by dagger attacks. So many people had their noses cut off that medieval medical textbooks speculated about techniques for growing them back.

14   Historians attribute this decline to the consolidation of a patchwork of feudal territories into large kingdoms with centralized authority and an infrastructure of commerce. Criminal justice was nationalized, and zero-sum plunder gave way to positive-sum trade. People increasingly controlled their impulses and sought to cooperate with their neighbors.

15   The third transition, sometimes called the Humanitarian Revolution, took off with the Enlightenment. Governments and churches had long maintained order by punishing nonconformists with mutilation, torture and gruesome forms of execution, such as burning, breaking, <u>disembowelment</u>, <u>impalement</u> and sawing in half. The 18th century saw the widespread abolition of judicial torture, including the famous prohibition of "cruel and unusual punishment" in the eighth amendment of the U.S. Constitution.

16   At the same time, many nations began to whittle down their list of capital crimes from the hundreds (including <u>poaching</u>, sodomy, witchcraft and counterfeiting) to just murder and treason. And a growing wave of countries abolished blood sports, dueling, witch hunts, religious persecution, absolute <u>despotism</u> and slavery.

17   The fourth major transition is the respite from major interstate war that we have seen since the end of World War II. Historians sometimes refer to it as the Long Peace.

18 Today we take it for granted that Italy and Austria will not come to blows, nor will Britain and Russia. But centuries ago, the great powers were almost always at war, and until quite recently, Western European countries tended to initiate two or three new wars every year. The cliché that the 20th century was "the most violent in history" ignores the second half of the century (and may not even be true of the first half, if one calculates violent deaths as a proportion of the world's population).

19 Though it's tempting to attribute the Long Peace to nuclear deterrence, non-nuclear developed states have stopped fighting each other as well. Political scientists point instead to the growth of democracy, trade and international organizations — all of which, the statistical evidence shows, reduce the likelihood of conflict. They also credit the rising valuation of human life over national grandeur — a hard-won lesson of two world wars.

20 The fifth trend, which I call the New Peace, involves war in the world as a whole, including developing nations. Since 1946, several organizations have tracked the number of armed conflicts and their human toll world-wide. The bad news is that for several decades, the decline of interstate wars was accompanied by a bulge of civil wars, as newly independent countries were led by inept governments, challenged by insurgencies and armed by the cold war superpowers.

21 The less bad news is that civil wars tend to kill far fewer people than wars between states. And the best news is that, since the peak of the cold war in the 1970s and '80s, organized conflicts of all kinds — civil wars, genocides, repression by autocratic governments, terrorist attacks — have declined throughout the world, and their death tolls have declined even more precipitously.

22 The rate of documented direct deaths from political violence (war, terrorism, genocide and warlord militias) in the past decade is an unprecedented few hundredths of a percentage point. Even if we multiplied that rate to account for unrecorded deaths and the victims of war-caused disease and famine, it would not exceed 1%.

23 The most immediate cause of this New Peace was the demise of communism, which ended the proxy wars in the developing world stoked by the superpowers and also discredited genocidal ideologies that had justified the sacrifice of vast numbers of eggs to make a utopian omelet. Another contributor was the expansion of international peacekeeping forces, which really do keep the peace — not always, but far more often than when adversaries are left to fight to the bitter end.

24 Finally, the postwar era has seen a cascade of "rights revolutions" — a growing revulsion against aggression on smaller scales. In the developed world, the civil rights movement obliterated lynchings and lethal pogroms, and the women's-rights movement has helped to shrink the incidence of rape and the beating and killing of wives and girlfriends.

▶

25   In recent decades, the movement for children's rights has significantly reduced rates of spanking, bullying, paddling in schools, and physical and sexual abuse. And the campaign for gay rights has forced governments in the developed world to repeal laws criminalizing homosexuality [LGBTQ+] and has had some success in reducing hate crimes against gay people.

*　*　*

26   Why has violence declined so dramatically for so long? Is it because violence has literally been bred out of us, leaving us more peaceful by nature?

27   This seems unlikely. Evolution has a speed limit measured in generations, and many of these declines have unfolded over decades or even years. Toddlers continue to kick, bite and hit; little boys continue to play-fight; people of all ages continue to snipe and bicker, and most of them continue to harbor violent fantasies and to enjoy violent entertainment.

28   It's more likely that human nature has always comprised inclinations toward violence and inclinations that counteract them—such as self-control, empathy, fairness and reason—what Abraham Lincoln called "the better angels of our nature." Violence has declined because historical circumstances have increasingly favored our better angels.

29   The most obvious of these pacifying forces has been the state, with its monopoly on the legitimate use of force. A disinterested judiciary and police can defuse the temptation of exploitative attack, inhibit the impulse for revenge and circumvent the self-serving biases that make all parties to a dispute believe that they are on the side of the angels.

30   We see evidence of the pacifying effects of government in the way that rates of killing declined following the expansion and consolidation of states in tribal societies and in medieval Europe. And we can watch the movie in reverse when violence erupts in zones of anarchy, such as the Wild West, failed states and neighborhoods controlled by mafias and street gangs, who can't call 911 or file a lawsuit to resolve their disputes but have to administer their own rough justice.

31   Another pacifying force has been commerce, a game in which everybody can win. As technological progress allows the exchange of goods and ideas over longer distances and among larger groups of trading partners, other people become more valuable alive than dead. They switch from being targets of demonization and dehumanization to potential partners in reciprocal altruism.

32   For example, though the relationship today between America and China is far from warm, we are unlikely to declare war on them or vice versa. Morality aside, they make too much of our stuff, and we owe them too much money.

33   A third peacemaker has been <u>cosmopolitanism</u>—the expansion of people's <u>parochial</u> little worlds through literacy, mobility, education, science, history, journalism and mass media. These forms of virtual reality can prompt people to take the perspective of people unlike themselves and to expand their circle of sympathy to embrace them.

34   These technologies have also powered an expansion of rationality and objectivity in human affairs. People are now less likely to privilege their own interests over those of others. They reflect more on the way they live and consider how they could be better off. Violence is often <u>reframed</u> as a problem to be solved rather than as a contest to be won. We devote ever more of our brainpower to guiding our better angels. It is probably no coincidence that the Humanitarian Revolution came on the heels of the Age of Reason and the Enlightenment, that the Long Peace and rights revolutions coincided with the electronic global village.

35   Whatever its causes, the implications of the historical decline of violence are profound. So much depends on whether we see our era as a nightmare of crime, terrorism, genocide and war or as a period that, in the light of the historical and statistical facts, is blessed by unprecedented levels of peaceful coexistence.

36   Bearers of good news are often advised to keep their mouths shut, lest they lull people into <u>complacency</u>. But this prescription may be backward. The discovery that fewer people are victims of violence can thwart cynicism among compassion-fatigued news readers who might otherwise think that the dangerous parts of the world are irredeemable hell holes. And a better understanding of what drove the numbers down can steer us toward doing things that make people better off rather than congratulating ourselves on how moral we are.

37   As one becomes aware of the historical decline of violence, the world begins to look different. The past seems less innocent, the present less sinister. One starts to appreciate the small gifts of coexistence that would have seemed utopian to our ancestors: the interracial family playing in the park, the comedian who lands a zinger on the commander in chief, the countries that quietly back away from a crisis instead of escalating to war.

38   For all the <u>tribulations</u> in our lives, for all the troubles that remain in the world, the decline of violence is an accomplishment that we can <u>savor</u>—and an <u>impetus</u> to cherish the forces of civilization and enlightenment that made it possible.

W4.6 Exploration

Decoding Difficult Language in "Violence Vanquished"

You may have noticed that some words and phrases in "Violence Vanquished" (W4.5, p. 46) are underlined. Working individually or in your group, write a definition of each underlined word or phrase, using one of these five strategies for dealing with difficult language:

1. Derive the meaning from context.
2. Analyze the parts of the word.
3. Back up and reread the passage.
4. Keep reading to see if the writer explains the difficult word or phrase.
5. Look the word up in a dictionary.

If you decide the word is not important to understanding Pinker's essay, skip the word and keep reading. (For more information about these strategies, see R2.11, Dealing with Difficult Language, p. 271.)

W4.7 Exploration

Recognizing Development Strategies in "Violence Vanquished"

Working individually or in your group, think about the kinds of evidence that Steven Pinker uses and how he makes clear to his readers how that evidence supports his assertions in "Violence Vanquished" (W4.5, p. 46).

1. Identify at least one example of each of the five types of evidence listed below:

   - analysis of trends
   - examples
   - expert testimony
   - facts
   - statistics or numerical evidence

2. For two of the pieces of evidence you identified, analyze how—and how effectively—Pinker connects that evidence to his assertion. (The assertion he is supporting may appear in a previous paragraph.)

3. Identify at least two places where Pinker makes assertions without providing any evidence. What kinds of evidence would you find convincing to support these claims?

Be prepared to share your findings with the class.

W5 ▸ Organizing Ideas

W5 discusses strategies for ensuring that when you write, your ideas are organized to have the maximum impact on the reader.

Unity

Unity is the quality of belonging to a whole. A football team has unity when all its members—the linemen, the running backs, the defense, and even the coaches—work together as a team. An essay has unity when all its parts—thesis, supporting claims, evidence—work together.

W5.1 Advice

Creating Unity

To create unity, an essay's thesis must be well supported by the assertions or claims made in supporting paragraphs, and the evidence in those supporting paragraphs must be relevant to the claim it's supporting. Weed out any unrelated material that creeps in, and make sure the essay's thesis remains the same from the beginning to the end of the essay.

Ensuring the Thesis Doesn't Evolve

The draft essay that appears later in this section, by a student named Jason, has a unity problem because the thesis evolves as the paper progresses. There is a clear thesis in paragraph 1:

> Lying to protect others—what psychologists call *prosocial* lying—is okay. (par. 1)

In the last paragraph, the writer again seems to restate the thesis:

> Lying is acceptable to protect other people, as long as your lie isn't for selfish reasons, and it won't do harm to another person. (par. 8)

The problem is that the writer has changed his mind. He is no longer arguing that lying is okay if it is intended to protect others. He has added two more conditions: the lie must not be for selfish reasons, and it cannot harm others.

It's easy to see why the thesis evolved as Jason wrote this draft. As he wrote, he thought hard about different examples of lying and realized that even lies that protect other people are not acceptable if they are selfish or harm others. The solution to this problem is easy: he needs to revise his thesis the first time it appears so that it matches the final version.

Cutting Unrelated Material

The second kind of unity problem occurs when material eases its way into an essay even though it doesn't address the thesis. Take a look at Jason's essay below. Jason's paragraph 3, for example, addresses the *topic*—lying—but doesn't address the thesis. It says nothing about when it's okay to lie. Paragraph 5 has the same problem. As hard as it can be to do so, paragraphs that don't address the thesis must be cut from the essay.

The Little White Lie

As a nine-year-old Cub Scout, I firmly believed that it was never okay to lie: "A scout is trustworthy, loyal, helpful, friendly, courteous, kind, obedient, cheerful, thrifty, brave, clean, and reverent"! But by the time I joined the Boy Scouts, I knew it wasn't that simple. How could you be trustworthy *and* courteous? What I hadn't figured out yet was when it was okay to lie. Now, I've got a new rule of thumb: <u>Lying to protect others—what psychologists call *prosocial* lying—is okay.</u>

> *This is the essay's thesis.*

Let's try out this rule on a few examples. We'll start with an easy case: You tell a little kid that there really *is* a Santa Claus. Okay, we all know this is a lie—at least all we adults know it. There are no jolly elves and reindeer at the North Pole.

> *This paragraph supports the thesis; it provides the first example of when it is okay to lie and explains how this example follows the rules for prosocial lying.*

~~In most societies, there is broad disapproval of lying because a society in which everyone trusts each other will function more effectively for everyone. If we expected everyone to lie, how would we~~

~~know who to trust? And if we can't trust anyone, how could we have friends, believe in reviews, and so on? Society is not perfect; people still do lie to each other. But, in general, we all try to avoid excessive lying.~~

Here's another example. Imagine that your mother comes home with a new haircut and asks whether you like it. Do you tell the truth—that it's way too short and makes her head look too small? No, that would hurt her feelings, and she can't glue the hair back on. In this case, it's perfectly okay to tell her it looks great. You've protected your mother's feelings, and eventually your mother's hair will grow out. Once it does, you might want to tell her she looks better with her hair a bit longer, so she doesn't run out and cut it really short again. But telling little white lies to avoid hurting someone's feeling is another case when it's okay to lie.

~~When you tell a lie, it often becomes necessary to tell more lies to conceal the first one. One time, I told my boss I had inventoried all the sweaters in the storeroom. I hadn't. When we sold out of black turtleneck sweaters, he told me to get some more from the storeroom. A few minutes later, I returned and told him there were no black turtleneck sweaters there. He asked how that could be since I had just done an inventory the day before. I told another lie. I said we discovered the turtleneck sweaters were all extra smalls, which we hardly ever sell, so I had shipped them back to the supplier. A few days later he asked me why we hadn't been reimbursed by the supplier for the turtleneck sweaters. I was caught. I confessed all the lies and was fired on the spot.~~

Now consider this example: Let's say you are trying to sell your three-year-old car. A potential buyer asks if it has any problems. Your mechanic told you that the brakes need to be relined, but if you tell potential buyers that, you'll be out a good bit of money. What should you do? In this case you would be lying for a selfish reason, and you could be harming the buyer—so don't do it!

This paragraph is about the topic — lying — but it doesn't support the thesis. It's not about when it is or isn't okay to lie. It should be cut.

This paragraph supports the thesis. It gives another example of an acceptable lie, and it explains why this lie is okay.

This paragraph is about the topic — lying — but it's another example of a paragraph that doesn't support the thesis because it's not about when it is or isn't okay to lie. It should be cut, too.

This paragraph supports the thesis because it offers an example of what is *not* prosocial lying.

This final body paragraph supports the thesis because it offers another example of what is *not* acceptable lying.

A final example: your friend Jesse asks you to read over her paper and give her some feedback. As you read, you realize her paper has no focus, it provides little evidence to support the assertions it does make, and it doesn't do what the assignment asked it to do. But you know she worked really hard on the paper. You want to protect her feelings, to avoid making her feel crushed, so you tell her the essay is fine. She turns it in and gets an F on it. Your attempt to protect your friend's feelings actually did her harm, and, therefore, you should not have lied.

The thesis here is quite different from the one in the opening paragraph.

It's clear from these examples, that the Scouts had it wrong: all lying is not wrong. Lying is acceptable to protect other people, as long as your lie isn't for selfish reasons, and it won't do harm to another person.

W5.2 Exploration
Evaluating Thesis and Unity

Working individually or in your group, read the following essay, identify the thesis, and identify any places where there are unity problems. Be prepared to explain to the class what you think the writer should do to improve unity.

Motorcycle Helmets and Individual Freedom

Many states have laws requiring motorcyclists to wear helmets when riding their bikes. These laws violate the principle of individual freedom. Henry David Thoreau wrote in "Civil Disobedience," "That government is best that governs least," and Lincoln is reported to have said, "My freedom to swing my arms ends where your nose begins."

I agree with Thoreau that the government should pass as few laws as possible, thereby maximizing individual freedom. And I agree with Lincoln that we only need laws to prevent one person's freedom from harming another person. The law requiring motorcycle helmets is a violation of these principles and an attack on the individual freedom of Americans.

I recognize that some laws are necessary. We need a law that says I must drive on the right side of the road so I don't crash into people coming from the opposite direction. I understand laws that say I can't fire a weapon in a public place because I could kill or injure someone. I understand laws that require people who own factories to provide necessary safety measures because, if they didn't, they could harm their workers and nearby residents.

But why do we need laws requiring employers to check the immigration status of their employees? These laws don't protect the employees from being harmed by their employer; they are a restriction on the employer's individual freedom. How about laws requiring that I get my children vaccinated against childhood diseases like measles and mumps? Don't I have individual freedom to make decisions about my own children's health?

Clearly the law requiring motorcycle helmets violates personal freedom. I understand that people think these helmets save lives, and I suppose they do. But if I choose to take chances with my own life, isn't that my choice? If I choose not to wear a helmet and then crash into a tree, I'm the only one who suffers. I haven't done harm to anyone else.

There is nothing more exhilarating than cruising down a highway on a spring afternoon with the wind blowing through my hair. I can smell the flowers blooming along the sides of the road and hear the songs of the birds. It's just not the same experience if I'm wearing a helmet.

I'm fine with the government passing laws requiring me to drive on the right side of the road, to have headlights that work, and to have brakes that work. Those laws are there to prevent me from harming other people. But laws like the helmet law—laws that protect me only from myself—are a gross violation of individual liberty.

W5.3 Writing

One Unusual Thing

Write a brief, one-page essay in which you describe one unusual thing about your family, your high school, or the neighborhood you grew up in. Your instructor will be reading these papers not only to get to know each of you but also to begin a discussion of how to make your writing more effective. Be sure your essay has a clear and consistent thesis and that everything in the essay supports that thesis.

W5.4 Exploration

Thesis and Unity in One Unusual Thing

You may recall from W5.1 (p. 53) and W5.2 (p. 57) that most college essays focus on a single idea or main point, which English teachers call a *thesis*. In W5.3, you were asked to write an essay in which you told your instructor about one unusual thing about your family, your high school, or the neighborhood where you grew up.

Your instructor will either conduct a class discussion about a selection of those papers or will have you discuss them in groups. In either case, you will evaluate each paper for thesis and unity. You will need to decide if each paper is about just "one unusual thing." If a paper discusses two or three different "unusual things," it would not have a single clear thesis, and it would not be following the assignment. If a paper starts out discussing a particular "unusual thing," but changes its focus to something different by the end, again, it doesn't have a single, clear thesis.

Checking for Unity: Chunking, Ordering, and Outlining

Problems with unity can be avoided by using strategies like chunking and ordering or outlining.

W5.5 Video

Chunking and Ordering

You can launch this video presentation on chunking (separating ideas into groups) and ordering (arranging those groups logically) from Achieve with *The Hub*.

Using Chunking and Ordering

In W3.3, Using Invention Strategies to Select a Topic (p. 27), we used brainstorming to generate possible topics for an essay. From that list, if you had decided you would write on the topic "freedom of speech at college," your next step would be to brainstorm ideas for content for your essay. You might have come up with a list of ideas for content something like this:

free speech and political ideas	the First Amendment
free speech and hate speech	what is speech?
free speech in the classroom	fighting words
free speech in the college newspaper	academic freedom
speech that creates a hostile environment	artistic freedom
free speech and obscene language	political correctness
free speech by professors	slander
free speech and invited speakers	fire in a crowded theater
free speech and incitement to violence	students' freedom of speech
free speech and microaggression	cancel culture

You've generated a good list of ideas, but they're completely random; they're just listed in the order they popped into your head. So your next task is to organize them into logical groups, a process known as *chunking* or *grouping* or *clustering*.

As you read over the list looking for logical clusters, you notice that the first two items are about free speech and the content of that speech, so you create a cluster labeled "Issues about the Content of Speech." Next you look for other items related to the content of speech, and you find six more. (See the yellow box on the following page.) Next, you return to the brainstormed list and look for another cluster topic. You notice the third item is "free speech in the classroom." Now you look for other items that discuss free speech issues in various locations and you find two more. (See the light blue box on the next page.)

Continuing this process, you end up with the six clusters listed below.

Issues about the Content of Speech	Free Speech in Various Locations
free speech and political ideas	free speech in the classroom
free speech and hate speech	free speech in the college newspaper
speech that creates a hostile environment	fire in a crowded theater
free speech and obscene language	
free speech and incitement to violence	
free speech and microaggression	
fighting words	
slander	

Some Basic Concepts	Free Speech by Various Individuals
what is speech?	free speech by professors
the First Amendment	free speech and invited speakers
	students' freedom of speech

Additional Freedoms	Principles Affecting Free Speech
academic freedom	political correctness
artistic freedom	cancel culture

Your next task is to decide what order to discuss these clusters in, a process known as *ordering*. In this case, the following might be the order you decide on.

1. Some Basic Concepts

2. Issues about the Content of Speech

3. Free Speech by Various Individuals

4. Free Speech in Various Locations

5. Principles Affecting Free Speech

6. Additional Freedoms

At the end of this process, you have generated lots of content, clustered it into logical groups, and decided on an order for the clusters. You have created a plan for your essay.

W5.7 Exploration

Practicing Chunking

In W3.4, Using Brainstorming to Narrow a Topic (p. 28), you were asked to brainstorm a list of ideas you might write about for one of ten broad topics. Below is a brainstormed list for one of those topics—religion. The ideas are listed in the order they popped into the writer's head while brainstorming. Now you're going to work on organizing this list of ideas by chunking them. In other words, organize them into logical groups or chunks of related ideas. Then give each chunk a label.

Is religion dying out?

How does someone choose a religion?

What do most religions have in common?

Religions provide guidance for how to lead a good life.

Definition of religion

What is not a religion?

Is it possible for a religion not to be based on the existence of a god or gods?

Religions provide comfort when people experience tragedy or loss.

What do religions say about other religions?

What do people get from religion?

Religion helps people to accept death.

Is Alcoholics Anonymous a religion?

Religions provide community and companionship.

Religions can motivate people to go to war.

Religion is the opiate of the people.

Religion motivates people to resist giving in to animal instincts.

How do religions start?

Religions provide support for the needy.

W5.8 Exploration

Practicing Ordering Ideas

In W5.7, Practicing Chunking (p. 61), you grouped brainstormed ideas into logical "chunks" and gave each "chunk" a name. For this activity, you will decide on the order in which you would like to discuss your "chunks" of ideas in an essay. In the process, you may think of some ideas to add or decide to move some ideas from one "chunk" into another. When you finish, you will have a thoughtful and well-organized plan for an essay, almost an outline.

W5.9 Advice

Outlining

You've already seen (in W5.6, Using Chunking and Ordering, p. 59) how you can group your ideas into clusters and arrange them in a logical order. Another way to accomplish these goals is to create an outline. Outlines range from quick lists of three or four ideas to highly structured documents complete with indentations, capital and lowercase letters, and Roman and Arabic numbers. For short writing assignments, or assignments when you don't have much time, such as an exam, a scratch outline can still be very helpful.

However, when you are working on an essay assignment, creating a more detailed outline can be really useful once you have narrowed your topic, drafted a working thesis statement, and generated some supporting evidence. An outline helps you to organize your ideas, decide on what order to present them, and identify where you need more support; it provides a road map for your essay that will guide your writing.

When asked in a history class to write an in-class essay on the beginnings of slavery in America, Javier jotted down a few quick ideas before beginning to write.

- Indentured servitude brought many poor Europeans to the colonies in the 17th century
- How it worked
- First Africans brought to Virginia in 1619 — treated as indentured servants
- Slavery legalized in Massachusetts in 1641, in Virginia in 1661

If, instead of writing for a class test, Javier had had three weeks to work on his paper on indentured servitude and slavery, he might have come up with a much more elaborate outline, something like the following.

Draft Thesis: As an increasing number of Africans became indentured servants in the 17th-century colonies, indentured servitude evolved fairly quickly into slavery.

I. Indentured servitude was a system for bringing workers to the colonies.

    A. The earliest indentured servants were poor Europeans who couldn't afford to pay for their voyage to the Americas.

    B. They promised to work 4 to 7 years to pay off the cost of their voyage.

II. Although not always followed, there were rules protecting indentured servants.

    A. When they completed their servitude, they were then granted complete freedom.

    B. Most were also given their "freedom dues" of something like 25 acres of land, seed for a year, fresh clothes, and a firearm.

III. Although initially classified as indentured servants, Africans were never treated the same way as Europeans.

    A. Most were captured in Africa and *forcibly* transported to the colonies.

    B. Beginning in 1619, Africans were brought to Virginia and categorized as indentured servants, but even then, their treatment was not the same as the treatment of the Europeans.

        1. Some Africans actually achieved freedom after serving out their period of indenture, but most of these were not given "freedom dues."

        2. By 1650, the total number of Africans in Virginia had risen to only 400; the total number of Europeans was nearly 19,000.

IV. Indentured servitude evolves into slavery.

    A. Slavery in England had been reserved for "non-Christians," and was not usually related to race.

    B. The number of freed Europeans in the colonies was growing and creating pressure on land ownership.

C. The colonists began to see slavery as a more economically feasible option than indenture.

    1. Enslaved individuals could be enslaved for life.

    2. The children of enslaved people would become enslaved as well.

    3. Slavery, originally based on religion—only non-Christians could be enslaved—had a problem: enslaved people could convert to Christianity and demand freedom.

    4. Gradually, the basis for slavery changed from religion to race, an unchangeable and easily identified category.

A formal outline like this is different in several ways from the scratch outline Javier used when he had to write a paper quickly.

1. It is much more detailed. Although he started with a brief outline, as Javier did more research and thinking, he added more and more detail.

2. An elaborate system of letters, numbers, and indentation is used to indicate where the ideas fit in the hierarchy of the argument.

3. Each entry is a complete sentence. This is only necessary in the most formal kind of outline—a sentence outline. In a less formal topic outline, each entry could just be a phrase.

4. At every level, notice that there are at least two entries: there are no 1's without 2's; no A's without B's.

Some instructors require that an outline like this one be turned in at the early stages of writing a research paper.

Most writers who use an outline to guide their writing consider it a very fluid document that is constantly revised, pruned, and added to. In many cases, as the writer fleshes out the outline, the draft thesis is revised significantly, paragraphs are reordered, new evidence is added, and support that is not relevant is deleted.

Creating Coherence

Coherence is simply the connection of ideas within a piece of writing to make logical sense to readers and ensure they can follow the writer's line of thought. When people read a coherent text, they easily understand the parts, how they fit together, and why they are in the order presented. A piece of writing is not coherent when readers have trouble following the writer's argument because the ideas do not connect smoothly or obviously.

Strategies for Creating Coherence

There are numerous strategies for creating coherence, including sequencing ideas logically, repeating key words and pronouns strategically, and using appropriate transitional words and phrases.

Logical Organization

One way to ensure coherence is to organize a sequence of ideas in a recognizably logical order—from general to specific, most important to least important (or vice versa), first to last (chronological), near to far (or far to near), bottom to top (or top to bottom), or left to right (or right to left).

General to Specific

Travel can be very educational. You learn all kinds of new information when you visit a place you've never been to before, but you also meet new people with new ways of looking at the world. Most enjoyable, you experience new kinds of food—tastes you never would have sampled at home.

Most Important to Least Important

The primary reason I am going to college is to gain the skills and credentials that will lead to a good job when I graduate. A secondary reason is that I want to learn about ideas and people and ways of seeing the world that are different from what I experienced growing up in my hometown of Lawton, Oklahoma. A third reason is that it is important to me that I understand political issues better. I sometimes listen to debates on television about issues I should care about, but I don't know enough to follow the argument.

First to Last (Chronological)

When I first came to Lakeland Community College, I felt totally confused. I was supposed to pay my bill in the Bursar's Office, but I didn't even know what a bursar was. When I sat down in my first class and the instructor started explaining the syllabus, her policy on plagiarism, and office hours, I had the vague notion that these things were important, but I didn't really know what they were. Today, after two years at this school, I feel like an expert. I know my way around. In fact, this summer I will be working as a student guide for new students who come to orientation.

Near to Far

Out of my window, I see tree branches crisscrossing the panes of glass. They belong to the maple tree beside the front door, and now, in winter, they are bare except for a few withered brown leaves. Beyond the branches, behind a row of trees, stretches the front lawn, carpeted in snow, and scattered with branches from a recent storm. Far in back to the left, insulated with tarpaper and surrounded by an electric fence is the beehive, warm and still quietly humming despite the subzero temperatures.

Bottom to Top

My grandparents live in an eight-story building in downtown Denver. As you approach the building at street level, you'll see a series of small shops—a men's clothing store, a bookstore, a computer store, and, of course, a Starbucks. As you look up, you'll notice seven floors of apartments with large glass windows and little balconies cantilevered out into space. If you lean back and look all the way up to the top, you may get a glimpse of people sitting around in chairs reading or chatting with their neighbors.

Left to Right

It's a small room with slanted ceilings and windows facing south and east. On the left side there is a shelf filled with books, a window hung with glass ornaments and a shell wind chime, and a calendar. In the middle, in front of the south-facing window, is a desk and chair, a computer, a phone, and containers of pens and pencils. On the right side is another desk with drawers full of files and an odd-shaped closet, without a door, lined with shelves jammed with office supplies.

Repetition of Key Words and Pronouns

Coherence in a text can be enhanced by strategic repetition of a key word, the use of synonyms for that word, and the repetition of pronouns referring to that word. In the following text, note the repetition of the term *scientist*, the use of *these experts* as a synonym for the word *scientists*, and the use of the pronoun *they* to refer to the scientists.

Scientists studying the warming of the planet are increasingly worried. They point to the melting of the Arctic ice cap as one alarming development. A recent study by these scientists announced that Arctic sea ice is melting at a rate of about 13% per decade. When these experts looked at melting in Antarctica, they found that melting there is contributing more to rising sea levels than previously thought. In addition, other scientists suggest that the warming of the oceans is proceeding at a faster rate than predicted. If nothing is done, these experts predict that within twenty years sea levels will rise by more than two feet and 32 to 80 million people will experience coastal flooding.

Use of Transitional Expressions

Another way to improve coherence is to use transitional expressions, words and phrases such as *for example*, *as a result*, and *finally*. These expressions serve as signposts, helping the reader follow the text and the connections being made within it. The following chart shows common transitional expressions organized by their function.

To signal sequence	again, also, then, first, second, last, next, before, after
To signal time	later, subsequently, in the meantime, the next day, a week later, after a while, in a few days, within minutes, earlier that day
To signal examples	for example, for instance, specifically, such as, to illustrate, namely, specifically
To signal location	in front of, beside, behind, nearby, next to, adjacent to, below, beyond, elsewhere, to the left, to the right, near, far
To signal summary	hence, in summary, to summarize, in brief, in conclusion, as a result, as I have demonstrated
To signal comparison	in the same way, likewise, similarly, also
To signal contrast	in contrast, on the other hand, however, instead, nevertheless, regardless, but, yet, on the contrary
To signal causation	as a result, therefore, thus, so, accordingly, fortunately, consequently

The following two paragraphs demonstrate how much transitional expressions help make a piece of writing coherent. In Paragraph 1, the transitional expressions have been omitted. Read it first. With a little effort, you should be able to understand what it says. Then read Paragraph 2, in which transitional expressions have been inserted.

Paragraph 1

When Jeanine started her new job as a server at Ciao, a high-end Italian restaurant, she was a little nervous because of her lack of experience. She didn't know how to pronounce many of the Italian words on the menu. The more experienced servers were very helpful. They showed her how to put in a drink order at the bar and how to let the kitchen know if a customer had an allergy. She became more comfortable and more confident. She is one of those experienced servers who help out the newcomers, but she still has trouble pronouncing *bruschetta*.

Paragraph 2

When Jeanine started her new job as a server at Ciao, a high-end Italian restaurant, she was a little nervous because of her lack of experience. <u>For example</u>, she didn't know how to pronounce many of the Italian words on the menu. <u>Fortunately</u>, the more experienced servers were very helpful. <u>For instance</u>, they showed her how to put in a drink order at the bar and how to let the kitchen know if a customer had an allergy. <u>As a result</u>, she became more comfortable and more confident. <u>Today</u>, she is one of those experienced servers who help out the newcomers, but she still has trouble pronouncing *bruschetta*.

W5.11 Exploration

Editing for Coherence

Working on your own or in your group—your instructor will tell you which—revise the following essay by making the organization more logical, repeating key words and phrases strategically, and adding appropriate transitional words and phrases.

Making Millions

I'm working on becoming a millionaire. It's a good thing I have lots of energy, because I'm going to need it. I'm only twenty-five, but I'm handling a lot more than the average young adult. I juggle 15 credit hours of school, a 48-hour work week, and two kids.

I'm not talking about your average Monday through Friday, 9-to-5–type of job, either. I work at my local Olive Garden from 1 in the afternoon to 9 at night, five days a week. And, I don't get to rest up on weekends either. Saturdays, you'll find me making cappuccinos at the Starbucks in my neighborhood from 10 to 6.

I have one daughter, Lakia, age 5 (Kindergartner Extraordinaire) and one son, Blake, age 3 (The Accident King). Lakia, while good at heart, already has the curse of the brilliant child—boredom—so she requires constant attention and a lot of work on my part. I need to be the source of all things entertaining or suffer the consequences of her overactive imagination. Even under the most intense supervision, my son, Blake, is an accident always waiting to happen. I thank God that he has "Super Powers" that allow him to feel no pain. I have never had to clean up so many spills or take so many trips to the emergency room as I do now. After school and after work is when I really need a supply of it. Off I go to the Kiddie Academy in Brookdale to pick up my two gregarious children.

Multiple family members warned that I was "already too busy to take on any more responsibilities." My most stressful activity is school. I was slow in starting to begin with. I started back to college this semester. I came back with a vengeance. I wasn't going to go to school part-time and have it take forever. Five classes and 15 credits later, here I am, running a little low on enthusiasm.

What it takes to be a full-time mom, student, and professional adult is phenomenal. Yet, somehow, I do it 24/7, 365 days a year with a reasonable amount of sanity. If I could figure out a way to bottle all that stuff—could you imagine the millions I would make?

W6 ▸ Using Language Powerfully

As Mark Twain pointed out, "The difference between the *almost right* word and the *right* word is really a large matter—t'is the difference between the lightning bug and the lightning." In W6 you're going to learn about putting some lightning in your language. You're going to learn how to choose your language thoughtfully, so your writing is not just correct but clear, exact, powerful, and expressive of who you are.

Writing Accurately

The first step toward writing effectively is writing accurately: using words that will convey your ideas to your readers.

W6.1 Advice

Using a Dictionary to Understand Words

Writers sometimes find themselves unsure about a word they are thinking about using. One solution to this hesitation is to look the word up in a dictionary. The entries there can help you with spelling, determining the word's part of speech, pronunciation, meaning(s), word origin, and usage. For many words, the dictionary will also suggest synonyms, words with similar meanings that might even more precisely express what you want to say.

The following is an annotated sample entry from *The American Heritage Dictionary of the English Language* for the word *periodic*.

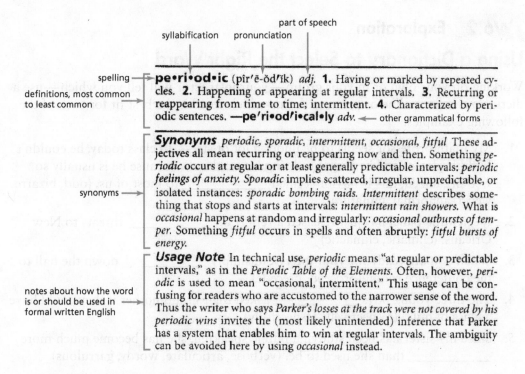

syllabification pronunciation part of speech

spelling → **pe•ri•od•ic** (pîr′ē-ŏd′ĭk) *adj.* **1.** Having or marked by repeated cycles. **2.** Happening or appearing at regular intervals. **3.** Recurring or reappearing from time to time; intermittent. **4.** Characterized by periodic sentences. —**pe′ri•od′i•cal•ly** *adv.* ← other grammatical forms

definitions, most common to least common

Synonyms *periodic, sporadic, intermittent, occasional, fitful* These adjectives all mean recurring or reappearing now and then. Something *periodic* occurs at regular or at least generally predictable intervals: *periodic feelings of anxiety. Sporadic* implies scattered, irregular, unpredictable, or isolated instances: *sporadic bombing raids. Intermittent* describes something that stops and starts at intervals: *intermittent rain showers.* What is *occasional* happens at random and irregularly: *occasional outbursts of temper.* Something *fitful* occurs in spells and often abruptly: *fitful bursts of energy.*

synonyms

Usage Note In technical use, *periodic* means "at regular or predictable intervals," as in the *Periodic Table of the Elements.* Often, however, *periodic* is used to mean "occasional, intermittent." This usage can be confusing for readers who are accustomed to the narrower sense of the word. Thus the writer who says *Parker's losses at the track were not covered by his periodic wins* invites the (most likely unintended) inference that Parker has a system that enables him to win at regular intervals. The ambiguity can be avoided here by using *occasional* instead.

notes about how the word is or should be used in formal written English

In most online dictionaries, you can click a button to hear the word said aloud, so you can learn to pronounce it correctly. You can also click on the listed synonyms to be taken to a definition of that word, making it easier to decide which word best fits the meaning you are trying to express. Below is a definition from the *Merriam-Webster Online Dictionary.*

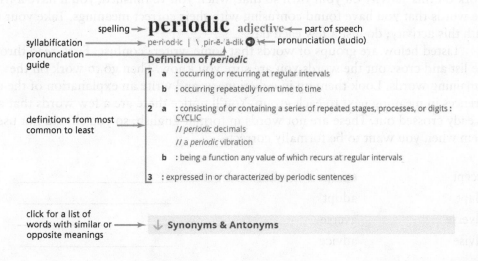

spelling → **periodic** adjective ← part of speech

syllabification → pe·ri·od·ic | \ ˌpir-ē-ˈä-dik 🔊 ← pronunciation (audio)
pronunciation guide

Definition of *periodic*

1 **a** : occurring or recurring at regular intervals

b : occurring repeatedly from time to time

2 **a** : consisting of or containing a series of repeated stages, processes, or digits : CYCLIC
// *periodic* decimals
// a *periodic* vibration

b : being a function any value of which recurs at regular intervals

3 : expressed in or characterized by periodic sentences

definitions from most common to least

click for a list of words with similar or opposite meanings → ↓ **Synonyms & Antonyms**

W6.2 Exploration

Using a Dictionary to Select the Right Word

Working on your own or in your group—your instructor will tell you which—use a dictionary, either online or print, to decide which word is the best fit for each of the following examples.

1. My math professor seems to be under a lot of stress. In class today, he couldn't find his glasses and he forgot to bring his textbook. Because he is usually so well organized, this behavior seemed _____ to most of us. (odd, bizarre, weird, abnormal, unnatural)

2. A scientific panel has just released a report on _____ threats to New Orleans. (climatic, climactic)

3. When you are ready for your interview, simply _____ down the hall to the conference room. (proceed, precede)

4. The three young boys _____ asked their grandmother if they could have a glass of milk. (respectively, respectfully)

5. Since my sister has been studying public speaking, she has become much more _____ than she used to be. (verbose, articulate, wordy, garrulous)

W6.3 Exploration

Determining the Meanings of Confusing Words

Work on this activity on your own so that, when you've finished, you'll have a list of the words that you have found confusing with their correct meanings. Take your time with this activity; do just a few each day.

Listed below are groups of words that some writers confuse. First, read through the list and cross out the words you are sure you know. Then go to work on the remaining words. Look them up in a dictionary, and write an explanation of the differences in meaning next to each group. You'll notice there are a few words that are already crossed out. These are not words in formal English, so you should not use them when you want to be formally correct.

accept	except	_____
adapt	adopt	_____
adverse	averse	_____
advise	advice	_____

affect	effect	
aggravate	annoy	
agree to	agree with	
all right	~~alright~~	
all together	altogether	
allusion	illusion	
a lot	~~alot~~	
already	all ready	
among	between	
amoral	immoral	
amount	number	
angry at	angry with	
ante-	anti-	
anxious	eager	
anyone	any one	
assure	ensure	insure
awhile	a while	
beside	besides	
between	among	
bring	take	
capital	capitol	
censor	censure	
cite	site	sight
climatic	climactic	
coarse	course	
compare to	compare with	
complement	compliment	
conscience	conscious	
continual	continuous	
could have	~~could of~~	
couldn't care less	~~could care less~~	
council	counsel	
desert	dessert	
different from	different than	
disinterested	uninterested	
elicit	illicit	

emigrate	immigrate	
eminent	imminent	
everyone	every one	
explicit	implicit	
farther	further	
fewer	less	
hanged	hung	
hopefully	hopeful	
imply	infer	
in	into	
its	it's	
lie	lay	
passed	past	
precede	proceed	
principal	principle	
quotation	quote	
raise	rise	
respectfully	respectively	
sensual	sensuous	
sit	set	
sometime	some time	sometimes
supposed to	~~suppose to~~	
their	there	they're
then	than	
to	too	two
try to	~~try and~~	
used to	~~use to~~	
wear	we're	where
weather	whether	
whose	who's	
would have	~~would of~~	
your	you're	

W6.4 Advice

Connotation and Denotation

To use language effectively, you have to be careful to choose words that convey your tone, your attitude or perspective, exactly. Take a look at the twelve words or phrases listed below.

mogul	fat cat	well to do
billionaire	person of means	moneyed
tycoon	wealthy	loaded
magnate	affluent	prosperous

In one sense, these words all *mean* the same thing. They all refer to someone who has a lot of money. But in another sense, their meanings are quite different. If you say someone is *prosperous*, you are implying that they worked hard and earned a lot of money; if you say someone is *moneyed*, it is more likely you are suggesting they were born into wealth. To say someone is a *fat cat* means something very different from saying someone is a *person of means*. Describing someone as *loaded* is not the same as describing them as *wealthy*.

The basic meaning, shared by all these words, is that the people referred to have a lot of money. This basic meaning of a word is known as its *denotation*. *Connotation* is the term used to refer to the secondary meanings that have come to be associated with words, meanings that often have cultural or emotional overtones. For example, the term *fat cat* is often used to refer to powerful businesspeople or politicians to indicate disapproval of the way they use their wealth or influence, while calling someone a *person of means* is more neutral but can suggest the person is not only wealthy but has inherited money or belongs to the upper class. Saying someone is *loaded* is slang for saying they are wealthy: you might use *loaded* when talking to friends but *person of means* in an academic essay.

When writing, be careful to select words that capture not only the correct denotative meaning, but also the precise connotative meaning you want to convey. Also take into account the rhetorical situation: words with an informal level of diction are appropriate in texts or Instagram posts for friends, but they are not necessarily the right choice in college assignments (like essay exams and research projects) or workplace writing (like sales reports and correspondence with customers).

W6.5 Exploration

Explaining Differences in Connotation

Working individually or in your group—your instructor will tell you which—explain the differences in connotation among the four words in each set below.

Set 1

    unusual   bizarre   odd   weird

Set 2

    voluble   glib   talkative   verbose

Writing with Flair

While writing accurately is crucial to writing effectively, adding a bit of flair to your writing will make your audience want to read what you've written.

W6.6 Exploration

Seeing How Concrete Language Works

Working individually or in your group—your instructor will tell you which—read and discuss the following two versions of the same passage. These paragraphs describe how the U.S. Senate appeared to Senator Barack Obama when he first arrived in 2005.

Passage 1

On most days, when I enter the Capitol, a train carries me from the building where my office is located through a tunnel lined with flags and seals. The train halts and I make my way, past people, to the elevators that take me to the second floor. Stepping off, I walk around the press who normally gather there, say hello to the Capitol Police, and enter, through double doors, onto the floor of the U.S. Senate.

The Senate chamber is not the most beautiful space in the Capitol, but it is imposing nonetheless. The walls are set off by panels and columns. Overhead, the ceiling is an oval, with an American eagle in its center. Above the visitors' gallery are statues of the nation's first twenty vice-presidents.

Passage 2

On most days, I enter the Capitol through the basement. A small subway train carries me from the Hart Building, where my office is located, through an underground tunnel lined with the flags and seals of the fifty states. The train creaks to a halt and I make my way, past bustling staffers, maintenance crews, and the occasional tour group, to the bank of old elevators that takes me to the second floor. Stepping off, I weave around the swarm of press that normally gathers there, say hello to the Capitol Police, and enter, through a stately set of double doors, onto the floor of the U.S. Senate.

The Senate chamber is not the most beautiful space in the Capitol, but it is imposing nonetheless. The dun-colored walls are set off by panels of blue damask and columns of finely veined marble. Overhead, the ceiling forms a creamy white oval, with an American eagle etched in its center. Above the visitors' gallery, the busts of the nation's first twenty vice presidents sit in solemn repose.

—**Barack Obama**, *Audacity of Hope*, pages 13–14

Which do you think is most effective and why?

W6.7 Advice
Using Concrete Language to Bring Writing to Life

Abstract language is used to describe ideas and qualities that do not have a physical presence. Words like *democracy*, *success*, *freedom*, or *love* are all abstract terms conveying concepts. All of them are open to different interpretations depending on how they are used, by whom, and in what context.

Concrete language refers to specific sensory details—descriptive words related to sight, sound, touch, smell, and taste—that bring writing to life. Examples of these types of words are *black velvet curtains*, *golden daffodils*, *knives and forks*, *sewage fumes*, *hurricane winds*, and *screeching brakes*, all of which relate to the physical world and can be perceived through the senses.

Here is a paragraph from *The Painted Drum* by Louise Erdrich. The narrator, Faye Travers, who handles estate sales, uses concrete and sensory language to describe an old house she is visiting to assess the contents.

The Tatro house is not grand anymore. The original nineteenth-century homestead has been renovated and enlarged so many times that its style is entirely obscured. Here a cornice, there a ledge. The building is now a great clapboard mishmash, a warehouse with aluminum-clad storm windows bolted over the old rippled glass and a screen porch tacked darkly across its front. The siding is painted the brown-red color of old blood. The overall appearance is rattling and sad, but the woman who greets me is cheerful enough, and the inside of the house is comfortable, but dim. The rooms are filled with an odor I have grown used to in my work. It is a smell that alerts me, an indefinable scent, really, composed of mothballs and citrus oil, of long settled dust and cracked leather. The smell of old things is what it is. My pulse ticks as I note that even on the ground floor an inordinate number of closets have been added during some period of expansion. Some run the length of whole walls, I estimate, roughly the room's proportions.

Erdrich uses concrete details to describe the look of the house: "nineteenth-century homestead," "[h]ere a cornice, there a ledge," "aluminum-clad storm windows," and siding "painted the brown-red color of old blood." She describes how it smells, an "indefinable scent . . . composed of mothballs and citrus oil, of long settled dust and cracked leather," and how it makes her feel, "[m]y pulse ticks," indicating her rising excitement at the treasures she might find. As you read these descriptive details, you can see and smell and experience what the narrator is seeing, smelling, and experiencing.

Adding these kinds of details to your writing will not only make it more interesting for your readers but also make it more accurate and informative. Whether you are telling a story, providing an example, describing a scene, or making a persuasive case, including concrete details will add color and life to your words.

W6.8 Exploration
Adding Concrete Language

Working on your own or in your group—your instructor will tell you which—edit the following text to make it more concrete and specific. To do this, you will need to make up relevant concrete details.

When I got home from work last night, I was exhausted. All I wanted was a quick dinner, a bottle of beer, and an early bedtime. Then I opened the refrigerator and discovered that the meat I planned to cook had gone bad.

Worse yet, my roommate had drunk my last bottle of beer. So off I went to the local store to purchase a few things. Coming out of the store with my supplies, I discovered I had a flat tire. After changing the tire and driving home, I was too tired to cook, so I headed straight to bed.

W6.9 Exploration

Words, Plain and Fancy

In this activity, think about the word choice that is most effective given the rhetorical situation. Think about when simple, clear language would work best and when more sophisticated language would be more effective. For most of the following items, there is room for argument about the best answer. In fact, that's the point of this activity: to get you thinking about the different options the English language offers.

For each of the items below, working individually or in your group—your instructor will tell you which—discuss the pros and cons of the different choices of words used to express the same idea.

1. You work as a supervising nurse in a large hospital. In a formal letter of reprimand for one of your subordinates who has violated hospital policy, which of the following sentences do you think would be the most effective?

   a. Nurse Baker's behavior on December 18 was dreadful.

   b. Nurse Baker's behavior on December 18 was atrocious.

   c. Nurse Baker's behavior on December 18 was unacceptable.

2. The financial aid office at your school has limited funds available for scholarships for low-income students. In a letter you write to that office, which of the following sentences do you think would be the most effective?

   a. My family has struggled financially since my mother lost her job four years ago.

   b. My family has been down on its luck since my mother lost her job four years ago.

   c. My family has been impoverished since my mother lost her job four years ago.

3. As a teacher of a fourth-grade class, you need to write a note to one of your students. Which of the following sentences do you think would be the most effective?

   a. Please ask one of your parents to write a terse note explaining why you are late for school so often.

    b.   Please ask one of your parents to write a short note explaining why you are late for school so often.

    c.   Please ask one of your parents to write a brief note explaining why you are late for school so often.

4. Which of the following sentences would be most appropriate in an email to your friends telling them how to get to the location of a picnic?

    a.   After about a half mile, the trail you are following will split. At this point, take the path to the left.

    b.   After about a half mile, the trail you are following will divide. At this point, take the path to the left.

    c.   After about a half mile, the trail you are following will bifurcate. At this point, take the path to the left.

5. In a letter asking for a refund from a plumbing company, which of the following sentences do you think would be the most effective?

    a.   I am writing to complain about the careless work done by the plumber you sent to my house on June 18.

    b.   I am writing to complain about the sloppy work done by the plumber you sent to my house on June 18.

    c.   I am writing to complain about the negligent work done by the plumber you sent to my house on June 18.

6. In a letter applying for a summer internship at an accounting firm, which of the following sentences do you think would be the most effective choice?

    a.   If I am hired as a summer intern at your firm, I will work hard to make your company's relationship with younger customers better.

    b.   If I am hired as a summer intern at your firm, I will work hard to ameliorate your company's relationship with younger customers.

    c.   If I am hired as a summer intern at your firm, I will work hard to improve your company's relationship with younger customers.

7. You want to carry a sign supporting your candidate Maggie Sloan at a political rally. Which of the following would be the most effective wording for your sign?

    a.   Maggie Sloan has what it takes to be mayor.

    b.   Maggie Sloan is eminently qualified to be mayor.

    c.   Maggie Sloan will be an outstanding mayor.

8. In your position as executive chef at an upscale restaurant, you are writing a letter to a newly hired cook. Which wording do you think would be the most effective?

   a. Before beginning work with us, please carefully look over the following policies.

   b. Before beginning work with us, please carefully read the following policies.

   c. Before beginning work with us, please carefully peruse the following policies.

9. In a cover letter for a job as a manager at a large department store, which of the following sentences do you think would be the most effective?

   a. In my job at Walmart last summer, I became an expert at handling customers.

   b. In my job at Walmart last summer, I became an expert at customer service.

   c. In my job at Walmart last summer, I became an expert at dealing with customers.

10. In an email to a group of interns starting work at your office, which of the following options would be most effective?

   a. Respect the limits on personal messages sent using the office's email system.

   b. Respect the parameters on personal messages sent using the office's email system.

   c. Respect the boundaries on personal messages sent using the office's email system.

W6.10 Advice

Blending "Englishes" (and Other Languages)

All languages change over time, across locations, and from group to group, and English is no exception. The English you hear at home over dinner is vastly different from the English spoken in Shakespeare's time. The English you hear in Mumbai, India, is vastly different from that spoken in Kingston, Jamaica; Sydney, Australia; Memphis, Tennessee; or Boston, Massachusetts. And the English spoken by surfer dudes is vastly different from that spoken by the elders at your place of worship or your English professors in class. In short, English isn't one uniform language but a collection of "Englishes." You yourself probably speak and write multiple Englishes, from the language you use when texting friends to that you use in a letter to your grandmother to that you use in a memo or report at work.

Some writers choose to blend their home language with formal English in ways that give them more options, more credibility, more authenticity, and more power. Let's look at a few examples of formal English blended with other versions of English—or even other languages—to create a unique blend.

In this example, Lee Tonouchi blends Hawaiian pidgin* ("planny Pidgin prejudice") with formal English ("ubiquitous"):

> In da real world get planny Pidgin prejudice, ah. Dey, da ubiquitous dey, dey is everywea brah, dey say dat da perception is dat da standard English talker is going automatically be perceive fo' be mo' intelligent than da Pidgin talker regardless wot dey talking, jus from HOW dey talking.
>
> —Lee Tonouchi, from "Da State of Pidgin Address,"
> *College English* (vol. 67, no. 1)

In this second example, Gloria Anzaldúa mixes Spanish with more and less formal English:

> In the fields, *la migra*. . . . Pedro ran, terrified of being caught. He couldn't speak English, couldn't tell them he was fifth generation American. *Sin papeles*—he did not carry his birth certificate to work in the fields. . . . *La migra* took him away while we watched.
>
> —Gloria Anzaldúa, *Borderlands/La Frontera*

In this third example, Geneva Smitherman, a widely respected professor of composition, blends Black English with formal, academic English to argue that we need to change what is considered "mainstream" English:

> Tellin kids they lingo is cool but it ain cool enough for where it really counts . . . is just like tellin them it ain cool at all. . . . [W]e all time talkin bout preparin people for the mainstream but never talkin bout changin the course of that stream.
>
> —Geneva Smitherman, "Response to Hunt, Meyers, et al.,"
> *College English* (vol. 35, no. 6)

Why Blend "Englishes" (and Other Languages)?

Tonouchi, Anzaldúa, and Smitherman blend languages to show that their home language has value, to express their individual identities, and to "chang[e] the

---

* A pidgin is a language that develops when two or more groups who speak different languages need to communicate. When a group has spoken a pidgin for several generations, it often evolves into a creole, a more stable language. Hawaiian pidgin is actually a creole spoken by more than 600,000 people.

course" of the "mainstream." For several reasons, you may also want to blend your home language with formal English:

- **To express your own identity.**   In one sense, you are your language, or, more accurately, *languages*. From Black English to Tejano Spanish to "Bostonese," from tech jargon to the language of the restaurant kitchen, the way you speak and the expressions you use can indicate the cultural group or geographic region you come from or identify with. In an educational environment that may, at times, feel like it's trying to change you into a different person, it can be helpful to assert your own identity.

- **To evoke a person or place.**   When writing about a particular person or place, you can often make that person or place come alive by capturing the language as it is spoken. My mother-in-law from Boston talks about it being "wicked cold" outside. In Hawaii, when someone is finished with something, they might say, "I'm all pau." People in Baltimore might report they are going "down the ocean" for the weekend.

- **To establish your credibility.**   When writing for an audience that is likely to share your home language, your use of that language can help you connect with the audience. When writing for an audience that doesn't share your home language, your use of that language can help establish your expertise in matters related to your community, your culture.

- **To make a strong point.**   Interrupting formal English to make a point in your home language can signal that what you are saying is important to you.

The Rhetorical Situation and Language Blending

Blending your home language and formal English may involve some risk. Your reader may think you are using language in a clever and powerful way, or they may disapprove completely of what you've done. Thinking about the rhetorical situation can help you decide whether you want to take that risk. (To learn more about the rhetorical situation, see W2.3, Components of Rhetorical Analysis, p. 11; W2.4, Thinking about Audience, p. 13; and W2.6, Thinking about Purpose, p. 16.)

- **Author.**   What version of you do you want to present? What part of your identity do you want to emphasize? Because language is so intimately connected to identity, the language choices you make can allow you to be your authentic self.

- **Audience.**   Who is your audience? How will your readers respond to language blending in your writing? Are you willing to challenge your audience's expectations, or do you want to satisfy them?

- **Purpose.** What do you want to happen as a result of your writing? What effect do you want it to have on your readers? Will language blending help you create that effect?

- **Topic.** What kind of language (or languages) is appropriate given your topic? Will using your home language make your writing on this topic more effective?

If you are writing for an audience that may not be familiar with your home English, you may want to think of ways to alert your readers to what they are about to encounter. You could do this in an introductory paragraph where you explain what you're going to do and why, or you may want to include phrases like "as my momma used to say" or "as we would say where I grew up." You won't need to include an alert every time. (Some writers choose not to include alerts at all.) Once readers get used to what you're doing, they'll able to understand what you're doing.

Another consideration is comprehension: How likely is it that your audience will understand the language you have used? Will readers be able to infer the meaning from the context? Consider this sentence from Leo Rosten's *The New Joys of Yiddish*:

> Why does a schlemiel like that ever try to fix anything?

Even readers unfamiliar with Yiddish will be able to infer that *schlemiel* here means an awkward or clumsy person without any futher explanation from you. If readers won't understand the word or be able to infer its meaning from the context, you may want to include a brief explanation following the unfamiliar word or phrase. Notice how Anzaldúa includes a definition for *sin papeles*:

> *Sin papeles*—he did not carry his birth certificate to work in the fields.

If multiple expressions require explanation, consider including footnotes or a glossary at the end of your paper.

W6.11 Writing

Blending "Englishes" (and Other Languages) in Your Own Writing

Using one of the three prompts below, write a short paper—a page would be plenty—in which you integrate words and phrases from your home language with more formal academic English.

1. Write an email to guidance counselors at your high school explaining what students need to know about the college experience.

2. Write a letter to your local school board in which you argue that they should or should not restrict teachers from addressing gender identity or racial justice in their classrooms.

3. Write an email to your manager at work proposing changes to make the establishment accommodating to a more diverse group of employees and customers.

As you give language blending a try, think about the strategies discussed in W6.10, Blending "Englishes" (and Other Languages), p. 81. How will the blending you're doing work given the audience, topic, and purpose for this writing?

W6.12 Exploration

Peer Reviewing Essays That Blend "Englishes" (and Other Languages)

Your instructor will distribute examples of the writing you and your classmates did for W6.11, Blending "Englishes" (and Other Languages) in Your Own Writing (p. 84). Working on your own or in your group—your instructor will tell you which—analyze how effectively writers have blended formal, academic English with their home languages. Use the following questions to guide your discussion:

1. Overall, did the language blending work? What was your overall response to the writing?

2. Were there places where the blended language was particularly effective? Can you suggest revisions that would make the blended language more effective, given the intended audience?

3. Are there places where you needed the writer to clarify the meaning of unfamiliar words and phrases? Point to specific instances.

Remember that it can be painful to hear criticism of your writing. Try to express your opinions in a way to minimize this discomfort, and offer encouragement whenever you can: Tell your classmates when they make a strong point or say something you had never thought of. When your writing is being discussed, listen respectfully and try to avoid being defensive.

W6.13 Advice

Using Figurative Language

Figurative language uses figures of speech, such as similes, metaphors, and personification, to convey information and ideas in more creative and powerful ways than ordinary language. For example, instead of writing "My professor spoke extremely rapidly," you could use a simile, "My professor talked *as* fast as an auctioneer." By comparing your professor's speech to that of an auctioneer, you create an image for readers that helps them to understand just how quickly your professor talks. Or you could use a metaphor and say, "My professor's words were claps of thunder that echoed off the classroom walls." Her words were not literally thunder, but this description conveys the idea that they were loud and strong. Personification involves attributing human characteristics or emotions to an inanimate object or something non-human, as in this example: My computer is a malevolent intelligence determined to see me fail.

Similes

If someone writes, "When he finally sat down to write his essay, Marcos spent fifteen minutes arranging the items on his desk like a dentist preparing his tools before beginning a root canal," they are using a simile. Similes make comparisons using the words *as* or, as in this case, *like*. Similes are effective because they use something most of us are familiar with — in this case, the careful arrangement of a dentist's tools — to explain something we don't know about — how carefully Marcos arranges everything on his desk before beginning writing. Similes are also effective because they are often clever, playful, or even funny — but not always. In this example, the comparison suggests that Marcos is about to embark on a serious project; this is a root canal job, not a cleaning. However, overused, worn-out similes have the opposite effect. Try to avoid such hackneyed similes as *ate like a pig*, *mad as a wet hen*, or *slept like a log*. Try to make fresh, new comparisons in your writing.

Metaphors

A metaphor is a figure of speech that is much like a simile, except that instead of saying X is *like* Y, a metaphor asserts that X *is* Y. Here's an example: "The IRS *is* a vulture circling my meager savings and preparing to swoop down on them." When you use a metaphor like this, you are comparing two dissimilar items that share one characteristic. Although there is not a literal connection, you are making an imaginative one in order to create a memorable image in your reader's mind. In this example, the writer is comparing the IRS to a vulture, suggesting that just as that bird will circle its prey endlessly until it tires or dies, the IRS will never give up, and your savings cannot be protected from it.

Here's another example. In *The Stuff of Thought: Language as a Window into Human Nature*, Steven Pinker writes, "A verb is the chassis of the sentence. . . . It is a framework with receptacles for the other parts — the subject, the object, and various oblique objects and subordinate clauses — to be bolted onto." He doesn't mean a verb literally *is* a chassis. He means that, in a sentence, the verb plays a role much like the role the chassis plays for a car.

One word of caution about metaphors: Once you introduce one into your writing, do not change your mind and switch to a different metaphor as the following example does.

> During the Great Recession, my family became *a ship tossed by violent seas*, but luckily we didn't get *too far over our skis* and do anything foolish.

This writer starts with a metaphor about a ship in rough seas, but switches to a metaphor about skiing, which is confusing for the reader.

Personification

An example of personification appeared in the opening paragraph: "My computer is a malevolent intelligence determined to see me fail." Note that this writer is treating her computer as though it is alive, personifying this inanimate object by suggesting it has the human traits of intelligence and malevolence, or ill will. "My utilities bill is telling me I need to lower my thermostat" is another example of personification.

Writers use personification to help readers relate to objects, animals, ideas, or other things, bringing them to life and making them easier to understand or care about. When a journalist talks about a "fire swallowing a forest whole," the reader gets a sense of the enormous destructive power of the flames and the feeling that they are almost alive, choosing their prey. When a novelist writes that "the wasted moon peered through the ragged clouds, too weak to throw a shadow or to reveal the fallen child," she creates a sense of foreboding; the moon, like the child, is weak and powerless.

It is wise to use personification sparingly to make a point, to add depth or color to your writing, or to engage readers with a subject they might not usually relate to.

When to Use Figurative Language

Using figurative language like similes, metaphors, and personification can be fun, both for the writer and for the reader. It can also be powerful and clever. You will most often find it used in works of fiction, such as novels, poems, and plays. Used sparingly in academic papers, it can help readers understand something they aren't familiar with by comparing it to something they are familiar with, help them to perceive something from a different perspective, or bring a dry topic to life. However, figurative language is not always appropriate. In most business writing and in some academic writing, it may seem flowery or pretentious. Also, given the content, it might not be appropriate. In the hard sciences, for example, a lot of writing is very technical, and specific formats must be followed.

There is no formula to help you decide whether or not to use figurative language, but it helps to think about your audience, to consider the context in which you are writing, and even to see what other writing for that audience in that context looks like.

W7 ▸ Thinking While Writing

Very often, the difference between mediocre writing and excellent writing is the quality of the *thinking* that went into the writing. In W7 you will explore strategies to make your writing more effective by thinking more broadly and deeply about your subject and thesis.

Getting Started

It might seem obvious, but in order to write something worth reading, you have to think. Let's start by considering what makes writing interesting.

W7.1 Writing
One Interesting Thing about You

Write a one-page essay on one interesting thing about the kind of person you are. Your instructor (your audience) will be reading these papers to get to know each of you in the class but also to begin a discussion of how to make your writing more effective. Remember this essay should be around a page long; don't take on too much. Please provide concrete examples to back up what you write about yourself.

W7.2 Exploration
Class Discussion on Interesting Writing

For this activity, you are going to make use of the papers you and your classmates wrote for the writing activity One Interesting Thing about You (W7.1), which asked you to write about one interesting thing about the kind of person you are.

Your instructor will make a numbered list of all the thesis statements in your papers and will pass out copies of the list to individuals or groups of students.

The task is to read over these statements and select the five that seem most likely to produce *interesting* papers. Remember that the assignment was to write about "one *interesting* thing about the kind of person you are."

Study the five you select and come up with some ideas about what makes a thesis statement interesting. Be prepared to share with the class your reasons for selecting the five thesis statements and your ideas about what makes a thesis interesting.

Developing an Interesting Essay

Now that you have a sense of what makes a thesis interesting, let's think about one surefire way to bore your reader: by proving the obvious. Then we'll consider a reliable way to avoid this: by thinking.

W7.3 Advice

Avoid Proving the Obvious

An effective essay argues something interesting and thoughtful. It does not argue something everyone already agrees with. Essays that are written to prove statements like the following are unlikely to be either interesting or thoughtful.

- Drunk driving is a terrible thing.
- Communication is important to a good relationship.
- Child abuse should not be tolerated.
- We should not tolerate racism.
- America must protect itself against terrorism.

Each of these statements is true, but none of them is likely to result in a very good essay. Why not? Because almost everyone already agrees with these statements. They belabor the obvious. Each of them argues a point that is not arguable because almost no one disagrees with it.

To avoid wasting your time making an argument that most people would already agree with, you might want to try this trick. Picture yourself standing in front of your class, reading your thesis out loud and then asking whether anyone disagrees. If you cannot picture more than one or two hands being raised, then you need to find a more interesting thesis.

W7.4 Advice

Use Thinking to Find an Interesting Thesis

Here are two examples showing how two students have thought their way to a thesis that isn't obvious, that makes a point that everyone doesn't already agree with, and that shows they've really given some thought to their topic. In each of these examples, the basic strategy is the same: simply thinking harder about the topic.

Example 1: Thinking about Helping Children "Get Ahead"

In a sociology class, students were asked to write about some aspect of "parenting." Charlene, a single mother with two young daughters, Carrie and Angel, decided on a draft thesis that it is important for parents to do everything they can to help their children "get ahead." She wanted her daughters' lives to be more comfortable and more successful than hers. She wanted to give them "every advantage" so they wouldn't be "left behind."

Charlene started writing about how she bought books and a computer for Carrie and Angel; enrolled them in a preschool program that she could barely afford; and, when her daughters were old enough for elementary school, moved to a neighborhood in her city that was known for the quality of its schools even though she had to take a second job in order to afford the rent.

As she thought she was almost finished with her essay, she saw a news report on television that bothered her greatly—a report that many wealthy parents had spent millions of dollars to hire a company that would get their children into highly competitive universities. This company bribed athletic coaches to write letters about the children's athletic ability when they had not actually participated in any sports. They even hired people to take college placement tests for the children.

Charlene was shocked. She knew these parents thought they were simply doing everything they could to help their children "get ahead," but they had clearly gone too far. Charlene began to rethink her essay. While she still thought parents should try to help their children "get ahead," she now recognized that there were also dangers to this approach.

The admissions cheating scandal she had seen on the news illustrated one danger, but Charlene wondered if there were others. She thought about parents she knew who were so eager to help their children that they did their children's home-work for them. She thought about a friend who was so determined that her son would get straight A's that she wouldn't allow him to try out for the school play because it would take too much time away from his school work. She thought about parents who put so much pressure on their children that they developed stress-related psychological problems.

After all this thinking, Charlene had arrived at a much more thoughtful and interesting thesis: while it is important for parents to help their children be successful, it is also important to avoid the dangers that can arise when this parenting approach goes too far.

Example 2: Thinking about Drunk Driving

In a criminal justice class, students were asked to write about a current criminal justice issue. One student wrote a wonderful paper about drunk driving that didn't just belabor the obvious. He argued that, while drunk driving is certainly a problem, we are placing all our attention on preventing drunk driving when more people in America are killed each year as a result of speeding. He reported that in 2011, 9,878 Americans died as a result of drunk driving, while 10,001 died in accidents caused by speeding. He wasn't arguing that drunk driving isn't a major problem; he was arguing that speeding is a slightly larger problem that people do not appear to be as upset about. There are no Mothers Against Speeding organizations. No one is tying ribbons on their door handles to protest speeding.

Each of the essays discussed above became more effective when the writer found something interesting and thoughtful to say after thinking more deeply about the topic.

One Word of Caution. Sometimes when students are told to write something that is not obvious, something that everyone doesn't already agree with, they go to the opposite extreme. They write a paper with a thesis that no one could ever agree with and that they have no chance of proving in any reasonable way: "Unicorns really do exist" or "The president is a literal zombie." This kind of farfetched thesis is not what is being suggested here. Instead, you are simply being asked to write a paper that argues something that is not obvious, something that results from doing some real thinking about your topic.

W7.5   Exploration

Thinking about Reserved Parking

A student named Alex got this assignment in his English class:

> Write a short paper, about a page, in which you propose who should get reserved parking spaces at your college or university. Be sure to provide evidence to support your assertions. The audience for this assignment is other students in your class.

Here is what Alex wrote in response to this assignment:

At this time of year, it is really difficult to find a parking place on campus. Several times I have been late to class because I've been driving around looking for a place to park. It would be great to have a reserved parking place, but after discussing this with several of my classmates and thinking about it for a long time, I have decided that the college should provide reserved parking places to disabled people, the faculty, and the college president.

People with disabilities deserve reserved parking because some simply could not make it to class if they had to park in the distant lots. This should be the highest priority for reserved parking.

If the faculty were not here, there wouldn't be a college. They play the most important role at the college. They teach the classes. If a faculty member doesn't make it to class, then twenty or thirty students suffer. This is why I think faculty should have reserved parking places.

Being the president of a college is a very prestigious position. I know our president worked for more than thirty years before she was promoted to president. If someone has worked his or her way to this position, we should recognize that accomplishment by providing reserved parking.

In conclusion, reserved parking at this college should be given to people with disabilities, faculty, and the president.

On your own or in your group, consider Alex's paper. What do you think of the *thinking* that went into this essay? Do you think Alex would want people who work for buildings and grounds to have reserved parking? Why do you think he didn't include them? Be prepared to share your assessment with the class.

W7.6 Advice

Thinking Deeply, Thinking Broadly

In W7.5, Thinking about Reserved Parking (p. 91), you read the essay in which Alex argued that three groups should get reserved parking on campus: people with disabilities, faculty, and the college president. Now we're going to think more deeply about one of Alex's three topics: people with disabilities.

When one group of students was asked to brainstorm about this topic and come up with a more specific list, here's what they suggested:

people who use a wheelchair	people with dyslexia
people who've had strokes	people who are pregnant
people with cystic fibrosis	older adults
people who are hard of hearing	people who are blind

The students then decided to group the first three items under the general category of people with mobility impairment. At this point, one student asked why people with hearing loss should get reserved parking. After some discussion, the group agreed that while having hearing loss was certainly a disability, it didn't impair movement, and so decided that those with hearing loss should not be given reserved parking. Another student quickly pointed out that people with dyslexia and, in fact, all people with learning disabilities, wouldn't benefit from reserved parking. For pregnant people and older adults, there was considerable discussion about "how pregnant" and "how much older," but the students generally agreed that at some point these two groups should get reserved parking. After a few minutes, they also agreed that blind people were unlikely to be behind the wheel—they would either take public transportation or get dropped off—so there was no need to include that group in the list.

At this point, one woman in the class raised an interesting issue. She agreed that pregnant people should get reserved parking, but she wasn't comfortable with placing pregnancy in the category of disability. The question was resolved when the class agreed to change the name of the category to "mobility impairment."

What this class did was think deeply. They drilled down into the phrase "people with disabilities" and discovered it was more complex than they had realized. They could have done the same thing with *faculty* and the *president*, but, instead, they decided to see what would happen if they thought more *broadly* about Alex's topic.

They made a list of all the groups who had received reserved parking on their campus or on other campuses. Here's what they came up with:

<u>people with mobility impairments</u>	vice presidents
<u>faculty</u>	staff
students with a GPA of 3.5 or higher	<u>buildings and grounds personnel</u>
the United Way lottery winner	the state champion volleyball team
the president	people who drive hybrid or electric cars

The class then asked this question: "What was the reason each group was given reserved parking?" The class focused first on the groups underlined above and agreed that they were given reserved parking so they could do their jobs, including the job of being a student.

Next, the class observed that some groups were rewarded with reserved parking in recognition of their accomplishments. They placed students with a GPA of 3.5 or higher, the president, vice presidents, and the state champion volleyball team in this category.

People were puzzled by the "the United Way lottery winner" category. One student explained that the college encourages everyone to donate to the United Way each fall. All the donors' names are placed in a hat, and a winner is drawn and awarded a reserved parking place for one year. Reserved parking was used to encourage behavior the college wanted—in this case, supporting the United Way. That left one group—people who drive hybrid or electric cars. The class quickly realized that this group belonged in the same category as the United Way donors: they were given reserved parking to encourage environmentally friendly behavior.

At this point, the class not only had a broad list of groups who could be given reserved parking—a lot more groups than the three Alex came up with—but they also had been able to organize those groups into three categories.

To make it possible for people to do their jobs	To recognize accomplishments	To encourage certain behaviors
• people with mobility impairments • faculty • staff • buildings and grounds crews	• students with a GPA of 3.5 or higher • the president • vice presidents • the state champion volleyball team	• people who drive hybrid or electric cars • the United Way lottery winner

By thinking deeply and broadly, the class generated both more and more interesting content for an essay, and by organizing that content into chunks, they arrived at a more thoughtful thesis for the paper: Reserved parking on campus is allocated for three different reasons.

W7.7 Video

Thinking about Alex's Paper

Those using Achieve with *The Hub* can watch a video presentation about the thinking that went into Alex's paper (W7.5, Thinking about Reserved Parking, p. 91).

W7.8 Video

Thinking Deeply

Those using Achieve with *The Hub* can watch a video presentation about the deeper thinking that could go into Alex's paper (W7.5, Thinking about Reserved Parking, p. 91).

W7.9 Video

Thinking Broadly

Those using Achieve with *The Hub* can watch a video presentation about the broader thinking that could go into Alex's paper (W7.5, Thinking about Reserved Parking, p. 91).

W7.10 Writing

Writing about a Campus Issue

Write a short essay—a page would be plenty—in which you argue for a change at your college or university. Think of this as an essay to be published in your school's newspaper, so the audience is readers of that paper. Use deep and broad thinking to make your paper as thoughtful and interesting as possible.

W8 ▸ Revising

Because effective revision is so important and takes time, be sure you schedule enough time for a rigorous review once you finish drafting a paper or other piece of writing.

Introduction to Revising

For most writers, revising begins almost as soon they start writing. They are constantly rereading and making changes as they write, but once they have a complete draft, they do a major revision.

W8.1 Advice
Revision Basics

When you are ready to revise, you want to be able to stand back from what you've written and view it objectively. Often it is easier to do this if you let some time pass between when you finish a draft and when you start revising it, ideally at least a day or two. However, if you finish your draft late the night before it's due, go to bed and revise it in the morning when you're fresh. If you don't have even that much time, at least get up from your desk and have a cup of coffee or take a walk around the block before you start revising. The important thing is to give yourself enough time to switch roles from being the writer of the draft to being an objective reader who can find ways to improve it.

Before you begin revising, it's always a good idea to get some feedback from others. Sometimes your instructor will schedule class time for peer review, a process that allows students to receive feedback on a draft from other students (see W1.6, Guidelines for Peer Review, p. 6, for details). Even if no peer review sessions are planned, ask a friend or even another student in your class to read over your paper and let you know what works and what could use some improvement.

It's also important to recognize the difference between revision and editing. *Revision* is when you look at the big issues in what you have written. Does it have a clear thesis? Is it unified? Does it provide enough evidence to support the points it makes? Is it organized effectively? *Editing* is when you look at the sentence-level issues like grammar, punctuation, spelling, and word choice. These are two different activities, and it is best not to try to do them both at the same time. Revise first, and when that is finished, you can more effectively edit for correctness. (For more details, see W9, Editing, p. 115.)

Some writers prefer to print out a copy of their draft and revise by marking up that copy and later transferring the changes to the draft on the computer. Others prefer to do their revising directly on the computer. Use whichever approach works best for you.

W8.2 Writing

How Do You Revise?

Write a short paper, no more than a page, in which you describe how revision fits into your writing process. How much time do you devote to revising? What sorts of things do you focus on when revising? The audience for this paper is your instructor.

Getting Started

The place to start is with the assignment: Does your essay do everything your instructor asked you to do?

W8.3 Advice

Revising for Assignment, Audience, and Purpose

When you are ready to start revising, it's a good idea to read your draft over quickly to refresh your sense of the essay as a whole and then to ask yourself these questions.

1. **What was the assignment your instructor gave for this essay?**   What exactly were you asked to do? Does your essay include everything the assignment calls for? Is it the right length? (For more details, see W2.1, Reading an Assignment, p. 10.)

2. **Who is the audience for this essay?**   Is there more than one? What do they already know? How technical can, or should, you be? Is your audience likely to agree or disagree with you? Have you written in a style, with a voice, that is appropriate for that audience? (For more details, see W2.4, Thinking about Audience, p. 13.)

3. **What is your purpose for writing this essay?** Is it to persuade, explain, express feelings or thoughts, or entertain? Is your purpose to request something, to recommend something, to reassure the audience, or to summarize something? Does your draft really address that purpose? (For more details, see W2.6, Thinking about Purpose, p. 16.)

W8.4 Advice

Backward Outlining

Backward outlining is a revision strategy that allows writers to step back and get an overview of the structure of their essay. Creating one is simple: Just take your rough draft and jot down a brief summary of each paragraph's main point. You can write your summary in the margin of your essay or in a separate document. Try it out for an essay you're working on now.

Here's an example that Zoey, a community college student, created for her first draft of a paper on happiness.

In Pursuit of Happiness

1 Happiness is something all humans strive for. We search for happiness our entire lives — happiness is the ultimate goal. We have searched for happiness since the dawn of time, yet even now, especially now, it seems impossible to attain.

¶1 Happiness is something humans have strived for since the dawn of time.

2 Happiness is subjective, everyone has their own unique ideas of what happiness is and how to find it, but how can we maintain it?

¶2 Everyone has their own idea of happiness.

3 Happiness is not something one achieves on their own. Happiness requires group effort. It is something that is impacted by our environment and those around us as much as it is impacted by ourselves, if not more. We are, in a way, pack animals, needing a community around us for our best chances for happiness.

¶3 Happiness requires a group effort.

4 The pursuit of happiness has been around for as long as humans have existed. It is mentioned in our religions, philosophies, mythologies and even written

¶4 Pursuit of happiness has been around forever.

in our government documents. We feel a natural urge to find happiness and why wouldn't we? Most people would love nothing more than for themselves and their loved ones to feel constant joy.

5   No one wants suffering or misery, but without it we cannot genuinely appreciate the positives in life. Perhaps happiness is not a constant but is fleeting so we can experience it again from a new perspective. Rarely, if ever, are people happy all the time or with everything they experience. This is just a part of life, the ups and downs our emotions take based on our environment or the people we are around.

¶5 Happiness is fleeting.

6   In Rashmi's passage, *Happiness in Sri Lanka?*, she thinks about her own happiness. "People often say to me, 'You must be very happy. You escaped such poverty gained such a wonderful education and are on your way to a very rewarding career. I usually respond that I am happy . . . , but my family back in Sri Lanka are very happy too. . . . They are surrounded by family and friends. They really seem to be even happier than I am." Even with her success, she still isn't completely happy. That is not to say someone like Rashmi does not ever experience joy from the life they have made for themselves. However, Rashmi may not be as happy as her family members who live a simple life together. Rashmi may be missing that community feeling of closeness. She may miss her family a lot due to being so far away and her family may be overall happier due to them being together. For these reasons I believe that Rashmi would agree with my view of happiness achievable in a solitary way. I think Rashmi would also say that happiness is dependent on not just you but the people around you and your environment.

¶6 Rashmi is not as happy as her family because she misses her family.

7   As humans, we crave intimacy and companionship, so it would make sense that happiness overlaps with that.

¶7 Happiness requires companionship.

8   Happiness in the traditional selfish sense can be less significant to our wellbeing than feeling joy from helping others and not necessarily ourselves.

¶8 The joy of helping others gives a greater happiness than selfishness.

9   Emily Esfahani Smith writes in *There's More to Life Than Being Happy* that, "While happiness is an emotion felt in the here and now, it ultimately fades away" (259). So then happiness cannot be something permanent and true to just a singular person.

¶9 Happiness cannot be permanent to a single person.

10   Perhaps it is something that comes with having love and companionship. Again, referring to Smith's writing, authors in a study discussed how "Happy people get a lot of joy from receiving benefits from others while people leading meaningful lives get a lot of joy from giving to others." So, to have a sustaining sense of happiness we need to be selfless more than selfish. That is not to say you cannot be selfish in certain situations (i.e., setting boundaries, cutting off connections with people who take advantage of or are toxic to you, etc.) but to add more meaning to your happiness, acting selflessly can help you maintain that happiness. A more fulfilling sense of joy can come from making those around you happy and helping them to have a pleasant life. The more we take care of each other the better off we all are.

¶10 Sustained happiness comes from giving to others.

11   Personally, I feel better and happier knowing I am making those around me happy. I love to give people gifts I think they will enjoy and do things for people as gestures of love or appreciation. It also

¶11 I feel happier when I make those around me happy.

brings me joy when I can see people being happy. Whether it is seeing them succeed with their goals or gaining momentary pleasure from sporting events, food, music or even television. Seeing those around me feeling good also allows me to feel good. It is a sense of safety and comfort. If my family and friends can feel at peace for even just a few moments, then I can feel that peace as well. That may be something instinctual, much like happiness, that if there is not a present danger that your group or you can sense, then we can pause for a moment and feel comfort and happiness in that situation.

12   When it comes to defining happiness, it is not a simple task. Happiness is an emotion we all feel and that we all look for in life. It has so many versions of itself, all unique to every person. One thing I believe is universal to everyone's version of happiness is that it is a very interconnected concept. We rely on others for our survival, our comfort, and naturally, our happiness as well. I would like to think writers like Rashmi and Emily Esfahani Smith, who both wrote about happiness and what it means to be happy, would agree with me that happiness is not something one person is likely to achieve alone. Focusing on community is a more likely path to happiness than focusing on self.

13   It seems ironic that if we pursue happiness in a solitary, selfish way, we are less likely to achieve it. If we give up that focus on self and, instead, turn our focus to the people around us, our family, our friends, our community, we will achieve greater happiness.

¶12 *Defining happiness.*

¶13 *Focusing on the people around us is the most likely path to happiness.*

Revising for Unity, Coherence, and Support of a Single, Clear Thesis

Unity, coherence, and support of a single, clear thesis: These are the basic ingredients of a well-constructed essay.

W8.5 Advice

Revising for Thesis and Unity

An important step in the revision process is checking to see whether

- your draft essay has a clear and consistent thesis
- the thesis at the end of the essay is the same as it was at the beginning (but expressed in different words)
- all your supporting reasons and evidence are relevant to that thesis

(For more details, see W3.5, Developing a Working Thesis, p. 29, and W5.1, Creating Unity, p. 53.)

Using her backward outline, Zoey checked for thesis and unity. Reading over the outline and asking herself "What is my thesis?" Zoey discovered a problem. At a number of points her paper argues that happiness is fleeting, that it doesn't last. But at other points it asserts that happiness is related to companionship, to a sense of belonging to a group.

For a minute Zoey thought that she might be able to combine these two ideas into a single thesis, something like "The only way to achieve lasting happiness is through companionship with other people," but she quickly saw this wouldn't work because she realized that no happiness is lasting, not even happiness that comes from companionship.

At this point, Zoey decided to make her thesis about achieving happiness through companionship, so she eliminated those points in her outline about happiness being fleeting:

¶1. Happiness is something humans have strived for since the dawn of time.

¶2. Everyone has their own idea of happiness.

¶3. Happiness requires a group effort.

¶4. Pursuit of happiness has been around forever.

¶5. ~~Happiness is fleeting.~~

¶6. Rashmi is not as happy as her family because she misses her family.

¶7. Happiness requires companionship.

¶8. The joy of helping others gives a greater happiness than selfishness.

¶9. ~~Happiness cannot be permanent to a single person.~~

¶10. Sustained happiness comes from giving to others.

¶11. I feel happier when I make those around me happy.

¶12. Defining happiness.

¶13. Focusing on the people around us is the most likely path to happiness.

Next, Zoey looked at the seven paragraphs in which she had written directly about happiness and companionship:

¶3. Happiness requires a community around us.

¶6. Rashmi is not as happy as her family because she misses her family.

¶7. Happiness requires companionship.

¶8. The joy of helping others gives a greater happiness than selfishness.

¶10. Sustained happiness comes from giving to others.

¶11. I feel happier when I make those around me happy.

¶13. Focusing on the people around us is the most likely path to happiness.

After rereading these paragraphs carefully, Zoey was able to formulate a clearer thesis that expressed what she really wanted to say about happiness:

The surest way to achieve the greatest happiness is through close ties with a community.

Zoey then looked at her four remaining ideas:

¶1. Happiness is something humans have strived for since the dawn of time.

¶2. ~~Everyone has their own idea of happiness.~~

¶4. Pursuit of happiness has been around forever.

¶12. Defining happiness.

She decided to group 1, 4, and 12 as an introduction and to eliminate 2 as not supporting the thesis.

W8.6 Writing

Applying Backward Outlining to Revising for Thesis and Unity

W8.4, Backward Outlining (p. 374), explains how to create a backward outline from your first draft. W8.5 (p. 98) explains how to use backward outlining to improve the thesis and unity of a draft. Now give it a try: Make a backward outline of a draft of one of your essays, and then use it to revise for thesis and unity.

W8.7 Advice

Revising for Organization

In W8.5, Revising for Thesis and Unity (p. 102), you saw how Zoey used her backward outline to revise for unity. Next, Zoey went to work on the organization of her essay, reorganizing the items in the most logical order so that her argument would be easy for the reader to follow.

The first thing she noticed was that paragraphs 1 and 4 are both about how the search for happiness has been around since the beginning of human existence. So Zoey combined them into a single paragraph 1.

Next, she noticed that the paragraph defining *happiness* came at the end of the paper. Defining this key word is a good idea, but it didn't make sense to leave that to the end of her essay, so she made the definition paragraph 2.

Now Zoey had the introduction (paragraphs 1, 2, and 3), and she had a concluding paragraph identified (paragraph 13, which becomes paragraph 8 in her reorganized scratch outline below). But what about the body of her essay? Are paragraphs 4 through 7 in the most effective order? Actually, they don't seem to be in any particular order at all, just the order they occurred to her when she was writing her first draft. Sometimes chronological order—earliest to latest—works for ordering the body paragraphs, but Zoey decided to organize them from most general to most specific, which is how they are ordered below. (You may want to take a look at W5.6, Using Chunking and Ordering, p. 59; W5.9, Outlining, p. 62; and W5.10, Strategies for Creating Coherence, p. 65, to learn more about options for ordering your ideas.)

The first two, paragraphs 4 and 5, are about happiness resulting in a general way from companionship and sharing. The last two, paragraphs 6 and 7, are about specific examples of how companionship and sharing work to create happiness.

Here's Zoey's revised outline:

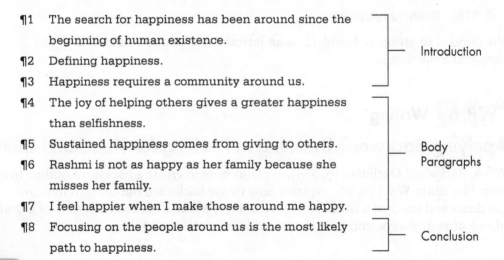

¶1 The search for happiness has been around since the beginning of human existence.

¶2 Defining happiness.

¶3 Happiness requires a community around us.

— Introduction

¶4 The joy of helping others gives a greater happiness than selfishness.

¶5 Sustained happiness comes from giving to others.

¶6 Rashmi is not as happy as her family because she misses her family.

¶7 I feel happier when I make those around me happy.

— Body Paragraphs

¶8 Focusing on the people around us is the most likely path to happiness.

— Conclusion

W8.8 Writing
Applying Backward Outlining to Revising for Organization

W8.4, Backward Outlining (p. 98), explains how to create a backward outline from your first draft. W8.7 (p. 104) explains how to use backward outlining to revise the organization of a draft. Now give it a try: Use a backward outline of a draft of one of your essays to revise for organization.

W8.9 Advice
Revising for Support

In W8.5 (p. 102) and W8.7 (p. 104), you saw how Zoey reorganized her draft essay, moving and deleting sections so that related sections were grouped together and irrelevant sections were cut. She next read over her outline looking for places she could make stronger by adding evidence. Those places are indicated in blue handwriting.

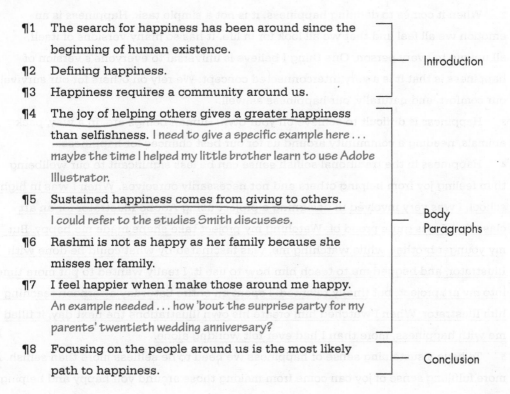

¶1   The search for happiness has been around since the beginning of human existence.

¶2   Defining happiness.

¶3   Happiness requires a community around us.

⎫ Introduction

¶4   The joy of helping others gives a greater happiness than selfishness. I need to give a specific example here . . . maybe the time I helped my little brother learn to use Adobe Illustrator.

¶5   Sustained happiness comes from giving to others.
I could refer to the studies Smith discusses.

¶6   Rashmi is not as happy as her family because she misses her family.

¶7   I feel happier when I make those around me happy.
An example needed . . . how 'bout the surprise party for my parents' twentieth wedding anniversary?

⎫ Body Paragraphs

¶8   Focusing on the people around us is the most likely path to happiness.

⎫ Conclusion

The items Zoey underlined in the revised outline are all assertions of her opinions. That's not a problem; making an argument always involves expressing your opinions. However, it would be a problem if any of these opinions appeared in the essay without adequate support or evidence. At this point, Zoey made notes about where she needs to add support and what that support might consist of. She then revised her essay. The new support she added is underlined. (W4.2, Types of Evidence, p. 42, discusses different approaches to providing support to back up the opinions you express in an essay with facts, anecdotes [stories] and examples, statistics or numerical evidence, and expert testimony.) She also included in-text citations for the sources she added, and she provided a works cited list at the end of her essay. (D2, MLA Documentation, p. 325, and D3, APA Documentation, p. 365, give details about citing sources in each style.)

In Pursuit of Happiness

1   Happiness is something all humans strive for. We have searched for happiness since the dawn of time, yet even now, especially now, it seems impossible to attain. It is mentioned in our religions, philosophies, mythologies and even written in our government documents. We feel a natural urge to find happiness and why wouldn't we? Most people would love nothing more than for themselves and their loved ones to feel constant joy.

2   When it comes to defining happiness, it is not a simple task. Happiness is an emotion we all feel and that we all look for in life. It has so many versions of itself, all unique to every person. One thing I believe is universal to everyone's version of happiness is that it is a very interconnected concept. We rely on others for our survival, our comfort, and naturally, our happiness as well.

3   Happiness is difficult to achieve on your own. Human beings are, in a way, pack animals, needing a community around us for our best chances for happiness.

4   Happiness in the traditional selfish sense can be less significant to our wellbeing than feeling joy from helping others and not necessarily ourselves. When I was in high school, I was very involved in designing a project using Adobe Illustrator for an art class that I was quite proud of. Watching my project take shape made me happy. But my younger brother, while watching me, was fascinated by what could be done with Illustrator, and begged me to teach him how to use it. I really wanted to put more time into my art project, but finally relented. 1 spent an entire Saturday afternoon teaching him Illustrator. When I watched him create his own illustrations the next day, it filled me with happiness, more than I had ever felt working alone.

5   To have a sustaining sense of happiness we need to be selfless more than selfish. A more fulfilling sense of joy can come from making those around you happy and helping

them to have a pleasant life. <u>Emily Esfahani Smith reports that studies have shown that "Happy people get a lot of joy from receiving benefits from others while people leading meaningful lives get a lot of joy from giving to others" (258).</u>

6   In Rashmi's passage, *Happiness in Sri Lanka?*, she thinks about her own happiness. "People often say to me, 'You must be very happy. You escaped such poverty and gained such a wonderful education.' I usually respond that I am . . . , but my family back in Sri Lanka are very happy too. . . . They are surrounded by family and friends. They really seem to be even happier than I am" (219). Even with her success, Rashmi misses that community feeling of closeness. She may miss her family a lot due to being so far away, and her family may be overall happier due to them being together. I think Rashmi would also say that happiness is dependent on not just you but the people around you and your environment.

7   Personally, I feel better and happier knowing I am making those around me happy. I love to give people gifts I think they will enjoy and do things for people as gestures of love or appreciation. It also brings me joy when I can see people being happy. Whether it is seeing them succeed with their goals or gaining momentary pleasure from sporting events, food, music or even television. Seeing those around me feeling good also allows me to feel good. It is a sense of safety and comfort. If my family and friends can feel at peace for even just a few moments, then I can feel that peace as well. <u>Last year was my parents' twentieth wedding anniversary. Secretly, I organized a celebration. I cooked for days and invited all their friends, but the biggest surprise was I drove to Texas and brought my brother home from college for the party. When he walked in the door, my mother and even my father burst into tears. I treasure that moment.</u>

8   It seems ironic that if we pursue happiness in a solitary, selfish way, we are less likely to achieve it. If we give up that focus on self and, instead, turn our focus to the people around us, our family, our friends, our community, we will achieve greater happiness.

(**NOTE:** The works cited list always starts on a new page.)

Works Cited

Rashmi. "Happiness in Sri Lanka?" In Peter Adams, *The Hub: A Place for Reading and Writing*, 2nd ed., Bedford/St. Martin's, 2023, pp. 218–19.

Smith, Emily Esfahani. "There's More to Life Than Being Happy." In Peter Adams, *The Hub: A Place for Reading and Writing*, 2nd ed., Bedford/St. Martin's, 2023, pp. 220–24.

W8.10 Writing

Applying Backward Outlining to Revising for Support

W8.4, Backward Outlining (p. 98), explains how to create a backward outline from your first draft. W8.9, Revising for Support (p. 105), explains how to provide stronger support for your essay by using a backward outline. (You may also want to take a look at W4.2, Types of Evidence, p. 42, which discusses backing up your opinions with facts, examples, statistics or numerical evidence, and expert opinion.) Now give it a try: Use a backward outline of a draft of one of your essays to revise for support.

W8.11 Advice

Revising for Coherence

When a piece of writing has coherence, it flows. It is easy for the reader to follow. Writers use three techniques to improve the coherence of their writing:

1. They organize their essay logically, something that Zoey worked on in W8.7, Revising for Organization (p. 104).
2. They strategically repeat key words and phrases.
3. They provide transitions.

(Repeating key words and phrases and providing transitions are discussed in more detail in W5.10, Strategies for Creating Coherence, p. 65.)

One way to revise for coherence is first to identify the key words and phrases in your essay. When Zoey went to work on revising for coherence, she quickly identified *happiness* as a key word, but in reading the essay over, she realized that the word *community* is also important to her argument. In the version of her essay that follows, the word *happiness* and other synonyms (words that mean about the same thing) or pronouns that refer to *happiness* are underlined; the word *community* is double underlined. When Zoey discovered that the word *community*, which is important to her argument, appeared only three times, she looked for words related to *community* and circled those. She found that the relationship between those words and *community* wasn't always clear, so she revised several of them to make the connection clear.

Transitional words and expressions are like road signs that help readers understand where they are going, what's coming up next, and how the parts of the essay relate to each other. When Zoey read over her paper looking for transitional words and expressions, she found very few. She added some—they are highlighted—at places where they would help the reader understand the relationships of different parts of her essay.

In Pursuit of Happiness

1 Happiness is something all humans strive for. We have searched for happiness since the dawn of time, yet even now, especially now, it seems impossible to attain. It is mentioned in our religions, philosophies, mythologies and even written in our government documents. We feel a natural urge to find happiness and why wouldn't we? Most people would love nothing more than for themselves and their loved ones to feel constant joy.

2 When it comes to defining happiness, it is not a simple task. Happiness is an emotion we all feel and that we all look for in life. It has so many versions of itself, all unique to every person. However, one thing I believe is universal to everyone's version of happiness is that it is a very interconnected concept. We rely on others for our survival, our comfort, and naturally, our happiness as well.

3 Happiness is difficult to achieve on your own. As a result, human beings are, in a way, pack animals, needing a community around us for our best chances for happiness.

4 Happiness in the traditional selfish sense can be less significant to our wellbeing than feeling joy from helping others and not necessarily ourselves. For example, when I was in high school, I was very involved in designing a project for an art class that I was quite proud of using Adobe Illustrator. Watching my project take shape made me happy. But my younger brother, while watching me, was fascinated by what could be done with Illustrator, and begged me to teach him how to use it. I really wanted to put more time into my art project, but finally relented. I spent an entire Saturday afternoon teaching him Illustrator. When I watched him create his own illustrations the next day, it filled me with happiness, more than I had ever felt working on my own project alone.

5 To be specific, to have a sustaining sense of happiness we need to be selfless more than selfish. A more fulfilling sense of joy can come from making those around you happy and helping them to have a pleasant life. Emily Esfahani Smith reports that studies have shown that "Happy people get a lot of joy from receiving benefits from others while people leading meaningful lives get a lot of joy from giving to others" (221).

6 In Rashmi's passage, *Happiness in Sri Lanka?*, she thinks about her own happiness. "People often say to me, 'You must be very happy. You escaped such poverty and

gained such a wonderful education and are on your way to a very rewarding career.' I usually respond that I am happy . . . , but my family back in Sri Lanka are very happy too. . . . They are surrounded by family and friends. They really seem to be even happier than I am" (p. 219). Even with her success, she is still missing happiness. Rashmi may be missing that community feeling of closeness. She may miss her family a lot due to being so far away, and her family may be overall happier due to them being together. I think Rashmi would also say that happiness is dependent on not just you but the people around you and your environment.

7   Personally, I feel better and happier knowing I am making those around me happy. For example, I love to give people gifts I think they will enjoy and do things for people as gestures of love or appreciation. Also, it brings me joy when I can see people being happy. Whether it is seeing them succeed with their goals or gaining momentary pleasure from sporting events, food, music or even television. Seeing those around me feeling good also allows me to feel good. It is a sense of safety and comfort. If my family and friends can feel at peace for even just a few moments, then I can feel that peace as well. For example, last year was my parents' twentieth wedding anniversary. Secretly, I organized a celebration. I cooked for days and invited all their friends, but the biggest surprise was I drove to Texas and brought my brother home from college for the party. When he walked in the door, my mother and even my father burst into tears. I treasure that moment.

8   It seems ironic that if we pursue happiness in a solitary, selfish way, we are less likely to achieve it. If we give up that focus on self and, instead, turn our focus to the people around us, our family, our friends, our community, we will achieve greater happiness.

(**NOTE:** The works cited list always starts on a new page.)

Works Cited

Rashmi. "Happiness in Sri Lanka?" In Peter Adams, *The Hub: A Place for Reading and Writing*, 2nd ed., Bedford/St. Martin's, 2023, pp. 218–19.

Smith, Emily Esfahani. "There's More to Life Than Being Happy." In Peter Adams, *The Hub: A Place for Reading and Writing*, 2nd ed., Bedford/St. Martin's, 2023, pp. 220–24.

W8.12 Writing

Applying Backward Outlining to Revising for Coherence

W8.4, Backward Outlining (p. 98), explains how to create a backward outline from your first draft. W8.11, Revising for Coherence (p. 108), explains how to use backward outlining to revise a draft for coherence. Now give it a try: Use a backward outline of a draft of one of your essays to revise for coherence.

W8.13 Advice

Strategies for Strengthening an Essay

At its most basic, an essay might look something like this:

- an introduction in which you, perhaps, catch the readers' attention and state your thesis
- three body paragraphs each giving support for your thesis
- a conclusion in which you restate your thesis in different words

This simplified five-paragraph essay might have been fine at an earlier stage of your education, but when writing college-level essays, you can make your writing more effective by including more than just the basics outlined above.

When revising an essay, in addition to improving thesis and unity, organization, support, and coherence, you can make your argument stronger, more convincing, and more interesting by doing more. Listed below are some ideas for what you might include. Some of these suggestions could be included in the introduction to the essay, others might mean adding additional body paragraphs, and still others might be added near the end of the paper or even as part of the conclusion. Use this list to give you ideas for how to strengthen your argument. (You may also want to take a look at W7, Thinking While Writing, p. 88.)

1. **Add more reasons.**   Don't stop thinking just because you've come up with three reasons that support the position you have taken in your thesis. Most essays can be made more convincing if they include more reasons, and more evidence, to support the thesis.

2. **Define key terms.**   If there are several words or phrases that are central to your argument, you may want to use a paragraph near the beginning of your essay to explain how you will be using them. For example, if you're writing

about juvenile delinquency, you may want to explain what that term will mean in your discussion. It's not that you think your reader has never heard of the term; it's just that it has a wide range of meanings, and you want to make clear what you mean when you use it. Does it, for example, include those under eighteen who commit murder? How about teenagers who spray-paint graffiti? (Take a look at W11.22, Strategies for Writing Simple Definitions, p. 226, for more on this topic.)

3. **Recognize negative effects.**   Your thesis may be a good idea, and you may have presented a number of positive outcomes that will result from it, but it is often a good strategy also to admit that there are some negative outcomes that may result. Recognizing these can add to your credibility. They demonstrate that you are knowledgeable enough to be aware of these negatives and honest enough to admit they exist. Of course, it is a good idea if you can also explain why these negatives are less serious than they appear or how they can be mitigated. (Take a look at W11.6, Responses to Positions Different from Yours, p. 203, for more on this topic.)

4. **Recognize what opponents may say.**   Closely related to recognizing negative effects is recognizing the perspectives of those who hold differing opinions, especially for controversies that are much discussed. Summarize alternative views as objectively as you can and then answer, rebut, or counter them. (Again, W11.6, Responses to Positions Different from Yours, p. 203, may be helpful.)

5. **Include some background for the topic you're writing about.**   How long has it been an issue? What positions have others taken about it?

6. **Make suggestions for implementation.**   If you are trying to convince your reader to agree with you about some issue, it can be a great idea to include some advice, toward the end of the essay, about what steps will be needed to implement the change you are proposing. (Take a look at W11.8, Strategies for Writing Proposals, p. 205.)

7. **Make a call to action.**   Even stronger than advice about implementation is a call to action, urging the reader not just to begin implementing some change but to actually commit to some cause.

8. **Include some personal background.**   Especially if it makes you a more credible author or demonstrates you are an author with a particular viewpoint, it can be very helpful to take a paragraph or two to give the reader some information about who you are and why you are writing about the topic.

W8.14 Advice

A Revision Checklist

Use the following checklist to ensure that the next time you are revising an essay, you think about every issue that might require revision.

Checklist

Assignment, Audience, Purpose

☐ Does the essay meet the requirements of the assignment? (See W2.1, Reading an Assignment, p. 10.)

☐ Is the style of the essay appropriate for the anticipated audience? (See W2.4, Thinking about Audience, p. 13.)

☐ Is the essay likely to accomplish the purpose of the assignment? (See W2.6, Thinking about Purpose, p. 16.)

Title and Introduction

☐ If your instructor expects a title, have you supplied one that captures the essence of your essay? (See W10.8, Strategies for Effective Titles, p. 194.)

☐ Does your introduction provide useful background information, include a clear statement of your thesis, and make your reader eager to read your paper? (See W10.2, Strategies for Effective Introductions, p. 189.)

Thesis

☐ Does your essay have a clear thesis? (See W3.5, Developing a Working Thesis, p. 29; W3.6, Using Invention Strategies to Arrive at a Thesis, p. 31; and W5.1, Creating Unity, p. 53.)

☐ Is the thesis at the end of the essay the same as earlier in the essay? (See W5.1, Creating Unity, p. 53.)

☐ Does your thesis assert something interesting and thoughtful? (See W7.4, Use Thinking to Find an Interesting Thesis, p. 90.)

☐ Do you avoid proving the obvious? (See W7.3, Avoid Proving the Obvious, p. 89.)

Support, Organization, and Unity

☐ Does everything in the essay support the thesis? (See W4.2, Types of Evidence, p. 42, and W8.9, Revising for Support, p. 105.)

☐ Do you provide convincing evidence to support every assertion in the essay?

- [ ] Are the main points of the essay organized in a logical order? (See W8.7, Revising for Organization, p. 104.)

- [ ] Are related ideas in your essay grouped together? (See W5.5, Chunking and Ordering, p. 58.)

- [ ] Do you provide transitional phrases to assist the reader in following your argument? (See W8.11, Revising for Coherence, p. 108.)

- [ ] Do you answer arguments you can imagine someone who disagrees with you raising? (See W11.6, Responses to Positions Different from Yours, p. 203.)

Conclusion

- [ ] Even though worded differently, does the thesis in the conclusion make the same statement as the thesis earlier in the essay? (See W10.5, Strategies for Effective Conclusions, p. 192.)

- [ ] Did you avoid introducing any new ideas in the conclusion? (See W10.6, Mistakes to Avoid in Conclusions, p. 192.)

W9 ▶ Editing

Formal English, the kind that is often expected in school and in the workplace, is just one version of English. There are many more. There's the English of Appalachia, the English of Minnesota, and the English of England. There's Spanglish and Tex-Mex. There are various pidgins and creoles. And each of these is a legitimate language with its own set of rules and its own vocabulary. (For more about mixing one or more of these "Englishes" and other languages in your writing, see W6.10, Blending "Englishes," p. 81.)

W9 addresses formal English. If you want or need to brush up on the rules of formal English, you've come to the right place. W9 consists primarily of a series of explorations designed to help you improve your ability to edit your writing in accordance with the conventions of formal English. You won't simply learn "the rules"; you'll figure out the rules for yourself and record them, in your own words, as you learn them.

Many of the units in W9 are designed to allow you to figure out for yourself a definition of a grammatical term or a grammar or punctuation rule. Keeping a journal in which you record the definitions and rules as you learn them is a useful idea; that way, you will have a written set to refer to later. After you have figured out the definition or rule for yourself, compare your version to the version provided in the section "Answers to Selected Explorations in W9" (p. 181). Your way of expressing the definitions and rules will, of course, not be identical to the ones in this section. Compare yours to the ones there to see if anything is missing in yours. **Throughout this chapter, an asterisk marks the units for which this section provides answers (see W9.5, p. 118, for example).**

Thinking about Grammar

To begin W9, do a little thinking about the concept of grammar in a very general way.

W9.1 Exploration

"Good" and "Bad" English

You've probably heard people talk about "good" English and "bad" English. You may have even used these terms yourself. In this activity, think about the meaning of the terms *good English* and *bad English*. On your own or in a group (your instructor will tell you which), consider the following questions:

1. What is the difference between "good" English and "bad" English?
2. Why do people consider "bad" English bad?
3. Who speaks and writes mostly in "good" English?
4. Why should someone want to become proficient in "good" English?

Be prepared to share your ideas with the class.

W9.2 Video
The Grammar in Your Head

Those using Achieve with *The Hub* can watch a video presentation about how much you may already know about the grammar of formal English (even if you don't think you know anything).

Punctuating to Avoid Fragments, Run-Ons, and Comma Splices

Because there is no punctuation in spoken English, the proper use of punctuation sometimes proves difficult for writers.

W9.3 Advice
What Is a Sentence?

In the past, you may have been taught this traditional definition of a *sentence*:

> A sentence is a group of words containing a subject and a verb and expressing a complete thought.

If that definition works for you, of course, continue to use it. But it doesn't work for all students—especially the "complete thought" part.

Here's another approach, devised by Rei Noguchi, a linguist and English teacher who taught for years at California State University, Northridge:

> According to Noguchi, a sentence is a group of words that makes sense when placed on the line below:
>
> They refused to believe the idea that _____

Here's how it works. If you have written a group of words and are not sure whether it is a sentence or not, you place the words on the blank line and then read the entire sentence out loud. If the word group makes sense, then it's a sentence. If it doesn't, then your word group isn't a sentence. Noguchi calls this sentence with the blank line a *test frame*.

For example, imagine you have written "The woman running after the bus." Now, you're not sure whether that group of words is actually a sentence, so you place it on the blank line in the test frame and then read the entire group of words out loud:

> They refused to believe the idea that <u>the woman running after the bus.</u>

Clearly, that doesn't make sense, so your original word group is not a sentence.

Here's another example. You've written "She put it in her refrigerator." To see whether that group of words is a sentence, you place it on the line and then read it out loud:

> They refused to believe the idea that <u>she put it in her refrigerator.</u>

That sounds fine, so the original group of words is a sentence.

One caution: This method of identifying sentences does not work for questions or commands, as the following examples demonstrate.

> **Question:** Did you finish the homework? (This *is* a complete sentence.)
>
> They refused to believe the idea that <u>did you finish the homework?</u>
>
> **Command:** Turn off the lights when you come to bed. (This *is* a complete sentence.)
>
> They refused to believe the idea that <u>turn off the lights when you come to bed.</u>

Identifying Sentences

Working individually or in groups (your instructor will tell you which), decide whether each of the following is or is not a sentence. You can use the traditional definition of a sentence or place each word group on the blank line in the test frame shown in W9.3 (p. 116). On the line before each number, enter an S for *sentence* or an N for *not a sentence*.

_____ 1. The woman smoking a cigarette in the parking lot.

_____ 2. I found it in the back seat of my car.

_____ 3. The teacher who gave me a D last semester in math.

_____ 4. When Jorge learned that he had been promoted to manager.

_____ 5. The children cried.

_____ 6. Felix knew the answer.

_____ 7. The only question that I missed on the exam.

_____ 8. If Tawanda answers the phone and starts laughing.

_____ 9. Dogs bark.

_____ 10. Saving money is not easy.

Recognizing Fragments*

A fragment is usually considered a serious grammatical mistake. Usually, but not always. In formal academic writing and also in most workplace writing, fragments are frowned upon. But they can be very effective in the right context. In written dialogue, fragments are useful. A fragment can be used for emphasis, to call attention to an important point. And, of course, they are used everywhere in advertisements: "Love. What makes a Subaru a Subaru." If you are thinking that a fragment or two might work in something you're writing in a college course, you might want to check with your instructor first. Because, in many contexts, they're considered serious errors. In this section and the next one, you'll explore how to recognize fragments and how to correct them.

The following pairs of items are labeled as either fragments or sentences, with the fragments printed in blue. In W9.3 (p. 116), you learned what a sentence is. Now, working on your own or in your group (your instructor will tell you which), study each of these paired examples and then write a definition of the term *fragment*.

Sentence	✓ I saw the damage to my car.
Fragment	✗ When I saw the damage to my car.
Sentence	✓ I had been studying for a math test.
Fragment	✗ The math test I had been studying for.
Sentence	✓ I love vegetables like Brussels sprouts, broccoli, and asparagus.
Fragment	✗ For example, Brussels sprouts, broccoli, and asparagus.
Sentence	✓ Because Lin was late for class, he had to sit in the front row.
Fragment	✗ Because Lin was late for class.
Sentence	✓ The woman wearing a purple sweater is my psychology teacher.
Fragment	✗ That woman wearing a purple sweater.

NOTE: Write your definition of a *fragment* in a notebook or online file for future reference.

W9.6 Exploration
Three Strategies for Correcting Fragments*

In each numbered item below, there is a fragment. Below it is a version of the same text with the fragment corrected. Working individually or in your group, first identify each fragment and then describe the strategy used to correct it.

1. I owe my success in high school to one person. The woman who taught me math. She was tough but fair.

   Corrected   I owe my success in high school to the woman who taught me math. She was tough but fair.

2. The man sitting at the counter and drinking coffee. He used to be the coach of my basketball team. Now, he's retired.

   Corrected   The man sitting at the counter and drinking coffee used to be the coach of my basketball team. Now, he's retired.

3. I think I saw the principal of my high school on Saturday when I was driving to Target. Jogging on the side of the road. I always admired him.

Corrected I think I saw the principal of my high school on Saturday when I was driving to Target. He was jogging on the side of the road. I always admired him.

W9.7 Exploration

Correcting Fragments

The following items include fragments. There are several ways to correct a fragment. Working on your own or in groups, first underline the fragment and then revise the item so that the fragment is eliminated.

1. When I learned Liz was going to be late. I was furious. She has not been on time for a single meeting this year.

2. The fact that Kayla was promoted. Made me determined to work even harder this year. I am going to get the same kind of promotion if I can.

3. The woman who rode to work on her bike and changed clothes in the restroom. She turned out to be a friend of Courtney's. Now she drives a BMW to work every day.

4. I have saved money out of my check every week for two years. Meaning I now can afford a vacation in Europe. When I return in three weeks. I expect to have some money left over.

5. The teacher in the red blouse and the gray skirt. She is the one who gave me an A in physical education. There was only one reason I got an A. The fact that I was never absent or late.

6. The car Sylvester was driving. It used to belong to L'Tanya. He does not know that it was badly damaged in an accident.

7. The binoculars I borrowed from Ms. Patel and then lost on my camping trip. They cost more than a hundred dollars. I will have to pay her back over the next six months.

8. Until Larry learns I won't be pushed around. I will continue to refuse to work with him. He is just too bossy.

9. To hunt for a cat for three weeks and not find him. That was almost more than I could bear. I had given up looking for him, and he just walked into the backyard.

10. The doctor whom Linda has been going to and who also treated my mother. He has an office on Pratt Street. I have an appointment with him next week.

W9.8 Exploration

What Is an Independent Clause?*

In the following sentences, the independent clauses have been underlined. Working individually or in groups, study these sentences and, using what you have already learned about sentences, figure out what an independent clause is. First, write a definition of *independent clause*. Then write an explanation of the difference between an independent clause and a sentence.

1. The phone rang, and my dog started barking.
2. When it rains, my knees ache.
3. Javier tried to solve the puzzle.
4. Raelyn laughed out loud when she heard the news about Earl.
5. Mark graduates in June, and his sister graduates next year.
6. Because of the snow, the parade was cancelled.
7. Paola is buying a new car this afternoon.
8. Riding a bicycle in the city can be dangerous.
9. Jayla made a salad, and Dion roasted a chicken.
10. If Sarah comes to class tomorrow, I will invite her to the party.

W9.9 Exploration

Recognizing Run-Ons and Comma Splices*

Run-ons and comma splices can cause problems for readers who have to puzzle out where one sentence ends and the next one begins. In this unit, you will learn to recognize these two errors. In W9.10 (p. 122), you will learn how to correct them.

In the following groups, the sentences without errors are printed in black, and the ones that are run-ons and comma splices are printed in blue. Working individually or in your group, study these examples. Then, write definitions of *run-on* and *comma splice*.

Group 1

Correct	✓ I used to live in Seattle. I worked at Boeing.
Run-On	✗ I used to live in Seattle I worked at Boeing.
Comma Splice	✗ I used to live in Seattle, I worked at Boeing.

Group 2

Correct	✓	Matt walked out of the meeting without saying a word. He was angry at the decision the group had made.
Run-On	✗	Matt walked out of the meeting without saying a word he was angry at the decision the group had made.
Comma Splice	✗	Matt walked out of the meeting without saying a word, he was angry at the decision the group had made.

Group 3

Correct	✓	Deon made a delicious lasagna. His wife made an avocado salad.
Run-On	✗	Deon made a delicious lasagna his wife made an avocado salad.
Comma Splice	✗	Deon made a delicious lasagna, his wife made an avocado salad.

Group 4

Correct	✓	All flights to Denver were cancelled. There was a terrible ice storm.
Run-On	✗	All flights to Denver were cancelled there was a terrible ice storm.
Comma Splice	✗	All flights to Denver were cancelled, there was a terrible ice storm.

NOTE: Write your definitions of *run-on* and *comma splice* in a notebook or online file for future reference.

W9.10 Exploration

Correcting Run-Ons and Comma Splices*

In W9.9 (p. 121), you learned to recognize run-ons and comma splices. Now, you'll learn how to correct them.

Each of the following groups includes a run-on and a comma splice (in blue) and then five correct sentences (in black) representing a variety of methods to correct run-ons and comma splices. There are more ways for correcting these errors, but the ones here should give you an idea of the range of options.

Working individually or in your group, make a list of at least five ways to correct run-ons and comma splices.

Group 1

Run-On	✗ I lived in Seattle in 2008 I worked at Boeing.
Comma Splice	✗ I lived in Seattle in 2008, I worked at Boeing.
Correct	✓ I lived in Seattle in 2008. I worked at Boeing.
Correct	✓ I lived in Seattle in 2008; I worked at Boeing.
Correct	✓ When I lived in Seattle in 2008, I worked at Boeing.
Correct	✓ While living in Seattle in 2008, I worked at Boeing.
Correct	✓ I lived in Seattle in 2008; at that time, I worked at Boeing.

Group 2

Run-On	✗ Matt walked out of the meeting without saying a word he was angry at the decision the group had made.
Comma Splice	✗ Matt walked out of the meeting without saying a word, he was angry at the decision the group had made.
Correct	✓ Matt walked out of the meeting without saying a word. He was angry at the decision the group had made.
Correct	✓ Matt walked out of the meeting without saying a word; he was angry at the decision the group had made.
Correct	✓ Matt walked out of the meeting without saying a word because he was angry at the decision the group had made.
Correct	✓ Angry at the decision the group had made, Matt walked out of the meeting without saying a word.
Correct	✓ Matt was angry at the decision the group had made; as a result, he walked out of the meeting without saying a word.

Group 3

Run-On	✗ Deon made a delicious lasagna his wife made an avocado salad.
Comma Splice	✗ Deon made a delicious lasagna, his wife made an avocado salad.
Correct	✓ Deon made a delicious lasagna. His wife made an avocado salad.
Correct	✓ Deon made a delicious lasagna; his wife made an avocado salad.
Correct	✓ While Deon made a delicious lasagna, his wife made an avocado salad.

Correct	✓ While Deon's wife made an avocado salad, he made a delicious lasagna.
Correct	✓ Deon made a delicious lasagna; meanwhile, his wife made an avocado salad.

Group 4

Run-On	✗ All flights to Denver were cancelled there was a terrible ice storm.
Comma Splice	✗ All flights to Denver were cancelled, there was a terrible ice storm.
Correct	✓ All flights to Denver were cancelled. There was a terrible ice storm.
Correct	✓ All flights to Denver were cancelled; there was a terrible ice storm.
Correct	✓ All flights to Denver were cancelled because there was a terrible ice storm.
Correct	✓ Because there was a terrible ice storm, all flights to Denver were cancelled.
Correct	✓ There was a terrible ice storm; as a result, all flights to Denver were cancelled.

NOTE: Record at least five ways to correct a run-on or comma splice in a notebook or online file for future reference.

W9.11 Exploration
Correcting Fragments, Run-Ons, and Comma Splices

In W9.7 (p. 120), you learned to correct fragments, and in W9.10 (p. 122), you learned to correct run-ons and comma splices. In this activity, you will put all that you learned together. In the following sentences, correct all the errors, which include fragments, run-ons, and comma splices.

1. I am getting a blister on my thumb, I will have to quit playing soon.
2. When she made a chocolate cake for my mother. She forgot to add any sugar.
3. The man wearing a plaid jacket. He is my math teacher.
4. When Aryelle opened the newspaper. She saw a picture of her old boyfriend.
5. There was no money in my account, the bank honored my check anyway.
6. Odelia's brother has done many foolish things. Such as getting four tickets for speeding. He also is in trouble for bouncing checks.

7. Because Jordan drank six cans of beer. We had to carry him home.

8. Anthony is trying to run two miles every morning. To get in shape before the soccer season starts.

9. The management at my apartment building does a great job. For example, having the parking lot plowed every time it snows. In addition, they keep the lawn in great shape.

10. I have never been to Las Vegas, I have no intention of going now.

11. The picnic has been called off let's all get together at Rab's house.

12. My father made a phone call, then he drove away without saying a word.

13. I hoped to get a part in the play. Even though I knew my chances were not very good. I thought the director might need an actor with a southern accent.

14. When Dexter got to the parking lot. He realized he had left his book in the classroom.

15. I wanted chocolate chip I got mocha chocolate.

16. I am experiencing some physical problems as I reach my fifties. My knees bother me a lot. Also, shortness of breath when I run.

17. Gus ran as hard as he could, he came in third.

18. The cake is delicious I cannot eat another bite.

19. Jessica spent fourteen dollars on specialty coffees this week, I spent only six.

20. Kayla bought a new computer. Using the money she had won in the lottery.

W9.12 Exploration
Punctuating Independent Clauses 1

In the following pairs of items, the sentence in black is correct, and the sentence in blue has an error. Study these sentences and figure out which punctuation rule they all demonstrate.

Pair 1

✓ Chin lives in Overlea, and his brother lives in Parkville.

✗ Chin lives in Overlea and his brother lives in Parkville.

Pair 2

✓ Drew bought a laptop, but he has not learned how to use it.

✗ Drew bought a laptop but he has not learned how to use it.

Pair 3

✓ Kyesha went to the ocean, and it rained every day.

✗ Kyesha went to the ocean and it rained every day.

Pair 4

✓ Maria works at a bakery, but she is looking for a second job.

✗ Maria works at a bakery but she is looking for a second job.

NOTE: Don't record anything in your notebook or online file until you have completed W9.14 (p. 127).

W9.13 Exploration

Punctuating Independent Clauses 2

In the following pairs, the sentence in black is correct, and the sentence in blue has an error. Study these sentences and figure out which punctuation rule they all demonstrate.

Pair 1

✓ Hector opened his biology book and started to study.

✗ Hector opened his biology book, and started to study.

Pair 2

✓ Mary opened the door and let a strange cat into the house.

✗ Mary opened the door, and let a strange cat into the house.

Pair 3

✓ Oklahoma is a great place to work and to raise children.

✗ Oklahoma is a great place to work, and to raise children.

Pair 4

✓ My mother has faced a lot of challenges but has overcome them all.

✗ My mother has faced a lot of challenges, but has overcome them all.

NOTE: While the first sentence in Pair 4 illustrates the official rule, many writers disregard the rule and use a comma before the *but* anyhow.

NOTE: Don't record anything in your notebook or online file until you've completed W9.14.

W9.14 Exploration

Punctuating Independent Clauses 3*

Now here are all the sentence pairs from W9.12 (p. 125) and W9.13 (p. 126). Sentences printed in black are correct; those printed in blue are incorrect. Study them carefully and figure out what the punctuation rule is for these kinds of sentences. You may want to refresh your memory of what an independent clause is before you work on these. (See W9.8, p. 121.)

Pair 1

✓ Chin lives in Overlea, and his brother lives in Parkville.

✗ Chin lives in Overlea and his brother lives in Parkville.

Pair 2

✓ Drew bought a laptop, but he has not learned how to use it.

✗ Drew bought a laptop but he has not learned how to use it.

Pair 3

✓ Kyesha went to the ocean, and it rained every day.

✗ Kyesha went to the ocean and it rained every day.

Pair 4

✓ Maria works at a bakery, but she is looking for a second job.

✗ Maria works at a bakery but she is looking for a second job.

Pair 5

✓ Hector opened his biology book and started to study.

✗ Hector opened his biology book, and started to study.

Pair 6

  ✓ Mary opened the door and let a strange cat into the house.

  ✗ Mary opened the door, and let a strange cat into the house.

Pair 7

  ✓ Oklahoma is a great place to work and to raise children.

  ✗ Oklahoma is a great place to work, and to raise children.

Pair 8

  ✓ My mother has faced a lot of challenges but has overcome them all.

  ✗ My mother has faced a lot of challenges, but has overcome them all.

NOTE: Record the punctuation rule these items demonstrate in a notebook or online file for future reference.

W9.15 Exploration

Punctuating Independent Clauses 4*

The sentences you have been working on in W9.12 (p. 125), W9.13 (p. 126), and W9.14 (p. 127) all used the conjunctions *and* or *but*. These are the most frequently used of the coordinating conjunctions, but there are others. Here's the complete list. You might want to use the word FANBOYS, which is spelled with the first letter of all seven, to remember them.

  For

  And

  Nor

  But

  Or

  Yet

  So

In the following sentence pairs, the black sentences are correct; the blue ones contain an error. Study these to see whether these five additional conjunctions follow the same grammar rules as *and* and *but*.

Pair 1

✓ In New York most people ride the subway to work, or they take a bus.

✗ In New York most people ride the subway to work or they take a bus.

Pair 2

✓ For breakfast I usually have a bowl of cereal or some scrambled eggs.

✗ For breakfast I usually have a bowl of cereal, or some scrambled eggs.

Pair 3

✓ Negotiations are going to continue all night, for the union has announced a strike for tomorrow morning.

✗ Negotiations are going to continue all night for the union has announced a strike for tomorrow morning.

Pair 4

✓ Nathan studied all weekend for the midterm test in his biology class.

✗ Nathan studied all weekend, for the midterm test in his biology class.

Pair 5

✓ There is an accident on the Expressway this morning, so I am driving through the city.

✗ There is an accident on the Expressway this morning so I am driving through the city.

Pair 6

✓ My daughter has grown so tall that she needs a new bed.

✗ My daughter has grown, so tall that she needs a new bed.

Pair 7

✓ I have applied for more than a dozen jobs, yet I have not been invited for a single interview.

✗ I have applied for more than a dozen jobs yet I have not been invited for a single interview.

Pair 8

✓ We haven't yet received any word from our daughter in Brazil.

✗ We haven't, yet received any word from our daughter in Brazil.

Pair 9

✓ The new café in my neighborhood doesn't serve espresso, nor does the café near my work.

✗ The new café in my neighborhood doesn't serve espresso nor does the café near my work.

Pair 10

✓ Neither the textbook for my math class nor the website explains how to factor polynomials.

✗ Neither the textbook for my math class, nor the website explains how to factor polynomials.

W9.16 Exploration

Punctuating Introductory Elements 1*

In the following pairs of sentences, the black versions are correct; the blue versions include an error. Study these to see what punctuation rule they illustrate.

Pair 1

✓ When it rains, my knees ache.

✗ When it rains my knees ache.

Pair 2

✓ Because I sprained my ankle, I cannot play tennis this weekend.

✗ Because I sprained my ankle I cannot play tennis this weekend.

Pair 3

✓ If I miss the bus, I will have to wait for an hour.

✗ If I miss the bus I will have to wait for an hour.

Pair 4

✓ Running after the bus, Jamey sprained his ankle.

✗ Running after the bus Jamey sprained his ankle.

Pair 5

✓ In the third drawer from the top, I found my iPhone.

✗ In the third drawer from the top I found my iPhone.

Pair 6

✓ To open a bank account, Susan had to fill out more than a dozen forms.

✗ To open a bank account Susan had to fill out more than a dozen forms.

NOTE: Don't record anything in your notebook or online file until you have completed W9.17.

W9.17 Exploration

Punctuating Introductory Elements 2*

The following pairs of sentences demonstrate one additional complication to the punctuation rule you worked on in W9.16 (p. 130). Study them to determine what this complication is. Again, the black sentences are correct; the blue ones have an error.

Pair 1

✓ When I graduate will be a time for celebrating.

✗ When I graduate, will be a time for celebrating.

Pair 2

✓ Being unemployed can produce much anxiety.

✗ Being unemployed, can produce much anxiety.

Pair 3

✓ To let the dog out without a leash was a big mistake.

✗ To let the dog out without a leash, was a big mistake.

Pair 4

✓ In the top drawer of my dresser is a collection of mismatched socks.

✗ In the top drawer of my dresser, is a collection of mismatched socks.

Pair 5

✓ Taking five courses this semester has been very stressful.

✗ Taking five courses this semester, has been very stressful.

NOTE: What complication to the punctuation rule you identified in W9.16 (p. 130) do these items illustrate? Record your answer in a notebook or online file.

W9.18 Exploration
Editing an Essay for Punctuation 1

Working individually or in your group, proofread the following essay and correct any errors you find. These errors will be in the following categories:

- fragments
- run-on sentences
- comma splices
- errors punctuating two independent clauses joined by a coordinating conjunction (*and, but, or, for, so, yet,* or *nor*)
- errors punctuating introductory elements

In some cases, you will be able to correct errors by simply adding or deleting punctuation; in other cases, especially when editing fragments, you may need to do a little rewording of the sentence.

Anticipation Can Kill the Moment

I don't remember my last day of college. It's an odd thing to admit but I don't remember such a major milestone in my life. I don't recall any tearful goodbyes to my favorite professors. Any solemn farewells to my friends and classmates. The whole day is a blank. All the celebration and sadness that I would imagine happened is simply missing from my memory.

For a while, I wondered why this was. After four years of late nights in the library or early mornings working in the dining hall the final day was a dark spot in my memory. I don't remember what I had for breakfast, or if I slept in. It's funny how the most important of days seems to slip by like that, they seem so brief in comparison to the time spent waiting for them.

What I came to realize, is that many days that held significance in my life were equally blank. My high school graduation, for one. That day was nothing but a commencement speech, as far as I know. Another important day that I can't remember, was my first date, I can't remember picking up my date, taking her home, or anything in between. Similarly, I can't remember the last playoff game that I played in high school. I know we lost but I don't know how that happened.

Thinking about all of these days I realized that the thing I remember most about graduating college was fear I had felt fear creeping up on me for the entirety of my final semester. There's nothing like realizing, after four years of relative safety, that there is nothing standing between you and adulthood. Like all the most important moments in life it's a plunge that has to be taken. A band-aid that has to be ripped off.

W9.19 Exploration
Editing an Essay for Punctuation 2

Working individually or in your group, proofread the following essay and correct any errors you find. These errors will be in the following categories:

- fragments
- run-on sentences
- comma splices
- errors punctuating two independent clauses joined by a coordinating conjunction (*and*, *but*, *or*, *for*, *so*, *yet*, or *nor*)
- errors punctuating introductory elements

In some cases, you will be able to correct errors by simply adding or deleting punctuation; in other cases, especially when editing fragments, you may need to do a little rewording of the sentence.

New or Used?

To buy a car, you need to make some decisions. First, you need to decide how much you can afford to pay. That decision will help you narrow down your options but you will still have more decisions to make, you'll need to decide what kind of car you want. If you tend to do a lot of sporting activities. Maybe consider a hatchback or an SUV for some extra storage space. If you have a long commute every day, maybe look at hybrid vehicles that get good gas mileage. It's essential to think long and hard about what your lifestyle will require, and then to look for the type of car that fits that lifestyle.

Next, you have to make the hard decision of whether to buy new or used. Without a doubt a new car will be more expensive. Even after you've spent hours haggling. It will end up costing thousands of dollars more than an older, used model with some mileage on it. In exchange for this upfront cost, though, the car should (theoretically) last for many years, and will include all of the latest technology available. Also, a warranty. Which will guarantee free repairs on certain parts of the vehicle for tens of thousands of miles. You also have the guarantee that the car has never been in an accident, never had coffee spilled on the seats, and has never had a shaggy dog shed all over the rugs.

A used car, sadly, can't give you that guarantee. First, there's the possibility of a sleazy used-car salesman who sells you an old junker with a promise and a trustworthy smile. When the junker breaks down in a cloud of steam and bitter feelings mere weeks later. Many dealers will try to take advantage of first-time car buyers. Selling damaged and even dangerous cars to unsuspecting drivers. A bad deal like this will not always result in injury or a broken-down vehicle, but may simply cost you a lot of money and aggravation. Used cars are often sold for more than they're worth, which is why it's important to use price-comparison tools like Kelley Blue Book for background research.

Although the consequences of a bad deal can be dire buying a used car means you also have the opportunity to get more than you pay for. Some people sell their car for thousands of dollars less than what they're worth, simply because they are in a hurry to get rid of the vehicle. When you buy a used car. You also avoid the immediate and steep drop in the car's value, which hits the moment you drive a new car off the lot. You might end up with a car that's been so well taken care of that it might as well be new. Even last year's model, with practically new features and very few miles on the odometer could be thousands of dollars cheaper used than new. To get these deals, is not easy, you have to be willing to put in some time.

Buying a car is a big decision, you need to be willing to invest some time in it. After you've visited several dealerships, checked with *Consumer Reports*, and done some internet research. You may make a decision that surprises you, you may decide not to buy a car at all.

Using Apostrophes to Show Possession and to Indicate Contractions

Apostrophes can be troublesome because they have two completely different uses in English: to show possession and to indicate contractions.

W9.20 Advice

Using Apostrophes to Show Possession

Possession in a grammatical sense can mean

- showing ownership or possession: *Maggie's car, the school's requirements*
- having made something: *Donna's risotto*

- having control or use of something: *Kevin's rental car, the veterans' club*
- being part of or connected to something: *the cat's meow, Miguel's hand*
- being a relative or member of a group: *Kobe's teammate, Peter's daughter*
- having a characteristic or quality: *Jane's obsession*
- being characteristic of a specific period of time: *July's heat*

W9.21   Exploration

Apostrophes with Possessives 1*

Working individually or in your group, study each set of sentences and write down the kind of relationship being represented by the possessives.

Set 1

Miguel's arm was fractured in the accident.

My car's windshield is cracked.

My school's roof was damaged in the storm.

Kind of relationship: _____

Set 2

LaDawn's sister was hired at the restaurant where I work.

Chris's mother will graduate from college this semester.

Kyle's niece is getting married this weekend.

Kind of relationship: _____

Set 3

Max's forgetfulness has caused him many problems.

Lizzie's thoughtfulness makes her a great friend.

I really enjoy Gillian's sense of humor.

Kind of relationship: _____

Set 4

Jake was not aware of the <u>college's policy</u> on withdrawing from classes.

<u>Toyota's logo</u> looks like a T made out of circles.

<u>Milano's menu</u> is mostly Italian dishes, but there are some American items too.

Kind of relationship: _____

Set 5

Many of <u>today's students</u> are working at least twenty hours a week.

A <u>one-hour's delay</u> would have caused us to miss our connection in Chicago.

<u>This year's tomatoes</u> are larger than ever.

Kind of relationship: _____

NOTE: The possessive word always appears in front of the word being possessed.

W9.22 Exploration

Apostrophes with Possessives 2*

Working individually or in your group, underline or highlight the possessive words in the following sentences. Not every sentence has a possessive word, and some may have two.

1. Marcella's umbrella is bright red.
2. Today's special is meatloaf and mashed potatoes.
3. I grabbed my boss's hand and shook it forcefully.
4. My professor's absence policy was stricter than the college's policy.
5. Several dogs were barking as I walked up the sidewalk.
6. I have often observed my biology professor's compassion for students.
7. I was very impressed with the soprano's voice.
8. My bicycle's tire was flat.
9. Yesterday's snow was completely melted by this morning.
10. Craig's book's cover had a large coffee stain.

Apostrophes with Possessives 3*

The following groups of sentences demonstrate one rule about the use of apostrophes. Again, the black sentences are correct; the blue ones have an error. Study these examples and figure out the grammar rule they illustrate.

Group 1

✓ Mariel's laptop was stolen from her car.

✗ Mariels laptop was stolen from her car.

✗ Mariels' laptop was stolen from her car.

Group 2

✓ Greg's car is a Volkswagen.

✗ Gregs car is a Volkswagen.

✗ Gregs' car is a Volkswagen.

Group 3

✓ Jan was sitting in her teacher's car.

✗ Jan was sitting in her teachers car.

✗ Jan was sitting in her teachers' car.

Group 4

✓ I found someone's purse in the restroom.

✗ I found someones purse in the restroom.

✗ I found someones' purse in the restroom.

NOTE: Record the grammar rule these items demonstrate in a notebook or online file for future reference.

Apostrophes with Possessives 4*

The following groups of sentences demonstrate a second rule about the use of apostrophes. Again, the black sentences are correct; the blue ones have an error.

In W9.23 (p. 138), the apostrophes were located before the s. In the correct sentences in this unit, the apostrophes are located after the s. Working individually or in your group, figure out when the apostrophe should be located before the s and when it should be located after the s.

Group 1

✓ These two students' essays are excellent.

✗ These two students essays are excellent.

✗ These two student's essays are excellent.

Group 2

✓ My grandparents' house is more than a hundred years old.

✗ My grandparents house is more than a hundred years old.

✗ My grandparent's house is more than a hundred years old.

Group 3

✓ The two candidates' speeches were long and boring.

✗ The two candidate's speeches were long and boring.

✗ The two candidates speeches were long and boring.

Group 4

✓ The three chairs' cushions were stained when Aris spilled a glass of wine.

✗ The three chairs cushions were stained when Aris spilled a glass of wine.

✗ The three chair's cushions were stained when Aris spilled a glass of wine.

NOTE: Record the grammar rule these items demonstrate in a notebook or online file for future reference.

W9.25 Exploration

Apostrophes with Possessives 5*

The following groups of sentences demonstrate a third rule about the use of apostrophes. This grammar rule affects only a small group of words, but it's the one that causes students the most trouble. Again, the black sentences are correct;

the blue ones have an error. Study these examples and figure out the rule they illustrate.

Group 1

✓ The children's coats were soaking wet, but they didn't seem to mind.

✗ The childrens coats were soaking wet, but they didn't seem to mind.

✗ The childrens' coats were soaking wet, but they didn't seem to mind.

Group 2

✓ The men's names were Jose and Juan.

✗ The mens names were Jose and Juan.

✗ The mens' names were Jose and Juan.

Group 3

✓ My wife asked the server where the women's room was.

✗ My wife asked the server where the womens room was.

✗ My wife asked the server where the womens' room was.

Group 4

✓ The two deer's footprints were clearly visible in the mud.

✗ The two deers footprints were clearly visible in the mud.

✗ The two deers' footprints were clearly visible in the mud.

NOTE: Record the grammar rule these items demonstrate in a notebook or online file for future reference.

W9.26 Advice

Using Apostrophes to Form Contractions

While the most common use for apostrophes is to indicate possession, they are also used to form contractions. Contractions are formed by combining two words into one and leaving out one or more letters. Note that the apostrophe is placed where the letter or letters have been left out, not at the place where the two words are joined.

is not → isn't

she will → she'll

I am → I'm

we had → we'd

can not → can't

Some teachers think contractions are inappropriate in college writing; others think they're fine. When possible, ask your instructor (or your manager) whether using contractions is acceptable.

W9.27 Exploration

Apostrophes for Contractions 1*

Working individually or in your group, form contractions using the following pairs of words:

they are	it is
he is	who is
could not	are not
had not	did not
you are	have not

W9.28 Exploration

Apostrophes for Contractions 2: Contractions versus Possessive Pronouns*

Students frequently create errors in their writing because they confuse contractions with possessive pronouns, especially the ones that are spelled quite similarly. Study the following examples and try to figure out when to use the version with an apostrophe and when to use the version without an apostrophe. The sentences in black are correct. The ones in blue include an error.

Working individually or in your group, write a paragraph in which you explain how to decide when an apostrophe is needed with pronouns like these and when it isn't.

Pair 1

    ✓ I hope it's not too late to sign up for the trip to Washington.

    ✗ I hope its not too late to sign up for the trip to Washington.

Pair 2

    ✓ Jill watched as her dog hid its bone under the bed.

    ✗ Jill watched as her dog hid it's bone under the bed.

Pair 3

    ✓ I hope you're coming to the movie with us.

    ✗ I hope your coming to the movie with us.

Pair 4

    ✓ Juanita saw your sister in the supermarket.

    ✗ Juanita saw you're sister in the supermarket.

Pair 5

    ✓ Jamard's parents are selling their house and moving to Florida.

    ✗ Jamard's parents are selling they're house and moving to Florida.

Pair 6

    ✓ They're making a new movie about Alexander Hamilton.

    ✗ Their making a new movie about Alexander Hamilton.

Pair 7

    ✓ I wonder whose car that is parked in front of my house.

    ✗ I wonder who's car that is parked in front of my house.

Pair 8

    ✓ Tamira knows who's driving to the beach this weekend.

    ✗ Tamira knows whose driving to the beach this weekend.

NOTE: Record the apostrophe rule these items demonstrate in a notebook or online file for future reference.

Editing an Essay for Apostrophes 1

The following essay has errors involving apostrophes. Working individually or in your group, edit the essay to correct these errors.

The Death Penalty

Were all familiar in America with the justice system. Due to the large police presence around the country, its virtually certain that, in some way or another, every single person in the country has had an interaction with law enforcement at some point. Most of us get a speeding ticket here and there, but for the worst offenders—murderers, serial rapists, and the like—the penalty goes all the way up to and including death. The United States is one of the only developed nation's in the world to still allow the death penalty, which raises the question: why? In many cases, the death penalty is not only an inhumane way to treat violence in society, but it can also come out to be more expensive and more time-consuming than comparable rehabilitation programs.

While the death penalty certainly instills fear in many who commit crimes, its never been enough to deter every one of them from committing a heinous crime like murder. So then the question becomes, why continue? It solves nothing to kill a murderer—if anything, it only serves to remind us that, as Gandhi once said, "An eye for an eye leaves the whole world blind." It also helps to remember that revenge is not the same as justice, and its' not worth pursuing if the real goal is to prevent future crimes. Families of a murderers' victims may desire to kill the person as payment for their loss, but in reality they only become a little more like the criminal, and in the process another life is taken.

Another more calculating reason to forgo the death penalty is it's extraordinary cost. While an actual execution may not be very expensive, according to a number of recent studies, imprisoning death row inmates can be upwards of fifty percent more expensive than imprisoning the general prison population.

And then theres the appeal process; most inmates are in a legal fight for their lives right up until the day that theyre killed. That means thousands of hours of legal work for public defenders and prosecutors as inmates work their way through the endless appeals of the American justice system, and those hours are billed directly to the taxpayer's. This compares to roughly two hundred hours of appeals on average for a general population inmate.

And while the drugs often used to execute prisoners are usually cheap, that has not been so in the last couple years. Ohio, Texas, and Oklahoma are just a few of the states that have experienced shortages of the drugs used for lethal injections, which has driven up they're price. Other states' have even considered bringing back the firing squad, although human right's groups are unlikely to be impressed by that proposal.

And then there are the cases where the police, or a prosecutor, or some other office along the way gets it wrong. These are cases where innocent peo-ple are sent to their death for crimes they didn't commit. According to a 2014 study, roughly one in twenty-five inmates sentenced to death is innocent—and yet not all of them are able to make their case before their execution is carried out. This amounts to murder by the justice system rather than justice for the victims.

Whether its the cost or the issue of human rights', the death penalty is a holdover from an older era that we could do without. Most countries in the world have done away with it already, leaving the United States as one of only fifty-eight nations that still allow it. Some U.S. states—such as Massachusetts, New York, and New Mexico—have even banned the practice. Meanwhile, other states have gone to increasing lengths to keep killing their worst criminals. But rather than trying to erase the problem of violent crime, what we as a society should be doing is working to treat the causes of violence. Treatment, early intervention, and better policing are all more effective ways to try to keep violent crime from occurring—and any of them is more humane than trading life for life.

Editing an Essay for Apostrophes 2

The following essay has errors involving apostrophes. Working individually or in your group, edit the essay to correct these errors.

Cooking in the Digital Age

We have a tradition in my family: every Christmas, my mom makes about a dozen small fruitcakes and sends them out to all our relative's households. Some go to New York to my moms sister, some to my dads' family in California, and one travels south to Florida. Its a tradition that weve repeated every year since I was just a little kid.

Every Thanksgiving, after the turkey had been eaten and the leftovers' stashed away for the next week of meals, my mom and I would break out the bowls and measuring cups, the fake maraschino cherries and the candied fruit chunks—and the dreaded figs—and set to work. The fruitcakes would be assembled, the batter would be sampled, and salmonella would be warned of. Then came the wrapping: in order to make a fruitcake properly, it had to sit wrapped in a bourbon-soaked gauze for roughly a month, which not only preserves it but also adds a little zip from the bourbon.

This is the tradition. Every Christmas we cut up the cake and enjoy a few slices (people may cringe, but its' the only genuinely good fruitcake in the known world). It's been this way for decades, ever since my mom got the recipe from my grandmother. But this kind of cooking and passing down of recipes' is falling out of fashion. Since the advent of the internet, family recipes have taken a backseat to quick and easy meals found online, leading more and more young cooks to start at they're phone or they're computer rather than at a cookbook.

A prime example of this trend is Buzzfeed. You might have heard of their news service or social media commentary, but Buzzfeed is also known for it's series of foody videos. These show time-lapse video's of someone making a certain recipe, often something exotic like a cheeseburger with buns made of fried mac and cheese. The videos are entertainment (and believe me, their as entertaining as they are mouth-watering), but theyre also meant to be instructive. Some episodes will have a guest chef come and teach a new cooking technique, or theyll have a Buzzfeed employees parent come and make their family recipe.

This has become the new norm. The internet is a vast reference book for those who seek tips or recipes or just want to dream about something juicy. Other outlets have gone a similar route to Buzzfeed, and they're videos now take up a great deal of space on everyones' Facebook feed. Its a "thing" for this generation to try out these videos, too; I myself am guilty of using a Buzzfeed recipe to make a "pizza bread boule." (Yes, it's exactly what you're picturing.)

New studies' are showing, however, that millennials are coming into the real world without real-world skills like cooking. The internet cooking craze may be part of the reason. It used to be that you learned a few recipes from someone at home and learned to improvise from there. But now its click, scroll, and read; some site's will even tell you what you can make from the leftover ingredients you find at the back of your fridge. Its' no longer solely a family experience—cooking has become both incredibly accessible and harder to learn properly at the same time.

There are pros and cons to this new way of doing things. On the one hand, not everyone can learn to cook or has someone at home to teach them. For those people, the internet is a welcome helper in the kitchen, where the endless combinations' of ingredients can be an overwhelming place to start. But whats lost are the traditional recipes like my moms' fruitcake, which is not something that will make it's way into a Buzzfeed video anytime soon. Learning to cook at home is learning to cook properly, to improvise, to figure out what combinations work, and to create your own recipes. That creativity may not make it to this generation—though at least well always have mac and cheese buns.

Ensuring Subject-Verb Agreement

Subject-verb agreement errors can greatly diminish the effectiveness of your writing; luckily, they are not that difficult to correct.

W9.31 Exploration
Identifying Verbs 1*

The double underlined words in the following sentences are all verbs. Working individually or in your group, try to figure out what makes them verbs. What do they all have in common? What's the same about all of them?

1. My sister and I <u>swim</u> every morning.
2. Jeanine <u>runs</u> five miles every day.
3. Arthur <u>drives</u> to work at five o'clock every morning.
4. My dog <u>eats</u> a can of dog food every day.
5. My sister <u>writes</u> our father once a week.

W9.32 Exploration
Identifying Verbs 2*

The double underlined words in the following sentences are also all verbs. Working individually or in your group, try to figure out what makes them verbs. What do they all have in common? What's the same about all of them? How are they different from the verbs in W9.31?

1. Mark <u>thinks</u> about basketball all the time.
2. My dog <u>sleeps</u> in the kitchen.
3. I always <u>sit</u> in the front row of the classroom.
4. My daughter <u>suspects</u> something.
5. I often <u>read</u> in the evening.

W9.33 Exploration

Identifying Verbs 3*

The double underlined words in the following sentences are also all verbs, but they are quite different from the verbs you encountered in W9.31 (p. 147) and W9.32 (p. 147). They are not expressing any action. They do not express what someone is doing. Working individually or in your group, try to figure out what makes them verbs. What do they all have in common?

1. Monday is the first day of spring.
2. My uncles are volunteer firefighters.
3. I am a Scorpio.
4. Friday was my birthday.
5. Sunday will be my parents' anniversary.

W9.34 Advice

Identifying Verbs 4

The verbs in W9.33 are all forms of the verb *be*, the most irregular and most common verb in English. Here is a list of these forms of the verb *be*.

am	were	had been
are	will be	will have been
is	have been	
was	has been	

These forms of the verb *be* are all used to link two parts of a sentence. When used this way, they are often called *linking verbs*.

W9.35 Exploration

Identifying Verbs 5*

Be verbs can be used to link as in W9.33, but they also have a second function as illustrated in the following sentences. Working individually or in your group, study the *be* verbs and then explain what their function is in these sentences.

1. Julio is taking his mother to the airport.
2. Kevin was reading a book about Harriet Tubman.

3. The students in this class <u><u>are working</u></u> on verbs.
4. My parents <u><u>were cooking</u></u> lamb vindaloo.
5. Lashanda <u><u>will be graduating</u></u> in a year.

W9.36 **Exploration**

Identifying Verbs 6*

In the following sentences, all the verbs have been double underlined. There are, however, some words that look like verbs, words that seem to express actions, but which are not underlined. Working individually or in your group, explain how to tell when an action word ending in *-ing* is a verb and when it is not.

1. Swimming <u><u>is</u></u> good exercise.
2. Karina <u><u>was swimming</u></u> this morning.
3. Amazon <u><u>will be sending</u></u> me a refund.
4. Sending fragile items through the mail <u><u>is</u></u> never a good idea.
5. Reading loudly, Miranda <u><u>impressed</u></u> the judges.
6. Miranda <u><u>was reading</u></u> a book by Toni Morrison.
7. Eugene <u><u>had been singing</u></u> in the shower.
8. Singing loudly, Eugene <u><u>woke</u></u> the baby.
9. Chasing cats <u><u>is</u></u> my dog's favorite activity.
10. My dog <u><u>was chasing</u></u> his own tail.

W9.37 **Advice**

Identifying Verbs 7

Because they are clearly derived from verbs, even though they are not functioning as verbs, these *-ing* words are called verbals. They can be a source of confusion for identifying verbs. Another source can be found in the following sentences. Again, all the verbs have been double-underlined.

1. To open a new restaurant in the middle of a pandemic <u><u>is</u></u> quite a challenge.
2. I <u><u>hope</u></u> to find a reliable car for under three thousand dollars.
3. Manuel <u><u>wanted</u></u> to buy a new computer.
4. To get my front door open, I <u><u>used</u></u> a crowbar.
5. To work forty hours a week <u><u>is</u></u> impossible for me.

There are other words in each sentence—*open*, *find*, *buy*, *get*, and *work*—that could be verbs in some other contexts, but here they are not. Each of those words is preceded by the word *to*. This combination of *to* + *verb* is never a verb. Like *-ing* words, they are called *verbals*—words that are clearly derived from verbs but are not functioning as verbs.

W9.38 Exploration

Identifying Verbs 8

Double underline all the verbs in the following sentences.

1. Luis is writing a letter to his senator.
2. Noticing the cost of grapes, Greg decided not to buy them.
3. The crying baby was getting on my nerves.
4. My brother had been sleeping for more than three hours.
5. Langston thought that the sleeping cat was his.
6. Meredith has been living in Houston for four years.
7. Driving to Chicago, I listened to NPR.
8. Halley will be paying in cash.
9. Joining the choir was a big mistake.
10. Signing the contract made me very nervous.

W9.39 Exploration

Identifying Subjects 1*

In the following sentences, the verbs have been double underlined and the subjects single underlined. Working individually or in your group, explain the relationship between a verb and a subject.

1. Jada opened the package in front of us.
2. Mercedes gave me a ride to work.
3. Running is good for your heart.
4. La'Quasia will bring the dessert for tonight's dinner.
5. Doctor Mauricio prescribed an antibiotic for me.

W9.40 Exploration

Identifying Subjects 2*

The following sentences illustrate a complication in identifying subjects. The verbs have been double underlined. Working individually or in your group, identify the subject for each of these verbs.

1. The cover of the book <u>was</u> wet.
2. The top of my refrigerator <u>is</u> dusty.
3. Some of the children <u>laughed</u> during the movie.
4. Many of the strawberries <u>were</u> moldy.
5. Most of the students <u>finished</u> the test early.
6. The man in a red sweater <u>gave</u> me a ride.
7. The pot on the stove <u>belonged</u> to my father.
8. The road to Wayne <u>is</u> always busy.
9. To find a twenty-dollar bill <u>was</u> lucky.
10. Moving into the city <u>was</u> very exciting.

W9.41 Exploration

Identifying Subjects and Verbs

Underline the subjects once and the verbs twice in the following sentences.

1. To get into the dance required a ticket.
2. Some of your answers are wrong.
3. Monique has booked a reservation for the whole group.
4. Hoping for a miracle, I turned in my test.
5. Greg was working on a degree in engineering.
6. One section of my roof is tile.
7. Spotting my brother in the crowd, I started yelling.
8. To forget her mother's birthday was thoughtless.
9. The handle of the lawn mower was broken.
10. My typewriter needs to be cleaned.
11. Joking about Regina's grade was not a good idea.
12. A friend of Juan's is running for mayor.

13. In a few minutes, we need to leave for the movie.

14. Katherine hopes to graduate next summer.

15. The restaurant next to the post office has closed.

16. Sunshine in the morning always cheers me up.

17. Taking the mustard out of the refrigerator, Vinnie noticed a beer on the back shelf.

18. A young boy was walking past my house.

19. Next to my car, a frowning police officer was waiting for me.

20. Listening to the radio, I heard the news about the fire.

W9.42 Exploration

Subject-Verb Agreement 1*

In the following pairs, the sentence in black is correct, and the sentence in blue has an error. Working individually or in your group, figure out the grammar rule they demonstrate.

Pair 1

✓ One student rides a motorcycle to school.

✗ One student ride a motorcycle to school.

Pair 2

✓ Two students ride motorcycles to school.

✗ Two students rides motorcycles to school.

Pair 3

✓ A tree grows in Brooklyn.

✗ A tree grow in Brooklyn.

Pair 4

✓ Many trees grow in Brooklyn.

✗ Many trees grows in Brooklyn.

Pair 5

✓ Marcia's mother lives in California.

✗ Marcia's mother live in California.

Pair 6

✓ Marcia's parents live in California.

✗ Marcia's parents lives in California.

NOTE: Record the grammar rule these items demonstrate in a notebook or online file for future reference.

W9.43 Exploration

Subject-Verb Agreement 2*

In the following sentence pairs, the sentence in black is correct, and the sentence in blue has an error. Working individually or in your group, figure out the grammar rule they demonstrate.

Pair 1

✓ An essay is due on Friday.

✗ An essay are due on Friday.

Pair 2

✓ Four essays are required in this course.

✗ Four essays is required in this course.

Pair 3

✓ He is my cousin.

✗ He are my cousin.

Pair 4

✓ They are my best friends.

✗ They is my best friends.

Pair 5

✓ A car was parked in my driveway.

✗ A car were parked in my driveway.

Pair 6

✓ Two cars were parked in my driveway.

✗ Two cars was parked in my driveway.

Pair 7

✓ A police officer was waiting on my porch.

✗ A police officer were waiting on my porch.

Pair 8

✓ Two police officers were waiting on my porch.

✗ Two police officers was waiting on my porch.

NOTE: Record the grammar rule these items demonstrate in a notebook or online file for future reference.

W9.44 Exploration

Subject-Verb Agreement 3*

In the following sentence pairs, the sentence in black is correct, and the sentence in blue has an error. Working individually or in your group, figure out the grammar rule they demonstrate.

Pair 1

✓ A friend of my parents lives in Denver.

✗ A friend of my parents live in Denver.

Pair 2

✓ A box of cookies was left on my doorstep.

✗ A box of cookies were left on my doorstep.

Pair 3

✓ One of my friends was in a car accident.

✗ One of my friends were in a car accident.

Pair 4

✓ The box of crayons was on sale for ninety-nine cents.

✗ The box of crayons were on sale for ninety-nine cents.

Pair 5

✓ High levels of water pollution are a threat to health.

✗ High levels of water pollution is a threat to health.

Pair 6

✓ Many songs on the top-ten list are ballads.

✗ Many songs on the top-ten list is ballads.

NOTE: Record the grammar rule these items demonstrate in a notebook or online file for future reference.

W9.45 Exploration
Subject-Verb Agreement 4: Indefinite Pronouns 1*

In the following pairs, the sentence in black is correct, and the sentence in blue has an error. Study these sentences and figure out the grammar rule they demonstrate.

Pair 1

✓ Everyone in my math class is going to pass.

✗ Everyone in my math class are going to pass.

Pair 2

✓ Someone is waiting in your office.

✗ Someone are waiting in your office.

Pair 3

✓ Anyone with a question is invited to attend the meeting.

✗ Anyone with a question are invited to attend the meeting.

Pair 4

✓ Each of the puppies was adorable.

✗ Each of the puppies were adorable.

Pair 5

✓ Either of those sweaters is a good match with that skirt.

✗ Either of those sweaters are a good match with that skirt.

Pair 6

✓ One of these bicycles was stolen.

✗ One of these bicycles were stolen.

Pair 7

✓ Neither of these jobs offers medical insurance.

✗ Neither of these jobs offer medical insurance.

NOTE: Record the grammar rule these items demonstrate in a notebook or online file for future reference.

W9.46   Advice

Subject-Verb Agreement 5: Indefinite Pronouns 2

You probably noticed that the subject in each of the sentences in W9.45 (p. 155) is a pronoun; in fact, it is a special kind of pronoun known as an *indefinite pronoun*. Below is a list of common indefinite pronouns. Note that these indefinite pronouns are *always singular*.

Always singular			
anybody	everybody	neither/either	one
anyone	everyone	nobody	somebody
anything	everything	no one	someone
each	much	nothing	something

W9.47 Exploration

Subject-Verb Agreement 6: Indefinite Pronouns 3*

In W9.46 (p. 156), you encountered a group of indefinite pronouns that are *always singular*. In the following sentence pairs, the subjects are all indefinite pronouns, but these are quite different from the ones you were working with in W9.45 (p. 155). As usual, the sentences in black are correct; the sentences in blue have an error. Study these and figure out the grammar rule for this group of indefinite pronouns.

Pair 1

✓ Both of my brothers are going to work in my mother's restaurant for the summer.

✗ Both of my brothers is going to work in my mother's restaurant for the summer.

Pair 2

✓ Many of the patients in this hospital are from other states.

✗ Many of the patients in this hospital is from other states.

Pair 3

✓ A few of the houses in my neighborhood were damaged by the hurricane.

✗ A few of the houses in my neighborhood was damaged by the hurricane.

Pair 4

✓ Several of my favorite songs are by Beyoncé.

✗ Several of my favorite songs is by Beyoncé.

NOTE: Record the grammar rule these items demonstrate in a notebook or online file for future reference.

W9.48 Advice

Subject-Verb Agreement 7: Indefinite Pronouns 4

W9.46 (p. 156) listed the sixteen indefinite pronouns in English that are always singular. The four listed in the box below are the only indefinite pronouns in English that are always plural.

Always plural	both	few	many	several

Subject-Verb Agreement 8: Indefinite Pronouns 5*

There is a third group of indefinite pronouns that function in a third way. Study the following groups of sentences, in which those in black are correct and those in blue have an error. Working individually or in your group, figure out what the grammar rule is for this group of indefinite pronouns. What determines whether the indefinite pronouns in this group are singular or plural?

Group 1

✓ All of my cookies are gone.

✗ All of my cookies is gone.

✓ All of my cake is gone.

✗ All of my cake are gone.

Group 2

✓ Some of my relatives are living in Florida.

✗ Some of my relatives is living in Florida.

✓ Some of my essay is about Florida.

✗ Some of my essay are about Florida.

Group 3

✓ None of the children were absent today.

✗ None of the children was absent today.

✓ None of the lecture was about grammar.

✗ None of the lecture were about grammar.

NOTE: Record the grammar rule these items demonstrate in a notebook or online file for future reference.

Subject-Verb Agreement 9: Indefinite Pronouns 6

In W9.46 (p. 156), you were introduced to the sixteen pronouns that are always singular. In W9.48 (p. 157), you encountered four pronouns that are always plural. Now consider the six pronouns, listed in the box below, that are sometimes singular and other times plural, depending on the noun that follows them.

Singular or plural	all any	more most	none	some

Editing an Essay for Subject-Verb Agreement 1

Working individually or in your group, proofread the following essay and correct any errors you find. These errors will all involve subject-verb agreement. To correct these errors, you will need to change the subject so it agrees with the verb or change the verb so it agrees with the subject.

Stress-Relieving Workouts

Millions of individuals experience stress at some point in their lives. Stress is how our bodies react to a threat or adjust to a change. According to recent studies, stress is something that affects at least 80% of people in some way. Though useful in the short term, long-term stress can have negative effects on the body like aches and pains, muscle tension, and high blood pressure. Finding a way to cope with stress can sometimes be difficult. Some remedies is too expensive or not easily accessible, but one method that may be flexible and inexpensive is fitness. Everyone are able to do yoga, cardio, or strength training, fitness strategies that do more than just boost physical fitness. They improves mental health as well.

A fitness strategy that tackles the body and the mind, known as yoga, is the ideal workout. Yoga is not just about poses and headstands. It is about control and inner peace. It helps a person manage their stress levels and also allows them to improve their body flexibility and control their breathing. Most of the yoga classes charges a fee, but yoga can also be done at home for free. Everyone are able to access hundreds of yoga sessions through online platforms like YouTube. These allows them to pick from countless yoga styles and levels and to practice at their own pace. Everyone are able to choose to meditate, develop body strength, or restore body posture from the comfort of their own home. Everyone in my yoga group do yoga at least four times a week.

Another common fitness workout that can be beneficial to people's physical and mental health is cardio—or cardiovascular activity. In recent studies most of the cardio workouts has been found to be extremely beneficial. They are an inexpensive and noninvasive method to deal with mental health as they causes the body to release endorphins, natural hormones that relieve pain and improve overall mood. Cardio can be a range of different activities, such as running, dancing, kickboxing, swimming, hiking, and many others. The possibilities are endless and can be done for free at home, at a park, or even at a public recreation center. While cardio, like yoga, helps people regulate their blood sugar, build breathing capacity, and develop muscle strength, it can also help the body combat stress, anxiety, and depression by releasing hormones that make people feel happy after blowing off some steam.

Strength training, a fitness method that has gotten more attention in recent years, focuses on physical fitness, but it also can tackle a person's mental well-being. It helps to improve one's fitness by combining functional movements and weights. Unlike others that are more common, this method require equipment that, for some, can be too expensive. However, you can use random objects around the house that weigh the same amount as the weights would and do squats, pushups, planks, and other functional movements at home for free. Though it help with overall body strength, bone health, and posture, it is also a mood booster and can aid people's sleeping patterns.

Any of these inexpensive workouts can help with people's overall fitness and mental well-being. It is just a matter of what works best for each person.

Everyone's body are different; they will respond and need different things. It's about doing what works for them. Stress may be something that affects everyone, but it is also something that can be managed through a variety of fitness strategies—while also working on physical fitness.

W9.52 Exploration
Editing an Essay for Subject-Verb Agreement 2

Working individually or in your group, proofread the following essay and correct any errors you find. These errors will all involve subject-verb agreement. To correct these errors, you will need to change the subject so it agrees with the verb or change the verb so it agrees with the subject.

Do We Exist? How Do We Know?

"I think, therefore I am." It's a statement meant to answer the age-old question, "How do we know we exist?" The question of consciousness have bothered philosophers since time has been recorded, asking us to wonder whether or not our world is real, whether or not we are real, and how we can prove it. Though the subject has been probed by many over time, it's only recently that we've seen attempts at a scientific answer. But despite the influx of modern study and thought, an absolute answer still eludes us.

First, a rough definition: Merriam-Webster defines consciousness as "The state of being characterized by sensation, emotion, volition, and thought." In other words, each of us experience the state of being alive, mentally present, and aware of ourselves. For the sake of not muddying the waters here, we'll leave animals out of this and say that humans are the only beings who fully experience this state (although certain primates and even elephants have been shown to have some basic understanding of self). This is, as far as we can tell, what sets us apart from the rest of the animal kingdom. It's our greatest advantage and the source of all the thought, art, science, and history that we knows today.

Although it was the French philosopher René Descartes who first coined the phrase, "ego cogito, ergo sum" (usually translated to English as, "I think, therefore I am") in the mid-1600s, the idea of higher cognition and the self had already been in existence for millennia. But the focus of early philosophers were often more on the soul than on the mind; for example, Judeo-Christian ideology hones in on the idea of "free will," a gift supposedly given to man by God to separate him from the animals and to allow him to create his own destiny. Similarly, Egyptian and Greek theologies tell of a soul that remains conscious after death, traveling to the underworld to (potentially) live on.

But in modern times, everyone have developed modern perceptions of reality. The age of computers have given rise to a theory that everything we see, the entire universe around us, including our own minds, are all part of an advanced computer simulation being run by a more evolved race of beings. While it may sound like science fiction, it's hard to argue with some of the points the theory makes about our reality. They are perhaps best summarized by the character Morpheus in the first movie of the Matrix trilogy: "If real is what you can feel, smell, taste and see, then 'real' is simply electrical signals interpreted by your brain." An advanced enough computer, or artificial intelligence (AI), could (theoretically) hijack the senses the mind relies on and replace the real world with a simulated alternative—or create humans and place us in what we call Earth. What we perceive as consciousness could be no more than an ordered array of 1's and 0's, generated by a hyper-advanced version of Sim City. How would we know the difference?

Stranger still may be the idea of "panpsychism." According to the Stanford Encyclopedia of Philosophy, followers of this theory holds that everything in the world possesses its own brand of consciousness. From humans to animals, all the way down to the grains of sand that cover the beach, everything have some kind of experience. What it's like to be a rock, most of us can never say, but this odd theory tells us that because a rock exists, it has an experience. It may not be able to think like a human, and it most certainly can't tell us what it's like to be itself, but it has the most basic level of consciousness possible. For followers of this odd field, that's enough to say it has some parts of a mind, just not enough to rival our own.

Each of these theories—the soul, the simulation hypothesis, panpsychism—have never been completely proven—and maybe they never will be. Maybe one day neuroscience or some other field will give us the answer to what consciousness is. At the moment, however, scientists can't even agree on exactly when consciousness arises in human beings. It will undoubtedly take more time and further study to discover the origin of human thought. For now, we may just have to accept that Descartes was right: the best way to know that we exist is that we can wonder about whether we do.

Avoiding Pronoun Reference and Agreement Errors

Pronouns are extremely useful words, but errors with them can confuse readers and detract significantly from the effectiveness of your writing.

W9.53 Exploration

Pronouns and Antecedents*

A *pronoun* is a word that takes the place of a noun. In each of the sentences in the following activity, a pronoun is printed in blue. The noun that the pronoun is taking the place of—is standing in for—is called its *antecedent*.

Working individually or with your group, identify the antecedent in each sentence that the pronoun in blue refers to. Pay particular attention to the last two. They are a little different.

1. Our state senator has announced that he will retire at the end of next year.
2. Before my sister could finish dinner, she remembered to call me.
3. This lasagna will taste great after it is baked for an hour.

4. The jury members told the judge **they** wanted to continue deliberating all weekend.

5. My grandparents knew that **they** would be invited to my graduation.

6. Kristin bought a computer from her uncle. **He** fixed it when it broke down.

7. My cousins had a party for the young man who moved in next door. **They** invited everyone in the neighborhood.

8. The book I was reading was about ancient Greece. **It** started with the earliest settlements on the island of Crete.

9. When **she** arrived at work, Imani was surprised to find the office closed.

10. Because **they** live in Hawai'i, my parents don't have any winter clothes.

The pronouns in these sentences work just the way pronouns are supposed to work. Each one is clearly taking the place of a specific noun, its antecedent. Notice that in 6, 7, and 8 the antecedent is actually located in a previous sentence. In 9 and 10, the pronoun comes earlier in the sentence than its antecedent. These are all perfectly correct.

W9.54 Exploration

Vague Pronoun Reference 1*

In W9.53 (p. 163), you saw the way a pronoun takes the place of a noun, its antecedent. The next set of sentences is a little different. Working individually or in your group, try to identify the antecedent for the pronouns in blue in these sentences. If you cannot identify an antecedent, be prepared to explain why not.

1. Mr. Nowak sent a package to my father when **he** received a promotion.

2. Maria told Christine that **she** had passed the final exam.

3. When Isaiah shook George's hand, **he** never looked at **him**.

4. Helen's brothers never came to see her parents while **they** were in the hospital.

5. After Juanita paid the salesclerk, **she** whistled.

This problem—having more than one possible antecedent for a pronoun—is known as *vague pronoun reference*. Revise each of the sentences above to correct this problem.

W9.55 Exploration
Vague Pronoun Reference 2*

In W9.54 (p. 164), you discovered one kind of error with pronoun reference—a pronoun that has two possible antecedents. In this section, you will discover another. Working individually or in groups, try to identify the antecedent for the pronouns in blue in these sentences. If you cannot identify an antecedent, be prepared to explain why not.

1. In Hawai'i, they all live near the ocean.
2. Scott bought a pair of skis, but he has never even tried it before.
3. By early April the dogwoods had flowered, and by the middle of May, they had fallen to the ground.
4. In New York City, they were much friendlier than I expected.
5. At the Department of Motor Vehicles, they told me I needed to get a new title to my car.

This problem—a pronoun that simply has no antecedent—is another form of *vague pronoun reference*. Revise each of the sentences above to correct this problem.

W9.56 Exploration
Vague Pronoun Reference 3*

The sentences in this activity are different from any that you've seen so far. Working individually or in your group, try to identify the antecedent for the pronouns in blue in these sentences. If you cannot identify an antecedent, be prepared to explain why not.

1. It rained every day during my vacation to Myrtle Beach. Also, my sister and her family had to cancel at the last minute. This is what was so disappointing to me.
2. I bought these shoes at Target during the spring sale. This is why they were so cheap.
3. I got my résumé typed and after three interviews, I was hired as a data processor for the Social Security Administration. I really appreciated Maxine's help with this.
4. The sky was beginning to get darker, and I had missed the last bus to Washington. This was making me very worried.
5. My mother wants to take us to Portland, and my father is hoping that we come to his house in Boston. This seems like a very nice offer.

The problem—using the pronoun *this* to refer back to some general idea that is hard to identify—is yet another form of *vague pronoun reference*. Revise each of the sentences above to correct this problem.

W9.57 Advice

Pronoun-Antecedent Agreement 1: Introduction

Formal English grammar has an additional rule about the use of pronouns. Take a look at the example sentences below to see if you can figure it out. The black versions are correct, and the blue versions have an agreement issue.

✓ My brother lives in California, but he is coming to visit this weekend.

✗ My brother lives in California, but they are coming to visit this weekend.

✓ When Bernie Sanders ran for president, he surprised everyone.

✗ When Bernie Sanders ran for president, they surprised everyone.

✓ If people in America work hard, they expect to get ahead.

✗ If people in America work hard, he expects to get ahead.

You probably noticed that, in each of the blue sentences, the pronoun and its antecedent don't match up. The pronoun is singular and the antecedent is plural, or the other way around. Pronouns must agree with their antecedents in number (singular or plural). We call this matching of pronouns and their antecedents *agreement*. (To learn about using the pronoun *they* in a singular sense, see W9.59, p. 168.)

The following sentences illustrate another issue with pronoun-antecedent agreement.

✓ My mother owns a convertible, but she never puts the top down.

✗ My mother owns a convertible, but he never puts the top down.

✓ When my father was in high school, he got straight A's.

✗ When my father was in high school, she got straight A's.

In traditional versions of formal English, pronouns must also match up with their antecedents in gender. According to that tradition, the blue versions above would have an issue with pronoun-antecedent agreement. Today, however, definitions of gender are much more fluid, and pronoun-antecedent agreement must reflect that fluidity.

The blue versions of sentences below reflect more common issues of pronoun-antecedent agreement.

✓ I admire women who can stand up for themselves.

✗ I admire women who can stand up for herself.

✓ My Macintosh was much less expensive than I expected it to be.

✗ My Macintosh was much less expensive than I expected them to be.

✓ Janice is one of those women who will make names for themselves.

✗ Janice is one of those women who will make a name for herself.

In these pairs of sentences you can see that ensuring that pronouns agree with their antecedents can be a little tricky. The third pair is especially difficult. Note that the sentence is saying that there are a number of women who will make names for themselves, so *themselves* refers to *women*, not *Janice*.

W9.58 Advice

Pronoun-Antecedent Agreement 2: Indefinite Pronouns

Many writers have difficulty with pronoun agreement when the antecedent is not a noun but an indefinite pronoun. The following chart lists the most common indefinite pronouns and indicates whether they are singular or plural.

Always singular	anybody anyone anything each either	everybody everyone everything much	neither nobody no one nothing	one somebody someone something
Always plural	both	few	many	several
Singular or plural	all any	more most	none	some

The indefinite pronouns that are always singular are a little confusing because words like *everyone* and *each* seem to be standing for a number of people, and so seem to be plural. That's the hard part. Even though they *seem* to be plural, all the pronouns in the first row of the chart are *always* singular.

In the second row of the chart, the pronouns seem to be plural, and they are, so they're not so hard.

In the third row, singular or plural, things are a little trickier. These pronouns are singular if they are followed by a prepositional phrase ending in a singular noun. They are plural if they are followed by a prepositional phrase ending in a plural noun. In the sentences below, the prepositional phrases are in italics. Here are some examples that show how this works:

- Most *of the songs* are from the sixties. (*Most* is plural because *songs* is plural.)

- Most *of the music* is from the sixties. (*Most* is singular because *music* is singular.)

- Some *of the books* were damaged in the flood. (*Some* is plural because *books* is plural.)

- Some *of the test* was very easy. (*Some* is singular because *test* is singular.)

- Any *of the beers* in this bar are organic. (*Any* is plural because *beers* is plural.)

- Any *of the wine* on this list is too expensive for my budget. (*Any* is singular because *wine* is singular.)

W9.59 Advice

Pronoun-Antecedent Agreement 3: Singular *They*

Before the 1970s, writers typically used the pronoun *he* in the generic sense to refer to a person when that person's gender was unknown. (But not always: Before the eighteenth century, and even after, the use of *they* as a singular pronoun was common. Shakespeare used it: "There's not a man I meet but doth salute me / As if I were *their* well-acquainted friend [*A Comedy of Errors*, 4.3.1–2]; so did Jane Austen: "'But to expose the former faults of any person, without knowing what *their* present feelings were, seemed unjustifiable'" [*Pride and Prejudice*, ch. 47].)

Since then, linguists have recognized that the *generic he* is sexist, as it implies that men are the norm and women a variation on that norm. To avoid using *he* in a generic sense, writers began using *he or she* or *s/he* or even alternating pronouns:

Everyone wants an A in *his or her* writing class.

Some grammarians groused about the change, but the English language moved on, and *he or she* became commonplace.

Now we recognize that not all people identify with one or the other gender; instead, they may identify with both—or neither. And others may prefer a non-gender-specific pronoun out of solidarity with the nonbinary or simply because they find gender irrelevant in most cases.

Some writers devised non-gender-specific pronouns (like *zie* and *hir*) to replace *he/she* and *his/her*. But the more popular option has been to use *they* in a singular sense:

> Each member of a jury must make up their own mind about the guilt or innocence of the accused.

Right now, the language is in flux. Most style manuals—including *The MLA Handbook*, *The Publication Manual of the American Psychological Association* (APA), and *The Chicago Manual of Style*—endorse using *they* in a singular sense when it is a person's preferred pronoun:

> Jesse earned an A in *their* writing class.

But not all agree that singular *they* should be used in formal writing when used generically:

> Everyone wants an A in *their* writing class.

Some would prefer writers to find a way of making the same statement without having to use a singular antecedent like *everyone*.

> All students want an A in *their* writing class.

Since instructors may want to be sure that you understand pronoun-antecedent agreement before breaking what they see as the rules, check with your instructor before you use singular *they* in formal writing assignments.

W9.60 Exploration

Correcting Pronoun Errors

Working individually or in your group and using what you learned in W9.53–W9.59 (pp. 163–169), edit the following sentences. All errors will involve pronoun reference (W9.54–W9.56) or pronoun-agreement issues (W9.57–W9.59).

1. When young children are read to, he or she is beginning to learn to read.
2. Before she had time to sit down, Joy Reid asked Jill Biden a question.

3. In New York City, they are voting in a special election this Tuesday.

4. The clerk agreed to refund my father's deposit before he had even asked for it.

5. In this election, they are spending millions of dollars on advertising.

6. Regina paid too much for her microwave, and she really doesn't like to microwave food. This is why she tried to sell the microwave on Craig's List.

7. Reggie and Joshua got into a huge argument last night, so this morning he called to apologize.

8. The football team had committed themselves to playing on Sundays.

9. When customers want help with a purchase, he shouldn't have to wait fifteen minutes.

10. Politicians sometimes make promises that she can't keep.

W9.61 Exploration
Editing an Essay for Pronoun Errors 1

The following essay contains errors involving vague pronoun reference and pronoun agreement. Working individually or in your group, edit the essay to correct these errors.

Voter Registration

Most countries around the world today are democracies. It's the first time in history that that can be said; the number of democracies only surpassed other forms of government in the twentieth century, making it the dominant method of choosing leadership. But this means that each nation has to choose their representatives, and that means there needs to be a method for doing so: voting. In the United States, a single day each year is set on which people vote for their representatives. But in order to get to the voting booth in the first place, citizens must navigate the voter registration laws in his or her home state. In some places, these processes are so arduous that it is difficult or impossible for people to vote—meaning that some people in this democracy are effectively denied a voice.

The United States has been a democracy since the late 1700s when it won its independence from Great Britain. At the time it was one of the only democracies in the world—and perhaps *the* only one. But while other modern democracies have developed over the last 200 years, the United States has done relatively little to adapt to the changing times. It is an embarrassment. We still use paper ballots, we still bubble in the name of the person we vote for, and we still have to register ourselves to vote.

In some countries, the registration process is streamlined. In Estonia, for example, voter registration is automatic. They send a voter identification card to each citizen and even allow it to be used to vote online because it wants people to vote. This not only makes voting more convenient—as it can literally be done from the comfort of one's own home—but also increases voter turnout. When voting is easier, and even encouraged by policies like automatic voter registration, voter turnout rises dramatically.

Other countries have tried a different approach. Australia, for one, has mandatory voting. The fine is about $20 if you don't cast a ballot, and if you think they won't find you, you'll find you're mistaken rather quickly. The government cross-references addresses, tax records, and any other data about each citizen to guarantee that everyone votes or pays their fine. This ensures that the country has a virtually 100% voter turnout each year, and every citizen has a voice in his government.

A more relaxed approach to this process is taken in Sweden, where voting is not compulsory but registration is. Once citizens hit 18, he or she is immediately registered to vote. The same goes for immigrants, who are also registered the moment they become citizens. In Sweden, they really want everyone to vote.

These countries compare starkly with the United States. Each American state has their own registration process, and the wait times to be processed can be weeks or even months. When an American mails in their registration forms, they can take weeks to process them and issue voter ID cards.

Americans also don't get the day off from work to vote; in many countries, Election Day is a national holiday. This is another problem that needs immediate attention. In America, many people can't afford to miss time at their job and therefore won't be able to vote. There is also the issue of voter identification: some states now require a photo ID to vote, and this has become a problem for many low-income, older, and racial and ethnic minority voters, who do not have easy access to identification. That process, too, costs money and can take weeks to carry out.

Compared to many other countries, America has a very complex voting process. Registering can be slow and arduous, and the process of voting itself can be equally so. Many other countries have set better examples and moved into the twenty-first century with their election practices. Though America has one of the oldest democracies around, it is not the most evolved; with some time and some clear guidance from overseas, however, it one day might be.

W9.62 Exploration
Editing an Essay for Pronoun Errors 2

The following essay has errors involving vague pronoun reference and pronoun agreement. Working individually or in your group, edit the essay to correct these errors.

Wildlife Refuges

It's easy to forget that wildlife refuges exist; we never really see them, as they occupy a space that most humans never set foot in. Their purpose is to shelter animals from human beings and give them respite from pollution and development. But they also provide access for people who want to see the outdoors as it is meant to be: untouched and undisturbed.

The National Wildlife Refuge System (NWRS) was founded over a hundred years ago by President Theodore Roosevelt as a means to preserve certain wildlife species. He ordered Ethan Hitchcock, his Secretary of the Interior, to start work on refuges before he had even been sworn in. At the time, they had been over-hunting animals and driving many species to dangerously low levels, threatening their survival. The creation of the wildlife refuges not only stabilized many of those populations but also created a massive network where scientists could continue making gains on conservation work. Since then, the system has grown to include hundreds of refuges across the country, protecting thousands of animal species and millions of acres of land. This is why the system of wildlife refuges is so important.

While the refuges' original intent was to preserve wildlife for the sake of sustainable hunting and resource conservation (i.e., fur, feathers, and other products taken from animals), they have evolved into a haven for species protected by the Endangered Species Act. And they have also become test sites for conservation work, places where universities and other interest groups can study animal and plant life. This allows them an undisturbed habitat, where they can test new conservation methods and habitat management techniques.

Refuges are essential territory for biologists, but they're also beneficial for the public. They're a great place to go hunting—and with some species, like turkey or deer, it's essential for some of those herds (or flocks) to be culled. A periodic cull controls populations, allowing for greater competition and bio-diversity among species. However, in some refuges, the hunters outnumber the biologists, and they don't respect the other's rights.

Another benefit the public gets to enjoy is the trails and other maintained areas where they can walk and enjoy nature. They provide free, curated access to the outdoors that can be hard to find elsewhere. Some of the best trails in the country are on refuges, and they're free and open to the public at all hours of the day.

Wildlife refuges aren't places we think about very often—in fact, people could be driving through a refuge and not even know it. But despite their place on the periphery, they are essential sites for study and research. They provide easy access to nature not only for those who want to conserve it, but also for people who simply enjoy it. They know how important these refuges are. For access to the outdoors, there is no better place.

Combining Sentences in Interesting Ways

The exercises in this section will give you the opportunity to explore the flexibility of language, discover the many options for expressing a single idea, and practice the grammar conventions covered earlier in this chapter.

W9.63 Advice

Sentence Combining 1

Most students find sentence-combining activities to be fun, perhaps because there is no single correct answer. The following activities give you a series of short, simple declarative sentences and ask you to combine them into one longer and more complex sentence. They invite you to be inventive, to be playful, and to experiment with different combinations. The only rule is that the one sentence you come up with must include all the information that was in the original short sentences. Of course, you will also need to make sure your sentences follow the rules of formal English grammar.

Here are two examples of how this works:

Example 1

Short Sentences to Combine

Daris is a student in my English class.

Daris gave me a ride this morning.

Some Possible Combinations

Daris is a student in my English class, and he gave me a ride this morning.

Daris, a student in my English class, gave me a ride this morning.

A student in my English class named Daris gave me a ride this morning.

Example 2

Short Sentences to Combine

My car is twelve years old.

My car is a Honda Civic.

I bought my car from my father.

Some Possible Combinations

I bought my twelve-year-old Honda Civic from my father.

My Honda Civic, which I bought from my father, is twelve years old.

My car is a twelve-year-old Honda Civic, which I bought from my father.

W9.64 Exploration

Sentence Combining 2

Below are five sets of short, simple sentences. Working individually or with your group, combine each set into one longer and more complex sentence. Make sure your one sentence contains all the information from the set of short sentences.

Set 1

I like a good cappuccino.

A cappuccino is coffee with lots of warm milk.

A cappuccino usually has whipped cream on top.

Set 2

I read a novel this weekend.

The novel was about a totalitarian state.

It was written by George Orwell.

Set 3

I was sitting by a beautiful stream.

I was reading a book.

The woman sat down near me.

She was reading the same book I was.

Set 4

I need to go shopping.

I am out of coffee.

I am out of money.

I can't go shopping.

Set 5

My daughter started the first grade last week.

She loves going to school.

Two of her best friends are in her class.

Her teacher seems to be very nice.

W9.65 Exploration

Sentence Combining 3

Below are five sets of short, simple sentences. Working individually or with your group, combine each set into one longer and more complex sentence. Make sure your one sentence contains all the information from the set of short sentences.

Set 1

That man is wearing a bright purple sweater.

That man is playing a harmonica.

That man was here yesterday.

I think that man is a busker.

Set 2

Angelique took a deep breath.

She walked to the end of the diving board.

She launched herself into the air.

She entered the water with almost no splash.

Set 3

Asher was planting irises in his garden.

It started to rain.

Asher refused to stop.

He got soaking wet.

Set 4

My English professor walked up.

My English professor was carrying a box of test tubes.

I looked at her more closely.

I discovered she wasn't my English professor.

Set 5

The dancers were waiting for the music to begin.

Their faces looked excited.

They had rehearsed well.

They were ready to perform.

W9.66 Exploration

Sentence Combining 4

Following are five sets of short, simple sentences. Working individually or with your group, combine each set into one longer and more complex sentence. Make sure your one sentence contains all the information from the set of short sentences.

Set 1

I live in the city.

I am used to lots of noise.

I am used to cars honking.

I am used to the sirens of fire engines.

I probably couldn't sleep in the country.

Set 2

I made risotto.

Risotto is one of Donna's favorite dishes.

Donna grilled chicken.

We drank some wine.

The wine was a Chianti.

Set 3

A roar erupted.

People stood up.

People stamped their feet.

Dolly came out again.

Dolly took a bow.

Set 4

Arun was studying chemistry.

The phone rang.

Arun answered the phone.

It was his girlfriend.

Arun forgot about chemistry.

Set 5

I applied for a job at the new steak house.

I have an AA degree in culinary arts.

I worked for four years in my parents' restaurant.

My parents owned an Italian restaurant.

I was offered a position as sous chef.

Language and Computers

Here, at the end of this chapter, explore using computers to edit your writing.

W9.67 **Exploration**

Computers and Editing 1

Paragraph 1, below, has nine grammar errors that have been underlined. Paragraph 2 is identical to Paragraph 1 except the errors have been corrected. You may want to compare each of the nine underlined errors in Paragraph 1 with the corresponding corrections in Paragraph 2 to make sure you understand what the errors are.

Paragraph 1

Lots of problems for the work force have been solved by the minimum wage. The work force actually has a <u>Government</u> backing the<u>m, and</u> saying <u>its</u> not fair to pay someone pennies when it takes quarters to survive. Before the minimum wage was en<u>acted businesses</u> could pay their employees anything they wanted, sometimes leaving their employees without the money to buy simple necessities such as food, w<u>ater cloth</u>ing, or shoes. This was a very unfair system, exploiting the workers, who had no way to defend themselves. Many of these workers didn't even have a <u>choice, many</u> had families that they supported. If <u>you</u> decided to leave your current job to find a better paying one, <u>you</u> never knew how long it was going to take to find one. Spending every penny they earned just to surv<u>ive, left</u> no savings to rely on while they looked for a new job.

Paragraph 2

Lots of problems for the work force have been solved by the minimum wage. The work force actually has a <u>government</u> backing the<u>m and</u> saying <u>it's</u>

not fair to pay someone pennies when it takes quarters to survive. Before the minimum wage was enacted, businesses could pay their employees anything they wanted, sometimes leaving their employees without the money to buy simple necessities such as food, water, clothing, or shoes. This was a very unfair system, exploiting the workers, who had no way to defend themselves. Many of these workers didn't even have a choice. Many had families that they supported. If they decided to leave their current job to find a better paying one, they never knew how long it was going to take to find one. Spending every penny they earned just to survive left no savings to rely on while they looked for a new job.

Now type Paragraph 3, below, into a word processor and run the computer's grammar checker to see what it locates as errors. Compare the grammar checker's list of errors with those in Paragraph 1. How good a job did the grammar checker do?

Paragraph 3

Lots of problems for the work force have been solved by the minimum wage. The work force actually has a Government backing them, and saying its not fair to pay someone pennies when it takes quarters to survive. Before the minimum wage was enacted businesses could pay their employees anything they wanted, sometimes leaving their employees without the money to buy simple necessities such as food, water clothing, or shoes. This was a very unfair system, exploiting the workers, who had no way to defend themselves. Many of these workers didn't even have a choice, many had families that they supported. If you decided to leave your current job to find a better paying one, you never knew how long it was going to take to find one. Spending every penny they earned just to survive, left no savings to rely on while they looked for a new job.

W9.68 Advice

Computers and Editing 2

Most word processing programs have one simple tool that can be very useful when you are editing your writing: the Find function, usually found on the Edit menu. As you are writing this semester, keep track of the grammar, punctuation, and word choice rules that you have trouble with most often.

When you have finished writing and revising your essay, use the Find function to search for each of the problematic terms. Here's one student's list:

to, too, two

its, it's

's, s'

your, you're

This student first used Find to search for every place she had written *to*. As the computer found each one, she checked to see if it was used correctly. Then she searched for *too* and checked each of those. Next, she searched for *two* and checked each of those. Then she did the same for each of the other terms on her list.

As you saw in W9.67 (p. 179), the computer is not so good at deciding whether something you have written is grammatically correct, but it is infallible at finding every instance of a word or phrase. So I recommend that you use the Find function to locate every place you've used a word or phrase from your list, but then use your own understanding of the rule involved, as you've learned it in this chapter, to decide whether you've used the word or phrase correctly.

Answers to Selected Explorations in W9

W9.69 Advice

Punctuating to Avoid Fragments, Run-Ons, and Comma Splices

Exploration W9.5 (p. 118): A fragment is a group of words that is not a sentence but is punctuated as if it were.

Exploration W9.6 (p. 119): The fragments are underlined and a brief description of the strategy used to correct them appears below the corrected version.

1. I owe my success in high school to one person. <u>The woman who taught me math.</u> She was tough but fair.

    Corrected   I owe my success in high school to one person, the woman who taught me math. She was tough but fair.

    Strategy   The fragment was merged with the preceding sentence.

2. <u>The man sitting at the counter and drinking coffee.</u> He used to be the coach of my basketball team. Now, he's retired.

> **Corrected**   The man sitting at the counter and drinking coffee used to be the coach of my basketball team. Now, he's retired.
>
> **Strategy**   The fragment was merged with the following sentence.

3. I think I saw the principal of my high school on Saturday when I was driving to Target. <u>Jogging on the side of the road.</u> I always admired him.

> **Corrected**   I think I saw the principal of my high school on Saturday when I was driving to Target. He was jogging on the side of the road. I always admired him.
>
> **Strategy**   The missing subject and verb were added to the fragment.

Exploration W9.8 (p. 121): An independent clause is any group of words that could be a sentence all by itself. (See W9.3, What Is a Sentence?, p. 116.) Some independent clauses are sentences by themselves. Others are parts of larger sentences.

Exploration W9.9 (p. 121): A run-on is two independent clauses run together with no punctuation. A comma splice is two independent clauses separated by a comma. Both are considered errors.

Exploration W9.10 (p. 122): Strategies for correcting run-ons and comma splices include the following:

1. Make the two independent clauses into two sentences by adding a period at the end of the first and capitalizing the first word of the second.
2. Join the two independent clauses with a semicolon.
3. Revise one independent clause so it is no longer an independent clause and place it after the remaining independent clause.
4. Revise one independent clause so it is no longer an independent clause and place it before the remaining independent clause.
5. Join the two independent clauses with a semicolon followed by a transitional expression, such as *therefore, however, furthermore, for example, as a result,* or *meanwhile.* The transitional expression should be followed by a comma.

Exploration W9.14 (p. 127): A comma must precede *and* or *but* when it is joining two independent clauses. A comma must not precede *and* or *but* when it is not joining two independent clauses.

Exploration W9.15 (p. 128): A comma must precede any coordinating conjunction when it is joining two independent clauses. A comma must not precede the coordinating conjunction when it is not joining two independent clauses.

Exploration W9.16 (p. 130): In each of these examples, a word, phrase, or clause—called an *introductory* element—comes before an independent clause. Introductory elements must be followed by a comma.

Exploration W9.17 (p. 131): Each of the sentences in blue, bolded type begins with an introductory element, but the second half of the sentence is not an independent clause. Combining what you learned in W9.16 with what you learned in this unit, you can infer that the punctuation rule for introductory elements is this:

> When an introductory element appears before an independent clause, it must be followed by a comma. When the part of the sentence after the introductory element is not an independent clause, the introductory element cannot be followed by a comma.

W9.70   Advice

Using Apostrophes to Show Possession and to Indicate Contractions

Exploration W9.21 (p. 136): For this discussion, the word with the *'s* will be called the "possessive word"; the word following the possessive word will be called the "possessed word." Possession in these sets of sentences represents the following relationships:

Set 1: The possessed word is part of, is connected to, the possessive word.

Set 2: The possessed word is a relative of the possessive word.

Set 3: The possessed word has the characteristic or quality of the possessive word.

Set 4: The possessed word belongs to an organization.

Set 5: The possessed word is a characteristic of a period of time.

Exploration W9.22 (p. 137):

1. <u>Marcella's</u> umbrella is bright red.
2. <u>Today's</u> special is meatloaf and mashed potatoes.
3. I grabbed my <u>boss's</u> hand and shook it forcefully.
4. My <u>professor's</u> absence policy was stricter than the <u>college's</u> policy.

5. Several dogs were barking as I walked up the sidewalk.
6. I have often observed my biology <u>professor's</u> compassion for students.
7. I was very impressed with the <u>soprano's</u> voice.
8. My <u>bicycle's</u> tire was flat.
9. <u>Yesterday's</u> snow was completely melted by this morning.
10. <u>Craig's</u> <u>book's</u> cover had a large coffee stain.

Exploration W9.23 (p. 138): This exploration seems to suggest that when you make a word possessive, you must add an *'s*. The next two explorations, however, complicate this rule.

Exploration W9.24 (p. 138): In W9.23, the possessive words were all singular, and the apostrophe went before the *s*. Here they are all plural, and the apostrophe goes after the *s*.

Exploration W9.25 (p. 139): All the plural words in W9.24 ended in an *s*. The plural words here end in a letter other than *s*, and in this case the apostrophe goes before the *s*.

Exploration W9.27 (p. 141):

> they are = they're
>
> it is = it's
>
> he is = he's
>
> who is = who's
>
> could not = couldn't
>
> are not = aren't
>
> had not = hadn't
>
> did not = didn't
>
> you are = you're
>
> have not = haven't

Exploration W9.28 (p. 141): Use an apostrophe with these pronouns only when they are contractions. To decide whether they are contractions, separate the possibly contracted word into the two words that formed the contraction. In the first pair, for example, if you are trying to decide whether *its* or *it's* is correct, separate the contraction *it's* into two words—*it* and *is*—and insert these two words back into the sentence:

> I hope it is not too late to sign up for the trip to Washington.

It is makes perfect sense here, so the contraction *it's* is correct.

W9.71 Advice

Ensuring Subject-Verb Agreement

Exploration W9.31 (p. 147): These verbs all express actions, something you can do. (You could express this idea in other ways, but these two should give you the gist.)

Exploration W9.32 (p. 147): While these verbs—*thinks, sleeps, sit, suspects,* and *read*—don't express much action (as did the verbs in W9.31), they do express something you can do.

Exploration W9.33 (p. 148): Look at the first sentence: *Monday is the first day of spring.* No action here. No one is doing anything. Instead the verb, *is,* is linking the two parts of the sentence. It's almost like Monday = the first day of spring. And then if you look at the other sentences, they work the same way, except in the last two, the statement is not about the present. Number 4 is about the past, and number 5 is about the future, but in every case the verb is linking the subject and another word or phrase in the second half of the sentence.

Exploration W9.35 (p. 148): In these sentences, some form of the verb *be* is used in combination with an action verb. When used in this way, these *be* verbs are called *helping* or *auxiliary verbs.* Note that the action verbs all end in *-ing.*

Exploration W9.36 (p. 149): There are a lot of *-ing* verbs in these sentences. Note that only the *-ing* verbs with a helping verb are double underlined as verbs. The others— the *-ing* verbs without a helping verb—are not verbs. They are called verbals. Verbals cannot serve as verbs in sentences, but they can serve as nouns or adjectives. When functioning as a noun, verbals can even be the subject of a sentence, as shown in W9.40.

Exploration W9.39 (p. 150): The subject in each of these sentences is the *do-er* of the verb, the person taking the action. To find subjects, first find the verb and then ask yourself who or what is *doing* the verb, taking the action.

Exploration W9.40 (p. 151): These sentences are a little trickier because the subject in each case is followed by a prepositional phrase . . . often a prepositional phrase beginning with *of.* Sometimes students think the noun in the prepositional phrase (for example, *book* in the prepositional phrase *of the book* in number 1) is the subject, but it is not. In number 2, the whole refrigerator isn't dusty, just the top. In number 3, all the children didn't laugh, just some of them. Notice that in the last two sentences, the verbal *to find* and *moving* are the subjects.

Exploration W9.42 (p. 152): When the subject is singular, the verb ends in *s*. When the subject is plural, the verb doesn't end in *s*.

Exploration W9.43 (p. 153): In sentences with *be* verbs, if the subject is singular, the verb must be *is* for present tense or *was* for past tense (both of these verbs do end in *s*); if the subject is plural, the verb must be *are* for present tense or *were* for past tense.

Exploration W9.44 (p. 154): As you saw in W9.40, the verb must agree with the subject, not the noun in the prepositional phrase. (The subject cannot be in a prepositional phrase.)

Exploration W9.45 (p. 155): This group of indefinite pronouns includes all the combinations of *any*, *every*, *no*, and *some* with *body*, *one*, and *thing* as well as the pronouns *each*, *much*, and *one*. They are always singular and so take a singular verb.

Exploration W9.47 (p. 157): This group of pronouns—*both*, *many*, *few*, and *several*—are always plural and must take a plural verb.

Exploration W9.49 (p. 158): This group of pronouns can be singular or plural depending on the noun in the prepositional phrase that follows them.

W9.72 Advice

Avoiding Pronoun Reference and Agreement Errors

Exploration W9.53 (p. 163): The antecedents are underlined in the following sentences.

1. Our state <u>senator</u> has announced that **he** will retire at the end of next year.
2. Before my <u>sister</u> could finish dinner, **she** remembered to call me.
3. This <u>lasagna</u> will taste great after **it** is baked for an hour.
4. The jury <u>members</u> told the judge **they** wanted to continue deliberating all weekend.
5. My <u>grandparents</u> knew that **they** would be invited to my graduation.
6. <u>Kristin</u> bought a <u>computer</u> from her uncle. **He** fixed it when it broke down.
7. My cousins had a party for the young man who moved in next door. **They** invited everyone in the neighborhood.
8. The <u>book</u> I was reading was about ancient Greece. **It** started with the earliest settlements on the island of Crete.
9. When **she** arrived at work, <u>Imani</u> was surprised to find the office closed.
10. Because **they** live in Hawai'i, my <u>parents</u> don't have any winter clothes.

Exploration W9.54 (p. 164): There are two possible antecedents for the pronoun in each of these sentences. For example, the pronoun *he* in number 1 could refer to Mr. Nowak or the father. Of course, such confusion should be avoided. In the following sentences, the vague pronoun reference has been corrected.

1. When my father was promoted, Mr. Nowak sent him a package.
2. When Maria passed the final exam, she told Christine.
3. Isaiah shook George's hand without ever looking at him.
4. While Helen's parents were in the hospital, her brothers never came to see them.
5. Juanita whistled as she paid the salesclerk.

Exploration W9.55 (p. 165): In these sentences, there is no antecedent for the pronouns. For example, in number 1, the *they* doesn't refer back to any noun or pronoun. The problems have been corrected in the following sentences.

1. Everyone in Hawai'i lives near the ocean.
2. Scott bought a pair of skis, but he has never even tried skiing before.
3. By early April the dogwoods had flowered, and by the middle of May, the flowers had fallen to the ground.
4. In New York City, people were much friendlier than I expected.
5. At the Department of Motor Vehicles, a clerk told me I needed to get a new title to my car.

Exploration W9.56 (p. 165): In each of these sentences, it is not clear what the antecedent for the pronoun *this* is. In number 1, *this* may refer to the rainy weather or the sister's family not being able to join them or both. It's simply not clear. The problems are solved in the following sentences.

1. It rained every day during my vacation to Myrtle Beach. Also, my sister and her family had to cancel at the last minute. Their cancellation was so disappointing to me.
2. I bought these shoes at Target during the spring sale. Because the spring sale was a good one, they were very cheap.
3. I got my résumé typed, and after three interviews, I was hired as a data processor for the Social Security Administration. I really appreciated Maxine's help with the typing.
4. The sky was beginning to get darker, and I had missed the last bus to Washington. The weather was making me very worried.
5. My mother wants to take us to Portland, and my father is hoping that we come to his house in Boston. These both seem like very nice offers.

W10 Introductions, Conclusions, and Titles

W10 discusses three brief but important parts of an essay—the introduction, the conclusion, and the title—and provides strategies for ensuring that these three components enhance the effectiveness of your essay.

Writing the Introduction

Because getting started on a piece of writing can often be the hardest part, writing the introduction can sometimes have a debilitating effect. To ease this effect, keep in mind, as you start a piece of writing, that you are only writing a draft introduction. As you work on the paper, you will undoubtedly revise the introduction several times.

This section will also offer you some options to help you avoid this kind of paralysis. When you get started, remember to think about your audience: What kind of introduction will be most effective given your readers? (For more about audience, see W2.4, Thinking about Audience, p. 13.) You will also want to keep in mind your thesis and your purpose for writing. (See W3.5–W3.7, pp. 29–31, and W2.6, Thinking about Purpose, p. 16.)

W10.1 Advice

Elements of an Effective Introduction

Regardless of how you organize your introduction, certain elements are almost always included:

- **Background information or history.** Provide any background or context readers will need to know. You may need to explain, for example, what problem occurred to make your proposal necessary, or what solutions had been tried—and had failed—in the past.

- **Establishment of *ethos*.** Convince your audience that you can be trusted, that you know what you're talking about, and that you will not exaggerate or mislead.

(To learn more about *ethos*, see W11.4, Three Types of Appeal: *Logos, Ethos,* and *Pathos*, p. 198.)

- **The thesis.** The position you are taking—the point you are making, your stand on your topic—is your thesis and is customarily stated in the introduction, though it may appear elsewhere in the paper. You may also want to preview the main points in your essay briefly. (For more information on drafting a thesis and where to place it, see W3.5–W3.8, pp. 29–32.)

W10.2 Advice
Strategies for Effective Introductions

Sometimes, especially for shorter pieces of writing, the introduction is just a single paragraph, but writers may devote several paragraphs to the introduction. As you read the following options, bear in mind that some of them may be a separate paragraph within the introduction.

Define a Key Term

It can be very helpful to the reader if you define any key terms in the introduction. Often you will be giving more than just a dictionary definition; you'll be explaining exactly how *you* will be using the term or terms in this essay. For more on writing definitions, see W11.22, Strategies for Writing Simple Definitions (p. 226), and W11.24, Strategies for Writing Extended Definitions (p. 229).

> In this essay, I will be using the term *juvenile delinquency* in a very specific way: any behavior by someone under eighteen years of age that violates a criminal statute. I do not mean minor misbehavior like truancy from school, posting graffiti, or running a stop sign. Nor do I mean crimes, like murder or rape, that are far too serious to be classified as delinquency.

Problem to Solution

One highly effective option for an introduction (especially for argument essays or proposals) is to identify a problem, providing some evidence that the problem exists, offering some discussion of the history of the problem, and finally suggesting a solution to the problem, which becomes the thesis of the essay.

> Are you tired of spending more than an hour in traffic each morning and each evening? In this essay I will propose three steps this city could take that would drastically reduce traffic congestion.

Preview Your Support

It can also be effective to start your introductory paragraph with a preview of the kind of evidence you will be presenting in the essay. Be careful not to give away too much, though. Follow this brief preview with your thesis.

> After decades of the population of this city declining every year, that trend has been reversed for the last three years. The price of housing and the cost of rent are now at the lowest level in more than a decade. The center of the city has come back to life, with new restaurants, bars, and coffee shops opening every month. This is the perfect time to think about moving into the city.

Start with a Quotation

> The American transcendentalist Ralph Waldo Emerson once proposed that "a foolish consistency is the hobgoblin of little minds." In this essay, I will explore the variety of situations in which being consistent is counterproductive.

Start with a Key Question

> Have you ever wondered whether going to college was the right decision for you? I will explore a variety of reasons why students might decide college is not the right choice for them, and I will explain why each of these reasons is invalid.

Open with a Brief Anecdote or a Story

> My first day in college was almost my last. It started when the bus I was taking got into an accident. The driver insisted everyone stay on the bus until the police had arrived and questioned us. I was sitting next to another young woman, Maxine, who turned out to be heading to the same college I was. When the police finally finished with us, Maxine and I decided to share an Uber to get to school. When we arrived—twenty minutes after my first class had started—I didn't know where to go. Maxine led me to my classroom and suggested we meet for lunch. Having friends at school can make a big difference.

W10.3 Advice

Mistakes to Avoid in Introductions

A strong introduction will typically avoid pitfalls like the following:

1. Don't repeat the language of the assignment ("In this five-hundred-word essay discussing the causes of . . .").
2. Don't make an announcement ("In this essay, I will prove . . .").
3. Don't apologize by saying something like "Even though I am not an expert . . ."
4. Don't be overly chatty or informal, especially in academic writing ("I'll bet you've never heard of . . .").
5. Don't include information everyone—especially your instructor—already knows ("The Declaration of Independence was signed on July 4, 1776").
6. Don't include a dictionary definition ("According to *Webster's New World Dictionary* . . .").

W10.4 Writing

Writing Introductions

Write an introduction for one of the following essay topics:

1. an article to be published in your local newspaper proposing ways to make it safer for bicyclists on public roads
2. an essay for a class in nursing or another health field in which you propose a change in the way nurses or other health care workers are educated
3. an article for next year's students explaining a good strategy for making a course schedule
4. an essay explaining to students who don't have a disability some principles of non-ableist language
5. an essay for a business or sociology course discussing tipping practices in the United States

Keep in mind the advice in W10.2, Strategies for Effective Introductions (p. 189), and W10.3, Mistakes to Avoid in Introductions, as well as the audience you are writing for.

Writing the Conclusion

To choose the most effective strategy for your conclusion, remember your audience and purpose. (See W2.4, Thinking about Audience, p. 13, and W2.6, Thinking about Purpose, p. 16.)

W10.5 Advice

Strategies for Effective Conclusions

In your essay's conclusion, you want to wrap things up in a memorable and engaging way. In most essays, you will want to restate your thesis in fresh language. In longer essays, you may want to remind readers of your main supporting points (this isn't usually necessary in briefer essays). You may also want to use one or more of these strategies:

- **Remind readers of why your thesis is important or relevant.** "If we don't make this change . . ."

- **Close with a witty, funny, or moving anecdote or example that reinforces your thesis.** "If we make this change, the young girl I described in the opening paragraph, and many other young girls, will have a chance at a fulfilling life." If you began with an anecdote or example in your introduction, you may want to refer back to it in your conclusion.

- **Remind readers of a powerful or surprising fact or statistic you have presented.** "Remember that almost everyone, sooner or later, will be physically disabled or will be taking care of someone who is."

- **End with a powerful quotation.** "We must act now because, as UN Secretary General Nan Ki-Moon said, 'There is no Planet B.'" If you began your essay with a quotation, you will probably want to refer back to it in your conclusion.

- **Urge readers to take action.** "If you want to support those affected by this devastating hurricane, make as large a donation as you can afford to the American Red Cross . . . today."

W10.6 Advice

Mistakes to Avoid in Conclusions

A strong conclusion will typically avoid pitfalls like the following:

1. Don't introduce a major new reason or a new piece of supporting evidence.
2. Don't make an announcement ("In this essay, I have shown . . .").

3. Don't include an overused and obvious phrase like "In conclusion . . ." or "As I have shown . . ."

4. Don't apologize by saying something like "Even though I am not an expert . . ."

5. Don't restate your thesis in the same words or phrases you used previously. Instead, make the same point using wording that is fresh and memorable.

W10.7 Writing
Writing Conclusions

Write a conclusion for one of the essay topics listed below. (It's okay to select the same topic you chose for W10.4, Writing Introductions, p. 191.)

1. an article to be published in your local newspaper proposing ways to make it safer for bicyclists on public roads

2. an essay for a class in nursing or another health field in which you propose a change in the way nurses or other health care workers are educated

3. an article for next year's students explaining a good strategy for making a course schedule

4. an essay explaining to students who don't have a disability some principles of non-ableist language

5. an essay for a business or sociology course discussing tipping practices in the United States

Keep in mind the advice in W10.5, Strategies for Effective Conclusions (p. 192), and W10.6, Mistakes to Avoid in Conclusions (p. 192), as well as the audience you are writing for.

Coming Up with a Title

The first thing a reader sees in your essay is the title, so it's important. But coming up with one is probably best left to the end of the writing of the essay. At that point, you'll have a clear idea of what the essay is about and what you want to bring to the reader's attention in the title.

In coming up with a title, as with everything else you write in an essay, you want to think about the audience you are writing for and your purpose for writing.

(For more information about audience and purpose, see W2.4, Thinking about Audience, p. 13, and W2.6, Thinking about Purpose, p. 16.)

W10.8 Advice

Strategies for Effective Titles

An effective title should convey your topic and give your readers an idea of your position, or *take*, on your topic. Start by asking yourself, "What will be most effective with my reader? How can I best convey the gist of my paper and indicate my purpose?"

In college writing, readers are, in most cases, instructors who are already interested in the topic. They want to see if you understand the topic and can write something thoughtful about it, so they are unlikely to appreciate cutesy titles. In fact, in most college writing, titles tend to be direct and stick to conveying the writer's topic and position toward that topic.

Outside of college, readers are more varied, and an effective title may need to entice your reader, so you could try one of these options:

- **Include a brief quotation.** For a bicycling blog, a title like this might grab readers' attention:

  "Cyclist Fatalities on the Roads Have Increased Almost Every Year Since 2010": How We Can Do Better?

- **Use alliteration (repeating the beginning sounds of words)**

  Scientific Cycling: Maximizing the Benefits of Bike Share Programs on Campus

- **Use parallelism**

  Sensible Class Schedules: Balancing Your Needs, Your Wants, and Your Life

- **Include a play on words**

  At the Tipping Point: The Need for a Fairer Wage for Waitstaff

- **Ask a question**

  Does Nursing Education Prepare Us for Today's Jobs?

W10.9 Advice

Mistakes to Avoid in Titles

An effective title will avoid pitfalls like the following:

1. Avoid cutesy titles, especially in papers for college courses.
2. Don't suggest more in your title than your paper covers.
3. Don't use language from the assignment.
4. Avoid lengthy titles: in academic contexts, you may need a long title to convey your main point, but in other contexts, shorter is usually better.

W10.10 Exploration

Writing Titles

Working individually or in your group (your instructor will tell you which), write at least three titles for one of the essay options below.

1. an article to be published in your local newspaper proposing ways to make it safer for bicyclists on public roads
2. an essay for a class in nursing or another health field in which you propose a change in the way nurses or other health care workers are educated
3. an article for next year's students explaining a good strategy for making a course schedule
4. an essay explaining to students who don't have a disability some principles of non-ableist language
5. an essay for a business or sociology course discussing tipping practices in the United States

Keep in mind the advice in W10.8, Strategies for Effective Titles (p. 194), and W10.9, Mistakes to Avoid in Titles, as well as the audience you are writing for.

W11 ▶ Writing Strategies

The strategies discussed in W11 are useful in many different writing situations—essay assignments, reports, summaries, fiction and nonfiction writing, book and movie reviews, lab reports, and more—but the focus here is on writing college essays. Writers will sometimes write essays that use a single one of these types of writing: an elaborate extended definition might be a three- or four-page essay, for example, or an explanation of the multiple causes of a complex event like the January 6, 2021, attack on the Capitol could easily be an essay all by itself. More commonly, however, although an essay or article may have one overall organizing principle, such as argument, cause and effect, or classification, it will also include several other strategies in order to present information effectively. For example, after an introductory paragraph in a proposal, a writer might define several key words, narrate an example or anecdote illustrating the problem, and compare two possible solutions. This weaving back and forth among various writing strategies can produce a sophisticated argument that convincingly presents and supports its position.

Argument

In this section on argument, two approaches will be considered. The first—classical argument—originated in ancient Greece and aims to win the reader over to the writer's position. The second—Rogerian argument—is much more recent. Psychologist Carl Rogers developed the underlying concept in the 1950s, and University of Michigan professors Richard Young, Alton Becker, and Kenneth Pike popularized it in the 1970s and 1980s. Rogerian argument aims to find common ground with those who hold alternative views.

W11.1 Advice

What Is an Argument?

An argument—whether classical or Rogerian—is a piece of writing that takes a position on an issue and provides evidence to support that position. In fact, it is sometimes suggested that all writing is argument.

In college courses, argument essays are typically three or four pages long, but they can sometimes be much longer, especially if they involve significant research. They can also be much shorter: an argument could be as short as a single paragraph. The crucial factor is that an argument takes a position on an issue.

W11.2 Advice

Classical Argument

Despite being thousands of years old, classical argument is still the most common form. The five parts of a classical argument are described below.

1. **Introduction: Interest and ethos.** In a classical argument, the introduction (one or more paragraphs) usually seeks to gain the reader's attention and make the writer's qualifications clear. It also establishes common ground with the reader and demonstrates the fairness and reasonableness of the writer. Finally, it usually includes the thesis statement, although sometimes writers withhold the thesis statement until later in the paper. (See W3.8, Where Should the Thesis Be Located?, p. 32.)

2. **Background and context.** Here the writer provides any information that will help the reader understand the context in which the argument is situated. This might include history of the topic, research that has taken place, definitions of key terms (see W11.22, Strategies for Writing Simple Definitions, p. 226, and W11.24, Strategies for Writing Extended Definitions, p. 229), and even relevant personal stories (see W11.14, Strategies for Writing Narratives, p. 212).

3. **Reasons and evidence.** This section of the argument presents reasons to support the thesis and evidence to support those reasons. The reasons should be logical and relevant to the argument. The evidence could include facts, data, examples, quotations from experts, and narration. (See W4.2, Types of Evidence, p. 42.) This section may also make appeals to the reasoning, ethics, and emotions of the audience. (See W11.4, Three Types of Appeal: *Logos*, *Ethos*, and *Pathos*, p. 198.)

4. **Response to alternative arguments.** In this section, the writer demonstrates awareness of alternative arguments, presenting them in a fair way and then refuting them with reasoning and evidence. Alternatively, the writer might acknowledge the positive results an opposing argument might produce but then show that their position will produce even greater positive results. (See W11.6, Responses to Positions Different from Yours, p. 203.)

5. **Summary and call to action.** In the concluding section, the writer usually summarizes the main points of the argument, emphasizes the importance of what is proposed, and urges the reader to take action.

W11.3 Advice

Rogerian Argument

W11.2 (p. 197) focused on classical argument in which the goal is to convince the audience to accept the writer's point of view, position, or proposed policy—in other words, to "win." Psychologist Carl Rogers proposed an alternative: perhaps arguments would be more fruitful if, rather than seeing arguments as having winners and losers, participants in arguments searched for a "both/and" position, so that all parties to the argument would benefit.

A Rogerian argument has four parts, all of which help to achieve a win/win solution:

1. **Introduction: Background and context.** The writer describes a problem or issue in enough detail to show understanding of and respect for alternative points of view.

2. **Alternative position(s).** The writer recognizes contexts in which alternative positions could be valid.

3. **Writer's position.** The writer presents the preferred position and explains the contexts in which that position could be valid.

4. **Conclusion.** The writer concludes by suggesting a middle ground on which writer and those who hold other views might agree or suggests how the reader would benefit by moving toward the writer's position.

In most academic and business writing, the classical form of argument is expected, but when thinking about your audience, you may identify situations—conflicts—in which it's important to get people from opposing sides of an issue to better understand each other's positions and, perhaps, find some common ground. In those circumstances, the Rogerian form of argument would be more effective.

W11.4 Advice

Three Types of Appeal: *Logos*, *Ethos*, and *Pathos*

As long ago as the fourth century BCE, the Greek philosopher Aristotle identified three strategies for argument—usually called *appeals*—that he called *logos*, *ethos*, and *pathos*. Think about a politician *appealing* for your vote or a nonprofit *appealing* for donations. In this sense, *to appeal* is to attempt to persuade by adopting a strategy likely to succeed with the audience.

- *Logos.* Arguments based on *logos* appeal to the head. They are based on evidence, reasoning, and logic. In fact, the English word *logic* is derived from *logos*. Arguments based on *logos* often make use of facts, quotations from experts, statistics, survey and poll results, interviews, and charts and graphs. Usually these kinds of factual evidence are tied together by sound reasoning, which can explain the causes, the results, the benefits, or the side effects of the factual evidence.

- **Ethos.** Arguments based on *ethos* have the goal of winning the reader's confidence in the writer. To accomplish this, writers include information that establishes their credibility or expertise by mentioning their credentials, awards they have won, or honors they have received. They also make clear the values and beliefs that underlie their arguments. Another way of gaining the reader's confidence is to write in a way that is clearly fair, a way that avoids mean-spirited personal attacks or distortions of the truth, and that recognizes that it is possible for reasonable people to disagree about an issue.

- **Pathos.** Arguments based on *pathos* appeal to the readers' feelings, to their hearts. Frequently, writers appeal to their readers' hearts by telling a story, especially a moving one, for example, about a young woman who overcomes her fears to climb Mt. McKinley, a high school dropout who founds a successful software company, or an orphan who spends ten fruitless years searching for her parents only to have her birth mother show up on her front porch one day.

Any one of these appeals, if relied on too heavily, may lose its effectiveness: An avalanche of factual evidence can sometimes overwhelm or bore readers. Spending too much time proclaiming one's honors and commitment to values may come across as bragging. Readers may be alienated by emotional appeals that seem manipulative or hokey. The most effective writing combines all three types of appeal—logical, ethical, and emotional—choosing the details that will most appeal to the audience.

The following essay, written by Kevin Turner (an older student), skillfully weaves all three appeals together to make his point.

W11.5 Advice

A Student's Argument Essay

Gifted and Talented Programs: More Harm Than Good?

KEVIN TURNER

1   My granddaughter called me a couple of years ago with big news. "I've been selected for gifted and talented," she announced with excitement and

joy in her voice. I shared her joy; I was elated to hear how excited she was as she got ready for the sixth grade. But I also felt a contradictory emotion: I felt guilty for feeling such elation. I had for years had serious reservations about gifted and talented programs and any other programs that separate kids according to our perceptions of their abilities.

2   I want to be clear. There are good arguments on both sides of this issue. Those who support "gifted and talented" programs have some powerful reasons for their support.

3   Some point out, for example, that our society needs to provide challenging curricula to the most talented students, those who will grow up to lead the country, to discover new treatments for diseases, and to produce art and music that challenge our souls. In a gifted and talented program, these students can be challenged to think more deeply and more creatively. They can experience the thrill of learning concepts they never thought they could understand. They can hone their thinking, writing, and speaking skills as they challenge and are challenged by other top students. Our nation will benefit in the future from the "gifts" and "talents" of these students.

4   A second argument for "gifted and talented" programs is that bright students, like my granddaughter, are too often bored in traditional classrooms with a range of students from those struggling to understand the material to those ready for more challenging material. A conscientious teacher will usually "teach to the middle," which means those students at the "top" will seldom be challenged and will frequently be bored. It was disheartening when my granddaughter told me one summer that she hated reading because the books she was assigned in school were too easy.

Kevin begins his essay with an appeal to the reader's feelings by discussing his own feelings (*pathos*).

In this paragraph, he tries to win the reader's confidence by demonstrating he understands both sides of the argument (*ethos*).

Using reasoning, here Kevin argues that students will benefit from these programs and so will the nation (*logos*).

Again, an appeal to logic or reasoning (*logos*).

5   My daughter was overcome with joy and pride that her daughter would be in the "gifted and talented" program. She, like most parents, wants what's best for her child. I understand that and love seeing her excitement about her daughter's success. So, I have tried, unsuccessfully so far, to explain to her why I have such reservations about the program.

In this paragraph, the author combines an appeal to feelings (joy and pride) with more effort showing he is being fair (*pathos* and *ethos*).

6   I point out that our system for identifying these bright students is seriously flawed. A multiple-choice test of arithmetic skills or reading comprehension doesn't measure a student's "gifts" or "talents." It, more likely, measures the child's socioeconomic background. Those who grow up in families struggling with poverty are less likely to have access to books. Those whose single mothers have to work two jobs are less likely to have had the experience of learning to add and subtract at home. When they are tested for entrance to a selective program, sometimes as early as the age of four or five, the test will favor children from more affluent homes.

Here Kevin uses logic to argue that the system for judging students is unfair (*logos*).

7   This bias is exacerbated in many large cities where wealthier parents are paying for tutoring services to make sure their children get into "gifted and talented" kindergartens. According to Leslie Brody, writing in *The Wall Street Journal,* a tutorial service in New York "charges $100 to $400 an hour for private sessions" and clients can receive "15 to 40 hours of tutoring over four to six months," resulting in fees of thousands of dollars (Brody).

In this paragraph, he is using facts combined with reasoning (*logos*).

8   Because the testing system favors children from more affluent families, the demographics of the students who qualify for "gifted and talented" kindergarten in New York City are heavily skewed against Black and Latinx students. According to "Making the Grade II," a 2019 report by the

New York School Diversity Advisory Group, Latinx children made up 41% of all kindergartners in New York City in 2018, but were only 10% of the students judged to be qualified for the "gifted and talented" programs. Black children were 24% of all kindergartners but only 8% of those who qualified for "gifted and talented" kindergarten (26).

More facts and logic to argue that there is racial bias in gifted and talented programs (logos).

9   To me, the most compelling reason to oppose "gifted and talented" programs is that they undermine the American Dream, the idea that in this country everyone who is willing to work hard can achieve success. The state of that dream can be seen in the enormous gap between the wealthy and the rest of us. In 2019, a report by the Federal Reserve Board entitled "Introducing the Distributional Financial Accounts of the United States" presented shocking statistics about the wealth gap in the United States. "In 2018," according to the Fed's report, "the top 10% of U.S. households controlled 70 percent of total household wealth, up from 60 percent in 1989." The report also notes that "the bottom 50% of the wealth distribution experienced . . . a fall in total wealth share from 4 percent in 1989 to just 1 percent in 2018" (Batty et al. 26). Not only has there been a large gap between the wealth of the top 10% and everyone else, but that gap is growing wider.

More facts and logic to argue that gifted and talented programs exacerbate the wealth gap and undermine the American Dream (logos).

10   Many factors contribute to this gap, but it is hard to deny that one factor is programs like "gifted and talented." Whatever gaps exist when four- and five-year-olds arrive in kindergarten are made larger by a system that results in mostly children from affluent backgrounds being placed into a program designed to help them advance faster.

Here he uses reasoning to argue his point (logos).

11   I fully recognize that those who support "gifted and talented" programs have good arguments to support their position. I completely

Again, Kevin assures the reader of his fairness, his recognition of the arguments on the other side (ethos).

understand the pride and joy of parents like my daughter when my granddaughter was accepted into such a program. I don't blame parents for wanting what's best for their children. And I recognize that programs for bright students have produced very talented scientists and entrepreneurs, creative artists and composers, and very productive engineers and architects, all of whom contribute greatly to making America the richest and most powerful nation on Earth. Those are positive results of our educational system, at least partially as a result of programs like "gifted and talented."

12   However, those same programs also contribute to the vast and growing gap between the wealthy and the rest of us in our society. Having to choose between these two goals, I would rather live in a country in which wealth is more evenly distributed, a country in which the American Dream is a reality, even if that country is less rich and less powerful.

Kevin ends with a reasoned explanation of why he comes down where he does on this issue (*logos*).

Works Cited

Batty, Michael M., et al. Introducing the Distributional Financial Accounts of the United States. Mar. 2019, https://www.federalreserve.gov/econres/feds/files/2019017pap.pdf.

Brody, Leslie. "Young, Gifted Students Facing a Gap." *The Wall Street Journal*, 13 Oct. 2015, https://www.wsj.com/articles/young-gifted-and-facing-a-gap-1444783939.

School Diversity Advisory Group. *Making the Grade II: New Programs for Better Schools*, Aug. 2019, https://steinhardt.nyu.edu/sites/default/files/2020-05/Making-the-Grade-II_0.pdf.

W11.6   Advice

Responses to Positions Different from Yours

The audience for your writing may be sympathetic, undecided, or even hostile. Those who already agree with you are easy: Just provide great evidence to support your claims.

To sway the undecided — and make the hostile a little more open to persuasion — think carefully about the values these readers hold, what they are likely to believe about your topic already, and what common ground you share. Use that assessment to help you figure out what reasons they might accept, and what evidence they might find convincing. Finally, consider what arguments they have already heard and been persuaded by, and what you can say to undermine their attachment to those positions.

It is sometimes tempting to simply ignore the positions that are different from yours. Why even bring them up? Here's the problem with that strategy. If you ignore them, your readers may conclude either you are not well informed or you are biased and not fair-minded. Ignoring positions different from yours will make your writing less effective.

The first step toward making an effective response is to develop a list of arguments that those who hold different positions from yours might offer. You can develop a list of opposing positions in three ways:

1. Conduct good research, which will probably unearth some of these arguments.

2. Talk to people who disagree with your position and listen carefully, thoughtfully, and empathetically to the arguments they make.

3. Imagine yourself in an argument with those who hold a different position from yours. What claims would they make?

Once you have identified the claims your opponents would make, respond to them, using any one of several strategies:

- Challenge the authenticity of the evidence, the data supporting the opposing view, if you have reason to suspect it is inaccurate or untrue.

- Produce evidence supporting your position that is stronger than the evidence supporting the opposing view.

- Challenge the interpretation of evidence and explain how yours better fits the facts.

- Critique the expertise of people holding the other view if there is evidence that they are not reliable, truthful, or experts in the field.

- Point out that the negative consequences that will result from the opposing position outweigh any positive results.

- If an opposing point cannot be refuted, concede it and argue that your other points far outweigh that one opposing point.

W11.7 Writing
Responding to Positions Different from Yours

The reasons for refuting alternative positions and strategies for doing so are discussed in W11.6, Responses to Positions Different from Yours (p. 203). Your instructor will assign this activity as part of the process of writing one of the essays that conclude each reading/writing project in Part P of *The Hub*.

Assignment. Write a short paper—less than a page—in which you state several of the positions that those who disagree with you might take. For each of these positions, explain how you would respond using the strategies listed in W11.6.

Proposals

In school, in your neighborhood, or in your workplace, if you want to innovate, to correct injustices, to improve efficiency, or, generally, to make things better, you need to be able to write an effective proposal.

W11.8 Advice
Strategies for Writing Proposals

Proposals are a kind of argument. They define a problem and argue for a solution to that problem. You could write a proposal to do any of the following:

- Convince your English teacher to give more time for revising essays.
- Prompt your local government to provide more lighting in your neighborhood.
- Convince your workplace to provide more employee parking.
- Persuade the federal government to improve the FAFSA application.

    A proposal has two essential components:

1. **Statement of the problem.** A proposal must clearly identify the problem you are addressing and present evidence to support the idea that it is a problem. You might give examples of how the problem has affected people or even how it could affect the audience you are writing for.
2. **Proposed solution.** A proposal must clearly describe your proposed solution. What is it? Who would have to do it? How much would it cost? How would it work?

Just identifying a problem and presenting a solution, though, is unlikely to convince your audience. Like other types of argument, to be effective, you have to do more:

- **Provide background.** Unless readers are experts, you will probably need to provide an overview of the problem's history—how and when it started, what its causes are, what attempts have been made to address it in the past and with what results. Is it getting worse? Sometimes this background information works best at the beginning of the proposal, but more often, it is more effective after you've explained what the problem is.

- **Show feasibility.** Once you've clearly explained your solution to the problem, you need to present evidence that it is feasible, that it is a realistic proposal to solve the problem (or at least reduce its severity) on time and within budget.

- **Address possible objections to your solution.** As with any type of argument, you will have greater success persuading readers if you show that you understand the concerns of those who hold alternative views and have considered other possible solutions. If people are worried about the cost, show how costs can be contained or explain that the costs of doing nothing will be greater. If others are likely to argue that your solution has already been tried and found to be ineffective, explain how the situation has changed or how implementation has been improved. If other solutions have been proposed, show that they won't work or won't work as well as your solution or that they will have more harmful side effects than your solution will have.

- **Urge action.** Close your proposal by urging readers to take specific actions. (You may want to review W11.6, Responses to Positions Different from Yours, p. 203.)

W11.9 Advice

A Student's Proposal

A Proposal to Substitute a Discussion Board for the Chat Room

LASHAWNA WILLIAMS

1   Dear Professor Jenkins, I want to bring to your attention a problem that is causing many students great difficulty. Your requirement that we join a chat room online for an hour every Sunday afternoon at 5:00 is having consequences you may not be aware of.

Clear statement of the problem

2   Many of us work on weekends to support our going to school. I am a cook at a restaurant on Saturdays and Sundays. I have to arrive by 3:00 to begin my prep work for dinner. I try to access your chat room on my cell phone at 5:00, but often we are simply too busy. I know that four of my classmates are having similar conflicts with their Sunday jobs.

Examples of how the problem is causing harm

3   While I can use my cell phone to access the chat room, three of my classmates that I know of don't own cell phones and, of course, don't own computers. They depend on computers in the writing center or in the library to access your website. The problem is that the library and writing center are not open on Sundays.

4   When we registered for your class, the schedule indicated the class meets on Monday, Wednesday, and Friday from 10:15 to 11:05. We built our class schedules and our work schedules around these times. Now we learn that we also are required to participate in the class chat room every Sunday afternoon, creating considerable hardship.

Background information about the problem

5   I would like to propose a solution to this problem which will still allow you to interact with us and read our thoughts about the readings in the course online, but will not cause the hardships for many of us that the Sunday afternoon chat room is causing. I propose that, instead of the chat room at a certain hour on Sundays, you establish a discussion board that we are required to post to at least six times each week.

Clear statement of the solution

6   There is a discussion board available in Blackboard, so there is no expense to the college, to you, or to the students. We could have the same kind of conversations you are calling for in the chat room, but there would not be a specific time we had to join the conversation. Just like with a chat room, you will be able to monitor the conversation, ask

Evidence the solution is feasible and will address the problem

us questions, clear up misunderstandings, and evaluate our performance. Last semester, I was in a class that required us to participate in a discussion board, and it was quite successful. There was much more participation by the class than we are getting in the chat room.

7 I know that you have announced that if we miss three chat room conversations, we can write an extra essay and be graded on that. This, however, is not nearly as good a solution as the discussion board I am proposing. First, it feels more like punishment than participation. Second, it means we do not benefit from the experience of being part of a discussion.

Argument that the proposed solution is superior to an alternative solution

8 I urge you to announce at our next class meeting that we are switching to the discussion board format instead of the Sunday chat room.

Strong argument for immediate action

Thanks for considering my proposal,
LaShawna Williams

W11.10 Writing

Making a Proposal to Solve a Problem

Think of a problem at your school, at your workplace, or in your town or city. Then think of a solution to that problem. Finally, think of the person to whom you could write to propose a solution. Address your proposal to that person. One or two pages for your proposal should be plenty, but if you need more space to make your case, a longer paper is fine too. (Refer to W11.8, Strategies for Writing Proposals, p. 205, for advice about how to write a successful proposal.)

Description and Observation

Writers use description to provide readers with a vivid picture of a person, place, or thing. Description is an important element of observations, writing assignments that ask you to provide a detailed description of an event, room, person, place, or performance. This section starts with a discussion of writing basic descriptions and then discusses how you can use descriptive writing in an observation.

W11.11 Advice
Strategies for Writing Descriptions

When writing descriptions, provide concrete details that appeal to the senses—how something looks, sounds, smells, feels, moves. (See W6.7, Using Concrete Language to Bring Writing to Life, p. 77.) Descriptions are usually easier for readers to process if they are organized in a logical order—for example, from bottom to top, left to right, or near to far. (See W5.10, Strategies for Creating Coherence, p. 65, for a discussion and examples of types of logical organization.)

The following is a well-written description of a character in the novel *The Magician's Assistant* by Ann Patchett.

> Mr. Howard Plate was big like his sons, with hair that might have been red when he was their age and now was that colorless sandy brown that red hair can become. But it was his face that drew attention, the way it was fine on one side and collapsed on the other, as if he had been hit very hard and the shape of the fist in question was still lodged beneath his left eye. It had the quality of something distinctly broken and poorly repaired. The bad light cast by the living room lamps threw a shadow into the cave of his cheek, where a random interlacing of scars ended and began. (pp. 205–206)

W11.12 Advice
Strategies for Writing Observations

Many writing assignments, whether for school or work, call for observation, a detailed description of something—an event, a room, a person, a place, or a performance. Observational writing can be useful in many situations, as shown in these examples:

1. An organization you belong to has asked you to visit a room to see if it is appropriate for a guest speaker your group has invited to give a lecture.
2. You and your neighbors have become concerned about a dangerous intersection and want to propose to your local government that steps be taken to make it safer.

3. As a nurse, you need to write reports detailing patients' appearances, including vital statistics (such as pulse rate and blood pressure) but also changes to appearance (such as a flushed complexion or swelling of the legs and ankles).

Each of these situations calls for a written document, perhaps a proposal or a report, and that document will include some description.

Here are some guidelines for writing a useful, focused observation.

1. **Make decisions before your visits.**   Ask yourself questions like these:
    - What is the purpose of the observation?
    - What kinds of information will be useful for that purpose?
    - How much time will you need for the observation?
    - Will the time of day or the day of the week make a difference in what you will observe?

2. **Arrange your visits.**   Make sure that you schedule them so that they occur at the most significant or typical times.

3. **Take careful notes.**   One good system for doing this is to use a computer file or pad of paper. Create two columns or draw a line down the center of the page. On the left, record the actual details you see, hear, smell, or otherwise observe; on the right, record your thoughts or reactions to those details.

4. **Record clear, concrete details.**   Be sure that your notes include evidence to support the purpose of your observation.

The two paragraphs below are descriptions of a lecture hall that the writer is observing as a possible site for a guest lecture. The highlighting indicates the different focus in each paragraph.

Paragraph 1

The Humanities Lecture Hall seats 175 people in chairs that provide pull-up desks for taking notes. The lights over the seating area can be dimmed leaving the stage brightly lit. The lectern on the stage has a microphone built in and a small light to illuminate the speaker's notes. The room is equipped with a powerful projector and a large screen that are controlled from the lectern.

Paragraph 2

The Humanities Lecture Hall is an attractive room whose walls are covered by beautiful walnut panels. The seats are covered in an attractive red, yellow, and blue material. The American and state flags hang on either side of the stage. The carpeting in the room is a red and yellow pattern which matches the seat coverings.

Both paragraphs contain concrete details, but the details in paragraph 1 will be helpful to the group trying to decide whether to book the lecture hall, while the details in paragraph 2 will not. The writer of paragraph 1 focused on details relevant to the hall as a possible site of a guest lecture: the number of seats with pull-up desks, the quality of the lighting, the presence of a well-equipped lectern, and easy access to a screen and projector. The writer of paragraph 2 seems to have forgotten the purpose of the observation and instead has focused on details of the hall's decoration.

It is important to organize your written observation in a logical fashion. Notice that paragraph 1 is organized spatially, beginning by reporting on the seating area, then moving to the speaker's lectern, and ending with the projection system available to the speaker.

Sometimes, instead of organizing an observation spatially, it will be more useful to organize it temporally—that is, according to time. Paragraph 3 was written as part of a letter urging improvements in the college bookstore's procedures during the first week of classes. Note the highlighted time-related phrases that help organize the observation for the reader.

Paragraph 3

I observed the check-out procedures at the bookstore on the first day of classes this semester, September 3, 2022, from 8:00 in the morning when the bookstore opened to noon. At 8:00, 43 students were in line waiting for the bookstore to open. In the first half hour, I was surprised to see that only two of the four cash registers were available for use. Employees, who I believe could have been staffing the other two registers, were actually unpacking boxes of books and placing them on the shelves. At 9:00, I asked twelve students as they purchased their books how long they had waited to be checked out. All twelve reported they had arrived at the bookstore at 7:30 and had gotten in the check-out line at about 8:15. Each hour for the remainder of the morning, I questioned twelve students about their wait time to be checked out. At 10:00, the bookstore opened the other two cash registers. The twelve students I questioned at that time had been waiting in the check-out line for an hour and a half or more. At 11:00, the twelve students had waited more than two hours. Again, at 12:00, the twelve students had waited more than two hours.

W11.13 Writing

Describing/Observing a Person, Place, Thing, or Event

In a short paper—less than a page is plenty—complete one of the following assignments.

1. **Describe one of the following.**   Be sure to provide plenty of concrete and sensory detail and to organize your description in a logical order.
    - your kitchen
    - your bedroom
    - the place where you work
    - someone in your family
    - your favorite possession

2. **Observe one of the following situations.**   Decide on the best time of day to make your observations and the kinds of information that would be useful to find out in order to achieve the stated purpose.

    - **Situation:**   A family tradition

      Purpose: To determine what makes it successful

    - **Situation:**   Everyday use of cell phones

      Purpose: To assess the impact of cell phones on face-to-face interactions

    - **Situation:**   A live performance you have attended

      Purpose: To determine whether it was a success or a failure

(See W6.7, Using Concrete Language to Bring Writing to Life, p. 77, for more about types of descriptive language, and see W5.10, Strategies for Creating Coherence, p. 65, for examples of types of logical organization.)

Narration

Human beings have been telling stories since the beginning of time. Narration is just a technical name for telling stories, and it is one of the most common and most useful writing strategies. Narration can not only make your writing more interesting, but it can also provide persuasive support for your thesis.

W11.14   Advice

Strategies for Writing Narratives

Normally when we write narration, we organize the content in chronological order—*first this happened, then this*—and so forth. Occasionally, writers may want to vary from this strictly chronological order. For example, a writer might start by telling the end of the story first, and then go back to the beginning to explain how that ending came about.

In college writing, narratives are more commonly part of a larger piece of writing. For example, if you were writing an essay arguing that your city needs to invest in safer bike lanes, your essay would probably contain facts and statistics about safety and the annual number of accidents involving motorists hitting cyclists. However, you might also include a narrative about the time you were badly injured when a car struck you as you were riding across an intersection even though you had the right of way. Narration can be a powerful way to provide support to your thesis. (You might also want to take a look at W11.4, Three Types of Appeal: *Logos*, *Ethos*, and *Pathos*, p. 198.)

In the book *The Immortal Life of Henrietta Lacks*, Rebecca Skloot mixes scientific reporting with the telling of very human stories. Below she narrates the events that occurred when Henrietta Lacks's cancer cells were first delivered to a lab at Johns Hopkins Hospital, where they would start their journey toward playing a major role in medical research. Dr. George Gey is the director of the lab, where he is assisted by his wife Margaret Gey. Mary Kubicek is Gey's twenty-one-year-old assistant.

Excerpt from Chapter 4, "The Birth of Hela"

Mary followed Margaret's sterilizing rules meticulously to avoid her wrath. After finishing her lunch, and before touching Henrietta's sample, Mary covered herself with a clean white gown, surgical cap, and mask, and then walked to her cubicle, one of four airtight rooms George had built by hand in the center of the lab. The cubicles were small, only five feet in any direction, with doors that sealed like a freezer's to prevent contaminated air from getting inside. Mary turned on the sterilizing system and watched from outside as her cubicle filled with hot steam to kill anything that might damage the cells. When the steam cleared, she stepped inside and sealed the door behind her, then hosed the cubicle's cement floor with water and scoured her workbench with alcohol. The air inside was filtered and piped in through a vent on the ceiling. Once she'd sterilized the cubicle, she lit a Bunsen burner and used its flame to sterilize test tubes and a used scalpel blade, since the Gey lab couldn't afford new ones for each sample.

Only then did she pick up the pieces of Henrietta's cervix—forceps in one hand, scalpel in the other—and carefully slice them into one-millimeter squares. She sucked each square into a pipette, and dropped them one at a time onto chicken-blood clots she'd placed at the bottom of dozens of test tubes. She covered each clot with several drops of culture medium, plugged the tubes with rubber stoppers, and labeled each one as she'd labeled most cultures they grew: using the first two letters of the patient's first and last names.

After writing "HeLa," for *Henrietta* and *Lacks*, in big black letters on the side of each tube, Mary carried them to the incubator room that Gey had built just like he'd built everything else in the lab (37–38).

This narrative illustrates many of the features of effective narrative writing.

1. *The author is using narrative to make a point.* By detailing all the steps Mary took to prepare to work with the HeLa cells, Skloot is illustrating the great care taken to sterilize the work space before culturing them and the process involved. Good narrative is usually shaped to convey a particular point of view or the point the writer wants to make.

2. *Skloot uses transitional expressions or time-related phrases throughout to help the reader keep track of the sequence of events (highlighted in blue).* Narratives are usually organized in chronological order — now one event happened, then this, and so on. However, they can jump around, for instance, first telling what is occurring now, and then providing the backstory, what happened before this event.

3. *There is at least one human character with a name, Mary, to provide human interest.* Narratives usually center around one or more people.

4. *The narrative is filled with concrete details (underlined) that help us see the lab and that establish Skloot's expertise as a writer.* She knows the names of things.

Here's another, much briefer, example from a personal narrative about a formative event in the life of Jenée Desmond-Harris, a Black writer, who grew up with her White mother in suburban California. The "private musings" she refers to were her thoughts about where she belonged, with the predominately White cheerleaders or the predominately Black dance team. Thea was her best friend; the rapper who died was Tupac Shakur.

Excerpt from "Tupac and My Non-thug Life" by Jenée Desmond-Harris

My private musings on identity and belonging . . . were interrupted when my mom heard me slam the front door and drop my bags: "*Your friend died!*" she called out from another room. Confused silence. "*You know, that rapper you and Thea love so much!*"

This brief excerpt illustrates two other characteristics often present in narratives:

5. *They sometimes use dialogue to emphasize key events or to depict characters or relationships.* The dialogue in the Desmond-Harris excerpt

effectively conveys a typical parent-teen relationship, while also calling attention to the event that will help Desmond-Harris decide where she belongs.

6. *They usually focus on some kind of underlying tension or conflict, arousing curiosity or suspense and then resolving it.* This brief snippet introduces drama and focuses the story: How will Desmond-Harris and her friend Thea respond to the bombshell that their favorite musical star has just died, and how will that relate to Desmond-Harris's "private musings"?

W11.15 Writing

Narrating an Event

For this assignment, you are going to write a short narrative—a page would be plenty—in which you tell the story of an important event in your life. Don't take on too much—don't try to tell the story of your first *year* in college; pick an event you can narrate in detail in a page. Here are some ideas to give you a jumping-off point.

- the first time you arrived on campus
- the first time you met someone you are now in a relationship with
- a time when you helped someone
- a time when you were really surprised
- a time when you learned a lesson

Be sure your story makes a point, includes many concrete and sensory details to illustrate it, and uses transitional expressions or time-related phrases to organize it. (See W6.7, Using Concrete Language to Bring Writing to Life, p. 77, and W5.10, Strategies for Creating Coherence, p. 65, for discussion and examples of types of logical organization and transitions signaling time.) You may also want to include dialogue or introduce and resolve tension or conflict.

Process

When writers find themselves needing to explain how to do something or how something works, they often use process writing.

W11.16 Advice

Strategies for Process Writing

Process writing is usually organized chronologically: *First*, you do this. *Next* you do that. In process writing, it is important to keep your audience in mind. How much detail do you need to explain the process so your reader will understand it? Can you use technical terms? If so, do you need to provide definitions of them? Are you writing for a general audience or for people already familiar with your subject?

How to Do Something

The following paragraph explains how to chop an onion.

> To chop an onion, you first need a little terminology. The sort of messy end of the onion, where there are hairy strands left from the root, is called the root end. The opposite end is called the stem end. You need to identify this root end of the onion before doing any cutting. Now cut the onion in half making sure your cut passes through the root end, leaving half of the root end on each half. For now, you can set aside one of the two halves. Next, cut away the stem end (not the root end) and then peel away and discard the outer layer or two of the onion. Your next step is to make a series of slices lengthwise, being careful not to slice through the root end. Now make three or four horizontal slices starting at the stem end and stopping before you reach the root end. Finally, make a series of cuts at a 90-degree angle to the horizontal cuts, and watch as the beautiful uniform diced pieces of onion appear.

Of course, many times explaining a process will be clearer if you present it as a numbered list. Illustrations can help as well.

> To chop an onion, you first need a little terminology. The sort of messy end of the onion, where there are hairy strands left from the root, is called the root end. The opposite end is called the stem end. You need to identify this root end of the onion before doing any cutting.
>
> 1. Cut the onion in half making sure your cut passes through the root end, leaving half of the root end on each half. For now, you can set aside one of the two halves.
>
> 2. Cut away the stem end (not the root end) and then peel away and discard the outer layer or two of the onion.

3. Make a series of slices lengthwise, being careful not to slice through the root end (Figure 1).

▲ **Figure 1.** Make a series of lengthwise slices.

4. Make three or four horizontal slices starting at the stem end and stopping before you reach the root end (Figure 2).

5. Make a series of cuts at a 90-degree angle to the horizontal cuts, and watch as the beautiful uniform diced pieces of onion appear (Figure 3).

▲ **Figure 2.** Make 3–4 horizontal slices.

▲ **Figure 3.** Make a series of cuts at a 90-degree angle to the horizontal slices.

How Something Works

While explaining how to do something (as in the example above) is the most common use for process writing, the same chronological organization can be used to explain how something works, as the following paragraph illustrates.

> #### How Impeachment of the President Works
>
> The impeachment process begins in the House of Representatives, when any member files charges. These charges are forwarded to the Judiciary Committee, which investigates, usually by holding hearings and interviewing witnesses. If a majority of the committee agrees, Articles of Impeachment are submitted to the full House for consideration. If a simple majority of those present and voting agrees, the House appoints managers to present the impeachment charges to the Senate. The Senate conducts a trial based on the impeachment charges. In the case of presidential impeachment, the Chief Justice of the Supreme Court presides. Conviction by the Senate requires a two-thirds vote by those present and may result in removal from office.

W11.17 Writing

Explaining a Process or How Something Works

Write a short paper—about a page—in which you either explain a process for doing something or explain how something works. You can come up with your own topic or use one of the topics listed below.

Explaining a Process

1. how to upload a document to your Learning Management System (such as Blackboard, Moodle, or Canvas)
2. how to stream a movie
3. how to use an application like Google Maps or Waze to find directions
4. how to request an incomplete grade for a course

Explaining How Something Works

1. how a constitutional amendment is passed
2. how a product is recalled
3. how the Most Valuable Player is selected for the American or National Baseball League
4. how the winner of the Nobel Peace Prize is selected

Comparison and/or Contrast

Writers often compare and/or contrast people, places, or ideas in order to point out similarities or differences.

W11.18 Advice

Strategies for Writing Comparison and/or Contrast

When you *compare*, you discuss similarities; when you *contrast*, you focus on differences. It is often useful to compare or contrast buildings, cities, proposals, ideas, even people. For instance, if you were recommending which of two job candidates should be hired, your recommendation could be based on comparing their qualifications and work experiences. If you were trying to explain why two approaches to the same problem produced such different results, it might be useful to contrast the methods and research involved in designing each. (Although comparing or contrasting two items can be very useful, comparing or contrasting more than two is, of course, also perfectly valid, but more difficult.)

While you may focus on similarities or differences, you will often need to discuss both similarities *and* differences. For example, if you were trying to explain why patients should receive quite different treatments for apparently similar illnesses, you might compare and contrast their symptoms, physical conditions, and histories, as well as the possible treatment options. Whether focusing on similarities or differences or both, be sure to discuss all the points of similarity or difference for all subjects, paying equal attention to each.

Two commonly used ways of organizing comparison and/or contrast writing are point by point and subject by subject.

Point-by-Point Method

Read the following paragraph in which journalist Timothy Noah compares two writers who had a profound influence on how Americans view opportunity and upward mobility.

The writers were Horatio Alger Jr. and James Truslow Adams. Alger wrote *Ragged Dick* (1868), *Luck and Pluck* (1869), and other dime novels for boys about getting ahead through virtue and hard work. To call these books popular would be an understatement: fully 5 percent of all the books checked out of the Muncie, Indiana, public library between November 1891 and December 1902 were authored by Alger. Adams was a more cerebral fellow who wrote books of American history, one of which (*The Epic of America*, 1931) introduced the phrase "the American dream" to our national discourse. Writing at the start of the Great Depression, Adams envisioned not "a dream of motor cars and high wages merely," but rather "a dream of a social order in which each man and each woman shall be able to attain to the fullest stature of which they are innately capable, and be recognized by others for what they are, regardless of the fortuitous circumstances of birth or position." Born a half century apart, neither Alger nor Adams could claim to have risen from the bottom. Both were born into well-established families whose American roots dated to the early seventeenth century. Alger could trace his lineage to three Pilgrims who in 1621 sailed to Plymouth Plantation on the *Fortune*, the second English ship to arrive there. Adams—no relation to the presidential Adamses—was descended from a man who arrived in Maryland in 1638 as an indentured servant and within three years possessed 185 acres. Alger's father was a Unitarian minister, Adams's a stockbroker. Both fathers were men of good breeding and education who struggled to make ends meet but were able—at a time when well over 90 percent of the population didn't finish high school—to obtain higher education for their sons. Alger went to Harvard, and Adams went to Brooklyn Polytechnic and, briefly, Yale. Both sons initially followed their fathers into the ministry and finance, respectively, before becoming full-time writers.

To understand the point-by-point method, let's analyze how Noah's paragraph is organized.

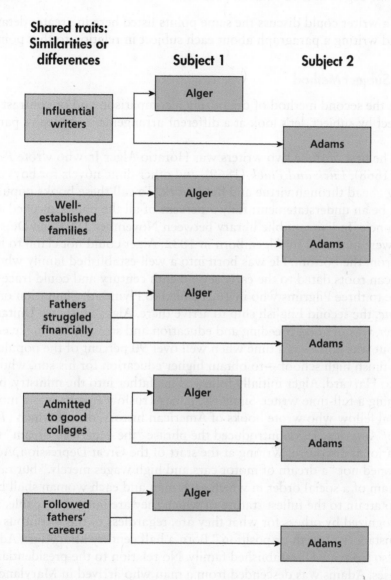

Noah basically tells us that there are five ways that the lives of Horatio Alger and James Adams were similar. He then addresses each point for both subjects:

1. Both Alger and Adams were influential writers.
2. Both came from well-established families.
3. Both had well-educated fathers who struggled financially.

4. Both fathers gave their sons a good education.

5. Both sons began in their fathers' professions but later became writers.

In an essay, a writer could discuss the same points listed here in greater detail, taking each one and writing a paragraph about each subject in relation to that point.

Subject-by-Subject Method

To illustrate the second method of organizing a comparison and/or contrast paragraph, subject by subject, let's look at a different arrangement of Noah's paragraph.

> The first of these two writers was Horatio Alger Jr. who wrote *Ragged Dick* (1868), *Luck and Pluck* (1869), and other dime novels for boys about getting ahead through virtue and hard work. To call these books popular would be an understatement: fully 5 percent of all the books checked out of the Muncie, Indiana, public library between November 1891 and December 1902 were authored by Alger. Born in 1832, Alger could not claim to have risen from the bottom. He was born into a well-established family whose American roots dated to the early seventeenth century and could trace his lineage to three Pilgrims who in 1621 sailed to Plymouth Plantation on the *Fortune*, the second English ship to arrive there. Alger's father, a Unitarian minister, was of good breeding and education and struggled to make ends meet but was able—at a time when well over 90 percent of the population didn't finish high school—to obtain higher education for his son, who went to Harvard. Alger initially followed his father into the ministry, before becoming a full-time writer. Similarly, James Truslow Adams was a more cerebral fellow who wrote books of American history, one of which (*The Epic of America*, 1931) introduced the phrase "the American dream" to our national discourse. Writing at the start of the Great Depression, Adams envisioned not "a dream of motor cars and high wages merely," but rather "a dream of a social order in which each man and each woman shall be able to attain to the fullest stature of which they are innately capable, and be recognized by others for what they are, regardless of the fortuitous circumstances of birth or position." Born a half century after Alger, Adams was also from a well-established family. No relation to the presidential Adamses, Adams was descended from a man who arrived in Maryland in 1638 as an indentured servant and within three years possessed 185 acres. Adams's father was a stockbroker who, like Alger's father, struggled financially but was nevertheless able to provide higher education for his son. Adams went to Brooklyn Polytechnic and, briefly, Yale. He initially followed his father into finance but then became a full-time writer.

This way of organizing comparison and/or contrast first makes all five points about Alger and then shows how each of the five points applies equally to Adams.

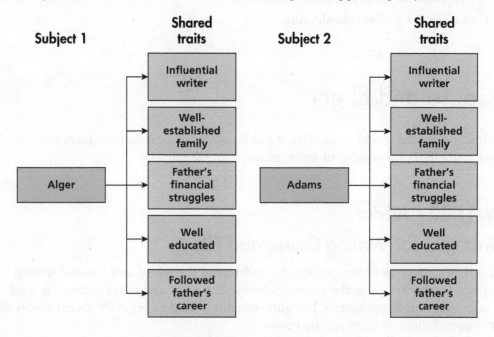

In an essay, a writer could take several paragraphs to discuss the points about Alger and several more to discuss the same points, in the same order, about Adams. He might add paragraphs between the two discussions and again after them, analyzing what the writer learned about the similarities between the two subjects and the conclusions he reached about them.

W11.19 Writing
Comparing and/or Contrasting Two Items

Write a short paper—no more than a page—in which you compare and/or contrast two items. You can either use one of the ideas from the list below or come up with your own.

Once you make your choice, you might do a little brainstorming to see how many points of similarity or difference you can come up with. This should help you decide whether you want to compare, contrast, or both.

- two places you have lived
- two candidates for political office

- the cuisine of two cultures
- two vacation spots you have visited
- two careers you are considering

Cause and Effect

To understand the world around us, it can be useful to explore the causes (or *reasons*) and effects (or *results*) of an event or phenomenon.

W11.20 Advice

Strategies for Writing Cause and Effect

Causal analysis is an important way to understand the world and a useful writing strategy. Sometimes, as in the examples below, the cause and effect strategy is used to organize a single paragraph, but quite often it is used to organize longer pieces of writing, including, at times, entire essays.

Causes and effects occur in many combinations.

- One cause can lead to a single effect.
- One cause can lead to multiple effects.
- Multiple causes can lead to a single effect.
- Multiple causes can have multiple effects.
- A causal chain can occur (a cause can have an effect, which in turn can cause another effect, and so on).

The following paragraph asserts that three causes resulted in one effect, that the candidate lost the election. The diagram that appears after the paragraph represents how the effect was the result of three different causes.

> My candidate for Congress lost the election even though everyone thought she would win. Now that the race is over, we can see that she assumed she would have strong support in the city, so she didn't really campaign very hard there; she ended up losing the city vote by 8 percent. She also didn't start fundraising until two months before the primary, so she couldn't buy as much TV time as her opponent did. In addition, her decision to support restrictions on fertilizer use cost her heavily among rural voters.

This graphic depicts how the paragraph is organized:

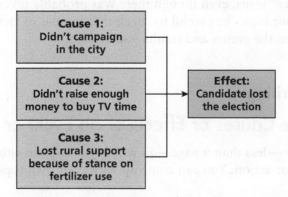

Now let's look at a paragraph that analyzes the effects of a single cause.

> The company where I work has decided to allow its employees to work on hybrid work schedules, meaning we can work from home several days a week. This hybrid scheduling has greatly improved employee morale. In addition, people are not constantly leaving the company for a different job the way they were before flextime. The number of applications for job openings has also doubled. Most important to management, productivity is up 18 percent over a year ago.

In this example, one cause, allowing flextime, resulted in four positive effects:

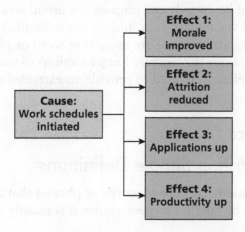

One word of caution: You should not assert that a cause-and-effect relationship exists when you are not sure that an event, or series of events, has resulted in a particular effect or effects. For example, you wore your "lucky" jeans to school today and you got an A on a test. You may be tempted to argue that your A on the test was caused by the "lucky" jeans, even though there was probably no connection. So, as you think about your topic, be careful to check that there is in fact a direct causal relationship between the events and results you discuss.

W11.21 Writing

Explaining the Causes or Effects of an Event or Action

Write a short paper—less than a page—in which you explain either the causes or effects of an event or action. You can come up with your own topic or use one of those listed below.

- a decision you made about your education
- a difficult choice you had to make
- a time someone helped you in a significant way
- a mistake you made
- a time you experienced bad luck

Definition

Providing definitions of key words and phrases is a useful writing strategy, especially when using specialized vocabulary your audience is unfamiliar with. It will ensure that the reader understands how you are using that word or phrase. It is also possible to use the definition strategy to structure longer sections of text. In fact, sometimes an entire essay can be effectively used to provide an extended definition.

W11.22 Advice

Strategies for Writing Simple Definitions

If you write an essay that makes use of words or phrases that are important to your argument but may not be familiar to your reader, it is usually a good strategy to define those terms.

Before discussing *how* to define a word, it may be useful to think for a minute about *why* you might want to define it. The first and most obvious reason is because you are using a word that your reader is unlikely to be familiar with. For example, you are writing for a general audience about economic issues and want to use the term *arbitrage*.

A second reason you might want to define a word you are using is to ensure your readers understand your particular definition of the word. For example, if you will be using the term *juvenile delinquency* in a paper, you may decide to define it because you want to make clear exactly what *you* mean by it. You might explain, "In this essay, I will be using the term *juvenile delinquency* to refer to serious criminal acts—not misdemeanors or minor vandalism—performed by people under the age of eighteen." Note that you are not trying to suggest that your way of defining the term is the only correct way to define it; you are merely making clear that *in this essay* this is how you will be using the term.

Defining a word at the most basic level consists of two steps:

1. Placing the word in a broad category
2. Identifying the features of the word that distinguish it from other members of that broad category

This process can be quite straightforward:

broad category   distinguishing characteristics
A dermatologist is a doctor who specializes in treating ailments of the skin.

Baseball is a sport played with bats and balls on a diamond-shaped field.

Other times it becomes a little more complicated. Consider the following example:

broad category distinguishing characteristics?
A bird is an animal that has feathers and can fly.

The problem here is that the definition is too narrow; the distinguishing characteristics (*feathers*, *ability to fly*) exclude birds like kiwis, ostriches, and emus, which are birds but can't fly.

Now consider another possible definition:

A bird is an animal with wings.

Now the definition is too broad—the distinguishing characteristic (*with wings*) lets in too many animals (like bats) that are not birds.

So let's try a third definition:

A bird is an animal that has feathers and wings.

Notice that this definition also solves the problem raised by bats. They don't have feathers.

There are also a few *don't*s when writing definitions:

1. **Don't use a form of the word being defined in your definition.**

   Expertise means being an ~~expert~~ in a particular field.

   Better: *Expertise* means having mastered the skills or knowledge of a particular field.

   Intimacy means being ~~intimate~~ with someone, like your partner or parent.

   Better: *Intimacy* means developing a close rapport or mutual attachment with someone, like your partner or parent.

2. **Don't use *is when* or *is where*.** The phrase *is when*—or sometimes its cousin, *is where*—is sometimes used mistakenly instead of placing the word being defined into a broad category or class.

   A metaphor *is when* one item is compared with another without using a word such as *like* or *as*."

   A better definition would be:

   A metaphor is a *figure of speech* in which a writer compares one object with another, without using a word such as *like* or *as*.

W11.23 Exploration

Revising Definitions

Below are six definitions. Working on your own or in your group, use the guidelines in W11.22, Strategies for Writing Simple Definitions (p. 226), to revise each one.

1. A *recession* means a lot of people are out of work because companies are laying off workers.
2. My definition of a *medical clinic* is a place where people go when they are sick or injured.
3. *Obscenity* is something vulgar or disgusting, such as a word or event or act.
4. A *socialist* is someone who supports socialism.
5. A *catastrophe* is when something truly terrible happens.
6. A *lie* is a statement that is far from the truth.

W11.24 Advice

Strategies for Writing Extended Definitions

The definitions in W11.22, Strategies for Writing Simple Definitions (p. 226), are fairly brief; each is just a sentence. But in college writing, it is often useful to provide a more extended definition, as here:

> A raptor is a bird that hunts and feeds on living animals or carrion. Raptors typically have a hooked beak, strong legs, and feet with sharp talons. Common species of raptors include hawks, eagles, owls, and falcons. Most raptors have excellent eyesight. Birds with long straight beaks like herons and egrets are not considered raptors.

After the one-sentence definition, this writer has included examples, description, and comparison, and also tells readers what a raptor is not. Other strategies you can use to flesh out an extended definition include the following:

- Discuss the origin of the term and how its meaning has changed over time.
- Tell a story that helps clarify what sets the term, phenomenon, or concept you're defining apart.
- Discuss the process by which the term, phenomenon, or concept occurs or comes into being.
- Discuss what causes the term, phenomenon, or concept you are defining or what effects follow from it.

With all of these ways of expanding upon what makes a term, phenomenon, or concept unique, you probably already realize that an extended definition can be as short as a paragraph or as long as many pages; it can be part of another essay or a full essay on its own.

W11.25 Writing

Providing an Extended Definition

Write an extended definition—at least a page—of one of the following:

- disability
- fake news
- delayed gratification
- fact

- freedom of speech
- happiness
- success

Classification

When writing about a large, complex topic, it is frequently useful to break it down into smaller parts, or categories, that are easier to understand, and then use the information about the parts to help explain the whole.

W11.26 Advice

Strategies for Writing Classification

At its simplest, classification divides things into just two categories: books are either fiction or nonfiction, athletes are either professional or amateur, and living things are either animal or vegetable. But often it is more helpful to divide things into several categories. Automobiles are either gasoline fueled, diesel fueled, electric, or hybrid. Nonflowing bodies of water can be oceans, seas, lakes, ponds, bays, gulfs, or fjords. Literature traditionally consisted of prose, poetry, or drama, but many today would add at least biography, autobiography, and creative nonfiction. Food can be classified according to the country of origin: Italian food, South African food, Chinese food, and so forth.

Classification is a particularly useful strategy if you want to say something different about the items in different categories within one larger topic. The paragraph below, for instance, divides victims in a mass casualty incident (the larger topic) into three categories and explains how different treatment is allocated to each of these categories.

> In a mass casualty incident such as an earthquake, a hurricane, or a terrorist attack, when medical personnel first arrive on the scene, patients are divided into three categories: those who will die regardless of treatment (Group 1), those who may live if treated quickly (Group 2), and those who will live even if not treated (Group 3). Because doctors' primary responsibility is to save lives, when the victims are many and the providers are few, all resources are focused on Group 2. When more medical personnel and resources become available, palliative care (reduction of pain and suffering) is administered to Group 1. When resources are plentiful, Group 3 will also be treated. During this time, patients are constantly monitored in case their condition changes and they need to be moved to a different group.

Use classification to help readers understand the content. For example, you might break complex subjects down into categories, grouping items that can be treated in a similar fashion or that must receive a different treatment or response.

Once you decide to write a classification, consider the following guidelines.

- **Select the categories according to a consistent principle of classification.** For example, it would be inconsistent to classify mattresses as twin, double, queen, king, and foam: the first four categories relate to size while the last one refers to content. Choose a principle of classification that is suitable for your purpose.

- **Make sure the categories make sense and serve a purpose.** Classifying students as pursuing certain disciplines such as science and technology, liberal arts, social sciences, and business allows a college to specify different required courses for each category. Classifying students according to the number of siblings they have does not serve any useful purpose in this context.

- **Decide how to classify examples that fit into more than one category.** If you classify literary texts into fiction, poetry, and drama, where do you place a play that is written in poetic form? One solution would be to add a category labeled *mixed*.

- **Give some thought to the most effective order of presentation of your categories.** One order might be to present the categories with the most members first and those with fewest members last. Another order could be to present the categories that need attention urgently first and those that need attention less urgently later.

W11.27 Writing

Breaking a Topic into Categories

Write a short paper — a half page is plenty — in which you break one of the following topics into smaller categories. State the principle of classification you chose and why.

- types of government
- sports
- college courses
- diseases
- bosses or professors
- lies
- games

Summary

Being able to write an effective summary in which you concisely restate the main points of a reading, novel, movie, lecture, textbook passage, or other longer piece of content will help you in many college courses as well as in the workplace.

W11.28 Writing

Summarizing Baldwin

You probably have a sense of what it means to write a summary. You write something short that briefly states the main ideas of something longer that you have read. For this assignment, try your hand at summary writing. After you've read James Baldwin's essay "On Being 'White' . . . and Other Lies," below, and perhaps made some notes, write a short paper—a half page is plenty—in which you summarize the text.

On Being "White" . . . and Other Lies

JAMES BALDWIN

James Baldwin (1924–1987) is the author of six novels including *Go Tell It on the Mountain* (1953) and *Giovanni's Room* (1956). He also wrote essays that explored race, racism, homophobia, the immigrant experience, and whiteness. "On Being 'White' . . . and Other Lies" first appeared in the magazine *Essence* in 1984. In this essay Baldwin questions the racial category "white" by pointing out it was only invented as a category when Europeans came to America.

1   The crisis of leadership in the white community is remarkable—and terrifying—because there is, in fact, no white community.

2   This may seem an enormous statement—and it is. I'm willing to be challenged. I'm also willing to attempt to spell it out.

3   My frame of reference is, of course, America, or that portion of the North American continent that calls itself America. And this means I am speaking, essentially, of the European vision of the world—or more precisely, perhaps, the European vision of the universe. It is a vision as remarkable for what it pretends to include as for what it remorselessly diminishes, demolishes or leaves totally out of account.

4   There is, for example—at least, in principle—an Irish community: here, there, anywhere, or, more precisely, Belfast, Dublin and Boston. There is a German community: both sides of Berlin, Bavaria and Yorkville. There is an Italian community: Rome,

Naples, the Bank of the Holy Ghost and Mulberry Street. And there is a Jewish community, stretching from Jerusalem to California to New York. There are English communities. There are French communities. There are Swiss consortiums. There are Poles: in Warsaw (where they would like us to be friends) and in Chicago (where because they are white we are enemies). There are, for that matter, Indian restaurants and Turkish baths. There is the underworld—the poor (to say nothing of those who intend to become rich) are always with us—but this does not describe a community. It bears terrifying witness to what happened to everyone who got here, and paid the price of the ticket. The price was to become "white." No one was white before he/she came to America. It took generations, and a vast amount of coercion, before this became a white country.

5   It is probable that it is the Jewish community—or more accurately, perhaps, its remnants—that in America has paid the highest and most extraordinary price for becoming white. For the Jews came here from countries where they were not white, and they came here, in part, because they were not white; and incontestably in the eyes of the Black American (and not only in those eyes) American Jews have opted to become white, and this is how they operate. It was ironical to hear, for example, former Israeli prime minister Menachem Begin declare some time ago that "the Jewish people bow only to God" while knowing that the state of Israel is sustained by a blank check from Washington. Without further pursuing the implication of this mutual act of faith, one is nevertheless aware that the Black presence, here, can scarcely hope—at least, not yet—to halt the slaughter in South Africa.

6   And there is a reason for that.

7   America became white—the people who, as they claim, "settled" the country became white—because of the necessity of denying the Black presence, and justifying the Black subjugation. No community can be based on such a principle—or, in other words, no community can be established on so genocidal a lie. White men—from Norway, for example, where they were Norwegians—became white: by slaughtering the cattle, poisoning the wells, torching the houses, massacring Native Americans, raping Black women.

8   This moral erosion has made it quite impossible for those who think of themselves as white in this country to have any moral authority at all—privately, or publicly. The multitudinous bulk of them sit, stunned, before their TV sets, swallowing garbage that they know to be garbage, and—in a profound and unconscious effort to justify this torpor that disguises a profound and bitter panic—pay a vast amount of attention to athletics: even though they know that the football player (the Son of the Republic, *their* sons!) is merely another aspect of the money-making scheme. They are either relieved or embittered by the presence of the Black boy on the team. I do not know if they remember how long and hard they fought to keep him off it. I know that they do not dare have any notion of the price Black people (mothers and

▶

fathers) paid and pay. They do not want to know the meaning, or face the shame, of what they compelled—out of what they took as the necessity of being white—Joe Louis or Jackie Robinson or Cassius Clay (aka Muhammad Ali) to pay. I know that they, themselves, would not have liked to pay it.

9   There has never been a labor movement in this country, the proof being the absence of a Black presence in the so-called father-to-son unions. There are, perhaps, some niggers in the window; but Blacks have no power in the labor unions.

10   Just so does the white community, as a means of keeping itself white, elect, as they imagine, their political (!) representatives. No nation in the world, including England, is represented by so stunning a pantheon of the relentlessly mediocre. I will not name names—I will leave that to you.

11   But this cowardice, this necessity of justifying a totally false identity and of justifying what must be called a genocidal history, has placed everyone now living into the hands of the most ignorant and powerful people the world has ever seen: And how did they get that way?

12   By deciding that they were white. By opting for safety instead of life. By persuading themselves that a Black child's life meant nothing compared with a white child's life. By abandoning their children to the things white men could buy. By informing their children that Black women, Black men and Black children had no human integrity that those who call themselves white were bound to respect. And in this debasement and definition of Black people, they debased and defamed themselves.

13   And have brought humanity to the edge of oblivion: because they think they are white. Because they think they are white, they do not dare confront the ravage and the lie of their history. Because they think they are white, they cannot allow themselves to be tormented by the suspicion that all men are brothers. Because they think they are white, they are looking for, or bombing into existence, stable populations, cheerful natives and cheap labor. Because they think they are white, they believe, as even no child believes, in the dream of safety. Because they think they are white, however vociferous they may be and however multitudinous, they are as speechless as Lot's wife—looking backward, changed into a pillar of salt.

14   However—! White being, absolutely, a moral choice (for there are no white people), the crisis of leadership for those of us whose identity has been forged, or branded, as Black is nothing new. We—who were not Black before we got here either, who were defined as Black by the slave trade—have paid for the crisis of leadership in the white community for a very long time, and have resoundingly, even when we face the worst about ourselves, survived, and triumphed over it. If we had not survived and triumphed, there would not be a Black American alive.

15   And the fact that we are still here—even in suffering, darkness, danger, endlessly defined by those who do not dare define, or even confront, themselves—is the key to the

crisis in white leadership. The past informs us of various kinds of people—criminals, adventurers and saints, to say nothing, of course, of popes—but it is the Black condition, and only that, which informs us concerning white people. It is a terrible paradox, but those who believed that they could control and define Black people divested themselves of the power to control and define themselves.

W11.29 Exploration

Analyzing Summaries

You will receive a selection of the summaries the class wrote in W11.28, Summarizing Baldwin (p. 232). Working individually or in your group, read over these summaries and make two lists: (1) what you found that worked well in one or more of the summaries, and (2) what you found that could be improved in one or more of the summaries. Be prepared to report out on your list.

W11.30 Advice

Strategies for Writing a Summary

The ability to tease out the most important points from a complex text, full of information and ideas, and present those key points in a coherent, concise summary is a crucial skill in college and beyond. After reading a complex text assigned in a course, you may find it helpful to write a paragraph or so in which you record the main ideas from what you read. After listening to a lecture or a class discussion, you may want to take a few minutes to summarize the most important points, which can help with your understanding of the class and your memory of it. After watching a movie, a play, or even a YouTube video, you may want to summarize the experience for later recall.

In the workplace, you may be asked to interview a candidate for a job and write a summary of what you learned from the interview. In your first job, it would not be unusual for you to be asked to investigate a complex topic like whether an office should switch to digital record keeping or not and to write a summary of your findings.

As you summarize, keep the following guidelines in mind:

1. **Carefully read the text, annotating as you read.** You will not be able to summarize the text if you don't understand it. (For a discussion of annotating, see R2.1, Why Annotate?, p. 257, and R2.2, Explaining Annotations, p. 257.)

2. **Consider how long your summary should be.** A good rule of thumb for written texts is that the summary should be a quarter to a third of the length of the original.

3. **Identify the source that is being summarized.**   Usually in the first sentence of your summary, you should name the author and the title of the text (or, for example, the director and title of a movie).

4. **Include only the writer's main ideas.**   Depending on your purpose, you will probably want to include only the thesis and key supporting points. Omit examples or details that are not crucial to understanding the writer's main point.

5. **Omit your own or others' opinions and ideas.**   Do not include your own opinions or ideas, or information from other sources.

6. **Write the summary in your own words and sentences.**   Don't rely heavily on the author's language, although occasionally, you may need to use a word the writer has already used—in an essay about elephants, it would be silly to use *pachyderms* as a replacement.

Reflection

Reflective writing asks you to think back, to "reflect," on an experience—an essay you have written, a major change in your life, a time when you weren't successful at something you wanted to do—and to examine how you now think and feel about that experience.

W11.31   Advice

Strategies for Writing a Reflection

Reflection makes us pause, sort through our experiences, consider what we've learned, consolidate our understanding, and create meaning. In this course, you are asked regularly to reflect on your experience reading and writing essays—what you learned, and what you'd like to learn next time, what you've done well (or not so well), what you enjoyed (or didn't)—but the process of writing down your reflections can be helpful in many other situations as well. After a job interview, writing a short reflection can help you figure out how best to "sell" your strengths or what kind of work environment will allow you to flourish. When a relationship ends, reflection can help you get over the breakup and move on. Even after making a mistake in your life—breaking a law, doing something cruel or thoughtless, cheating on a task at work or school—reflective writing can help you learn and move on from these experiences.

Reflecting on an Important Experience

Think of an experience you have had in the past couple of years. This could be a project you worked on in school or it could involve a job, a program you volunteered for, a family event of some kind, or an athletic endeavor. Almost any experience that you can remember fairly clearly will work, but it should not have been an event that was over in a few minutes. Try to pick something in which you invested considerable time and effort. Then write a short paper—a page or so—reflecting on this experience.

- **Report on what you learned.** What were the most important or most useful ideas you encountered? What mistakes did you make? Was there some part of the experience that you are proud of? Do you have any regrets?
- **Describe how you now feel about the experience.** Are you disappointed? Satisfied? Proud? Relieved? Eager to get on with some new experience?
- **How will you be different in the future?** What did you learn that will make a difference for you in the future? How will you be different?

Weaving Strategies into a Strong Essay

After discussing the writing strategies covered in this topic separately, in this final section you will see how they can be woven together into a powerful essay.

Using Multiple Writing Strategies in an Essay

Writing strategies have been discussed one by one in W11, but most often they are woven together to create a coherent and convincing essay. Although you might be writing an essay that is predominantly cause and effect, comparison and/or contrast, process, or argument, you will find that you need to use other strategies to flesh out your paper. Before you start drafting, consider your subject, audience, purpose, and assignment. Then consider which of the strategies discussed earlier in this chapter would work. If you are making an argument, for example, you might consider including the following:

- a paragraph or two defining one or more terms critical to that argument
- a narrative paragraph that provides some historical context for the issue

- a lengthy description of a place important to the argument
- several paragraphs that focus on the positive effects that would result from taking the proposed action

W11.34   Exploration

Identifying Multiple Writing Strategies in an Essay

The process of weaving various writing strategies together in a longer essay is a very effective way to organize a compelling essay, as Steven Pinker does in the excerpt below, which comes from his introduction to a book on language. (The several references to later chapters refer to the rest of the book.) Working on your own or in your group, identify as many different writing strategies Pinker uses in this excerpt as you can.

Words and Worlds

STEVEN PINKER

Steven Pinker, an experimental psychologist, was born in Montreal, Canada. He earned a bachelor's degree in experimental psychology from McGill University and a doctorate from Harvard. He has taught at Stanford and MIT and is currently the Johnstone Family Professor in the psychology department at Harvard. After early research on language development in children, he went on to focus on the cognitive, genetic, and neurobiological underpinnings of language. He has authored ten books and received nine honorary doctorates.

1   On September 11, 2001, at 8:46 A.M., a hijacked airliner crashed into the north tower of the World Trade Center in New York. At 9:03 A.M. a second plane crashed into the south tower. The resulting infernos caused the buildings to collapse, the south tower after burning for an hour and two minutes, the north tower twenty-three minutes after that. The attacks were masterminded by Osama bin Laden, leader of the Al Qaeda terrorist organization, who hoped to intimidate the United States into ending its military presence in Saudi Arabia and its support for Israel and to unite Muslims in preparation for a restoration of the caliphate.

2   9/11, as the happenings of that day are now called, stands as the most significant political and intellectual event of the twenty-first century so far. It has set off debates on a vast array of topics: how best to memorialize the dead and revitalize lower Manhattan; whether the attacks are rooted in ancient Islamic fundamentalism or modern revolutionary agitation; the role of the United States on the world stage

before the attacks and in response to them; how best to balance protection against terrorism with respect for civil liberties.

3   But I would like to explore a lesser-known debate triggered by 9/11. Exactly how many events took place in New York on that morning in September?

4   It could be argued that the answer is one. The attacks on the building were part of a single plan conceived in the mind of one man in service of a single agenda. They unfolded within a few minutes of each other, targeting the parts of a complex with a single name, design, and owner. And they launched a single chain of military and political events in their aftermath.

5   Or it could be argued that the answer is two. The north tower and south tower were distinct collections of glass and steel separated by an expanse of space, and they were hit at different times and went out of existence at different times. The amateur video that showed the second plane closing in on the south tower as the north tower billowed with smoke makes the twoness unmistakable: in those horrifying moments, one event was frozen in the past, the other loomed in the future. And another occurrence on that day—a passenger mutiny that brought down a third hijacked plane before it reached its target in Washington—presents to the imagination the possibility that one tower or the other might have been spared. In each of those possible worlds a distinct event took place, so in our *actual* world one might argue, there must have been a pair of events as surely as one plus one equals two.

6   The gravity of 9/11 would seem to make this entire discussion frivolous to the point of impudence. It's a matter of mere "semantics," as we say, with its implication of picking nits, splitting hairs, and debating the number of angels that can dance on the head of a pin. But this book is about semantics, and I would not make a claim on your attention if I did not think that the relation of language to our inner and outer worlds was a matter of intellectual fascination and real-world importance.

7   Though "importance" is often hard to quantify, in this case I can put an exact value on it: three and a half billion dollars. That was the sum in dispute in a set of trials determining the insurance payout to Larry Silverstein, the leaseholder of the World Trade Center site. Silverstein held insurance policies that stipulated a maximum reimbursement for each destructive "event." If 9/11 comprised a single event, he stood to receive three and a half billion dollars. If it comprised two events, he stood to receive seven billion. In the trials, the attorneys disputed the applicable meaning of the term *event*. The lawyers for the leaseholder defined it in physical terms (two collapses); those for the insurance companies defined it in mental terms (one plot). There is nothing "mere" about semantics!

8   Nor is the topic intellectually trifling. The 9/11 cardinality debate is not about the facts, that is, the physical events and human actions that took place that day.   ▶

Admittedly, those have been contested as well: according to various conspiracy theories, the buildings were targeted by American missiles, or demolished by a controlled implosion, in a plot conceived by American neoconservatives, Israeli spies, or a cabal of psychiatrists. But aside from the kooks, most people agree on the facts. Where they differ is in the *construal* of those facts: how the intricate swirl of matter in space ought to be conceptualized by human minds. As we shall see, the categories in this dispute permeate the meanings of words in our language because they permeate the way we represent reality in our heads.

9   Semantics is about the relation of words to thoughts, but it is also about the relation of words to other human concerns. Semantics is about the relation of words to reality—the way that speakers commit themselves to a shared understanding of the truth, and the way their thoughts are anchored to things and situations in the world. It is about the relation of words to a community—how a new word, which arises in an act of creation by a single speaker, comes to evoke the same idea in the rest of a population, so people can understand one another when they use it. It is about the relation of words to emotions: the way in which words don't just point to things but are saturated with feelings, which can endow the words with a sense of magic, taboo, and sin. And it is about words and social relations—how people use language not just to transfer ideas from head to head but to negotiate the kind of relationship they wish to have with their conversational partner.

10   A feature of the mind that we will repeatedly encounter in these pages is that even our most abstract concepts are understood in terms of concrete scenarios. That applies in full force to the subject matter of the book itself. In this introductory chapter I will preview some of the book's topics with vignettes from newspapers and the Internet that can be understood only through the lens of semantics. They come from each of the worlds that connect to our words—the worlds of thought, reality, community, emotions, and social relations.

11   Let's look at the bone of contention in the world's most expensive debate in semantics, the three-and-a-half-billion-dollar argument over the meaning of "event." What, exactly, is an event? An event is a stretch of time, and time, according to physicists, is a continuous variable—an inexorable cosmic flow, in Newton's world, or a fourth dimension in a seamless hyperspace in Einstein's. But the human mind carves this fabric into discrete swatches we call events. Where does the mind place the incisions? Sometimes, as the lawyers for the World Trade Center leaseholder pointed out, it encircles the change of state of an object, such as the collapse of a building. And sometimes, as the lawyers for the insurers pointed out, it encircles the goal of a human actor, such as a plot being executed. Most often the circles coincide: an actor intends to cause an object to change, the intent of the act and the fate of the object are tracked along a single time line, and the moment of change marks the consummation of the intent.

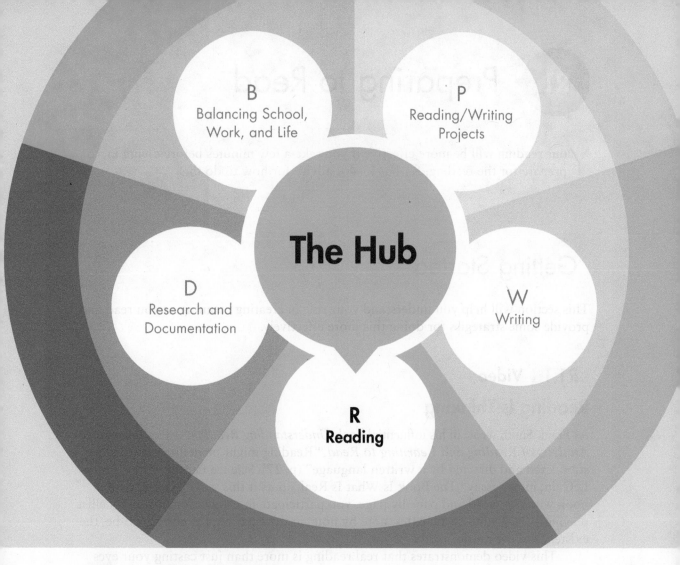

B
Balancing School,
Work, and Life

P
Reading/Writing
Projects

The Hub

D
Research and
Documentation

W
Writing

R
Reading

R Reading

R1 Preparing to Read 242
R2 Reading Actively 257
R3 Reading Critically 275

Students in college, particularly students in English courses in college, can expect to be required to read challenging texts regularly. Part R is a collection of advice, explorations, readings, and videos that will help you as you encounter these college-level texts.

R1 ▸ Preparing to Read

Your reading will be more effective if you take a few minutes before diving in, to prepare for the reading. R1 has lots of advice for how to do this.

Getting Started

This section will help you understand your role in creating meaning as you read and provide some strategies for doing this more effectively.

R1.1 Video
Reading Is Thinking

As Frank Smith wrote in his influential book *Understanding Reading: A Psycholinguistic Analysis of Reading and Learning to Read*, "Reading might be defined as thought stimulated and directed by a written language" (p. 27). Science fiction writer Ursula LeGuin, in her essay "The Book Is What Is Real," puts it this way: "As you read a book word by word and page by page, you participate in its creation, just as a cellist playing a Bach suite participates, note by note, in the creation, the coming-to-be, the existence of the music" (p. 127).

This video demonstrates that real reading is more than just casting your eyes over text. Reading—really reading—requires you to engage with the text, to apply the active and critical reading strategies discussed in R2 and R3, to puzzle out what you don't understand at first, and to connect what's in the text with what you already know. In short, reading is an act of creation; reading is thinking. (If you have access, you can launch this video from Achieve with *The Hub*.)

R1.2 Video
The Reading Process

Like writing, reading is a process. (See W1.3, How Effective Writers Go about Writing, p. 3.) Effective readers start by spending a few minutes previewing the text (see R1.6,

Previewing and Making Predictions about a Text, p. 245) and activating the appropriate schema (see R1.4, Activating Schema, p. 244). Activating schema sounds technical and unfamiliar, but all it really means is figuring out the appropriate framework for making sense of a text. Previewing simply means looking over the text to see if you can figure out what it's about, how difficult it will be to read, how long it is. When previewing, you may also want to consider the rhetorical situation of the text you're about to dive into: Who is the author? What is the text about? Who were its intended readers? What kind, or *genre*, of text is it (a lab report, say, or a scholarly article)?

While reading, effective readers interact with the text, figuring out what it means and challenging and interrogating it to figure out, not only what the author is saying, but also what they think about what the author is saying. While reading, effective readers may also make notes.

After reading, they may summarize the reading to consolidate what they've learned and to remember the key ideas. (R2, Reading Actively, p. 257, and R3, Reading Critically, p. 275, will give you strategies for tackling the kinds of challenging texts you're likely to be assigned in college.) The video in this unit demonstrates effective readers' process before, during, and after reading. (If you have access, you can launch this video from Achieve with *The Hub*.)

R1.3 Advice
Optimizing Your Reading

Reading takes concentration, so it makes sense to read when and where you can focus best. This differs from person to person. If even the smallest noise distracts you, find a quiet place where you won't be disturbed. This could be the library, a secluded bench on campus, or your apartment or dorm room when your roommates are at work or in class. If you do better when there's some background noise, play music, try a lounge in your dorm, or go to a coffee shop.

- **Try to read in the same place and at the same time.**   Block out time on your calendar for reading, and list your assignments and their due dates. Developing a routine of reading in the same place at the same time will help you to focus and become a more attentive reader.

- **Choose times to read when you are most alert.**   Some people find they can concentrate best in the morning while others prefer to read in the evening. Whatever time works best for you, plan to read your most difficult assignments first, when you have the most stamina and focus.

- **Avoid distractions.**   In today's world, you are always connected. In order to concentrate, silence your phone and turn off all social media. Resist checking for messages, updates, or breaking news until after you've finished reading.

- **Build in breaks and reward yourself for completing assignments.** College reading can be challenging and sometimes even dull. At the end of a long or difficult section, or after reading several smaller chunks, take five minutes to stretch your legs or get coffee. Reward yourself for completing an assignment by going for a walk, eating lunch with a friend, or checking your texts.

Activating Schema and Previewing

Carrying out these two interrelated activities—activating schema and previewing—will prepare you for reading a text.

R1.4 Advice

Activating Schema

Imagine you start reading a text that opens with this sentence:

> He plunked down twenty dollars at the window.

Right away, you might imagine a man placing a bet at a race track. You continue reading.

> She tried to give him ten dollars, but he refused to take it.

Continuing with the idea that the man was placing a bet at a racetrack, you think the cashier is trying to give him change. But then you read the next sentence:

> So when they got inside, she bought him a large tub of popcorn.

Once you read *when they got inside*, you understand that the *she* in the preceding sentence isn't the cashier but the man's companion—maybe a friend, maybe a date. And then there's popcorn. Where do you buy popcorn? At the movies, of course![1]

What you've just done is change your schema, your framework for understanding. You switched from a racetrack schema to a movie schema, and this one small change in your schema has changed your understanding of the text completely.

---

[1] Information from Allan Collins, John Seely Brown, and Kathy Larkin. "Inference in Text Understanding." In *Theoretical Issues in Reading Comprehension.* Edited by R. J. Spiro, B. C. Bruce, and W. F. Brewer. Routledge, 1980.

We all have schemas for all kinds of situations: baseball games, marriage ceremonies, dentist appointments. We know how these events take place and what to expect. Similarly for texts: We know that comic books combine cartoon-like drawings with words, textbooks are organized into chapters and usually have a table of contents and an index, and Instagram posts include photos that you can like, share, or comment on. When you activate the appropriate schema, your mind knows what to expect and has an easier time processing the text.

To activate a schema, you simply bring to your consciousness what to expect from the kind of text you are about to read. You make yourself aware of what this kind of text is like and what kinds of issues are associated with the topic this text addresses. To do this activating, take a few minutes to think about what you already know about what you're reading. Draw on your own experiences, other books or articles you've read, TV shows or movies you've watched, radio news or podcasts you've listened to, or social media you follow.

For example, if you're reading a chapter on infectious diseases for a health class, you might think of recent news items about the COVID-19 pandemic, the breakout of flu at your college last year that knocked you out for a week, or the hygiene precautions you have to take at your food service job to prevent the transmission of bacteria and viruses.

Activating the appropriate schema has two significant benefits: by connecting new information to something with which you are already familiar, it can make new information easier to understand and remember. If you're not sure you've activated the right schema, don't worry. As you keep reading, it will quickly become clear that you need to revise your schema or even switch to a different one . . . just as you did when you read the sentences about the man at the racetrack at the beginning of this unit.

R1.5 Exploration
Activating Your Schema

Working individually or in your group (your instructor will tell you which), take a look at an article you need to read. First decide what the article is about. Then, activate your schema by making a list of what you already know about that topic.

R1.6 Advice
Previewing and Making Predictions about a Text

When you set out to read a book, an article, an essay, a blog, a web page—when you set out to read any text—your strategy may be simply to dive in, to start reading at the beginning and plow your way through to the end. With the limited time in most of our busy lives, simply diving in can seem like the quickest way to get something read.

Most experienced readers, however, have found that taking a few minutes before diving in to get a sense of what it is they are about to read actually saves them time and makes their reading more effective because it allows them to activate the appropriate schema. This does not mean you need to spend hours previewing and predicting; just a few minutes will be very helpful when you start to read.

Use these guidelines to preview and predict:

- **Take a look at the title and subtitle.** The title and subtitle will often indicate the topic and may hint at the author's approach to or position on the topic.

- **Take a look at any biography or background on the author.** What can you learn about the author? Qualifications? Other publications? Biases?

- **Take a look at the actual text.** For books, look over the front and back covers (including the flaps, if present) and the table of contents. For magazine articles, look at any pull quotes (the quotations set in a large font and used as decoration). For journal articles, read the abstract (or summary).

- **Read the first paragraph or introduction.** These often provide an overview, and they will usually suggest whether the text is informative or persuasive and give you a sense of the author's tone (lighthearted or serious; positive, negative, or neutral).

- **Take a look at the headings.** Headings can act like an outline of the text, helping you to understand how the reading is organized.

- **Read the final paragraph or conclusion.** These sections often provide a summary.

- **Take a look at the list of references or works cited.** These will give you a sense of the kinds of sources the author cites.

- **Check to see how long the text is.** The reading selection's length may suggest its scope and help you decide how much time you will need to devote to the reading.

R1.7 Exploration

Previewing *The Stuff of Thought*, Steven Pinker

Put the previewing and predicting skills you learned in R1.6 (p. 245) into practice using the selections from Steven Pinker's book *The Stuff of Thought* reproduced below. Working on your own or in your group (your instructor will tell you which), answer as many of these questions as you can:

- What is the book about? What is its topic?

- Who is Steven Pinker? What is his background? Is he likely to be an expert on the book's topic?

- What do you think the author's main point is likely to be? What do you think he'll argue for?

- How would you characterize the author's tone (or attitude)? How does he come across?

- How challenging do you think this text will be to read and understand?

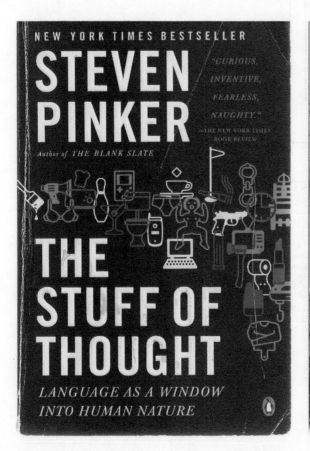

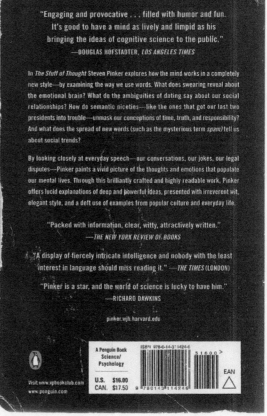

ABOUT THE AUTHOR

Steven Pinker is the Johnstone Family Professor of Psychology and Harvard College Professor at Harvard University. He is the author of seven books, including *The Language Instinct, How the Mind Works, Words and Rules,* and *The Blank Slate.* He lives in Boston and Truro, Massachusetts.

STEVEN PINKER

The Stuff of Thought

Language as a Window into Human Nature

PENGUIN BOOKS

CONTENTS

PREFACE

1   There is a theory of space and time embedded in the way we use words. There is a theory of matter and a theory of causality, too. Our language has a model of sex in it (actually, two models), and conceptions of intimacy and power and fairness. Divinity, degradation, and danger are also ingrained in our mother tongue, together with a conception of well-being and a philosophy of free will. These conceptions vary in their details from language to language, but their overall logic is the same. They add up to a distinctively human model of reality, which differs in major ways from the objective understanding of reality eked out by our best science and logic. Though these ideas are woven into language, their roots are deeper than language itself. They lay out the ground rules for how we understand our surroundings, how we assign credit and blame to our fellows, and how we negotiate our relationships with them. A close look at our speech—our conversations, our jokes, our curses, our legal disputes, the names we give our babies—can therefore give us insight into who we are.

2   That is the premise of the book you are holding, the third in a trilogy written for a wide audience of readers who are interested in language and mind. The first, *The Language Instinct*, was an overview of the language faculty: everything you always wanted to know about language but were afraid to ask. A language is a way of connecting sound and meaning, and the other two books turn toward each of those spheres. *Words and Rules* was about the units of language, how they are stored in memory, and how they are assembled into the vast number of combinations that give language its expressive power. *The Stuff of Thought* is about the other side of the linkage, meaning. Its vistas include the meanings of words and constructions and the way that language is used in social settings, the topics that linguists call semantics and pragmatics.

*   *   *

3   As in my other books on language, the early chapters occasionally dip into technical topics. But I have worked hard to make them transparent, and I am confident that my subject will engage anyone with an interest in what makes us tick. Language is entwined with human life. We use it to inform and persuade, but also to threaten, to seduce, and of course to swear. It reflects the way we grasp reality, and also the image of ourselves we try to project to others, and the bonds that tie us to them. It is, I hope to convince you, a window into human nature.

Reading Rhetorically

First proposed by the ancient Greeks, analyzing the rhetorical situation means thinking about the author, audience, topic, purpose, context, genre, and medium of a text.

R1.8 Advice
Reading and the Rhetorical Situation

In W2, Preparing to Write (p. 10), you looked at the rhetorical situation as a writer, as the author of a text. Now you're going to consider it from the reader's perspective:

1. **Author.**   Besides the author's name, what else can you learn? What evidence is there that the author really has some expertise about the subject? What biases might the author have? Is the author part of an organization? A corporation? What else has the author written?

    For most texts you read, the author's name will appear at the top of the text or, sometimes, at the end. Occasionally, there will be a brief biography. But sometimes there will be no biographical information. In these cases—or even if there is a biography—take a few minutes to do a quick search for the author on Google or another search engine to see what you can learn. Look for evidence of their expertise:

    - Do they have a credential or degree that indicates they are qualified to discuss the topic?
    - Have they published other relevant works?
    - Have they won any awards?
    - Does their job give them access to relevant knowledge?
    - Do other authors you have been reading refer to them?

2. **Audience.** Obviously, you're the audience, but did the author intend another group to be the reader or readers of this text? If so, how might that intended audience have affected what you're reading? If you're reading a scholarly article, for example, the intended audience is other experts on the subject, so the author may have used specialized jargon that you'll need to decipher. The author may also have taken for granted a familiarity with the topic, omitting background that would provide needed context for those new to the subject.

3. **Topic.** What is this text about? What do you know about it already? How interested are you in it? (You may want take a look at R1.4, Activating Schema, p. 244.)

4. **Purpose.** What do you think the author intended or, at least, hoped would happen as a result of this piece of writing? What did the author want the effect of this text to be on its audience?

5. **Context.** Where does the writing you're reading fit into the world? Is the topic the center of a firestorm of public argument? Is it a topic that most of the world views as already settled and not in need of more discussion? Thinking about where the text you're reading fits into the broader conversation will help you make sense of it.

6. **Genre.** What *kind* of writing are you reading? Understanding its genre—whether it's a lab report or a business plan, a romance novel or an article from a scholarly journal, for example—will help set your expectations.

7. **Medium.** Today people consume texts in many different media: print, audio files, on computer screens, and even on their phones. Reading on screen is a very different experience from reading on paper. If you are reading an article on your phone, you may be able to bring up a definition simply by clicking on an unfamiliar vocabulary word, for example, or get background or check sources just by clicking on the links. But reading online can be challenging as well. Reading a long, complex text on your phone might be convenient, but it also has disadvantages. Visuals are often too small to process. Your reading can be interrupted frequently by other messages. Jumping frequently to definitions can be distracting.

R1.9 Exploration

Analyzing the Rhetorical Situation of a Text

The following article appeared on a blog written by Mike Rose, a respected scholar in composition and long-time professor of education at University of California, Los Angeles. Working together or in your group (your instructor will tell you which), analyze the author, audience, topic, and purpose of the text. If time permits, you may also want to comment on the other three elements of the rhetorical situation: context, genre, and medium.

"Grit" Revisited: Reflections on Our Public Talk about Education

MIKE ROSE

23 JUNE 2016

1   One of the many frustrating things about education policy and practice in our country is the continual search for the magic bullet—and all the hype and trite lingo that bursts up around it. One such bullet is the latest incarnation of character education, particularly the enthrallment with "grit," a buzz word for perseverance and determination. . . .

2   In a nutshell, I worry about the limited success of past attempts at character education[*] and the danger in our pendulum-swing society that we will shift our attention from improving subject matter instruction. I also question the easy distinctions made between "cognitive" and "non-cognitive" skills. And I fear that we will sacrifice policies aimed at reducing poverty for interventions to change the way poor people see the world.

3   In this post, I would like to further explore these concerns—and a few new ones—by focusing on "grit," for it has so captured the fancy of our policy makers, administrators, and opinion-makers. . . .

4   [Psychologist Angela] Duckworth and her colleagues did something that in retrospect was a brilliant marketing strategy, a master stroke of branding—or re-branding. Rather than calling their construct "perseverance" or "persistence," they chose to call it "grit." Can you think of a name that has more resonance in American culture? The fighter who is all heart. The hardscrabble survivor. *True Grit*. The Little Train That Could.

5   Grit exploded. *New York Times* commentators, best-selling journalists, the producers of *This American Life*, Secretary of Education Arne Duncan, educational policy makers and administrators all saw the development of grit as a way to improve American education and, more pointedly, to improve the achievement of poor children who, everyone seemed to assume, lacked grit. . . .

6   But, of course, a good deal of the discussion of grit doesn't really involve all students. Regardless of disclaimers, the primary audience for our era's character education is poor kids. As I and a host of others have written, a focus on individual characteristics of low-income children can take our attention away from the structural inequalities

---

[*] Teaching intended to improve students' character — their manners, morality, hygiene, or, in this case, perseverance

they face. Some proponents of character education have pretty much said that an infusion of grit will achieve what social and economic interventions cannot. . . .

7   It is hard to finish what you begin when food and housing are unstable, or when you have three or four teachers in a given year, or when there are few people around who are able to guide and direct you. It is equally hard to pursue a career with consistency when the jobs available to you are low-wage, short-term and vulnerable, and have few if any benefits or protections. This certainly doesn't mean that people who are poor lack determination and resolve. Some of the poor people I knew growing up or work with today possess off-the-charts determination to survive, put food on the table, care for their kids. But they wouldn't necessarily score high on the grit scale.

8   Personality psychology by its disciplinary norms concentrates on the individual, but individual traits and qualities, regardless of how they originate and develop, manifest themselves in social and institutional contexts. Are we educators and policy makers creating classrooms that are challenging and engaging enough to invite perseverance? Are we creating opportunity for further educational or occupational programs that enable consistency of effort? Are we gritty enough to keep working toward these goals without distraction over the long haul?

R1.10   Advice
Evaluating the Source of a Text

In addition to evaluating the author of a text, you should also think about its publisher or sponsor: What affiliations does the publisher or sponsor have? What else have they published or posted? What else can you learn about the publisher or sponsor? All this information about the source of the text will help you better understand and evaluate it.

As you evaluate sources, ask these questions:

- Has the publisher published or posted material by other authors whom you recognize as having expertise in the subject? If yes, it increases the source's credibility.

- Is the source sponsored by a reputable organization—a university, a major foundation, or a government agency? If so, that adds to its credibility and that of the writers it publishes.

- Does the source provide references or documentation to support the legitimacy of the content it is providing? If not, be wary.

- Does the source publish material that seems biased? If yes, that doesn't mean you should ignore it, but be aware of the publication's slant.

- Is the content in the source current? For many subjects—especially those relating to science, technology, medicine, and other rapidly changing fields—information becomes outdated quickly, so you want to make sure the source is providing the most current data.

- Is the source well-written and the content presented in a logical, well-organized fashion? Anyone can post and share information online. Legitimate, professional sources take time to edit their content, check the credentials of the writers whose work they host or present, and provide a well-organized homepage. If the content is inaccurate or poorly written, if links are broken, if navigation is difficult, and if you cannot find out information about the publisher, look for more reliable alternatives. If it is not possible to learn much about the publisher of a text or owner of a website, that may be an indication that the source is not reliable.

R1.11 Exploration

Evaluating Sources of Texts

A cochlear implant is a small electronic device implanted behind the ear of a person with severe hearing loss in an attempt to improve their hearing. If you were doing research into cochlear implants, you might come across articles like those listed below. Working individually or in your group (your instructor will tell you which), locate these articles and evaluate the author and source for each article. You can launch these articles from Achieve with *The Hub*. If you are *not* using Achieve, type the article's title into your favorite search engine. If the link is broken or your search fails, you will find an updated list of URLs at macmillanlearning.com/thehublinks. When you Google these, you will find that several ads appear first; be sure to scroll down to the actual articles before clicking.

1. "Position Statement on Early Cognitive and Language Development and Education of Deaf and Hard of Hearing Children," National Association for the Deaf

2. "Cochlear Implants—A Cultural Threat," Michelle Jay, StartASL (This text starts with an article by Michelle Jay and then includes several articles by students. Evaluate only the Jay article, not the ones by students.)

3. "Cochlear Implants: What Are They and How Do They Work?" Joy Victory, Healthy Hearing

R1.12 Exploration
Your Purposes for Reading

Not only do writers have a purpose for their writing, but readers usually read with a purpose. Working in your group, make a list of the different kinds of reading the members of your group do. Then list what the purpose is for each different kind of reading, as illustrated in the following chart.

Kind of Reading	Purpose for Reading
A text from a friend	To meet up for coffee, to vent, to learn what they're doing, thinking
A recipe for something you plan to make for dinner	To make a shopping list of ingredients

R1.13 Advice
Purposes for Reading

We read for many different purposes: to find out when the next bus leaves campus, to find a recipe for a special meal, to locate sources for a research paper, to learn what's happening in the world of politics, or to relax with a crime novel. A list of some of the many purposes we have for reading might look like this:

- to learn new information
- to understand a difficult concept
- to evaluate and critique different perspectives on a topic
- to find specific information in a text
- to get a general sense of a text (skimming)
- to locate specific information, such as the date of a historical event (scanning)
- for practical purposes (e.g., to learn how to change brake fluid or build a set of shelves)
- for a class assignment
- for pleasure

These variations in purpose require the use of different reading techniques, as can be seen in the following examples.

1. You scan an email or a program to find the location of room in which a meeting you are supposed to attend is being held.

2. You are reading a novel for pleasure. You read attentively but in a relaxed manner, savoring the experience.

3. You are reading a letter from a company to which you have applied for a job to find out whether you have been invited for an interview. You read fairly quickly, skimming the document to find out whether you are invited for an interview or not.

4. You are reading a textbook about the causes of the War of 1812 in preparation for a test. You read slowly with great focus, annotating the text, making notes to help you understand and remember the details, summarizing important events, and creating and answering questions you think your instructor might ask.

5. You are previewing a challenging article in a scholarly journal before you dive in for a detailed read. You read the abstract, title, headings, and first and last paragraphs; note the name of the author; review any graphic aids, such as charts and graphs; and consider how difficult the article will be to read and how much time you will need.

6. You are reading a half dozen articles on global warming to see if any of them discuss the effect of rising sea levels in Florida, a topic you are writing about. You preview each and then skim through those that sound promising, looking for references to Florida.

Notice how your reading techniques change depending on your purpose. It's a good idea, before you start reading anything, to think for a minute about your purpose for reading and to adjust your approach to match that purpose.

R1.14 Exploration

Purpose for Your Recent Reading

Working individually or in your group (your instructor will tell you which), identify three texts you've read in the past forty-eight hours. Then explain the purpose of each of those readings. Remember that everything you read—an email, a sign at work, a memo from your boss, and, of course, a book or an article—can be considered a reading.

Reading Actively

Reading is not just a matter of processing words. It demands wrestling with those words, thinking about their various implications, discovering hidden meanings, and even applying their meaning to the world outside the text—a process called active reading. In R2, you will learn and practice some strategies for reading actively.

Annotating and Taking Notes

Interacting with a text by highlighting, underlining, and writing comments, questions, and reactions directly on the text is called *annotation*, and it almost automatically increases how carefully and thoughtfully readers engage with the text. Other ways of taking notes on a text include keeping a reading journal and creating visual tools, like timelines and family trees.

R2.1 Advice

Why Annotate?

Annotating while reading helps you to slow down and think about what you are reading, identify key passages, comment on what strikes you, decide whether you agree or not, ask questions, make connections with other texts, and add examples from your own experience. It is a powerful tool for improving how well you understand a text. Annotations can also serve as a kind of index to the text: they can refresh your memory when you return to the text later, and they can help you locate specific information you may need to study for a test or write in response to a reading.

R2.2 Exploration

Explaining Annotations

Following is a text annotated by a thoughtful reader. Read the text and the annotations to see the variety of reasons a reader might annotate.

Prologue: The Woman in the Photograph

(A) — Look this up

There's a photo on my wall of a woman I've never met, its left corner torn and patched together with tape. She looks straight into the camera and smiles, hands on hips, dress suit neatly pressed, lips painted deep red. It's the late 1940s and she hasn't yet reached the age of thirty. Her light brown skin is smooth, her eyes still young and playful, oblivious to the tumor growing inside her—a tumor that would leave her five children motherless and change the future of medicine. Beneath the photo, a caption says her name is "Henrietta Lacks, Helen Lane, or Helen Larson."

(B) was the original photo in color?

(C) is she African-American?

No one knows who took that picture, but it's appeared hundreds of times in magazines and science textbooks, on blogs and laboratory walls. She's usually identified as Helen Lane, but often she has no name at all. She's simply called HeLa, the code name given to the world's first immortal human cells—*her* cells, cut from her cervix just months before she died.

(D) Can cells really be immortal?

(E)

Her real name is Henrietta Lacks.

I've spent years staring at that photo, wondering what kind of life she led, what happened to her children, and what she'd think about cells from her cervix living on forever—bought, sold, packaged, and shipped by the trillions to laboratories around the world. I've tried to imagine how she'd feel knowing that her cells went up in the first space missions to see what would happen to human cells in zero gravity, or that they helped with some of the most important advances in medicine: the polio vaccine, chemotherapy, cloning, gene mapping, in vitro fertilization. I'm pretty sure that she—like most of us—would be shocked to hear that there are trillions more of her cells growing in laboratories now than there ever were in her body.

There's no way of knowing exactly how many of Henrietta's cells are alive today. One scientist estimates that if you could pile all HeLa cells ever grown onto a scale, they'd weigh more than 50 million metric tons—an inconceivable number, given that an individual cell weighs almost nothing. Another scientist calculated that if you could lay all HeLa cells ever grown end-to-end, they'd wrap around the Earth at least three times, spanning more than 350 million feet. In her prime, Henrietta herself stood only a bit over five feet tall.

(F) wonder why Henrietta is called by her first name, Defler by his last

I first learned about HeLa cells and the woman behind them in 1988, thirty-seven years after her death, when I was sixteen and sitting in a community college biology class. My instructor, Donald Defler, a gnomish balding man, paced at the front of the lecture hall and flipped on an overhead projector. He pointed to two diagrams that appeared on the wall behind him. They were schematics of the cell reproduction cycle, but to me they just looked like a neon-colored mass of arrows, squares, and circles with words I didn't understand, like "MPF Triggering a Chain Reaction of Protein Activations."

G
can't follow this, why was she in college

I was a kid who'd failed freshman year at the regular public high school because she never showed up. I'd transferred to an alternative school that offered dream studies instead of biology, so I was taking Defler's class for high-school credit, which meant that I was sitting in a college lecture hall at sixteen with words like *mitosis* and *kinase inhibitors* flying around. I was completely lost.

F
wonder why Henrietta is called by her first name, Defler by his last

"Do we have to memorize everything on those diagrams?" one student yelled.

Yes, Defler said, we had to memorize the diagrams, and yes, they'd be on the test, but that didn't matter right then. What he wanted us to understand was that cells are amazing things: There are about one hundred trillion of them in our bodies, each so small that several thousand could fit on the period at the end of this sentence. They make UP all our tissues—muscle, bone, blood—which in turn make up our organs.

H
like the way she said this

I
☆

J
cute

Under the microscope, a cell looks a lot like a fried egg: It has a white (the *cytoplasm*) that's full of water and proteins to keep it fed, and a yolk (the *nucleus*) that holds all the genetic information that makes you *you*. The cytoplasm buzzes like a New York City street. It's crammed full of molecules and vessels endlessly shuttling enzymes and sugars from one part of the cell to another, pumping water, nutrients, and oxygen in and out of the cell. All the while, little cytoplasmic factories work 24/7, cranking out sugars, fats, proteins, and energy to keep the whole thing running and feed the nucleus—the brains of the operation. Inside every nucleus within each cell in your body, there's an identical copy of your entire genome. That genome tells cells when to grow and divide and makes sure they do their jobs, whether that's controlling your heartbeat or helping your brain understand the words on this page.

K
can sugar be plural?

All it takes is one small mistake anywhere in the division process for cells to start growing out of control, he told us. Just *one* enzyme misfiring, just *one* wrong protein activation, and you could have cancer. Mitosis goes haywire, which is how it spreads.

M

what is culture?

L

important

"We learned that by studying cancer cells in culture," Defler said. He grinned and spun to face the board, where he wrote two words in enormous print: HENRIETTA LACKS.

Next to each annotation is a letter in a yellow circle. Working on your own or in your group (your instructor will tell you which), explain what each annotation accomplishes. Does it ask a question, challenge an assertion, add the writer's own thought or example, mark something important, or do something else (or a combination of things)? Be prepared to compare your explanations with those written by other people or groups and to share your ideas with the rest of the class.

R2.3 Exploration

Annotating a Text

Working individually or in your group (your instructor will tell you which), annotate a text your instructor has assigned. Annotations may ask a question, challenge an assertion, add your own thoughts or examples, mark something as important, or do a combination of things.

R2.4 Advice

Highlighting

Sometimes readers may also use a highlighter to mark passages of a text while they are annotating. Highlighting can be a useful way to identify the main idea and key supporting points, but be careful of highlighting too much or too little. Highlighting too much suggests that everything is of equal importance. Highlighting too little hints that the reader either did not understand the text or was reading too quickly to identify the main idea and key supporting points. Neither will be effective strategies when it comes time to study or write in response to the text.

One strategy to avoid over- or under-highlighting is to read first and then highlight: read a paragraph all the way through before trying to identify and mark what's important. Another strategy is to think beforehand about what you want to highlight. You might decide to identify the thesis and key reasons in an argument, or you might highlight key metaphors or words related to a specific theme in a work of literature. (Or you could do both, using different colors for each element you're identifying.)

R2.5 Advice

Keeping a Reading Journal

A different tool for recording your thoughts and reactions is to keep a reading journal. Whether you use a notebook, a plain piece of paper, or a Google Doc, all you need to do to turn it into a reading journal is make two columns. If you want, you can label the left side something like "Ideas from Text" and the right side "My Thoughts about the Ideas."

An excerpt from "Words and Worlds" appears below. It comes from an extremely interesting but challenging book called *The Stuff of Thought* by Harvard psychology professor Steven Pinker. This is not a book you can read quickly and get much out of. It requires slow, deliberate reading and thinking, the kind of reading assisted by keeping a reading journal, so it will be used to illustrate what a reading journal looks like. Following the excerpt, you will find one student's writing journal for this text. The numbers in the writing journal correspond to the numbered underlined passages in the text.

Words and Worlds

STEVEN PINKER

1   On September 11, 2001, at 8:46 A.M., a hijacked airliner crashed into the north tower of the World Trade Center in New York. At 9:03 A.M. a second plane crashed into the south tower. The resulting infernos caused the buildings to collapse, the south tower after burning for an hour and two minutes, the north tower twenty-three minutes after that. The attacks were masterminded by Osama bin Laden, leader of the Al Qaeda terrorist organization, who hoped to intimidate the United States into ending its military presence in Saudi Arabia and its support for Israel and to unite Muslims in preparation for a restoration of the caliphate.

▶

2   9/11, as the happenings of that day are now called, stands as **①** <u>the most</u> <u>significant political and intellectual event of the twenty-first century so far</u>. It has set off debates on a vast array of topics: how best to memorialize the dead and revitalize lower Manhattan; whether the attacks are rooted in ancient Islamic fundamentalism or modern revolutionary agitation; the role of the United States on the world stage before the attacks and in response to them; how best to balance protection against terrorism with respect for civil liberties.

3   But I would like to explore a lesser-known debate triggered by 9/11. Exactly how many events took place in New York on that morning in September?

4   It could be argued that the answer is one. The attacks on the building were part of a single plan conceived in the mind of one man in service of a single agenda. They unfolded within a few minutes of each other, targeting the parts of a complex with a single name, design, and owner. And they launched a single chain of military and political events in their aftermath.

5   Or it could be argued that the answer is two. The north tower and south tower were distinct collections of glass and steel separated by an expanse of space, and they were hit at different times and went out of existence at different times. The amateur video that showed the second plane closing in on the south tower as the north tower billowed with smoke makes the twoness unmistakable: in those horrifying moments, one event was frozen in the past, the other loomed in the future. And another occurrence on that day—a passenger mutiny that brought down a third hijacked plane before it reached its target in Washington—presents to the imagination the possibility that one tower or the other might have been spared. **②** <u>In each of those possible</u> <u>worlds</u> a distinct event took place, so in our *actual* world one might argue, there must have been a pair of events as surely as one plus one equals two.

6   The gravity of 9/11 would seem to make this entire discussion **③** <u>frivolous to</u> <u>the point of impudence</u>. It's a matter of mere "semantics," as we say, with its implication of picking nits, splitting hairs, and debating the number of angels that can dance on the head of a pin. But this book is about semantics, and I would not make a claim on your attention if I did not think that **④** <u>the relation of language to our inner and</u> <u>outer worlds was a matter of intellectual fascination and real-world importance</u>.

7   Though "importance" is often hard to quantify, in this case I can put an exact value on it: three and a half billion dollars. That was the sum in dispute in a set of trials determining the insurance payout to Larry Silverstein, the **⑤** <u>leaseholder of</u> <u>the World Trade Center</u> site. Silverstein held insurance policies that stipulated a maximum reimbursement for each destructive "event." If 9/11 comprised a single event, he stood to receive three and a half billion dollars. If it comprised two events,

he stood to receive seven billion. In the trials, the attorneys disputed the applicable meaning of the term *event*. The lawyers for the leaseholder defined it in physical terms (two collapses); those for the insurance companies defined it in mental terms (one plot). There is nothing "mere" about semantics!

8   Nor is the topic intellectually trifling. The 9/11 cardinality debate is not about the facts, that is, the physical events and human actions that took place that day. Admittedly, those have been contested as well: according to various conspiracy theories, the buildings were targeted by American missiles, or demolished by a controlled implosion, in a plot conceived by American neoconservatives, Israeli spies, or a cabal of psychiatrists. But aside from the kooks, most people agree on the facts. Where they differ is in the *construal* of those facts: how ❻ the intricate swirl of matter in space ought to be conceptualized by human minds. As we shall see, ❼ the categories in this dispute permeate the meanings of words in our language because they permeate the way we represent reality in our heads.

9   ❽ Semantics is about the relation of words to thoughts, but it is also about the relation of words to other human concerns. Semantics is about the relation of words to reality—the way that speakers commit themselves to a shared understanding of the truth, and the way their thoughts are anchored to things and situations in the world. It is about the relation of words to a community—how ❾ a new word, which arises in an act of creation by a single speaker, comes to evoke the same idea in the rest of a population, so people can understand one another when they use it. It is about the relation of words to emotions: the way in which words don't just point to things but are saturated with feelings, which can endow the words with a sense of magic, taboo, and sin. And it is about words and social relations—how ❿ people use language not just to transfer ideas from head to head but to negotiate the kind of relationship they wish to have with their conversational partner.

10   A feature of the mind that we will repeatedly encounter in these pages is that ⓫ even our most abstract concepts are understood in terms of concrete scenarios. That applies in full force to the subject matter of the book itself. In this introductory chapter I will preview some of the book's topics with vignettes from newspapers and the Internet that can be understood only through the lens of semantics. They come from each of the worlds that connect to our words—the worlds of thought, reality, community, emotions, and social relations.

11   Let's look at the bone of contention in the world's most expensive debate in semantics, the three-and-a-half-billion-dollar argument over the meaning of "event." What, exactly, is an event? ⓬ An event is a stretch of time, and time, according to physicists, is a continuous variable—an inexorable cosmic flow, in Newton's world, ▶

or a fourth dimension in a seamless hyperspace in Einstein's. But **13** <u>the human mind carves this fabric into discrete swatches we call events.</u> Where does the mind place the incisions? Sometimes, as the lawyers for the World Trade Center leaseholder pointed out, it encircles the change of state of an object, such as the collapse of a building. And sometimes, as the lawyers for the insurers pointed out, it encircles the goal of a human actor, such as a plot being executed. Most often the circles coincide: an actor intends to cause an object to change, the intent of the act and the fate of the object are tracked along a single time line, and the moment of change marks the consummation of the intent.

*　　*　　*

12   The 9/11 cardinality debate highlights another curious fact about the language of thought. In puzzling over how to count the events of that day, it asks us to treat them as if they were objects that can be tallied, like poker chips in a pile. The debate over whether there was one event or two in New York that day is like a disagreement over **14** <u>whether there is one item or two at an express checkout lane,</u> such as a pair of butter sticks taken out of a box of four, or a pair of grapefruits selling at two for a dollar. The similar ambiguity in tallying events is one of the many ways in which space and time are treated equivalently in the human mind, well before Einstein depicted them as equivalent in reality.

13   As we shall see in Chapter 4, **15** <u>the mind categorizes matter into discrete things (like a *sausage*) and continuous stuff (like *meat*),</u> and it similarly categorizes time into discrete events (like *to cross the street*) and continuous activities (like *to stroll*). With both space and time, the same mental zoom lens that allows us to count objects or events also allows us to zoom in even closer on what each one is made of. In space, we can focus on the material making up an object (as when we say *I got sausage all over my shirt*); in time, we can focus on an activity making up an event (as when we say *She was crossing the street*). This cognitive zoom lens also lets us pan out in space and see a collection of objects as an aggregate (as in the difference between *a pebble* and *gravel*), and it allows us to pan out in time and see a collection of events as an iteration (as in the difference between *hit the nail* and *pound the nail*). And in time, as in space, we mentally place an entity at a location and then shunt it around: we can *move a meeting from 3:00 to 4:00* in the same way that we move a car from one end of the block to the other. And speaking of an *end*, even some of the fine points of our mental geometry carry over from space to time. **16** <u>*The end of a string* is technically a point, but we can say *Herb cut off the end of the string*, showing that an end can be construed as including a snippet of the matter adjacent to it. The same is true in time: the *end of a lecture* is technically an instant,</u>

but we can say *I'm going to give the end of my lecture now*, construing the culmination of an event as including a small stretch of time adjacent to it.

14   As we shall see, **🔟7** language is saturated with implicit metaphors like EVENTS ARE OBJECTS and TIME IS SPACE. Indeed, space turns out to be a conceptual vehicle not just for time but for many kinds of states and circumstances. Just as a meeting can be moved from 3:00 to 4:00, a traffic light can go from green to red, a person can go from flipping burgers to running a corporation, and the economy can go from bad to worse. Metaphor is so widespread in language that it's hard to find expressions for abstract ideas that are *not* metaphorical. What does the concreteness of language say about human thought? Does it imply that even our wispiest concepts are represented in the mind as hunks of matter that we move around on a mental stage? Does it say that **18** rival claims about the world can never be true or false but can only be alternative metaphors that frame a situation in different ways? Those are the obsessions of Chapter 5.

Ideas in the Text	My Thoughts about the Ideas
1. "9/11" was "the most significant . . . event of" this "century so far" (p. 538)	That "so far" seems very ominous. It implies that worse events are ahead of us.
2. "In each of those possible worlds" (p. 538)	This is hard to follow. I think he's saying that because, in our imaginations, either plane could have been prevented from striking its target, we are forced to consider, even in the actual world where both towers were struck, that there were two events.
3. "frivolous to the point of impudence" (p. 538)	I guess that's very frivolous.
4. "the relation of language to our inner and outer worlds was a matter of intellectual fascination and real-world importance" (p. 538)	Hmmm. Inner and outer worlds? The world in our minds and the world we actually live in?
5. "leaseholder of the World Trade Center" (p. 538)	Was the leaseholder just renting the towers? Odd. I would expect the person with the insurance would be the owner.

Ideas in the Text	My Thoughts about the Ideas
6. "the intricate swirl of matter in space" (p. 539)	I don't get this. Is he talking about some kind of nebula or something? What does this have to do with anything?
7. "the categories in this dispute permeate the meanings of words in our language because they permeate the way we represent reality in our heads" (p. 539)	These "categories in this dispute" I think refers to whether there was one event or two. What does he mean about the way we represent reality in our heads?
8. "Semantics is about the relation of words to thoughts" (p. 539)	I think words simply stand for thoughts. The word "chair" stands for the thought we have of a thing that is a chair.
9. "a new word, which arises in an act of creation by a single speaker" (p. 539)	Interesting. I wonder how a new word gets into a language spoken by millions of people?
10. "people use language . . . to negotiate the kind of relationship they wish to have with their conversational partner" (p. 539)	Interesting. I wish he had said more about this.
11. "even our most abstract concepts are understood in terms of concrete scenarios" (p. 539)	I wonder what he means by this.
12. "An event is a stretch of time" (p. 539)	So far, so good. I get this. Makes sense.
13. "the human mind carves this fabric into discrete swatches we call events" (p. 540)	Still okay, although I don't see why he decides to call time a fabric.
14. "whether there is one item or two at an express checkout line" (p. 540)	A great example of how hard it is to count the number of events.
15. "the mind classifies matter into discrete things (like a *sausage*) and continuous stuff (like *meat*)" (p. 540)	Isn't this the same as the distinction between count and noncount nouns?

Ideas in the Text	My Thoughts about the Ideas
16. "the end of a string" compared to "the end of a lecture" (p. 540)	The end is technically the end, except when it also includes stuff just before the end.
17. "language is saturated with implicit metaphors like EVENTS ARE OBJECTS and TIME IS SPACE" (p. 541)	This seems to be a major point.
18. "rival claims about the world can never be true or false but can only be alternative metaphors that frame a situation in different ways" (p. 541)	So here's the answer to the World Trade Center legal argument, but he doesn't tell who actually won in court!

You can include quotations, paraphrases, or summaries in column 1, but if you mainly include quotations (as this student did), be sure to include quotation marks and page numbers, so it will be clear later which words are the author's and where the quotations came from. (To learn more about avoiding plagiarism, see D1.13, p. 317; for quoting and paraphrasing, see D1.10, p. 309; for summarizing, see W11.30, p. 235.)

R2.6   Exploration

Keeping Your Own Reading Journal

Your instructor will assign a text for you to read. Working individually, keep a reading journal like the one in R2.5 (p. 261).

R2.7   Advice

Creating Timelines and Family Trees

When reading longer and more complicated works, it is sometimes helpful to keep track of what you're reading and thinking by creating graphics, such as timelines and family trees. You might think of these as the visual equivalents of taking notes.

Timelines

If you're reading a narrative text, one that is telling a story or describing how events happened over time, it may be helpful to create a timeline. Here's an example of what such a timeline might look like.

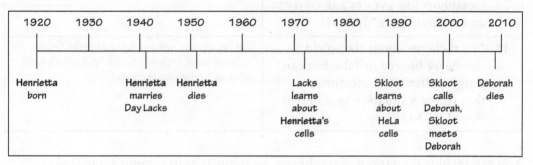

Peter Adams

The student who constructed it was reading *The Immortal Life of Henrietta Lacks*. Early in the book, she learned that the main character, Henrietta Lacks, was born in 1920. Realizing that this book was going to cover events that took place over a number of years, she decided to construct a timeline in which she could post the major events in the story. She marked Henrietta's birth in 1920 at the left end of the timeline and 2010, the date the book was published, at the right end. Then she made a vertical mark for every ten years. As she read the book, she marked major events on the timeline.

The student did all this on a piece of plain paper, although she might have created a similar graphic using a computer. A timeline like this is especially helpful when you are reading a text that doesn't present information in chronological order but skips backward and forward in time, as *The Immortal Life of Henrietta Lacks* does.

Family Trees

If you are reading a text—especially a full-length book—with lots of characters, creating a family tree can help you keep their names straight and see the relationships among the different family members. *The Immortal Life of Henrietta Lacks* includes seven generations of one very large family, so making a family tree seemed to be a good strategy to another student. Here is his tree.

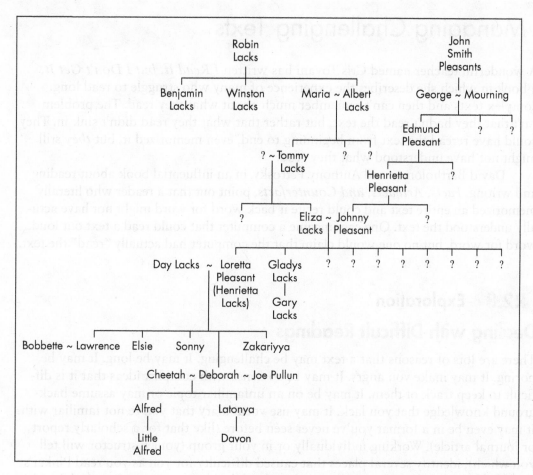

Peter Adams

These family trees can be very messy. Sometimes you discover that you haven't left yourself enough room for all the branches of a family, so you have to start over on a blank sheet. Often, there are several families who interact with each other, so you have to find a way to match up the generations and who married whom. Despite their potential messiness, though, in a book with lots of characters, family trees can be extremely helpful in keeping track of everyone.

Managing Challenging Texts

A wonderful teacher named Cris Tovani has written *I Read It, but I Don't Get It*, a book in which she describes the experience of many who struggle to read long, complex texts and then can't remember much about what they read. The problem isn't that they hadn't read the text, but rather that what they read didn't sink in. They could have reread the text from beginning to end, even memorized it, but *they* still might not have understood what they read.

David Bartholomae and Anthony Petrosky, in an influential book about reading and writing, *Facts, Artifacts, and Counterfacts*, point out that a reader who literally memorized an entire text and could recite it back word for word might not have actually understood the text. One can imagine a computer that could read a text out loud, word for word, but no one would claim that the computer had actually "read" the text.

R2.8 Exploration
Dealing with Difficult Readings

There are lots of reasons that a text may be challenging. It may be long. It may be boring. It may make you angry. It may be so dense with complex ideas that it is difficult to keep track of them. It may be on an unfamiliar topic or may assume background knowledge that you lack. It may use vocabulary that you're not familiar with. It may even be in a format you've never seen before (like that for a scholarly report or journal article). Working individually or in your group (your instructor will tell you which), identify several places that caused difficulty for you as you read Pinker's "Words and Worlds" (R2.5, p. 261). For each of the entries on your list, explain what it was that made the text difficult at that point.

R2.9 Advice
Chunking

One strategy for reading a long, challenging text is to break the reading assignment into smaller chunks. If you have been assigned a chapter, break it down into sections, maybe the content between two major headings, and stop after each chunk to check that you've understood what you've read. Write a brief summary of the main points or create a diagram or timeline that helps you to organize what you've learned. (Take a look at W11.30, Strategies for Writing a Summary, p. 235; W5.9, Outlining, p. 62; and R2.7, Creating Timelines and Family Trees, p. 267.)

R2.10 Advice

Slowing Down

Another strategy for challenging readings is to break the text into even smaller
chunks; even reading sentence by sentence may sometimes be necessary. You may
recall reading an excerpt from "What Is Independence and Interdependence?."
That reading was especially challenging because it is an excerpt from a scholarly
article written by two highly trained social psychologists for an audience of similarly
trained social psychologists. To make sense of the excerpt, you had to slow down and
read it sentence by sentence, sometimes backing up and rereading.

Look again at just the first few sentences of that passage. Some of the elements
you might find challenging—or even confusing—are highlighted below.

> One particularly powerful and important set of [personality] patterns is that
> which prescribe the normatively appropriate relations between the self (the
> individual) and others (other individuals). Social scientists in various fields (e.g.,
> Dumont, 1977; Marx, 1857–1858/1973; Mead, 1934; Triandis, 1995) have
> repeatedly theorized two distinct types of sociality or social relations that can
> be linked to divergent modes of being or senses of self. One type of sociality
> assumes that social relations are formed on the basis of instrumental interests
> and goals of participating individuals. Labels for such social relations include
> *gessellschaft*, independent, egocentric, and individualist. Another type of soci-
> ality assumes that individuals are inherently connected and made meaningful
> through relationships with others. Labels for such social relations include
> *gemeinschaft*, interdependent, sociocentric, communal, and collectivist (see
> Fiske et al., 1998; Shweder & Bourne, 1984; Tönnies, 1887/1988, for reviews).

Scholarly articles like this one require a type of reading you may not be used to: slowing down, reading carefully, and thinking hard about the language being used. To
make sense of this passage, you need to figure out how the authors are using terms like
prescribe, a word you have probably used but in a different sense. You'll also have to
figure out what other, unfamiliar specialist vocabulary means. (See R2.11, Dealing with
Difficult Language.) Finally, you'll have to put it all together to create meaning.

R2.11 Advice

Dealing with Difficult Language

Readers frequently have difficulty when they bump into a word or phrase that they
don't know. The most common strategy for dealing with an unfamiliar word is to look

it up in a dictionary. Now, this is not a bad strategy; in fact, sometimes it's very good advice, but looking it up in a dictionary is only one of a number of available strategies.

In fact, in many situations it is not the best strategy. When you interrupt your reading to consult a dictionary, it's easy to lose track of the meaning of the text you've been reading. If you encounter a number of unfamiliar words that you look up, you can end up having read an entire passage with little idea of what it meant. To avoid these interruptions to the flow of your reading, you can first use one or more of the following strategies when you encounter unfamiliar words or phrases.

Use Context Clues

Suppose you came across the following sentence in something you were reading:

> She grabbed her portmanteau, which she had packed the night before, and left for the train station.

Chances are, you are not familiar with the word *portmanteau*, but from the rest of the sentence, it would not be hard to guess that it must be some kind of a suitcase. It is often possible to work out the meaning of a word by carefully reading not only the sentence in which it appears but those that immediately precede or follow it. Basically, you infer from the information provided what a word or term means.

Figuring out the meaning of a word from its context often gives you only a general sense of the word. For instance, using the example above, a portmanteau is actually a large suitcase, usually made of leather, and opening into two halves of equal size. You would never figure out all that detail from the context, but in most cases recognizing that it was a type of suitcase would be all you needed to understand what you were reading.

Use Word Parts

Another strategy that can be useful in figuring out what an unfamiliar word means without looking it up is to break it into its parts. Consider the following sentence:

> Karina's essay was filled with polysyllabic words.

If you are unfamiliar with the word *polysyllabic*, you may be able to figure out its meaning by breaking it into parts. You've probably encountered the prefix *poly-* in other words. Do you remember what a polygon is? It's a two-dimensional figure with many sides. How about polygamy? It means being married to multiple partners. By now, it seems clear that *poly-* means *many*, and as the second half of the word is fairly close to *syllable*, a polysyllabic word is apparently a word with many syllables.

Being familiar with word parts, the building blocks of words, can be useful, especially if you are studying in the sciences. Words can contain one or more roots, prefixes, and suffixes. Roots are the core of words and carry their basic meaning. Prefixes are added to the beginning of root words to change their meaning; for example, adding the prefix *un-* to the word *happy* creates *unhappy*, which means the opposite of the original word. Suffixes are placed at the ends of root words and can change their part of speech; for example, adding *-less* to the root word *clue* changes the word from a noun to an adjective, *clueless*. Suffixes can also change the root word's tense; for example, adding *-ed* to the root word *raid* changes it from the present to the past tense, *raided*.

No one expects you to memorize word parts, but if you do a quick search of the internet you will find all sorts of charts listing roots, prefixes, and suffixes with their meanings, which you can download or print out for easy reference. Many scientific terms are built from word parts, and familiarizing yourself with the most common ones, such as *bio-*, *geo-*, *mono-*, or *-itis*, can help you to make sense of terms as you read.

Reread the Passage

Another strategy when you encounter a word or phrase that you don't understand is to back up and reread the passage. Sometimes the meaning will become clearer on a second reading.

Look for Synonyms, Antonyms, or Definitions Close By

A different strategy is to keep reading. Often writers, realizing they have used a term some readers may not know, will explain the term in the next sentence or even later in the same sentence, including words with similar meanings (synonyms) or opposite ones (antonyms) to provide clues to their meanings. Textbook authors will even put important terms in bold or italics and follow them with definitions. Writers often use punctuation to indicate they are about to provide a definition or explanation of a term, introducing it with a colon, setting it off with commas or dashes, or placing it in parentheses.

Decide the Word Is Not Important

Sometimes it is perfectly acceptable to decide that a word is not going to be important, at least in the text you're reading, and you can move on without worrying about what it means. Suppose you were reading a mystery novel and came across this sentence:

The murdered woman was wearing a cerise sweater.

Does it matter what color cerise is? Probably not. You will likely be able to follow the action of the novel just fine even though you're not sure of the color of the woman's sweater. But what if, later in the novel, you find out that a suspect had tiny fragments of cerise-colored thread under his fingernails? Now does it matter what color cerise is? Actually, it does not. It is important to remember that the victim's sweater was cerise, but it doesn't really matter what color that is. (By the way, *cerise* is a bright or dark red. It comes from the French word for *cherry*.)

Use a Dictionary

Some readers are interested in expanding their vocabulary when they read. If you fit into this group, it is probably still better not to interrupt your reading to look up words unless knowing the meaning of a particular word is crucial to understanding the text. Instead, underline or circle each word whose meaning you can't guess at from the context. After you've finished reading the text, you can go back, look up all the words you marked, and write their definitions either in the margin beside them or in a log you keep of new words. (Note that online dictionaries are quick and easy to use and provide lots of useful information, including the option to hear how a word is pronounced. It's worth bookmarking a site, such as dictionary.com or merriam-webster.com, for easy reference.)

R2.12 Exploration
Decoding Difficult Language

You can work with "Words and Worlds," the excerpt from Steven Pinker's *The Stuff of Thought* (R2.5, p. 261), or your instructor may assign a reading that includes some challenging words. Working individually or in your group (your instructor will tell you which), identify the words you have difficulty with. Make a list with three columns as shown in the following example. Then use one or more of the six strategies listed in R2.11, Dealing with Difficult Language (p. 271), to figure out the meaning of each word. Save using a dictionary as a last resort.

Challenging Words	Strategy Used	Meaning
multifarious	word parts	having many parts
laminated	dictionary	made of thin layers bonded together
restitution	from context	giving something back that had been wrongfully taken away

R3 Reading Critically

Being a critical reader means reading thoughtfully—evaluating the assertions in a text, the support for those assertions, the assumptions underlying them, and the credibility of the author.

Analyzing the Evidence

R3.1 Advice

Distinguishing between Facts and Opinions

W4.1, Evidence and Assertions (p. 37), illustrates the relationship between facts (evidence) and opinions (assertions) from the point of view of the *writer*. It is also important that *readers* recognize this relationship and are able to distinguish between facts and opinions. It's even more important for readers to recognize that many ideas expressed as if they are facts are merely opinions masquerading as facts.

What Are Facts?

Exactly what is a fact? How can you recognize what is factual in what you read? It has often been said that facts are not arguable. Facts are statements that have been proven to be true. Facts are what the experts agree is true. Some factual statements satisfy these definitions without any difficulty. The capital of California is Sacramento. Mt. Everest is the highest mountain in the world. English 101 is a required course at most colleges.

But sometimes facts are stated as if they apply universally when they don't. Consider the "fact" that water boils at 212° Fahrenheit. This is a fact—but only at sea level. Those who live at higher elevations, in places like Denver, know that water boils at a lower temperature there. The statement that "Native Americans' primary food source was the bison" needs to be examined carefully. It turns out to be true for Native Americans in the Great Plains but not true for Native Americans who lived in other parts of North America.

It's also the case that what are considered facts can change. (That's the nature of science: what's considered a fact changes in response to new evidence or a new understanding of the evidence.) As recently as the early 2000s, it was considered a fact that there were nine planets in our solar system. However, in 2006, the International Astronomical Union downgraded Pluto to a dwarf planet. Today, the fact is that our solar system has just eight planets. For years, scientists have agreed that the earliest members of the human genus to use stone tools were *Homo habilis*, who evolved around 2.8 million years ago. But in 2015, stone tools and fossils of early humans that are 3.3 million years old were discovered in Kenya. So the facts about when humans began using tools have also changed.

As a reader, you should carefully examine and think deeply about statements that authors clearly intend that you will accept as facts. Make sure the "fact" is worded carefully so that it is true and that it is *currently* considered a fact, that experts haven't learned new information that modified what used to be considered factual.

How to Decide Whether the Experts Agree?

It is generally safe to assume that a statement is a fact if the experts agree that it is. The problem is that it is rare for 100 percent of experts to agree about anything. It is unreasonable to insist that something is not a fact unless there is 100 percent agreement about it by every expert in the world; statements about which the vast majority of experts agree can safely be understood to be facts.

Where should we draw the line? How great must the agreement be for something actually to be considered a fact? Perhaps the answer to these questions is that, as a reader, you could accept opinions on which a great many experts agree as evidence, just not quite as strong evidence as actual facts. You may also find it useful to investigate the experts who don't agree. Are they legitimate experts? What reasons do they give for their disagreement? Do you find their reasons sensible? (Take a look at D1.7, Evaluating Sources, p. 305, for some tips.)

You also should be aware that experts who have devoted their lives to their profession may not be unbiased about that profession. Experts on nuclear energy are likely to favor expansion of nuclear power plants. Doctors whose lives have been dedicated to curing people are likely to find it hard to accept the idea that some people don't think they need to be cured. Police officers who have devoted their lives to their careers are unlikely to accept arguments that we should replace some police officers with people who have more experience in calming disputes and de-escalating violence. Of course, we should listen to expert opinion, but we should also be aware of the biases that often accompany expertise.

How Should Readers Respond to Conclusions, Claims, and Opinions?

It is a *fact* that college tuition has gone up faster than inflation for years, and it is a *fact* that the cost of textbooks has increased dramatically. Further, it is a *fact* that other fees at colleges have gone up at a steep rate. But it is *not* a fact that college is too expensive. That last statement is an *opinion*. It is based on facts, but it is an assertion that someone might make after thinking about the facts, which doesn't make it a fact. Someone else might look at the same set of facts and reach a different conclusion. Still others might know of a different set of facts that could be used to argue that college is not too expensive.

There is, of course, nothing wrong with writers asserting their opinions, but as a critical reader, you need to make sure that such assertions are actually supported by convincing evidence. When reading a text that makes an assertion followed by factual evidence or a text that presents a series of facts and then makes an assertion based on those facts, it's a good idea to stop and think about the conclusions the authors have reached. Do they seem reasonable? Could the same facts lead to a different conclusion? Are enough facts presented to justify the conclusion? This kind of analysis can lead to a more insightful reading of the text, and being able to distinguish between facts and opinions is essential to this kind of analysis.

Finally, some alternative vocabulary. You've been reading about the differences between facts and opinions. What about *conclusions, assertions,* and *claims*? These terms are usually used to mean the same thing as *opinions*. In any case, as a reader, if you encounter statements that you would consider fitting any of these categories, you should carefully examine the evidence provided to support them.

R3.2 Exploration

Recognizing Facts and Opinions

R3.1 (p. 275) discusses the difference between facts and opinions (sometimes called *conclusions, claims,* or *assertions*). It is important for readers to be able to distinguish between these types of statements, because opinions without factual evidence to support them should be given little credence.

Working individually or in your group (your instructor will tell you which), decide whether the following statements are facts, statements about which most experts agree, or opinions.

1. The cost of healthcare is too high.
2. The cost of healthcare has risen every year for the past forty years.
3. More Democrats support background checks for the purchase of guns than do Republicans.
4. Global warming is caused by human behavior.
5. Every parent should have their children vaccinated against childhood diseases.
6. Immigration takes jobs away from American workers.
7. There are more electric cars on the road today than ever before.

8. Completing a college degree improves your chances of economic success in America.

9. Gasoline prices are too high.

10. Donald Trump was the forty-fifth president.

R3.3 Exploration

Evaluating Evidence

R3.1, Distinguishing between Facts and Opinions (p. 275), discusses the difference between facts, statements most experts agree on, and opinions. Here, you're going to think about evaluating the facts or evidence writers provide to support their opinions.

Imagine that your college needs to know, on average, how many students eat in the cafeteria each week. This information will be used for budgeting purposes. Below are reports written by three different student employees who were assigned this task. Working in your group, read each of the three reports, evaluate the evidence that supports the assertion made in each one, and decide which report is most convincing.

Report 1

At this college, on average, 1,578 students eat in the cafeteria each week. To arrive at this number, I sat in the cafeteria each day for a week and counted the number of students in the cafeteria. Below are my totals for the week. The cafeteria is closed on weekends.

Monday: 310

Tuesday: 330

Wednesday: 301

Thursday: 349

Friday: 288

Report 2

At this college, on average, 1,316 students eat in the cafeteria each week when classes are in session. To arrive at this number, I sat in the cafeteria each day for a week in September, December, January, and March and counted the number of students in the cafeteria. Below are my data for each month.

September		December		January		March	
Mon.	310	Mon.	285	Mon.	192	Mon.	301
Tue.	330	Tue.	301	Tue.	186	Tue.	244
Wed.	301	Wed.	280	Wed.	228	Wed.	289
Thu.	349	Thu.	338	Thu.	199	Thu.	260
Fri.	88	Fri.	275	Fri.	165	Fri.	143
Totals	1,578		1,479		970		1,237

I arrived at the figure of 1,316 students each week by averaging the four weekly totals I had observed.

Report 3

At this college, an average of 845 students eat in the cafeteria each week when classes are in session. At first, I thought I would sit in the cafeteria for a week at several different times during the academic year and count the number of students in the cafeteria. Then I realized two things: first, to do this would be extremely time-consuming and boring, and, second, it would be inaccurate. Not all students in the cafeteria are eating; many are there simply to do homework while waiting for their next class.

Faced with this realization, I asked the cafeteria manager if the cash registers recorded the number of students who paid for food each week. When she said, "Yes," I asked if she could give me a copy of those weekly totals for a year. She said, "Sure." All I had to do was average the weekly totals she gave me to arrive at an accurate average number of students who ate in the cafeteria each week when classes were in session.

Below are the totals produced by the cash registers for one complete year:

January	Week 1	764	March	Week 1	928
	Week 2	770		Week 2	919
	Week 3	759		Week 3	908
	Week 4	803		Week 4	Spring break
February	Week 1	965	April	Week 1	889
	Week 2	971		Week 2	891
	Week 3	954		Week 3	868
	Week 4	949		Week 4	860

May	Week 1	869		Week 2	985
	Week 2	858		Week 3	976
	Week 3	840		Week 4	969
	Week 4	No classes	October	Week 1	962
June	Week 1	No classes		Week 2	965
	Week 2	619		Week 3	957
	Week 3	625		Week 4	956
	Week 4	625	November	Week 1	950
July	Week 1	618		Week 2	954
	Week 2	611		Week 3	948
	Week 3	No classes		Week 4	946
	Week 4	623	December	Week 1	943
August	Week 1	629		Week 2	941
	Week 2	622		Week 3	931
	Week 3	618		Week 4	No classes
	Week 4	609		Total	36,327
September	Week 1	980	Average weekly total: 36,327 ÷ 34 = 845		

Analyzing the Author's Language

Often, paying close attention to the language an author uses can provide helpful clues to the meaning of a text and the intentions of the author.

R3.4 Advice

Recognizing the Author's Tone

Understanding what an author is saying and, more important, the effect the author wants to have on readers—the author's purpose—can be assisted by paying attention to the author's tone. *Tone* is the writer's attitude or perspective as conveyed by the connotations (the emotional resonance) of the words used. Consider these words and phrases: *freedom fighter*, *rebel*, and *terrorist*. Each could be used to describe a soldier fighting for Ukraine or Russia, a member of Fatah or of the Israeli army, depending on the side the writer supports.

As you read, consider the author's tone. Does the author sound angry? Sad? Perplexed? Sarcastic? Pleading? Serious? Compassionate? Condescending? Consider, too, how the writer's tone is likely to affect readers. What does the writer want readers—including you—to do, think, or feel? Being attentive to tone will allow you to be a more perceptive reader.

R3.5 Advice

Recognizing Euphemisms

A euphemism is a word or phrase that a writer uses to avoid a harsher, more offensive, or even more hurtful expression. Using *passed away* in place of *died*, *meat-packing company* in place of *slaughterhouse*, or *let go* in place of *fired* are all euphemisms.

Sometimes writers employ euphemisms to avoid offending or shocking their readers: using *passed away* at a funeral is perfectly acceptable. But sometimes people use euphemisms to lessen resistance to something they are proposing. A company preparing to fire a large percentage of their workforce might use a term like *smartsizing* or *rightsizing* or even *delayering* or *workforce optimization* rather than *layoffs*. And, sometimes writers use euphemistic language to conceal something they don't want the reader to recognize. Governments might use phrases like *enhanced interrogation techniques* or *severe tactics* when they are reluctant to admit to torture, or they might use *ethnic cleansing* to avoid a word like *genocide*.

If you find euphemisms in texts you are reading, ask yourself why the author is using them. If they are used to avoid language readers might find hurtful or offensive, fine. On the other hand, if the writer is using euphemisms to conceal or camouflage the text's true message, ask yourself what the writer is concealing and why, and read the entire message with greater skepticism.

R3.6 Advice

Analyzing Figurative Language

Figurative language is more beautiful, more powerful, more creative than more ordinary language. Figures of speech add power, depth, and sometimes humor. The three most common figures of speech are *simile*, *metaphor*, and *personification*.

- **Simile.** Similes compare one thing to something very different, using words such as *like* or *as*: "My grandfather sat on his bench all afternoon like a frog sunning himself on a log."

- **Metaphor.** Like a simile, a metaphor compares two unlike things, but it does so without using *like* or *as*: "My professor's suggestion was the seed that grew into my first published poem."

- **Personification.** In personification, human qualities are attributed to an inanimate object. "My cell phone reminded me it was time to go to class." In this case, the cell phone is treated as if it's a person issuing reminders.

When you encounter a figure of speech in a text, think about why the author used it. What purpose did it serve? What was the author's motive? In most cases, writers use figurative language to surprise and delight their readers. But in some cases their motives may be less pure. Figurative language may sometimes be used to associate one thing (a politician or a position, for example) with positive qualities or to insinuate the opposite about an opponent. When a flag waves in the background or a bald eagle soars above, consider the motives of the writer with skepticism. (To learn more about figurative language, see W6.13, Using Figurative Language, p. 85.)

Reading between the Lines

This section will encourage you not only to read between the lines but also to dive under the lines to find meanings not so obvious, and it will suggest techniques for doing these kinds of deep reading.

R3.7 Advice

Believing and Doubting

The believing and doubting game is an approach to engagement with a text that was developed by Peter Elbow at the University of Massachusetts. It's a wonderful way for getting readers to engage more deeply with a text.

At its heart, the believing and doubting game simply asks you to read a text two different ways. It asks you to read it once as a "believer," someone who agrees with the author and is reading because you want to understand exactly what the author's point is and why the author came to that conclusion. Then it asks you to read the text a second time from the point of view of a skeptic, someone who doubts that the central argument of the text is correct. This time you are reading to find flaws in the argument, weaknesses in the logic, and reasons to refute the conclusions.

One way to use this approach is to write two short—less than a page—summaries of a text. In the first, you write as a believer, someone who agrees with the author, and you focus on the points you agree with. In the second, you write as a doubter, someone who is trying to explain why you disagree with the argument.

R3.8 Exploration

Reading as a Believer and a Doubter

In R3.7, Believing and Doubting (p. 282), you read about a strategy that helps you to think deeply about a text as you read it. Now try out this approach to engaging with a text using an article supplied by your instructor. Read the article once as a believer, someone who is in agreement with the author. Don't allow any doubts or disagreements to creep in while you read as a believer. Then write a "believer's summary" in which you summarize the article briefly, emphasizing the points you agree with. Try to limit this summary to a half page. When you've finished that, read the article again, this time as a doubter, someone who disagrees with the author. Then write a second brief summary in which you focus on the points you disagree with. Again, a half page is plenty.

R3.9 Advice

Making Inferences

We all make inferences every day. We look out the window and infer from the gray sky and looming clouds that it's going to rain. We encounter backed-up traffic on a usually quiet road and think about possible causes: an accident, roadwork, or maybe dangerous driving conditions if there is snow or freezing rain. To make these inferences, we use clues in what we see or hear and draw conclusions about them based on our knowledge and previous experiences.

Writers do not always directly state their point. Sometimes they rely on the reader to piece together their message from the information they provide. To make an inference when you read a text, you have to think about what you already know about the subject, notice the details and language the writer uses, add up the facts the writer provides, and combine all these to come up with an idea of what the text means.

Here are some tips for making inferences as you read:

- **Read the text carefully.** Make sure you understand the main ideas and details the writer presents.

- **Consider the author's audience and purpose.** Who would the writer have expected to be reading this text, and what might those readers have in common? What does the writer want to accomplish, that is, what does the writer want to make readers think, do, or feel?

- **Look for unusual details.** Ask yourself what clues the details provide about what the author is saying, especially any details that seem unusual.

- **Put the facts and details together.** Considering all the facts and details, what point do they seem to be making? Why were these facts and these specific details included and not others?

- **Evaluate the author's choice of language.** What is the overall tone of the text? What does this suggest to you about the author's meaning?

- **Compare what you know with what you've read.** Think about what you already know about the subject. Does what the writer says fit with the information you already have? Have you had experiences that would help you understand his or her point?

- **Recheck the text.** Finally, once you have made your inference, reread the text to check that your conclusion fits all the evidence in the text. Consider whether other conclusions could be made based on the evidence. Is there additional evidence in the text or from other sources that would confirm your hypothesis or cause you to revise it?

Let's look at an example, a text written by a young college professor about a class he is teaching:

> Before I could even get to my classroom, I had to pass through a metal detector and wait as a heavy metal gate slammed shut behind me and another one opened in front of me. When I arrived in my classroom, right away I saw that only about a dozen of my twenty students were there. I asked where everyone else was, and one young man replied, "Eight of us are on 'lock down.'"

To make an inference about this passage, you first have to read it carefully. Then you need to notice details like the *metal detector*, the *heavy metal gates*, and the fact that eight students are on "*lock down*." When you've added up these details, you probably realize that the instructor is in a prison. But he's a professor, so what's he doing in prison? Ah, he's teaching a class to inmates. You've made an inference. The text didn't exactly say the professor is teaching in a prison, but by noticing the details, connecting them to what you already know, and thinking about them, you inferred that he must be teaching a class in a prison.

So that's what's meant by making an inference—reading a text, noticing the details, and, using your own knowledge to come up with a meaning that isn't directly expressed in words.

R3.10 Exploration

Practice Making Inferences

Working in your group, see what inferences you can make from reading each of the two passages below.

Passage 1: Excerpt from *Better: A Surgeon's Notes on Performance*

This passage comes from Dr. Atul Gawande's book about what is involved in providing good patient care.

> In 1847, at the age of twenty-eight, the Viennese obstetrician Ignac Semmelweis famously deduced that, by not washing their hands consistently or well enough, doctors were themselves to blame for childbed fever. Childbed fever, also known as puerperal fever, was the leading cause of maternal death in childbirth in the era before antibiotics (and before the recognition that germs are the agents of infectious disease). It is a bacterial infection most commonly caused by *Streptococcus*, the same bacteria that causes strep throat—that ascends through the vagina to the uterus after childbirth. Out of three thousand mothers who delivered babies at the hospital where Semmelweis worked, six hundred or more died of the disease each year—a horrifying 20 percent maternal death rate. Of mothers delivering at home, only 1 percent died. Semmelweis concluded that doctors themselves were carrying the disease between patients, and he mandated that every doctor and nurse on his ward scrub with a nail brush and chlorine between patients. The puerperal death rate immediately fell to 1 percent—incontrovertible proof, it would seem, that he was right. Yet elsewhere, doctors' practices did not change. Some colleagues were even offended by his claims; it was impossible to them that doctors could be killing their patients. Far from being hailed, Semmelweis was ultimately dismissed from his job.

Passage 2: Excerpt from *Outliers: The Story of Success*

This passage is an excerpt from Malcolm Gladwell's book, which explores some of the complex factors that contribute to the success of people like Bill Joy, who created UNIX and Java computer languages; Bill Gates, founder of Microsoft; and John Lennon of the Beatles.

Exhibit A in the talent argument is a study done in the early 1990s by the psychologist K. Anders Ericsson and two colleagues at Berlin's elite Academy of Music. With the help of the Academy's professors, they divided the school's violinists into three groups. In the first group were the stars, the students with the potential to become world-class soloists. In the second were those judged to be merely "good." In the third were students who were unlikely to ever play professionally and who intended to be music teachers in the public school system. All of the violinists were then asked the same question: over the course of your entire career, ever since you first picked up the violin, how many hours have you practiced?

Everyone from all three groups started playing at roughly the same age, around five years old. In those first few years, everyone practiced roughly the same amount, about two or three hours a week. But when the students were around the age of eight, real differences started to emerge. The students who would end up the best in their class began to practice more than everyone else: six hours a week by age nine, eight hours a week by age twelve, sixteen hours a week by age fourteen, and up and up, until by the age of twenty they were practicing—that is, purposefully and single-mindedly playing their instruments with the intent to get better—well over thirty hours a week. In fact, by the age of twenty, the elite performers had each totaled ten thousand hours of practice. By contrast, the merely good students had totaled eight thousand hours, and the future music teachers had totaled just over four thousand hours.

R3.11 Advice

Recognizing Assumptions and Biases

As discussed in R3.9, Making Inferences (p. 283), it is important to look beyond the words in the texts you read for a deeper level of meaning. Careful reading can help you to accurately infer from clues in a text the unstated assumptions and biases of the author. Recognizing the assumptions and biases authors bring to what they write, as well as the ones you bring to the text as you read what they say, will help you to better understand, evaluate, and comment on the written material you encounter in college.

Assumptions

All of us make assumptions. In most parts of America, if you want to ask someone where the nearest gas station is, you don't start by asking, "Do you speak English?"

Even though there are many people in America, even many American citizens, who don't speak English, when we approach someone on the street to ask directions, we *assume* they speak English. When we walk into a store to buy a hot dog and a Coke, most of us *assume* that we can pay with a credit card. When we sign up for a course in a college, we *assume* that the course will be taught by someone with some expertise in the subject. When our doctor prescribes a medicine for us to take, we *assume* that the medicine is safe and may alleviate the problem we are taking it for. We assume all the time. There's nothing wrong with making assumptions; in fact, they make modern life possible.

However, when you are reading, it is often a good idea to take a few minutes to ask yourself what assumptions lie behind the text, not because there is something inherently wrong with assumptions, but because you need to decide whether you agree that the assumptions the author is making are reasonable. For example, you are reading an article arguing for increased funding to build prisons, and you discover that the authors think we need more funding for prisons because they support mandatory sentences for drug offenses. But you believe that drug treatment programs are a more effective response to substance-related crimes than are longer prison terms. So it would be reasonable for you to question the argument for more funding for prisons because you do not share the assumption on which it rests. Understanding the assumptions underlying an argument and deciding whether you share these assumptions will help you decide whether you agree with the conclusions reached by the writer.

Recognizing Your Own Assumptions

We all have ways of thinking about the world that we learn from our families, communities, or religious and political institutions. These ways of thinking can be so familiar that we don't even recognize that we have them. We don't question them. But in order to fully evaluate the assumptions of authors, we must also be aware of and evaluate our own assumptions about the topic being discussed. Maybe you disagree with a writer because the writer doesn't support what you believe to be true. Are you sure your assumptions are correct? What evidence do you have to support them? Once you become more aware of the assumptions that underpin your thinking, you will be better able to recognize and evaluate those of the people you read.

Biases

You've probably been told to avoid biased writers, to look for writers who are even-handed and present both sides of an argument. In reality, the situation is more complicated than that. First, almost everyone is biased. It's next to impossible to find a writer who isn't. The fact that a writer is producing a piece of writing is good evidence that the writer has a bias in favor of that thesis. Second, we as readers often are not aware of an author's bias unless we make it a priority to be aware of it.

We should read any given piece of writing with healthy skepticism, questioning the writer's assertions and evaluating carefully the evidence presented.

Here are three ways to identify a writer's biases:

1. **Investigate the author's background.** If a brief biography is provided with the text you are reading, take a look at it. If not, do a little digging on the internet. If the author works for an organization with a known bias or writes regularly for publications with a known bias, that can indicate the author's biases.

2. **Look for evidence of bias in the text itself.** Does the writer use loaded language? For example, does the writer label opponents as immature, stupid, or narrow-minded? Does the writer use demeaning adjectives to describe those with alternative viewpoints, adjectives like *so-called*, *self-proclaimed*, or *ill-informed*? Or does the writer use loaded verbs, such as *spewed*, *would have you believe*, and *whined*? Evidence of bias may be subtler than this; authors may use words with positive connotations to depict their own positions and words with negative connotations to depict the positions of others. (If you need a refresher on connotation and tone, take a look at W6.4, Connotation and Denotation, p. 75, and R3.4, Recognizing the Author's Tone, p. 280.)

3. **Look for openness to alternative positions.** Ask yourself if the writer demonstrates an awareness that there are reasonable arguments on other sides of the issue. If not, this can indicate bias and a point of view that does not encompass all the relevant information on the subject. (For a refresher on responding to other views, take a look at W11.6, Responses to Positions Different from Yours, p. 203.)

Evaluating Your Own Biases

Just as with assumptions, it is important to be aware of your own biases in order to identify and evaluate the biases of writers. For instance, are you prejudiced in favor of or against particular groups of people, politicians, institutions, books, movies, and so on? Would your particular biases make it hard for you to entertain opposing views? Can you put your point of view aside so that you can fairly assess a different perspective, weighing the evidence provided to see if the alternative argument has merit?

R3.12 Exploration

Recognizing Assumptions and Biases in Three Passages

Working individually or in your group (your instructor will tell you which), analyze any assumptions or biases in the following passages.

1. **Gun Control. Now.**

> Sutherland Springs, Texas. Las Vegas. Orlando. Sandy Hook. Columbine. Red Lake, Minnesota. Essex, Vermont. Lancaster. Aurora. Virginia Tech. How many more innocent victims must die at the hands of an antiquated and oft-misinterpreted amendment? Enough.
>
> It's time to stop the violence.
>
> Gun control doesn't have to mean no guns. I'm not suggesting we take guns away. I'm suggesting we put tighter controls on acquiring and owning them.
>
> Gun show loopholes must be stopped. Ammunition should not be sold online. Mandatory wait periods should be enforced, during which time a thorough background check, psychological and medical evaluation, and character references should be completed.
>
> —"Gun Control. Now." From the "People-Powered Petitions" section of the MoveOn.org website

2. **Medicare for All**

> The U.S. spends more on health care per person, and as a percentage of gross domestic product, than any other advanced nation in the world, including Australia, Canada, Denmark, France, Germany, Japan, New Zealand and the United Kingdom. But all that money has not made Americans healthier than the rest of the world. Quite simply, in our high-priced health care system that leaves millions overlooked, we spend more yet end up with less.
>
> Other industrialized nations are making the morally principled and financially responsible decision to provide universal health care to all of their people—and they do so while saving money by keeping people healthier. Those who say this goal is unachievable are selling the American people short.
>
> Americans need a health care system that works for patients and providers. We need to ensure a strong health care workforce in all communities now and in the future. We need a system where all people can get the care they need to maintain and improve their health when they need it regardless of income, age or socioeconomic status. We need a system that works not just for millionaires and billionaires, but for all of us.
>
> —"Medicare for All" page in the "Issues" section of Bernie Sanders's website

3. **Stop Animal Abuse**

Every day in countries around the world, animals are fighting for their lives. They are enslaved, beaten, and kept in chains to make them perform for humans' "entertainment"; they are mutilated and confined to tiny cages so that we can kill them and eat them; they are burned, blinded, poisoned, and cut up alive in the name of "science"; they are electrocuted, strangled, and skinned alive so that people can parade around in their coats; and worse.

The abuse that animals suffer at human hands is heartbreaking, sickening, and infuriating. It's even more so when we realize that the everyday choices we make—such as what we eat for lunch and the kind of shampoo we buy—may be directly supporting some of this abuse. But as hard as it is to think about, we can't stop animals' suffering if we simply look the other way and pretend it isn't happening.

Animals are counting on compassionate people like you to give them a voice and be their heroes by learning about the issues they face and taking action. Each of us has the power to save animals from nightmarish suffering—and best of all, it's easier than you might think. If you're ready to join the millions of other compassionate people who are working to create a kinder, better world for animals, please read on to learn how animals suffer in the food, animal experimentation, entertainment, clothing and pet-trade industries. Together, we can make a difference.

—From the "Animal Rights Issues" section of the PETA website

R3.13 Advice
Constructing Meaning

Sometimes the meaning of a text is fairly obvious. Sometimes authors state what they mean to say in the first paragraph, even in the first sentence. But at other times, writers aren't so direct. Sometimes the reader has to construct the meaning by reading carefully, weighing the evidence, evaluating the reasoning, and comparing what the text says with the reader's own experiences.

For example, two groups of students read a section of Rebecca Skloot's book *The Immortal Life of Henrietta Lacks* that describes Lacks's experience going to Johns Hopkins Hospital in Baltimore for treatment of what turned out to be cervical cancer. The book tells us that Lacks was admitted to the "colored" ward of the hospital, her tissues were used for medical research without her permission or knowledge, and, after her death, her surviving husband and children were tricked into signing an agreement to allow the hospital to perform an autopsy on her body. On the other hand, the book tells us that Hopkins was founded to provide healthcare for the poor, that Hopkins provided Lacks all the therapy for cervical cancer that medicine at that time had at its disposal, and that Hopkins didn't make any money from Lacks's cells.

Asked to write a brief statement summing up what the passage said about Johns Hopkins Hospital, the students in the first group wrote, "Johns Hopkins was a racist organization." The students in the second group wrote, "The good that Hopkins did for medical science far outweighed the racism it was also guilty of."

When asked why the two groups had arrived at such different "meanings" from the text, after much hesitation, a woman in the second group, made up of four African American women, volunteered an observation: "Group 1 is all white. I think they were afraid that if they didn't come down hard on the racism, we black students would jump all over them." At this point, one of the women in the first group suggested that the women in the second group were all studying to be nurses. It turned out three of the four were in the nursing program.

The point here is not that one group or the other had the "right answer." In fact, there can be more than one "right" reading. The point is that the meaning of a text is not something lying quietly on the page waiting to be discovered and underlined. The meaning of a text is something to be *constructed* by the reader. When readers read a text carefully and thoughtfully, weigh the evidence given, examine the assumptions underlying the text, evaluate the reasoning, and compare it all with their own experiences and thoughts, they are able to *construct* a meaning from the text. The kind of reading that will allow you to engage with a challenging text and construct a meaning after reading that text is what we mean by critical reading.

R3.14   Exploration

Constructing Mike Rose's Meaning in "'Grit' Revisited"

Reread the excerpt from Mike Rose's blog in R1.9, Analyzing the Rhetorical Situation of a Text (p. 251). Then, working individually or in your group (your instructor will tell you which), decide what the passage means. What is Rose saying? What's his point? Write your decision about the meaning of the essay in a sentence or two. A word of warning: the meaning of this excerpt is fairly subtle. You will need to pay attention to details, weigh the evidence, make inferences, and do some thinking in order to decide what the passage means.

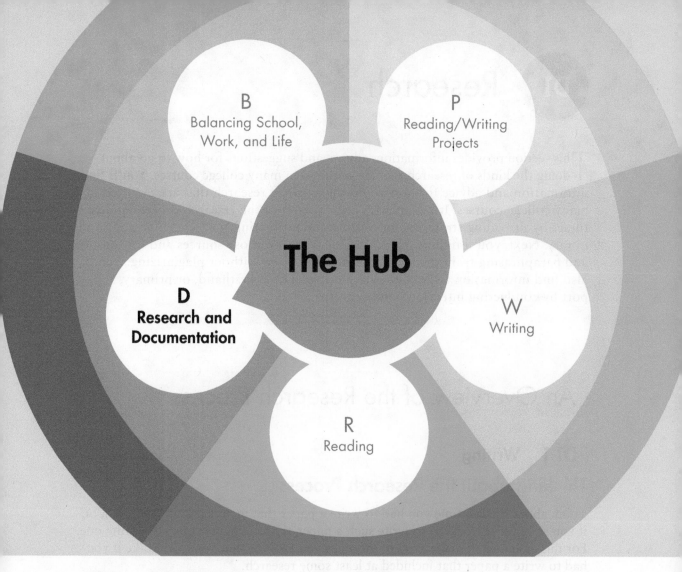

The Hub

B — Balancing School, Work, and Life

P — Reading/Writing Projects

W — Writing

R — Reading

D — Research and Documentation

D Research and Documentation

College writing assignments often require that you support your claims with ideas and information from reliable sources. This coverage of research will help you with finding relevant sources, incorporating evidence from sources in your writing, making clear which ideas are yours and which you have borrowed from other writers, and documenting the sources from which you have borrowed.

D1 Research

This section provides information, advice, and suggestions for how to go about doing the kinds of research that are required in many college courses. You'll find information and advice for how to do the kinds of research that are required in many college courses. It begins with a discussion of the research process and continues by providing strategies for finding and evaluating sources online and in the library. Next, you'll find advice for taking notes on those sources and for quoting and paraphrasing from them and synthesizing them without plagiarizing. You'll also find information to help you develop your own firsthand, or primary, support by conducting interviews and surveys.

An Overview of the Research Process

D1.1 Writing

Thinking about the Research Process

Think about the last time you had to write a paper that included doing research, or, if you've never been asked to write such a paper, try to imagine yourself writing one. For this assignment, make a list of the steps you took or that you might take if you had to write a paper that included at least some research.

D1.2 Advice

The Research Process: A Checklist

The checklist below offers a list of common research tasks. Read over the list and think about which ones you already do and which you should add to your own research process.

Checklist: Steps in the Research Process

Getting Started

☐ *Analyze the assignment:* Read and analyze the assignment, and consider the rhetorical situation. (See B4.2, Defining Terms for Writing Assignments, p. 416, and W2.3, Components of Rhetorical Analysis, p. 11.)

☐ *Make a schedule:* Working backwards, map the steps of the research and writing processes onto a calendar. Set workable deadlines for each step, making sure to consider the other tasks you may have to accomplish at the same time (from studying for a test in another class to working at your job to doing your laundry and even having a little fun).

☐ *Choose a topic:* Pick a general topic that is not only appropriate for your assignment but also one that you are interested in and want to learn more about.

Exploring Your Subject

☐ *Browse to get ideas:* Take some time to look at a variety of sources in different media and from a variety of perspectives. Follow links and references that look interesting, and make brief, informal notes about sources that seem promising, recording enough detail to find them again later. (See D1.4, Finding Sources Online, p. 298, and D1.6, Finding Sources in the Library, p. 300.)

☐ *Consider your audience and your ethos:* What kinds of sources is your audience likely to find convincing and compelling? What sources will help build your *ethos*. (See W11.4, Three Types of Appeal: *Logos, Ethos,* and *Pathos,* p. 198.)

Focusing Your Research

☐ *Focus your topic:* Once you've laid the groundwork, start drafting a tentative thesis statement. You don't have to commit to it at this point—you will probably need to tweak it at least, as your research progresses—but even a draft thesis can focus your search.

☐ *Devise research questions:* Think about the "how" and "why" questions that will help you delve into your focused topic. Your questions should be clear, focused, and require research and analysis or synthesis to answer. (See R3, Reading Critically, p. 275, and D1.14, Synthesis, p. 318.)

Doing the Research

☐ *Develop key terms:* As you work, keep a list of key terms to use in searching library catalogs and databases, and even searching with Google. Start with key terms from your thesis. Refine your list with terms used in the most promising sources you found in your exploratory search. Add terms from library catalogs and databases, and consider the words experts use (*heart attack* versus *myocardial infarction*, for example).

☐ *Use sources to find other sources:* Bibliographies and reference lists in your most promising sources are a great place to start. And the first part of catalog numbers for books can help you find other, related books.

☐ *Evaluate your sources:* Think about the authors: Are they experts? Will your audience consider them experts? Think about who publishes your sources: Interest groups with an agenda to push? Scholarly journals or academic presses that publish for other scholars? Popular newspapers, magazines, and books that hope to sell more copies? (See R1.11, Evaluating Sources of Texts, p. 254, and D1.7, Evaluating Sources, p. 305.)

☐ *Keep track of your sources:* You could go old school, by taking notes in a notebook, putting Post-it notes on books or printouts, or even making a stack of notecards (one per source). But you can also save copies of promising articles through the very databases you use to conduct your search, or use a citation manager, or even a program like Google Drive or Dropbox, to save copies of your sources and your notes.

D1.3 Exploration
Choosing Relevant Steps in the Research Process

For this activity, on your own or working in a group (your instructor will tell you which), select one of the following three assignments. Then decide which of the steps listed in the checklist in D1.2, The Research Process (p. 294), you would definitely have to do in order to write the assigned essay.

Assignment 1: Evolution of Thinking on Delayed Gratification

For this assignment, you will write an academic essay suitable for an English composition class in which you discuss the evolution of thinking over the past fifty years about delayed gratification. You will need to explain Walter Mischel's contribution in his famous "Marshmallow Experiment," then explore more recent thoughts on the subject, and, finally, present your own thoughts about the issue. The audience for this essay is your English composition instructor.

You must include information from at least six articles by quoting, paraphrasing, or summarizing relevant passages. When you do this, be sure to provide appropriate citations for any words you quote, paraphrase, or summarize from the websites and to include a list of works cited or references at the end of your essay. The essay is due one week from today.

Assignment 2: Freedom of Speech

For this assignment, you will write a ten- to twelve-page academic essay on a topic related to freedom of speech in America. In your essay, you will discuss what freedom of speech means in America through your focus on a specific topic like one of the following:

- The origins of the principle of freedom of speech at the time the country was forming
- Reservations about freedom of speech when it was proposed
- Changes in the principle of freedom of speech over time
- Threats to free speech over the years
- Controversies that have arisen involving free speech
- How the American version of free speech is different from that of other countries
- A topic of your choosing

Think of this essay as writing that would be appropriate in a college course on history, political science, law, or English composition. Your audience for this essay will be your instructor for that course.

Once you've settled on a topic to write about, you will need to do some research. Locate at least six articles or books that discuss your topic. Once you have your articles, write a brief evaluation of each using the questions that follow. Include these evaluations when you turn in your essay.

1. Who was the author(s)? What can you find out about the author(s)? What level of expertise does the author have on the subject?
2. Where was the article published? What kind of journal, book, or website did it appear in, and is that source reliable, accurate, and up-to-date?
3. Does the author or the publisher of the article have a particular bias? Does that bias make the article less valuable as a resource?
4. Who seems to be the audience this article was intended for?
5. Does the article provide convincing evidence to support its thesis?

Be sure to provide appropriate citations for any words you quote, paraphrase, or summarize from the websites and to include a list of works cited or references at the end of your essay. This assignment is due in six weeks.

Assignment 3: Taking a Position on the Minimum Wage

For this assignment, you are going to write a three- to four-page essay to convince government officials in your city or state of your position on the minimum wage. You will visit seven websites addressing the issue of raising the minimum wage—five are listed below and two you will find. Evaluate each of the websites using the questions listed in Assignment 2. Finally, recommend what the minimum wage should be in your city or state based on your research. Be sure to provide appropriate citations for any words you quote, paraphrase, or summarize from the websites and include a list of works cited or references at the end of your essay.

Here are the five websites. Remember: You need to locate two more that also address the effect of raising the minimum wage on employment. You can link to these websites from Achieve with *The Hub*. If you are *not* using Achieve or the links are broken, type their titles into your favorite search engine. (An updated list of links is also available at macmillanlearning.com/thehublinks.)

1. "Increase in Minimum Wage Kills Jobs," Employment Policies Institute
2. "Minimum Wage and Job Loss: One Alarming Seattle Study Is Not the Last Word," Arindrajit Dube, *New York Times*
3. "New Minimum Wage Hikes Set to Kill Jobs in 2018," Brendan Pringle, *Washington Examiner*
4. "The Controversial Study Showing High Minimum Wages Kills Jobs, Explained," Jeff Guo, *Vox*
5. "Study: Seattle's $15 Minimum Wage WORKED," David Pakman, *HuffPost*

Finding and Evaluating Sources, and Taking Notes

D1.4   Video

Finding Sources Online

This video discusses how to locate useful and relevant sources through online research. You can launch it from Achieve with *The Hub*; navigate to section D1, and open D1.4.

D1.5   Advice

Developing a List of Key Terms

Key terms are the words you use to search library databases and catalogs and even Google. Since computers are quite literal—they search for the exact terms you type in—you'll need to continually revise your key terms to get the best results.

Start by considering the rhetorical situation of the sources you are looking for. Magazines and newspapers, written for a general audience, may require different search terms than scholarly journals, written for experts. For example, general readers may use the term *emotion*, whereas psychologists may use the term *affect*, so you would want to include both terms in your list of key terms. Here are some other strategies to devise and revise key terms in your searches:

- Look for lists of subject terms or subject headings and add those to your list of key terms. In a catalog, look for a list of search terms in the detailed record. In a library database, these might appear in a tab labeled something like "search terms" or "thesaurus," or they may appear in the entry for the source.

- Look for key terms in or below the abstract (or summary) of a relevant article.

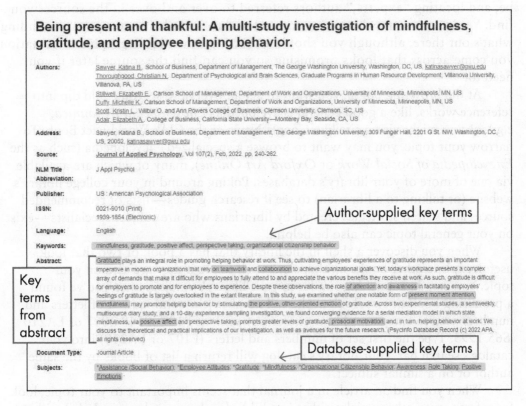

- Combine key terms to narrow your search.
- Try out terms in different databases, since different databases may use different key terms and yield different results.
- Mine bibliographies and lists of works cited to find relevant terms.
- Keep track of what has worked and what hasn't, modifying your list as needed.

D1.6 Advice

Finding Sources in the Library

Research, whether in the library or on the web, has two phases: a "browsing" phase and a "focused" phase. In the browsing phase, you have a general topic you know you want to explore, but you also know that the topic will probably need to be narrowed, focused, or even abandoned. Further, at this point you often have no more than a fuzzy idea about what you are going to argue about the topic or what your thesis will be.

During the browsing phase, you are educating yourself about the topic and getting a feel for the issues, discovering what the main arguments seem to be, and locating "experts," authors referred to over and over in the sources you find. You're not so much looking for material to include in your paper as finding what's out there, although you should be jotting down bibliographic information you come across that looks promising so you can find the source later if you need to.

At the browsing phase, you want to get an overview, so you could dip into reference works, like a good general encyclopedia (*Encyclopedia Britannica*, e.g.), or you might visit a site like Google News or the CIA's World Fact Book. To narrow your topic, you may want to browse a specialized encyclopedia (such as the *Encyclopedia of Social Work* or *Oxford Art Online*), many of which are available via one of more of your library's databases. Poking around in your college library's website (or talking to a librarian) to see if research guides—lists of recommended sources and search strategies created by librarians who are subject specialists—exist on your general topic can also be helpful.

When you discover a shelf in the library that has a book or two that look useful, explore other books on that same shelf to see if they are also on your topic. You can do something similar in your library's catalog: once you've found a promising book or two, look at the call number (the combination of letters and numbers used to categorize library holdings), such as P107 .P548 2007 or LA210 .S65 1993. Type the first set of numbers and letters (P107 or LA210) into your catalog's search bar. Your library's catalog will return a list of books by the same author or on a similar subject.

When you find an article in a journal that seems important to your topic, look for references to other articles either in a bibliography or perhaps included within the article itself. Again, as you browse, either make notes or make copies of pages so you can locate this material during the focused phase of research. (For more about notetaking, see D1.9, p. 307.)

Once you have a good feel for the topic you have been exploring and have identified the main arguments about it, discovered some "experts," and narrowed, focused, or even revised your topic, you are ready for phase two: the focused phase. At this point, you should have begun to formulate a thesis, with the understanding that it may change considerably as you continue researching and writing.

The second phase is organized around a narrowed topic and a tentative thesis. (See W3.3, Using Invention Strategies to Select a Topic, p. 27, and W3.5, Developing a Working Thesis, p. 29.) Now you will be searching the library focusing primarily on two types of materials: books and periodicals (journals, magazines, and newspapers). Because the tools and methods for searching for these two are quite different, we will discuss them one at a time.

Some libraries now offer unified search (sometimes called "Smart Search" or "Federated Search"), a kind of one-stop-shop for searching both a library's catalog and its databases at the same time. But strategies for locating books and for locating articles in periodicals differ somewhat and not all libraries offer unified search, so it makes sense to discuss each type of search separately.

Locating Books

The library catalog is your tool for locating books and other library holdings (such as videos, audio recordings, and rare books and documents). Today, most libraries' catalogs are computerized, which not only means books are much easier to find but also that you can do your search from home. If you are not familiar with accessing your college's catalog, there are two ways you can become familiar with the process. The first is through a library orientation session. Many college writing classes will schedule a day to meet in the library for such an orientation. Be sure to attend that session. A second way is to visit the library and ask a reference librarian to help you get started.

Once you have accessed the library's catalog, you are ready to begin searching for books. The most obvious way into the college's collection of books is to search by *subject* using the topic you have focused on. For example, imagine that you are going to write about the atomic bombing of Hiroshima during World War II, and you have focused on the specific topic of the ethical justification for the bombing. Each college library's catalog web page will look slightly different, but the procedures for locating materials will usually work in a similar way to the following example.

On the search page, begin by choosing to search by subject, typing the word "Hiroshima" into the search box and clicking the Search button.

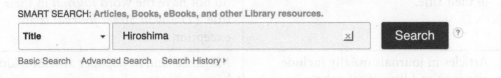

The catalog search engine returns results as follows (only the first two are shown):

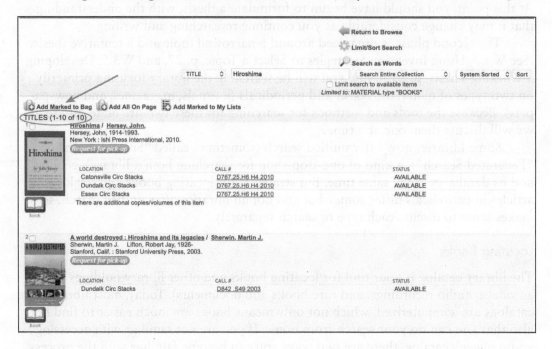

You can see, in the item circled in red, that the library owns ten books with "Hiroshima" in the title. Ten is too many for you to read or even to skim for this assignment, so you need to find a way to narrow down the list. Study the titles to find the books that seem most closely related to your working thesis. Also look for authors who were referred to frequently while you were in the browsing phase.

Distinguishing between Journals, Magazines, and Newspapers

It is important that you understand the difference between scholarly journals and popular magazines and newspapers. The following chart will help you with this distinction.

Journals	Magazines and Newspapers
Journals usually have the word *journal* in their title.	Magazines and newspapers usually do not have the word *journal* in their title. (*The Wall Street Journal* is an exception.)
Articles in journals usually include citations and lists of references.	Magazine and newspaper articles seldom have citations or lists of references.

Journals	Magazines and Newspapers
Journals are seldom glossy and seldom have full-color illustrations.	Magazines are usually glossy with full-color illustrations. Newspapers may also include color photos and advertisements.
Journals are usually found in libraries.	Some magazines and newspapers may be found in libraries, but they are also available by subscription or at a newsstand.
The authors of journal articles are usually identified by academic credentials.	Magazine and newspaper articles are usually written by journalists.
Journal articles often begin with a summary or abstract.	Magazine and newspaper articles usually do not include a summary or abstract, although the database you are using to search may supply one.

For most research you do in college, you will be expected to use scholarly sources, although for some topics, some audiences, and some contexts, popular magazines and newspapers may be appropriate.

Using Library Databases

Most libraries, especially those on college and university campuses, have powerful tools that allow you to locate articles on almost any topic you might want to write about: databases. Many students use Google to search for articles, but there are good reasons why searching using your library's databases is a better choice:

1. **Google will find thousands of articles but does not evaluate the expertise of their authors.** Using Google you'll get a list that includes excellent scholarly articles intermixed with the websites of high school students, blogs by conspiracy theorists, and people trying to sell a gimmick or a cure. Using Google Scholar will produce a list that is more scholarly but doesn't have some of the other benefits of using a library database that are discussed below.

2. **Many of the sources you locate with Google or Google Scholar will charge a fee if you want to access an article.** Most libraries pay a license fee in order for their students to access the sources listed in the databases for free.

3. **When you find articles from a library database that look useful for the paper you are writing, in most cases you can download the article directly to your computer.** You may even be able to save, annotate, and take notes on the article using the very same

database you used to locate the source. If you later quote from the article, you can cut and paste from the article directly into your paper ensuring that you quote accurately. (Don't forget to add quotation marks.) If you need a paper copy, you can print one from your computer.

4. **Most library databases can be accessed from home.**   Sometimes students decide to use Google because they can access it from home, not realizing that they can also access their college library from home. You may want to ask a reference librarian or perhaps your English teacher to show you how to do this.

Many students use Google to search for articles. If you choose to do this, use Google Scholar. Simply open Google, type "Google Scholar" in the search box, and press Enter. Clicking on the words "Google Scholar" at the top of the page opens the search engine.

General versus Specialized Databases

There are two different types of library databases for periodicals: general and specialized.

General Databases

General databases provide access to a wide range of scholarly journals as well as articles from reputable magazines and newspapers. They can be a good place to start your research if you haven't yet developed your focus or if you have chosen a topic but are not sure what discipline it belongs to. Some of the most widely used general databases are listed below. Your reference librarian can help guide you to the ones that will be most useful for the task you are working on.

- **Academic Search Premier** (or Complete or Elite, depending on the version your library subscribes to) includes general and scholarly sources in the humanities, education, social sciences, computer science, engineering, languages, linguistics, arts, literature, and ethnic studies.

- **Academic OneFile** (Gale) offers millions of articles from scholarly journals as well as magazine articles, podcasts, and videos from reliable sources.

- **JSTOR** provides access to more than 12 million academic journal articles, books, and primary sources; however, JSTOR does not include *current* issues.

- **Nexis Uni** (formerly Lexis/Nexis Academic) provides full-text news, business, and legal publications. It also provides transcripts of television and radio broadcasts and includes national and international sources.

- **ProQuest** includes dissertations and theses, e-books, newspapers, periodicals, historical collections, and governmental and cultural archives estimated to include more than 125 billion digital pages.

Specialized Databases

If you are searching for scholarly articles, specialized databases may be preferable once you have a focused topic to search for and you are confident about the discipline or disciplines where most scholarship on your topic takes place. Most libraries offer large numbers of these specialized databases. Your reference librarian can help guide you to the ones that will be most useful for the topic you are working on. A small sample is listed below.

- **ERIC–Education** provides an index to journal articles and other documents from the Educational Resource Information Center, 1966 to the present.
- **Medline Complete** includes articles from over 4,600 journals publishing on biomedical and health topics.
- **MLA International Bibliography** covers scholarship on all aspects of modern languages and literature. More than 70,000 sources are added annually, allowing access to very recent scholarship as well as articles dating back to the 1880s.
- **PsycArticles** (APA) provides access to articles published 1985 to the present in forty-two journals published by the American Psychological Association and others.
- **Web of Science** indexes scholarly journals in all disciplines and includes the Arts & Humanities Citation Index, Science Citation Index Expanded, and Social Sciences Citation Index.

D1.7 Advice

Evaluating Sources

Evaluating a source starts from the first moment you think to yourself "This looks interesting!" or "This isn't really related to my topic." The following questions will help you evaluate the sources you locate as you do research.

- **Who is the author?** How expert is the author on the subject? What can you find out about the author?
- **What kind of source is it?** For example, is it an article from a scholarly journal, a magazine, or a newspaper? A research report, review of the scholarly literature, or editorial?
- **Who published the source?** Is the publisher a well-respected newspaper or magazine, a scholarly journal, a major book publisher or university press, or an interest group trying to further a specific point of view? (It's fine to use sources from interest groups, but you should be aware of the point of view the group holds and point that out to readers when you refer to it in your essay.) What

can you find out about the organization or company that published it? (Hint: Wikipedia might help.)

- **What kind of quality control does the publisher use (if any)?** Scholarly publishers consult other experts in the field—a process called *peer review*; well-respected newspapers, magazines, and book publishers check their content against multiple sources, and they use fact checkers, copy editors, and proofreaders.

- **When was the source published?** If it's not recent, are you sure it has not been revised or challenged by more recent scholarship?

- **Who seems to be the audience for this source**—other experts or general readers?

- **What kind of evidence does the source use to support its claims?** Does it use firsthand (or *primary*) evidence (evidence the author has developed, say, from laboratory research or an examination of historical documents) or evidence synthesized from other published sources (secondary evidence)? Both kinds of evidence can be useful, but the combination of synthesized evidence backed up by firsthand evidence can be the most convincing.

- **Does the source use concrete evidence to support its claim?** Make sure you can verify the information using other reliable sources.

- **How does the source relate to other sources you have read?** Does it challenge, support, or extend claims? Does it add anything new to the discussion?

D1.8 Exploration
Evaluating Sources for an Assignment

A research assignment is listed below. After the assignment, several possible resources (books, blogs, articles, or websites) are listed. Take a look at the material provided or visit the website for each of these resources and decide how good a source it would be for a college research paper. Then compile a list of the strengths and weaknesses of each source you evaluated.

Assignment: Evaluating the Affordable Care Act

You are writing a research paper about the Affordable Care Act (Obamacare) and find the following sources. Evaluate them using the questions above. (Locate the sources using the search terms provided. If these search terms do not work, you will find an updated list of links at macmillanlearning.com/thehublinks.)

- The official government site for signing up for healthcare provided under the Affordable Care Act (Type "healthcare.gov" into your browser.)

- An article entitled "What Obamacare Achieved—and Didn't" (on Vox.com) (Type the entire title into your search engine.)
- An article entitled "Overwhelming Evidence That Obamacare Caused Premiums to Increase Substantially" in *Forbes* (Type "overwhelming evidence Obamacare premiums Forbes" into your search engine.)

D1.9 Advice

Notetaking

Much of the writing you do in college involves research, whether you are writing a lengthy formal research paper or a fairly short essay in which you want to include information or perhaps a quotation or two from some experts on your topic. An essential skill for effective research is effective notetaking. This section suggests a number of strategies for taking notes that will help you incorporate research into your writing.

Strategies for Effective Notetaking

As you locate articles, books, and websites with information about your topic, take note when a source

- has information that may be useful in supporting your thesis
- makes a statement you may want to argue against
- is written by an expert who supports your position, advocates a position you may want to refute, or convinces you to modify your position
- provides a concrete example that may be useful in your paper
- provides a fact that may be useful in your paper

What to Include in Your Notes

You will want to include four pieces of information in each note you take.

1. A subject heading that indicates what the note is about
2. Information about the source of the note. This information will be important when you construct a list of works cited or references. It will also make it easier for you to find the source again if you need to. Be sure to record the following:
   a. Title of the source
   b. Name of the author(s)

c. Name of the translator(s) or editor(s)

d. Version or edition

e. Volume and issue numbers for periodicals

f. Publisher

g. Date of publication

h. Page number for print sources or DOI (digital object identifier, a permanent code) or URL for online sources

i. The name of the database in which you found the source

Most sources won't include *all* these pieces of information, so include as much as you can.

3. A summary, paraphrase, or quotation of the ideas or information in the source. Be sure to indicate in the note what is summary, what is paraphrase, and what is quotation. (See W11.30, Strategies for Writing a Summary, p. 235, and D1.10, Quoting and Paraphrasing, p. 309.)

4. Your response to the information

How to Record Your Notes

There are at least five ways to record these notes.

1. **On notecards.** Taking notes on cards requires care to make sure quotations are accurate and the context is included, but notecards can easily be arranged in the order the information will appear in the paper.

2. **In a paper journal.** This option has all the disadvantages of notecards. In addition, it is not easy to arrange notes in any order.

3. **In a series of word processing documents.** Copying and pasting material directly from online sources is convenient and accurate. Notes are easy to arrange and to organize in files. In most cases, a chunk of text can be copied and the part to be used highlighted, allowing you to see the relevant content or quotation in context. But if not used carefully, copying and pasting can lead to accidental plagiarism or "patchwriting" (ineffective paraphrasing).

4. **By photocopying or printing out each article or page from a book and writing the source information somewhere on that copy.** Photocopying and printing cost money. You do end up with the entire page on which the relevant information or potential quotation appears, allowing you to see it in context. However, it is a little awkward, but not impossible, to arrange this type of material in order.

5. **By using a database or citation manager.** The database you use to conduct research may allow you to save, annotate, and document your sources. Citation managers, too, like *Zotero* (www.zotero.org), *Mendeley* (www.mendeley.com), and *EndNote*

(endnote.com), allow you to save, annotate, organize, and document your sources. For most purposes, databases and citation managers are free, or your library may have a subscription. But as with any software, there is a learning curve.

Each of these options has advantages and disadvantages. You should use the notetaking method that works best for you.

Supporting Your Ideas with Sources

D1.10 Advice

Quoting and Paraphrasing

The point of doing research is to find sources that include facts, expert opinion, examples, or other forms of evidence to support your thesis. Once you have located these kinds of evidence, you will include them in your essay in one of three ways: as quotations, as paraphrases, or as summaries. Quoting and paraphrasing are discussed here. Summarizing is discussed in W11.30, Strategies for Writing a Summary (p. 235).

Quotations

When you quote a source, you reproduce the words exactly as they appear in the source document. Use quotations when the author

- uses powerful or vivid language that would be less effective if paraphrased
- uses highly technical language that would be difficult to paraphrase accurately
- is highly respected, and the expert's exact words will be more convincing than your own

When quoting from a source, accuracy is essential. You must reproduce the source's words exactly, with a few exceptions that will be discussed below. Short quotations should be incorporated directly into your text. In MLA style, *short* means four typed lines or less; in APA style, *short* means forty words or fewer. Long quotations should be indented as a block half an inch from the left margin.

Short Quotation

According to the linguist John McWhorter, languages change so fast that no one "could converse with their ancestors from more than about a thousand years back" (*Word on the Street* 8).

Long Quotation

Most people think the English language is fairly stable—that the rules
governing English have changed very little over the years. Of course, slang
expressions come and go. As linguist John McWhorter points out, what
was "swell" in the thirties, was "keen" in the fifties, "groovy" in the sixties,
and "neat" in the seventies. Keeping up with the latest slang is a sign one is
"with it." However, in *Word on the Street*, his major study of the language,
McWhorter argues that language also evolves in more profound ways:

> It is less easy to perceive, however, that language is also always
> changing in a much deeper and more significant sense than mere
> colorful words and idioms. Sounds are always wearing off, other
> sounds are always evolving into different ones; endings are constantly
> wearing off, new endings are constantly developing; word meanings
> drift; and the order of words changes. These things happen so slowly
> that they are usually barely perceptible within a human lifetime.
> However, the changes are so relentless and so profound that there
> is no society in the world in which people could converse with their
> ancestors from more than about a thousand years back (8).

Framing Quotations

The way you frame the quotations in your essays will make the quotations more
effective. This framing (underlined in the following examples) provides context for
the quotation that follows.

Noted sociologist Annette Lareau, in her major study of child rearing in
American families, confides that she "was struck by how hard parents try,
how much effort they put into each day as they pursue their lives" (*Unequal
Childhoods* 360).

In her influential book *Grit*, MacArthur fellow Angela Duckworth explains
what grit really is: "Grit is about working on something you care about so
much that you're willing to stay loyal to it" (54).

So far in this essay, I have given several reasons why change is so difficult
to bring about in higher education. Cheryl Hyman, former president of
Chicago City Colleges, suggests another reason when she claims that if there
is one thing "educators don't want to hear, it's that education should be run
more like a business" (*Reinvention* 30).

Note that the framing material, called a *signal phrase*, includes two pieces of information:

- The name of the person being quoted (Annette Lareau, Angela Duckworth, and Cheryl Hyman)
- Some information to explain why this person has expertise ("Noted sociologist," "MacArthur fellow" and writer of an "influential book," and "former president of Chicago City Colleges")

Sometimes it's also useful to explain in the framing material how the quoted material relates to the essay itself. In the third example, taken from an essay exploring how difficult it is to make changes in higher education, the framing material explains that the quotation from Hyman will provide yet another reason for why it is so difficult.

One additional feature of the materials these authors have chosen to frame their quotations is the verbs they use: *confides*, *explains*, and *claims*. Notice how much more information these verbs provide than more ordinary verbs that might have been used, such as *says* or *writes*. *Confides* tells the reader that not only did Lareau write these words but that they are letting us in on her feelings about her findings. In the second example, *explains* signals that the quotation has something to say that could clear up any confusion the reader might have about grit. Finally, *claims* signals that the writer of the essay is not completely convinced that Hyman is right about faculty attitudes.

Here is a list of more expressive verbs for introducing quotations. Try using some of them the next time you include a quotation in your writing.

Expressive Verbs		
acknowledges	declares	observes
admits	denies	opposes
advises	discusses	points out
agrees	emphasizes	replies
argues	explains	reports
asserts	hypothesizes	responds
believes	implies	reveals
claims	insists	suggests
concludes	interprets	thinks
confirms	objects	

In the previous examples, the framing material was placed in front of the quoted material. The following examples illustrate that this is not the only way to position framing material.

> "India is named for the Indus River, along whose fecund banks a great urban civilization flourished more than four thousand years ago," writes historian Stanley Wolpert in the opening chapter of his monumental *New History of India* (3).

> "Greek drama grew out of religious ritual," argues Moses Hadad in his introduction to *Greek Drama*, "and was presented as part of a religious cult" (1).

There's one more thing to notice about framing quotations: The page number on which the quotation appears in the original source is inserted at the end of the quotation. Providing the page number lets readers know where they can find the quotation in context, and it also hints that the quotation is ending and that your own words will follow, usually some kind of analysis of the quotation or an explanation for its relevance to your paper.

Exceptions to Word-for-Word Quoting

This section on quotations began by saying "you reproduce the words exactly as they appear in the source document." However, there are three primary exceptions to this rule: (1) using ellipses to exclude irrelevant words in quoted material, (2) adding words (in brackets) to explain an author's meaning, and (3) adjusting the author's words (with brackets) to fit into your own sentence.

Using Ellipses to Indicate Omitted Words. Sometimes you want to include some words from one long sentence, or maybe two adjacent sentences, and not include the words between them that are not relevant to your point. *As long as you do not change the author's original meaning*, you can omit some words from a quotation. If you do this, indicate the omission with an ellipsis (three spaced periods). In the following example, unnecessary words have been deleted from the original text by Paul Tough. Note the ellipses the writer has used to indicate where words from the original have been omitted. The writer has also maintained the author's original meaning.

Original

"What matters most in a child's development, they say, is not how much information we can stuff into her brain in the first few years. What matters, instead, is whether we are able to help her develop a very different set of qualities, a list that includes persistence, self-control, curiosity, conscientiousness, grit, and self-confidence" (Tough, *How Children Succeed*, xv).

Quotation

Education writer Paul Tough insists that what "matters most in a child's development . . . is not how much information we can stuff into her brain in the first few years. What matters, instead, is whether we are able to help her develop . . . persistence, self-control, curiosity, conscientiousness, grit, and self-confidence" (*How Children Succeed*, xv).

Adding Words of Explanation.   Sometimes, it is necessary to add words to quoted text in order to explain what a writer is saying. To add clarifying words to the original text, enclose the added words in brackets.

Original

You can trace its contemporary rise, in fact, to 1994, when the Carnegie Corporation published *Starting Points: Meeting the Needs of Our Youngest Children,* a report that sounded an alarm about the cognitive development of our nation's children. The problem, according to the report, was that children were no longer receiving enough cognitive stimulation in the first three years of life, in part because of the increasing number of single-parent families and working mothers—and so they were arriving in kindergarten unready to learn. The report launched an entire industry of brainbuilding "zero-to-three" products for worried parents. Billions of dollars' worth of books and activity gyms and Baby Einstein videos and DVDs were sold.

Quotation

According to education writer Paul Tough, "The [Carnegie] report [*Starting Points: Meeting the Needs of Our Youngest Children*] launched an entire industry of brainbuilding 'zero-to-three' products for worried parents."

Adjusting the Author's Words to Fit into Your Own Sentence.   In addition to adding clarifying words to the original quotation, you may also sometimes need to adjust the quotation to fit into your sentence grammatically. You can do so using brackets and ellipses as needed. Take a look at the sentence that follows; it changes "trace" to "traces" and deletes some words to incorporate the quotation into the writer's own sentence.

Original

You can trace its contemporary rise, in fact, to 1994, when the Carnegie Corporation published *Starting Points: Meeting the Needs of Our Youngest Children,* a report that sounded an alarm about the cognitive development of our nation's children. The problem, according to the report, was that children were no longer receiving enough cognitive stimulation in the first three years of life, in part because of the increasing number of single-parent families and working mothers—and so they were arriving in kindergarten unready to learn. The report launched an entire industry of brainbuilding "zero-to-three" products for worried parents.

Quotation

Tough "trace[s] . . . an entire industry of brainbuilding 'zero-to-three' products" to one document: *Starting Points: Meeting the Needs of Our Youngest Children* (xv).

Paraphrases

When you use your own words to express an author's ideas fairly and accurately, you are paraphrasing. Being able to express someone else's ideas accurately is one way to ensure that you understand them. Use a paraphrase in these situations:

- to help you think through an author's ideas
- to record ideas that you might want to use in an essay
- to show a reader that you have understood an idea
- when the language in the source is not particularly effective
- when the source language doesn't fit well with your language

When you decide to paraphrase, it is important that you faithfully represent the thought in the source in your own words. Unlike summaries, paraphrases are usually about the same length as the original source, sometimes longer, as you are basically restating someone else's ideas in your own words and sentence patterns. You might include a word or two from the original source in quotation marks, but most of the wording should be your own, written in your style. As well as rewording, you might want to reorganize the material you are paraphrasing, or break complicated sentences in the original into shorter ones. In addition, you must include the name of the author and title of the source in your paraphrase and/or provide an in-text citation.

Reproduced below is the original text from Studs Terkel's *Working*, where he describes working Americans' search for meaning in their lives. An unacceptable paraphrase follows it. It does not mention or cite the passage it refers to, and it uses much of the language of the original, with just some synonyms swapped in. The words that come from the original that are still used in this unacceptable paraphrase are underlined. The sentence patterns also remain the same. This combination can lead to accusations of plagiarism. (The important topic of plagiarism is discussed in detail in D1.12, Questions about Plagiarism, p. 316, and D1.13, Avoiding Plagiarism, p. 317.)

Original

It is about a search, too, for daily meaning as well as daily bread, for recognition as well as cash, for astonishment rather than torpor; in short, for a sort of life rather than a Monday through Friday sort of dying. Perhaps immortality, too, is part of the quest. To be remembered was the wish, spoken and unspoken, of the heroes and heroines of this book (xiii).

Unacceptable Paraphrase

Working people's lives are about a search for meaning as well as daily bread, for recognition and not simply a pay check, for astonishment rather than torpor; in short, for a sort of life rather than a sort of dying. Perhaps immortality, too, is what workers may be looking for. To be remembered was the wish of many of the people interviewed, of the heroes and heroines of the working class (xiii).

Below is an acceptable paraphrase. Notice that only a few words from the original text are retained in this paraphrase, and they are marked by quotation marks to make it clear that they are Terkel's words. Notice, also, that just like with quotations, this paraphrase is framed by a signal phrase—"In his book *Working*, respected journalist Studs Terkel makes the point that,"—which identifies the author, his credentials, and the source of the paraphrased material.

Acceptable Paraphrase

In his book *Working*, respected journalist Studs Terkel makes the point that working people are seeking more than just a paycheck. He explains that people seek such intangible goals as "meaning," "recognition," and even "astonishment." He continues that they are seeking "life" and perhaps even "immortality" (xiii).

D1.11 Exploration

Quoting and Paraphrasing Shaughnessy

In this activity, you will use the following short passage from Mina Shaughnessy's book *Errors and Expectations: A Guide for the Teacher of Basic Writing* to practice quoting and paraphrasing. Shaughnessy was teaching at City University of New York in the 1990s and was present as "open admissions" transformed her school and many more, and hers was one of the earliest books to address the teaching of students who arrive in colleges and universities with less-than-college-ready writing skills. The following passage is from the first page of her book:

> Toward the end of the sixties and largely in response to the protests of that decade, many four-year colleges began admitting students who were not by traditional standards ready for college. The numbers of such students varied from college to college as did the commitment to the task of teaching them.

Practice Quoting

In an essay you are writing for an education class, you want to make the point that "open admissions" might have resulted in major transformations at some colleges, but it had little effect at others. Working individually or in your group, write a sentence or two in which you quote from the Shaughnessy passage to make that point.

Practice Paraphrasing

Working individually or in your group, make the point that "open admissions" might have resulted in major transformations at some colleges, but it had little effect at others. Write this in a sentence or two, paraphrasing Shaughnessy's passage.

In both cases, make sure you provide an effective frame for the material you quote or paraphrase.

D1.12 Exploration

Questions about Plagiarism

As you read Avoiding Plagiarism: Using Quotation Marks and Documenting Your Sources (D1.13, p. 317), make a list of questions you have about the topic.

D1.13 Advice

Avoiding Plagiarism: Using Quotation Marks and Documenting Your Sources

Sometimes plagiarism seems like a very complicated and scary concept, but it doesn't need to be. If you plagiarize, you use the words and ideas of another person without giving them credit; you use them as though they are your own words. In American colleges and universities, plagiarism is considered a very serious academic offense and can result in failing grades or even more serious consequences.

Avoiding plagiarism is really simple: if you use the exact words of another writer, you must place them in quotation marks and provide an in-text citation that links to a works cited or references list; if you use the ideas of another writer, credit and document the source. You cannot pretend that someone else's words or ideas are your own.

Hardly anyone has trouble understanding the first part: if you use someone else's words in something you're writing, you must put those words in quotation marks (see D1.10, Quoting and Paraphrasing, p. 309, for more details). That part's easy, but then you also must provide a citation—a note in parentheses after the quoted words that tells readers where the quoted words came from so they can find the original source if they're interested. There are several systems for formatting these citations, two of which are discussed in detail in *The Hub*: D2.2, MLA In-Text Citations (p. 325), and D3.2, APA In-Text Citations (p. 366). Make sure you know which citation system your instructor expects.

The definition of plagiarism above also discusses using someone else's *ideas*; that's the part that is sometimes harder to grasp. If, while doing research for a writing project, you read an article or a book in which the author makes a really good point that supports your thesis and if you take that idea and express it in your own words, you must *still* give the author credit for the idea. You must make it clear that the idea you are expressing, even if you express it completely in your own words, is an idea you got from another writer.

When you quote another writer's words exactly, you indicate that the words came from someone else by placing them inside quotation marks, but you don't use quotation marks if you are paraphrasing or summarizing someone else's ideas. In these cases, you must indicate where the idea came from and include an in-text citation that links to a works cited or references list, just as you do when you are quoting.

Note that these principles apply not only to print sources but also to online sources, handwritten documents, spoken words, and even the words of other students.

Here's another important distinction. It is plagiarism if you use someone else's words or ideas without giving them credit through quotation marks and citations.

However, if you make an error in the format of your citation, that is not plagiarism. It may be an error that affects your instructor's evaluation of your essay, but it is not plagiarism.

D1.14 Advice

Synthesis

A well-written essay that uses sources doesn't just present them as a laundry list: "Cunningham says this," "Nguyen says that," and "Marcos says something else." Instead, it weaves them together, points out similarities and disagreements, and compares the methods they use to reach their conclusions. This process of weaving sources into a single conversation, called *synthesis*, can improve the effectiveness of your research.

How to Synthesize Sources

Synthesis is a skill we all practice in our daily lives. Imagine you are looking for a work study job, for example. You might talk to friends and classmates who work in various on-campus venues and ask them what they like and dislike about their jobs, the advantages and disadvantages of each. After thinking about what they all have to say, and taking into account your class schedule, past work experiences, and time limitations, you make a decision that working evenings in the library is your best option. If you're buying new bluetooth headphones, you might read reviews, research prices, and talk to friends who already own a pair. Pulling together all this information and taking into account affordability and your needs is how you reach a decision about what to purchase.

In college, synthesis involves researching to locate a variety of sources on the topic you are going to write about, reading them carefully, comparing what they have to say, and then coming to your own conclusion about the issue. In fact, the goal of a research paper is not only to explain what other people have said or think about an issue and how they agree or disagree with each other but to come up with your own ideas about the subject.

In order to synthesize, keep the following in mind as you compare sources.

- What points do different sources agree on?
- What points do different sources disagree on?
- How are the sources different from each other? For example, are they looking at the same or different data, populations, time periods, solutions, and so on?

- How do the different sources support their positions? What types of evidence do they use, and how reliable and convincing is it?
- How do the sources treat the topic? Are they serious, providing significant support for their ideas, or are they expressing personal opinions with little hard evidence to support them?

Once you have a good idea of what your sources are saying, you need to think about what your position is on the issue. Are there sources that support your opinion? Are there ones that do not support your position but make a compelling argument you will need to consider? Once you know what you want to say, use synthesis to create a unified conversation among your sources and yourself.

Examples of Synthesis

Here are some examples of how a writer might synthesize sources in a paper.

1. A writer points out the agreement between two sources, but also acknowledges the differences between their analyses.

   Slowinski and Smith agree that the current procedure for applying for financial aid is flawed, but they disagree on what the flaws are.

2. A writer points out that several sources reached similar conclusions even though the subjects they studied were quite different.

   Based on studies of three different populations—farm workers in California, college students in Iowa, and hotel employees in the Hilton system—Stevens, Allen, and Crivello reach nearly identical conclusions.

3. A writer, while admitting there is disagreement about solutions to a problem, points to three sources' agreement on what the problem is.

   Even though they disagree about the solutions we should enact, all three economists I have quoted agree that the extreme wealth gap in America between the very affluent and everyone else is a serious problem.

4. A writer instead of synthesizing two or three sources, synthesizes one source with her own views.

   Fitzgerald's argument comes to the same conclusion that I have, but for very different reasons.

Conducting Interviews and Surveys

D1.15 Advice

Conducting Interviews: A Checklist

When thinking about how to provide evidence to support your thesis in a paper, don't overlook the possibility of interviewing an expert. Quoting the words of someone with direct experience can provide strong support for your argument:

- For an essay on a fairly recent military event, you might interview a relative or family friend who served in Vietnam, Afghanistan, or Iraq.
- For an essay on civil rights, you might interview someone who took part in a Black Lives Matter or other protest march.
- For an essay you are writing for your career counselor, you might interview someone working in the field you are considering.
- For your marketing or sales department, you might interview customers about their perceptions of your company's products or procedures.

The checklist below outlines the steps for setting up and conducting an interview.

Checklist: Conducting Interviews

Scheduling an Interview

- ☐ Identify an expert or someone with relevant lived experience to interview. (Faculty or graduates from your school may be good options.)
- ☐ Once your subject has agreed, establish a time and place for the interview as well as an understanding of how long the interview will last.
- ☐ Send an email or note confirming the time and place.
- ☐ Ask your subject if they mind being recorded.

Planning for an Interview

- ☐ Avoid asking questions you can answer from published sources. Instead, do some background research. Then think about what only the subject can tell you.
- ☐ Think about what you want to know from the subject and write questions in advance that will elicit that information.
- ☐ Prioritize your questions.
- ☐ Ask questions to clarify your interview subject's exact position, job, or role.

- [ ] Avoid simple yes or no questions. Instead, ask questions that will elicit a story ("Tell me about the time . . .") or allow for an open response ("How did you feel about . . . ?").
- [ ] On the page of questions you plan to use, leave plenty of space after each one to record the subject's responses.
- [ ] Make sure you have materials for taking notes—bring an extra pen, just in case—and make sure your recording device is working and you know how to use it.

Conducting an Interview

- [ ] Respect the subject's time. Arrive promptly and conclude within the timeframe you established.
- [ ] Note the date, time, and place of the interview.
- [ ] Take notes even if you are also recording.
- [ ] Be careful to distinguish in your notes between quotations, paraphrases, and summaries.
- [ ] If your subject provides useful responses to an early question and you want to continue that line of inquiry, do not feel you must get to all the questions you prepared.

Following Up on an Interview

- [ ] Flesh out your notes as soon as possible after the interview. The longer you wait, the harder it will be for you to accurately recall what was said.
- [ ] If you are not sure of what the person said or meant, contact them and ask. But consolidate all your follow-up questions to avoid irritating your interviewee.
- [ ] Send a thank-you note or email to the interviewee, and offer to send a copy of the final report.

D1.16 Advice

Conducting Surveys: A Checklist

Surveys are a useful way to gather evidence for an essay, but they take some time to construct, to administer, and to interpret. A good place to start is to clearly define what it is you want to learn from your survey. If you were writing a paper about the attention paid to politics by people under thirty years old as compared to those over thirty–fifty, conducting a survey to try to measure those differences would be a logical approach. You probably won't be able to draw a generalizable conclusion from the small sample you are likely to get, but you might get some interesting data to support a narrow claim about your campus or your town.

Checklist: Conducting Surveys

Developing Survey Questions

- ☐ List your goals—what you want to learn from the survey—in detail.
- ☐ Ask relevant biographical questions to gather information about the people (*respondents*) participating in your survey: name, age, gender, address, party affiliation, and so on.
- ☐ Ask questions to gather information about the respondent's attitudes or behaviors.

Developing Questions about Attitudes/Behaviors

- ☐ Keep your survey brief—the more questions you ask the fewer people will finish the survey. Ask only questions that are directly relevant to your goal—make every question count.
- ☐ Your survey can include close-ended questions (yes/no, multiple choice, ratings) and open-ended (free response) questions, but limit the number of open-ended questions to a few. (They take respondents more time to answer, and they will take you more time to assess.)
- ☐ Ask questions clearly: Make sure there will be no confusion about what you are asking.
- ☐ Ask only one question at a time; do not combine questions.
- ☐ Avoid leading questions (questions that suggest the answer you're looking for).
- ☐ When asking rating questions, make sure your options do not overlap (*not* 1–3, 4–6, 6+ *but* 1–3, 4–6, 7+), and label each answer option, rather than labeling just the first, last, and middle option.

Testing Your Survey

- ☐ Take your own survey. Time yourself—how long did it really take? Test your survey on classmates, friends, or family members, and revise questions based on their feedback and how long it took them to complete it.

Conducting Your Survey

- ☐ Survey as large a group as you can, and try to reach a wide array of people.
- ☐ If conducting a survey based on a large list, randomize the list and then choose every fifth, tenth, or twentieth name, as appropriate.
- ☐ Check your list to see if it is representative. Have you reached out to people from different regions, genders, political perspectives, and so on?

Writing Up Your Results

- ☐ Add up the responses and look for patterns.
- ☐ Discuss your overall findings and support your conclusions with evidence from your survey.
- ☐ In an appendix, include a copy of your survey and a tally of the responses.

D2 ▶ MLA Documentation

I n English and in some humanities classes, you may be asked to use the MLA (Modern Language Association) system for documenting sources. The guidelines below follow those set forth in the *MLA Handbook*, 9th edition (2021).

Rather than thinking of the MLA guidelines simply as rules to be followed, think of them as guidelines for participating in an academic community—a community in which the exchange and extension of ideas require a system. Even though the guidelines present a system for citing many different kinds of sources, they don't cover everything, and at times you will have to adapt the guidelines to the source you are using.

The sections that follow provide you with an overview of MLA style plus guidelines for how to cite and document sources using in-text citations and a works cited list. The last section contains information on how to format a paper using MLA style, with examples from several student papers.

Introduction to MLA Style

D2.1 Advice

Documenting Sources in MLA Style

There may be several ways to cite a source in the list of works cited. Think carefully about your context for using the source, so you can identify the pieces of information that you should include and any other information that might be helpful to your readers. The first step is to identify elements that are commonly found in works that writers cite.

Author and Title

The first two elements are the author's name and the title of the work. Each of these elements is followed by a period.

> Author.   Title.

Containers

The next step is to identify elements of what MLA calls the "container" for the work—any larger work that contains the source you are citing. For example, a magazine or newspaper "contains" its articles, an anthology or collection "contains" its stories or poems, and a television show or podcast contains its episodes.

The context in which you are discussing the source and the context in which you find the source will help you determine what counts as a container in each case. Some works are self-contained; if you watch a movie in a theater, the movie title is the title of your source, and you won't identify a separate container title. But if you watch the same movie as part of a DVD box set of the director's work, the container title is the name of the box set. And if you watch it on a streaming service, like Netflix or Amazon Prime, then the name of the streaming service or application is the movie's "container."

Some works may have more than one container. An article may appear in a scholarly journal, but if you access the article through a database, you will have to cite both the journal and the database as containers for the article you reference. Thinking about a source as nested in larger containers may help you to visualize how a citation works.

Basic container information

Author.   **Title.**

Container 1
Title of container, contributors, version/edition, volume/issue, publisher, date, location (pages, DOI, URL, etc.).

Container 2 (if needed):
Title of container (such as database), same elements as in Container 1 (if available).

The elements you may include in the "container" part of your citation include, in order, the title of the container; the name of contributors such as editors or translators; the version or edition; the volume and issue numbers or other numbers (such as season and episode); the publisher; the date of publication; and a location such as the page number(s), DOI, permalink, or URL. These elements are separated by commas, and the end of the container section is marked with a period.

Most sources won't include *all* these pieces of information, so include only the elements that are relevant and available for the source you are citing. If your container is itself a part of some larger container, such as a database, simply add information about the second container after the first one. You will find many examples of how elements and containers are combined to create works cited entries in section D2.3, MLA Works Cited List (p. 331). The Guidelines for the Works Cited List (p. 332) also provide details about the information required for each element.

Works Cited Entry (one container)

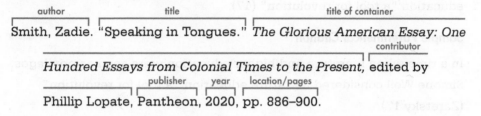

author title title of container

Smith, Zadie. "Speaking in Tongues." *The Glorious American Essay: One Hundred Essays from Colonial Times to the Present,* edited by Phillip Lopate, Pantheon, 2020, pp. 886–900.

contributor

publisher year location/pages

Works Cited Entry (two containers)

author title

Carey, Craig. "Realism and Recording: Remixing Literary and Media History."

title of container 1 volume, number date pages

American Literary Realism, vol. 3, no. 3, spring 2021, pp. 198–203.

title of container 2 location (DOI)

JSTOR, https://doi.org/10.5406/amerlitereal.53.3.0198.

D2.2 Advice

MLA In-Text Citations

MLA style requires you to supply an in-text citation each time you quote, paraphrase, summarize, or otherwise integrate material from a source. In-text citations are made with a combination of signal phrases and parenthetical references and include the information your readers need to locate the full citation in the works cited list at the end of the text.

Guidelines for In-Text Citations

A signal phrase introduces information taken from a source; usually the signal phrase includes the author's name. Include both first and last names the first time you mention a source; include just the last name in later citations. Parenthetical references include at least a page number (except for unpaginated sources, such as those found online). The works cited list provides publication information about the source.

There is a direct connection between the signal phrase or parenthetical citation and the first word(s) in the works cited entry.

Sample Citation Using a Signal Phrase

In a time when literature and higher education were seen as privileges, historian Robert Zaretsky notes that Simone Weil considered literature education "a tool for revolution" (17).

Sample Parenthetical Citation

In a time when literature and higher education were seen as privileges, Simone Weil considered literature education "a tool for revolution" (Zaretsky 17).

Works Cited Entry

Zaretsky, Robert. *The Subversive Simone Weil: A Life in Five Ideas.*
    U of Chicago P, 2021.

Directory to MLA In-Text Citation Models

Guidelines for In-Text Citations

1. Author named in a signal phrase   Ordinarily, introduce the material being cited with a signal phrase; include both first and last name the first time you mention an author and last name only after.

> Lee claims that his comic-book creation Thor was "the first regularly published superhero to speak in a consistently archaic manner" (199).

2. Author named in a parenthetical citation   When you don't mention the author in a signal phrase, include the author's last name before the page number(s), if any, in parentheses. Don't use punctuation between the author's name and the page number(s).

> The word *Bollywood* is sometimes considered an insult because it implies that Indian movies are merely "a derivative of the American film industry" (Chopra 9).

3. Digital or nonprint source   Give enough information in a signal phrase or in parentheses for readers to locate the source in your list of works cited—at least the author's name or the title. If the source lacks page numbers but has numbered paragraphs, sections, or divisions, use those numbers with the appropriate abbreviation in your parenthetical citation. Don't add such numbers if the source itself does not use them. For audio or video sources, include a time stamp for the material you are citing.

> As a *Slate* analysis notes, "Prominent sports psychologists get praised for their successes and don't get grief for their failures" (Engber).
>
> Kalika Bali explains that as the "digital divide between languages" with and without technological resources grows, "the divide between the communities that speak these languages is expanding" (00:04:40–51).

4. Two authors   Name both authors in a signal phrase or in parentheses.

> Sandra Gilbert and Susan Gubar point out that in the Grimm version of "Snow White," the king "never actually appears in this story at all" (37).

5. Three or more authors   Use the first author's name followed by *and colleagues* or *and others* in a signal phrase or *et al.* (Latin for "and others") in parentheses.

> Similarly, as Mary Field Belenky and colleagues assert, examining the lives of women expands our understanding of human development (7).

> Similarly, a "misreading of women" is the unfortunate result of defining human development by men's intellectual development (Belenky et al. 7).

6. Organization as author   Give the group's full name in a signal phrase; in parentheses, shorten the name to the first noun and any preceding adjectives, omitting *A*, *An*, or *The*.

> According to a survey by the Girl Scouts of the United States of America, seventy-five percent of young people want to elect more women to Congress.

> One survey reports that seventy-five percent of young people want to elect more women to Congress (Girl Scouts).

7. Unknown author   Use the full title, if it is brief, in your text—or a shortened version (the first noun and any preceding adjectives, omitting *A*, *An*, or *The*) in parentheses.

> Coca-Cola and other similarly well-known companies often avoid public politics to uphold their images as "emblems of American harmony" ("CEO Activism").

8. Two or more works by the same author   Mention the title of the work in the signal phrase or include a short version of the title in the parentheses.

> Old Man Warner complains that the younger people calling for change will next "be wanting to go back to living in caves" (Jackson, "The Lottery" 295).

9. Two or more authors with the same last name   Include the author's first and last name in the signal phrase or first initial and last name in the parentheses.

> One approach to the problem is to introduce nutrition literacy at the K–5 level in public schools (E. Chen 15).

10. Indirect source (source quoted in another source)   Use the abbreviation *qtd. in* to indicate that you are using a source that is cited in another source.

> Jordan "silently marveled" at her Black students' dismissal of Black language in the novel (qtd. in Baker-Bell 24).

11. Multivolume work   If you cite more than one volume of a multivolume work, include the volume number, a colon, and then the page number; if not, omit the volume number and colon.

> Modernist writers prized experimentation and gradually even sought to blur the line between poetry and prose, according to Forster (3: 150).

12. Work in an anthology or a collection   Use the name of the author of the work, not the editor of the anthology, but use the page number(s) from the anthology.

> In "Love Is a Fallacy," the narrator's logical teachings disintegrate when Polly declares that she should date Petey because "[h]e's got a raccoon coat" (Shulman 391).

In the list of works cited, the work is alphabetized under Shulman, the author of the story, not under the name of the editor of the anthology.

> Shulman, Max. "Love Is a Fallacy." *Current Issues and Enduring Questions*,
>   edited by Sylvan Barnet and Hugo Bedau, 9th ed., Bedford/St. Martin's,
>   2011, pp. 383–91.

13. Government source   In a signal phrase, include the name of the author (if there is one) or full name of the agency or governing body, as given in the works cited list. In a parenthetical citation, shorten the name if you use the agency or governing body in the author position.

> The National Endowment for the Arts notes that social media and online events play a significant role in "showcasing the importance of the arts to the vitality of the nation" (15).

> Social media and online events play a significant role in "showcasing the importance of the arts to the vitality of the nation" (National Endowment 15).

If you cite more than one agency or department from the same government in your essay, you may choose to standardize the names by beginning with the name of the government. In that case, when shortening the names, give enough information in each parenthetical citation to differentiate the authors: (*United States, National Endowment*); (*United States, Environmental Protection*).

14. Entire work Use the author's name in a signal phrase or a parenthetical citation.

> Michael Pollan explores the issues surrounding food production and consumption from a political angle.

15. Two or more sources in one citation List the authors (or titles) in alphabetical order and separate them with semicolons.

> Economists recommend that employment be redefined to include unpaid domestic labor (Clark 148; Nevins 39).

16. Personal communication or social media source Use the author's name or screen name as given in the works cited list.

> According to @grammarphobia, the expression *if you will* "had a legitimate usage" before it became "empty filler."

17. Literary work (novel, play, poem) Because literary works are often available in many different editions, cite the page number(s) from the edition you used followed by a semicolon; then give other identifying information that will lead readers to the passage in any edition. For a novel, indicate the part or chapter.

> In utter despair, Dostoyevsky's character Mitya wonders aloud about the "terrible tragedies realism inflicts on people" (376; bk. 8, ch. 2).

For a play, indicate the page number, then the act and/or scene (*37; sc. 1*). For a verse play, give only the act, scene, and line numbers, separated by periods.

> Marullus expresses his anger at the commoners' celebrations, shouting, "You blocks, you stones, you worse than senseless things!" (Shakespeare 1.1.40).

For a poem, cite the part (if there is one) and line(s), separated by a period.

> Whitman speculates "All goes onward and outward, nothing collapses, / And to die is different from what anyone supposed, and luckier" (6.129–30).

If you are citing line numbers on their own, with no part or book number, use the word *line(s)* in the first reference (*lines 21–22*) and the line numbers alone in later references (*34–36*).

18. Sacred text   In the first citation, give the work's title as in the works cited entry, followed by book, chapter, and verse, or their equivalent, separated with periods.

> He ignored the admonition "Pride goes before destruction, and a haughty spirit before a fall" (New Oxford Annotated Bible, Prov. 16.18).

In later citations, omit the work's title (*Prov. 16.18*). Common abbreviations for books of the Bible are acceptable in a parenthetical citation.

19. Encyclopedia or dictionary entry   For reference works without an author, start the citation with the title of the entry in quotation marks.

> The word crocodile has a complex etymology ("Crocodile" 139).

20. Visual   To cite a visual that has a figure number in the source, use the abbreviation *fig.* and the number in place of a page number in your parenthetical citation: (*Manning, fig. 4*). If you refer to the figure in your text, spell out the word *figure*. To cite a visual that does not have a figure number in the source, use the visual's title or a description in your text and cite the author and page number as for any other source. Each visual that appears in your own project should include a caption with the figure or table number and information about the source. (See D2.4, MLA-Style Formatting, p. 352.)

21. Legal source   For a legislative act (law) or court case, name the act or case either in a signal phrase or in parentheses. Italicize the names of cases but not the names of acts.

> The Jones Act of 1917 granted U.S. citizenship to Puerto Ricans.

> *Dred Scott v. Sandford* may have been the Supreme Court's worst decision; it concluded that both free and enslaved Black people could not be U.S. citizens.

D2.3   Advice
MLA Works Cited List

An alphabetized list of works cited, which appears at the end of your project, gives publication information for each of the sources you have cited.

Guidelines for the Works Cited List

In the list of works cited, include only sources that you have quoted, summarized, or paraphrased in your project. MLA's guidelines apply to a wide variety of sources, but you may have to adapt them, combining the guidelines and models in this section to fit the source types you use in your research project.

Organization of the List

Ideally, a works cited entry includes the following pieces of information (although in reality, they may not all be available for every source):

- The author
- The title of your source
- The title of the larger work (if any) in which your source is located. (MLA calls this larger work a *container*; the container might be an anthology or collection, a journal, a magazine, a website, a television series, a database, and so on.)
- As much of the following information as is available about your source and its container (if any), listed in this order:
  - Contributors, such as the editor, translator, director, or performer
  - Version or edition
  - Volume and issue or other similar numbers
  - Publisher or sponsor
  - Publication date
  - Location of the source (such as page numbers, DOI, permalink, URL, or time stamp)

Not all sources will require every element. For more information on identifying and organizing source elements, see D2.1, Documenting Sources in MLA Style (p. 323), and the specific models in this section for more details.

Authors

- Arrange the list alphabetically by authors' last names or by titles for works with no authors.
- For the first author, place the last name first, a comma, the first name and any initials. The second author's name is in normal order (first name followed by last name). For three or more authors, use *et al.* after the first author's name.
- Spell out *editor, translator, director*, and so on.
- For organizations as authors, list the name as it appears in the source, but omit any article (*a, an,* or *the*).

Titles

- In titles of works, capitalize all words except articles (*a, an, the*), prepositions (such as *of, with*), coordinating conjunctions (such as *and*), and the *to* in infinitives (*How to Run a Marathon*)—unless the word is first or last in the title or subtitle.
- Use quotation marks for titles of articles and other works within a larger work.
- Italicize titles of books, websites, and other standalone works.

Publication Information

- MLA does not require the place of publication for a book publisher.
- Use the complete version of publishers' names, except for business terms such as *Inc.* and *Co.*; retain terms such as *Books* and *Press*. For university publishers, use the letters *U* and *P* for *University* and *Press*, respectively. Omit initial articles from group or publisher names (*Trevor Project*, not *The Trevor Project*).
- Take the name of the publisher from a book's title page (or copyright page if it is not on the title page). A website's publisher might be at the bottom of a page or on an *About* page.
- If the title of a website and the publisher are the same or similar, use the title of the site but omit the publisher.

Dates

- For a book, give the most recent year on the copyright page. For an article from a periodical (journal, magazine, newspaper, or blog), use the most specific date given: month and day (*May 2022*); day, month, and year (*28 May 2022*); or season and year (*spring 2022*). For a web source, use the post date, copyright date, or most recent update; use the complete date as given in the source.
- Abbreviate all months except May, June, and July and give the date in inverted form: *13 Mar. 2022*.
- If the source has no date, give your date of access at the end: *Accessed 24 Feb. 2022*.

Page Numbers

- For most articles and other short works, give page numbers when they are available in the source, preceded by *p.* (or *pp.* for more than one page).
- Do not use the page numbers from a printout of an online source.
- If an article does not appear on consecutive pages, give the number of the first page followed by a plus sign: *35+*.

URLs and DOIs

- If a source has one, give the DOI (digital object identifier, a permanent code) in URL form, with the protocol and host (https://doi.org/) at the beginning. (See the second example in item 10.)

- If a source does not have a DOI, include a permalink.

- If there is no permalink, include the URL. (See the first example in item 10.) Keeping the URL's protocol (*http://* or *https://*) is optional, but retain it if you want your readers to be able to click on the links.

- If a URL is longer than three lines in your works cited list, you may shorten it, but keep at least the website host (for example, *www.usda.gov* or *npr.org*).

- Book publishers may divide a URL or DOI to create even lines, but writers should not; short lines before a URL or DOI are acceptable.

Directory to MLA Works Cited Models

Guidelines for Listing Authors

Alphabetize entries in the list of works cited by authors' last names (or by title if a work has no author). The author's name is important because citations in the text refer to it and readers will look for it to identify the source in the list.

1. One author   Give the author's last name, followed by a comma, then give the first name, followed by a period.

> Gay, Roxane.

2. Two authors   List the authors in the order in which the source lists them. Reverse only the first author's name.

> Stiglitz, Joseph E., and Bruce C. Greenwald.

3. Three or more authors   List the author whose name appears first in the source followed by *et al.* (Latin for "and others").

> Lupton, Ellen, et al.

4. Organization or group author   When the author is a company, organization, or other group, begin with the name of the organization but omit initial articles.

> Coca-Cola Company.

5. Unknown author   Begin with the work's title. Titles of works that appear within another work (or "container") appear in quotation marks. Titles of standalone works are italicized.

> **Article, Television or Podcast Episode, or Other Work within a "Container"**
>
> "California Sues EPA over Emissions."
>
> "Fast Times at West Philly High."
>
> **Book, Television or Podcast Series, or Other Standalone Work**
>
> *Women of Protest: Photographs from the Records of the National Woman's Party.*
>
> *Frontline.*

6. Author using a pseudonym (pen name)   Use the author's name as it appears in the source, followed by the author's real name in brackets, if you know it. Alternatively, if the author's real name is better known, you may start with that name, followed by *published as* and the pen name in brackets.

> Saunders, Richard [Benjamin Franklin].
>
> Franklin, Benjamin [published as Richard Saunders].

7. Screen name or social media account   Start with the account display name, followed by the screen name or handle (if available) in brackets. If the account name is a first and last name, invert it.

> Gay, Roxane [@rgay].
>
> Pat and Stewart [@grammarphobia].

If the account name and handle are very similar (for example, *ACLU SoCal* and *@ACLU_SoCal*), you may omit the handle. See items 41 and 42 for more on citing social media.

8. Multiple works by the same author Alphabetize the works by title, ignoring the article (*A*, *An*, or *The*) at the beginning. Use the author's name for the first entry only. For later entries, use three hyphens or dashes followed by a period.

> Coates, Ta-Nehisi. *Between the World and Me*. Spiegel and Grau, 2015.
>
> ---. *We Were Eight Years in Power: An American Tragedy*. One World, 2018.

9. Multiple works by the same group of authors Alphabetize the works by title. For the first entry, use the authors' names in the proper form (see items 1–4). Begin later entries with three hyphens or dashes and a period. Use three hyphens or dashes only to replace the exact same names, in the exact same order, as in the first entry.

> Agha, Hussein, and Robert Malley. "The Arab Counterrevolution." *The New York Review of Books*, 29 Sept. 2011, www.nybooks.com /articles/2011/09/29/arab-counterrevolution/.
>
> ---. "This Is Not a Revolution." *The New York Review of Books*, 8 Nov. 2012, www.nybooks.com/articles/2012/11/08/not-revolution/.

Articles and Other Parts of Longer Works

10. Journal article Give the volume and issue numbers for all journals.

> Bryson, Devin. "The Rise of a New Senegalese Cultural Philosophy?" *African Studies Quarterly*, vol. 14, no. 3, Mar. 2014, pp. 33–56, asq.africa.ufl.edu /files/Volume-14-Issue-3-Bryson.pdf.
>
> Diala, Isidore. "M. J. C. Echeruo and Igbo Folk Drama." *Research in African Literatures*, vol. 51, no. 2, fall 2021, pp. 1–26. *Academic Search Premier*, https://doi.org/10.2979/reseafrilite.51.2.01.
>
> Matchie, Thomas. "Law versus Love in *The Round House*." *Midwest Quarterly*, vol. 56, no. 4, summer 2015, pp. 353–64.

MLA Citation at a Glance   Article in a Journal

To cite an article in a scholarly journal in MLA style, include the following elements:

1 Author(s)

2 Title & subtitle (if any) of article

3 Journal title

4 Volume & issue number

5 Date of publication

6 Page numbers of article, if available

7 DOI (digital object identifier), Permalink, or URL if available

First Page of Article

Journal Table of Contents

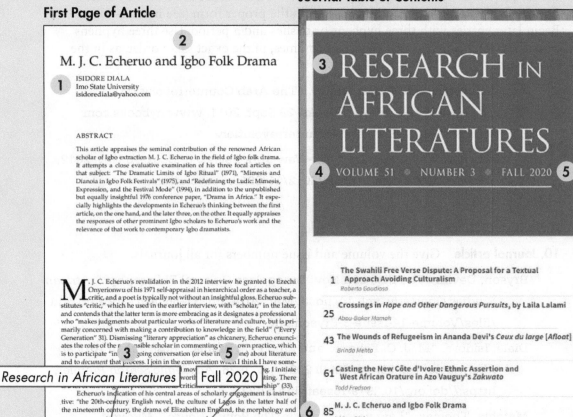

2 M. J. C. Echeruo and Igbo Folk Drama

1 ISIDORE DIALA
Imo State University
isidorediala@yahoo.com

ABSTRACT

This article appraises the seminal contribution of the renowned African scholar of Igbo extraction M. J. C. Echeruo in the field of Igbo folk drama. It attempts a close evaluative examination of his three focal articles on that subject: "The Dramatic Limits of Igbo Ritual" (1971), "Mimesis and Dianoia in Igbo Folk Festivals" (1975), and "Redefining the Ludic: Mimesis, Expression, and the Festival Mode" (1994), in addition to the unpublished but equally insightful 1976 conference paper, "Drama in Africa." It especially highlights the developments in Echeruo's thinking between the first article, on the one hand, and the later three, on the other. It equally appraises the responses of other prominent Igbo scholars to Echeruo's work and the relevance of that work to contemporary Igbo dramatists.

M. J. C. Echeruo's revalidation in the 2012 interview he granted to Ezechi Onyerionwu of his 1971 self-appraisal in hierarchical order as a teacher, a critic, and a poet is typically not without an insightful gloss. Echeruo substitutes "critic," which he used in the earlier interview, with "scholar," in the later, and contends that the latter term is more embracing as it designates a professional who "makes judgments about particular works of literature and culture, but is primarily concerned with making a contribution to knowledge in the field" ("Every Generation" 31). Dismissing "literary appreciation" as chicanery, Echeruo enunciates the roles of the responsible scholar in commenting on own practice, which is to participate "in going conversation (or else in one) about literature and to *document* that process. I join in the conversation when I think I have something worth ... ting. There ... criticism and ... larship" (33).

3 Research in African Literatures   **5** Fall 2020

Echeruo's indication of his central areas of scholarly engagement is instructive: "the 20th-century English novel, the culture of Lagos in the latter half of the nineteenth century, the drama of Elizabethan England, the morphology and

RESEARCH IN AFRICAN LITERATURES. Vol. 51, No. 3 (Fall 2020), doi: 10.2979/reseafrilite.51.3.05

4 Vol. 51, No. 3

7 https://doi.org/10.2979/reseafrilite.51.3.05

Journal Table of Contents

3 RESEARCH IN AFRICAN LITERATURES

4 VOLUME 51 • NUMBER 3 • **5** FALL 2020

Adapted from Hacker Handbooks (Bedford/St. Martin's).

Database Record

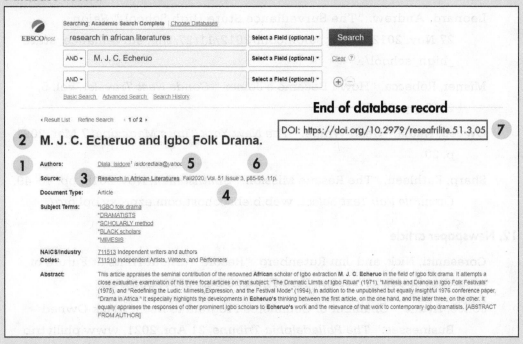

End of database record

DOI: https://doi.org/10.2979/reseafrilite.51.3.05   **7**

Reference List Entry for a Journal

Diala, Isidore. "M. J. C. Echeruo and Igbo Folk Drama." *Research in African Literature*, vol. 51, no. 3, fall 2020, pp. 85–95, https://doi.org/10.2979/reseafrilite.51.3.05.

For more on citing articles from journals and other periodicals, see items 10–15.

11. Magazine article Use the full date plus volume and issue numbers if available.

Leonard, Andrew. "The Surveillance State High School." *Salon*,
27 Nov. 2012, www.salon.com/2012/11/27/the_surveillance_state
_high_school/.

Misner, Rebecca. "How I Became a Joiner." *Condé Nast Traveler*, vol. 5,
2018, pp. 55–56.

Owusu, Nadia. "Head Wraps." *The New York Times Magazine*, 7 Mar. 2021,
p. 20.

Sharp, Kathleen. "The Rescue Mission." *Smithsonian*, Nov. 2015, pp. 40–49.
OmniFile Full Text Select, web.b.ebscohost.com.ezproxy.bpl.org/.

12. Newspaper article

Corasaniti, Nick, and Jim Rutenberg. "Record Turnout Hints at Future of
Vote in U.S." *The New York Times*, 6 Dec. 2020, pp. 1A+.

Jones, Ayana. "Chamber of Commerce Program to Boost Black-Owned
Businesses." *The Philadelphia Tribune*, 21 Apr. 2021, www.phillytrib
.com/news/business/chamber-of-commerce-program-to-boost-black
-owned-businesses/article_6b14ae2f-5db2-5a59-8a67-8bbf974da451
.html.

13. Editorial, opinion, or commentary in a newspaper

Brooks, David. "The Great Unmasking." *The New York Times*, 27 May 2021,
https://www.nytimes.com/2021/05/27/opinion/coronavirusmasks
-vaccine.html. Editorial.

Editorial Board. "The Road toward Peace." *The New York Times*, 15 Feb.
1945, p. 18. Editorial. *ProQuest Historical Newspapers: The New York
Times*, search.proquest.com/hnpnewyorktimes.

14. Letter to the editor

Carasso, Roger. Letter. *The New York Times*, 4 Apr. 2021, Sunday Book
Review sec., p. 5.

Rushlow, Lee. "My Recent Postal Ballot Was the Best I've Ever Cast." *The Wall Street Journal,* Dow Jones, 8 Oct. 2020, www.wsj.com/articles /my-recent-postal-ballot-was-the-best-ive-ever-cast-11602183549?reflink =desktopwebshare_permalink.

15. Review If the review is untitled, use the label *Review of* and the title and author or director of the work reviewed. Then add information for the publication in which the review appears.

Jopanda, Wayne Silao. Review of *America Is Not the Heart*, by Elaine Castillo. *Alon: Journal for Filipinx American and Diasporic Studies*, vol. 1, no. 1, Mar. 2021, pp. 106–08. *eScholarship*, escholarship.org/uc/item/0d44t8wx.

Bramesco, Charles. "*Honeyland* Couches an Apocalyptic Warning in a Beekeeping Documentary." *The A.V. Club*, G/O Media, 23 July 2019, film.avclub.com/honeyland-couches-an-apocalyptic-warning-in-a -beekeepin-1836624795.

16. Selection in an anthology or a collection Begin with the name of the author of the selection, not with the name of the anthology editor.

Symanovich, Alaina. "Compatibility." *Ab Terra 2020: A Science Fiction Anthology*, edited by Yen Ooi, Brain Mill Press, 2020, pp. 116–23.

17. Multiple selections from the same anthology or collection Provide an entry for the entire anthology (second example) and a shortened entry for each selection (first and third examples). Alphabetize the entries by authors' or editors' last names.

Challinor, Nels. "Porch Light." Ooi, pp. 107–15.

Ooi, Yen, editor. *Ab Terra 2020: A Science Fiction Anthology.* Brain Mill Press, 2020.

Symanovich, Alaina. "Compatibility." Ooi, pp. 116–23.

18. Published interview (See item 56 for a personal interview.)

Harjo, Joy. "The First Native American U.S. Poet Laureate on How Poetry Can Counter Hate." Interview by Olivia B. Waxman. *Time*, 22 Aug. 2019, time.com/5658443/joy-harjo-poet-interview/.

19. Encyclopedia or dictionary entry   For an online source that is continually updated, such as a wiki entry, use the date of the most recent update.

> Robinson, Lisa Clayton. "Harlem Writers Guild." *Africana: The Encyclopedia*
> *of the African and African American Experience*, edited by Kwame
> Anthony Appiah and Henry Louis Gates Jr., 2nd ed., Oxford UP,
> 2005, p. 163.

> "House Music." *Wikipedia: The Free Encyclopedia*, Wikimedia Foundation,
> 8 Apr. 2021, en.wikipedia.org/wiki/House_music.

> "Oligarchy." *Merriam-Webster*, 2021, www.merriam-webster.com/dictionary
> /oligarchy.

Books and Other Standalone Works

20. Basic format for a book   For most books, supply the author name(s); the title and subtitle, in italics; the name of the publisher; and the year of publication.

> Cabral, Amber. *Allies and Advocates: Creating an Inclusive and Equitable*
> *Culture.* Wiley, 2021.

If you used an e-book, include *E-book ed.* before the publisher's name.

> Cabral, Amber. *Allies and Advocates: Creating an Inclusive and Equitable*
> *Culture.* E-book ed., Wiley, 2021.

For an online book, include the title of the site on which the book appears (in italics) and the DOI or URL (permalink preferred) for the work, following the book's publication information. If the book's original publication date is not available, include the date of online publication.

> Euripides. *The Trojan Women.* Translated by Gilbert Murray, Oxford UP,
> 1915. *Internet Sacred Text Archive*, www.sacred-texts.com/cla/eurip
> /trojan.htm.

MLA Citation at a Glance Book

To cite a print book in MLA style, include the following elements:

1 Author

2 Title & subtitle

3 Publisher

4 Year of publication

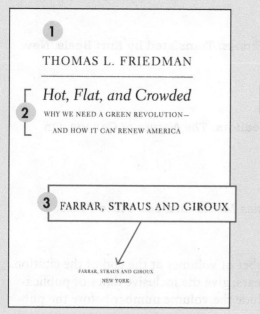

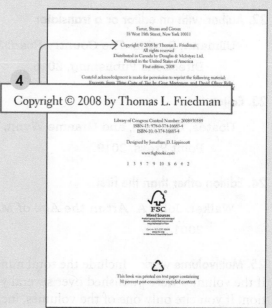

Reference List Entry for a Print Book

        1   **2**

Friedman, Thomas L. *Hot, Flat, and Crowded: Why We Need a Green Revolution—*

                                     3   **4**

   and How It Can Renew America. Farrar, Straus and Giroux, 2008.

For more on citing books and other standalone works in MLA style, see items 20–35.

Adapted from Hacker Handbooks (Bedford/St. Martin's).

21. Audiobook   Give the author's name and the title of the audiobook, each followed by a period. After the title, include the phrase *Narrated by* followed by the narrator's full name. If the author and narrator are the same, include only the last name. Then include the label *audiobook ed.*, the publisher, and the date of release.

> de Hart, Jane Sherron. *Ruth Bader Ginsburg: A Life.* Narrated by Suzanne
>   Toren, audiobook ed., Random House Audio, 16 Oct. 2018.

22. Author with an editor or a translator

> Ullmann, Regina. *The Country Road: Stories.* Translated by Kurt Beals, New
>   Directions Publishing, 2015.

23. Editor

> Coates, Colin M., and Graeme Wynn, editors. *The Nature of Canada.* On
>   Point Press, 2019.

24. Edition other than the first

> Walker, John A. *Art in the Age of Mass Media.* 3rd ed., Pluto Press,
>   2001.

25. Multivolume work   Include the total number of volumes at the end of the citation. If the volumes were published over several years, give the inclusive dates of publication. If you cite only one of the volumes, include the volume number before the publisher and give the date of publication for that volume.

> Brunetti, Ivan, editor. *An Anthology of Graphic Fiction, Cartoons, and True
>   Stories.* Yale UP, 2006–08. 2 vols.

> Brunetti, Ivan, editor. *An Anthology of Graphic Fiction, Cartoons, and True
>   Stories.* Vol. 2, Yale UP, 2008.

If you cite one volume that is individually titled, include information about both the volume and the complete set.

> Cather, Willa. *Willa Cather: Later Novels.* Edited by Sharon O'Brien, 1990.
>   *Willa Cather: The Complete Fiction and Other Writings*, edited by
>   O'Brien, vol. 2, Library of America, 1987–92.

26. Sacred text   Give the title of the edition of the sacred text (taken from the title page), in italics; the editor's or translator's name (if any); and the publication information. Add the name of the version, if there is one, before the publisher.

> *The Oxford Annotated Bible with the Apocrypha*. Edited by Herbert G. May and Bruce M. Metzger, Revised Standard Version, Oxford UP, 1965.

> *Quran: The Final Testament*. Translated by Rashad Khalifa, Authorized English Version with Arabic Text, Universal Unity, 2000.

27. Foreword, introduction, preface, or afterword   Begin with the author of the book part, the part title (if any), and a label for the part. Then give the title of the book, the author or editor preceded by *by* or *edited by*, and publication information. If the part author and book author are the same, use only the last name with the book title.

> Coates, Ta-Nehisi. Foreword. *The Origin of Others*, by Toni Morrison, Harvard UP, 2017, pp. vii–xvii.

28. Book with a title in its title   If the book's title contains a title normally italicized, do not italicize the title within the book title. If the book title contains a title normally placed in quotation marks, retain the quotation marks and italicize the entire title.

> Lethem, Jonathan. *"Lucky Alan" and Other Stories*. Doubleday, 2015.

> Masur, Louis P. *Runaway Dream: Born to Run and Bruce Springsteen's American Vision*. Bloomsbury Press, 2009.

29. Book in a series   After the publication information, list the series name and the book's number in the series (if there is one) as it appears on the title page.

> Denham, A. E., editor. *Plato on Art and Beauty*. Palgrave Macmillan, 2012. Philosophers in Depth.

30. Republished book   After the title of the book, cite the original publication date, followed by the current publication information.

> de Mille, Agnes. *Dance to the Piper*. 1951. The New York Review Books, 2015.

31. More than one publisher named   If the book was published by two or more publishers, separate the publishers with a slash, and include a space before and after the slash.

> Acevedo, Elizabeth. *With the Fire on High*. HarperTeen / Quill Tree Books, 2019.

32. Graphic narrative or illustrated work If the author and illustrator are the same, cite the work as you would a book with one author (see items 1 and 20). When the author and illustrator are different, begin with the contributor who is most important to your research. List other contributors after the title, labeling their contribution. If there are multiple contributors but you are not discussing a specific contributor's work in your essay, you may begin with the title.

> Martínez, Hugo, illustrator. *Wake: The Hidden History of Women-Led Slave Revolts.* By Rebecca Hall, Simon and Schuster, 2021.

> *Stealth.* By Mike Costa, illustrated by Nate Bellegarde, colored by Tamra Bonvillain, lettered by Sal Cipriano, vol. 1, Image Comics, 2020.

33. Pamphlet or brochure

> Sierra County Public Health. *Benefits of the COVID-19 Vaccine.* 2021, sierracounty.ca.gov/DocumentCenter/View/5522/Benefits-of-the -COVID-19-Vaccine-Brochure. Brochure.

34. Dissertation

> Kabugi, Magana J. *The Souls of Black Colleges: Cultural Production, Ideology, and Identity at Historically Black Colleges and Universities.* 2020. Vanderbilt U, PhD dissertation. *Vanderbilt University Institutional Repository,* hdl.handle.net/1803/16103.

35. Published proceedings of a conference

> Zhang, Baoshang, et al., editors. *A Dialogue between Law and History: Proceedings of the Second International Conference on Facts and Evidence.* Springer, 2021.

Online and Social Media Sources

36. Website

> *Lift Every Voice.* Library of America / Schomburg Center for Research in Black Culture, 2020, africanamericanpoetry.org/.

If the website does not have a date of copyright, publication, or update, include your date of access at the end. (See the first example in item 37.)

37. Web page or document on a website

Bali, Karan. "Shashikala." *Upperstall*, upperstall.com/profile/shashikala/.
  Accessed 22 Apr. 2021.

Enzinna, Wes. "Syria's Unknown Revolution." *Pulitzer Center*, 24 Nov. 2015,
  pulitzercenter.org/projects/middle-east-syria-enzinna-war-rojava.

38. Blog Cite a blog as you would a website. (See item 36.)

Horgan, John. *Cross-Check*. Scientific American, 2020, blogs
  .scientificamerican.com/cross-check/.

Ng, Amy. *Pikaland*. 2020, www.pikaland.com.

39. Blog post Cite a blog post as you would a web page or a document from a
website. (See item 37.)

Edroso, Roy. "No Compassion." *Alicublog*, 18 Mar. 2021, alicublog.blogspot
  .com/2021/03/no-compassion.html.

Horgan, John. "My Quantum Experiment." *Cross-Check*, Scientific
  American, 5 June 2020, blogs.scientificamerican.com/cross-check
  /my-quantum-experiment/.

40. Comment on a blog post or an online article List the screen name of the commenter and use the label *Comment on* before the title of the post or article. Include
the time posted (if available), following the date. Provide the URL to the comment
when possible; otherwise, use the URL for the post or article.

satch. Comment on "No Compassion," by Roy Edroso. *Alicublog*, 20 Mar.
  2021, 9:50 a.m., disq.us/p/2fu0ulk.

41. Tweet Give the author's display name and handle (in brackets). Use the text of
the tweet in quotation marks as the title, using the writer's capitalization and punctuation, or use a brief description (no quotation marks) if you are focusing on a visual
element of the tweet. Follow with *Twitter*, the date, and the URL. (See item 7 in this
section for how to style screen names.)

Abdurraqib, Hanif [@NifMuhammad]. "Tracy Chapman really one of
  the greatest Ohio writers." *Twitter*, 30 Mar. 2021, twitter.com
  /NifMuhammad/status/1377086355667320836.

42. Other social media posts   Cite as a web page or document from a website. (See item 37.) If it is brief, use the text accompanying the post as the title, in quotation marks; if it is long, use the first few words followed by an ellipsis. If the post has no title or text, or if you are focusing on a visual element, provide a description of the post (no quotation marks). (See item 7 for how to style screen names.)

> ACLU. "Public officials have . . ." *Facebook*, 10 May 2021, www.facebook
> .com/aclu/photos/a.74134381812/10157852911711813.

> Jones, James [@notoriouscree]. "Some traditional hoop teachings
> #indigenous #culture #native #powwow." *TikTok*, 6 Apr. 2021, www
> .tiktok.com/@notoriouscree/video/6948207430610226438.

> Rosa, Camila [camixvx]. Illustration of nurses in masks with fists raised.
> *Instagram*, 28 Apr. 2020, www.instagram.com/p/B_h62W9pJaQ/.

Visual, Audio, Multimedia, and Live Sources

43. Work of art   Cite the artist's name; the title of the artwork, in italics; and the date of composition. For works viewed in person, include the institution and the city in which the artwork is located. For works viewed online, include the title of the site and the URL of the work.

> Bronzino, Agnolo. *Lodovico Capponi*. 1550–55, Frick Collection,
> New York.

> Lange, Dorothea. *Migrant Mother, Nipomo, California*. Mar. 1936. *MOMA*,
> www.moma.org/collection/works/50989.

44. Cartoon or comic strip

> Shiell, Mike. Cartoon. *The Saturday Evening Post*, Jan.–Feb. 2021, p. 8.

> Munroe, Randall. "Heartbleed Explanation." *xkcd*, xkcd.com/1354/.
> Accessed 10 Oct. 2022.

45. Advertisement

> Advertisement for Better World Club. *Mother Jones*, Mar.–Apr. 2021, p. 2.

> "The Whole Working-from-Home Thing—Apple." *YouTube*, uploaded by
> Apple, 13 July 2020, www.youtube.com/watch?v=6_pru8U2RmM.

46. Map or chart   If the map or chart is located in another source, cite it as a short work within a longer work. If the title does not identify the item as a map or chart, add *Map* or *Chart* at the end of the entry.

"Australia." *Perry-Castañeda Library Map Collection*, U of Texas Libraries,

2016, legacy.lib.utexas.edu/maps/cia16/australia_sm_2016.gif.

"New COVID-19 Cases Worldwide." *Coronavirus Resource Center*, Johns

Hopkins University and Medicine, 3 May 2021, coronavirus.jhu.edu

/data/new-cases. Chart.

47. Sound recording   Begin with the name of the person or group you want to emphasize. For a single work from an album or collection, place the title in quotation marks and the album or collection in italics. For a standalone work, italicize the title. Provide the names of relevant artists and the orchestra and conductor (if any), record label, and date. If you listened to the recording online, include the name of the streaming service (in italics) and the URL for the recording or the name of the app.

Bach, Johann Sebastian. *Bach: Violin Concertos*. Performances by Itzhak

Perlman, Pinchas Zukerman, and English Chamber Orchestra, EMI,

2002.

Bad Bunny. "Vete." *YHLQMDLG*, Rimas, 2020. *Apple Music* app.

48. Film or video   If you focus on a particular person's work, start with that name. If not, start with the title; then name the director, distributor or production company, and year of release. Other contributors, such as writers or performers, may follow the director. If you viewed the film or video on a streaming service, include the app or the website name and URL at the end of the entry. See item 50 for how to cite online videos (*YouTube, Vimeo*).

Judas and the Black Messiah. Directed by Shaka King, Warner Bros.

Pictures, 2021.

Kubrick, Stanley, director. *A Clockwork Orange*. Hawk Films / Warner Bros.

Pictures, 1971. *Netflix*, www.netflix.com.

Youn, Yuh-Jung, performer. *Minari*. Directed by Lee Isaac Chung, Plan B

Entertainment / A24, 2020. *Amazon Prime Video* app.

49. Supplementary material accompanying a film Begin with the title of the feature, in quotation marks, and the names of any important contributors. End with information about the film, as in item 48, and the location of the supplementary material.

> "Sweeney's London." Produced by Eric Young. *Sweeney Todd: The Demon Barber of Fleet Street*, directed by Tim Burton, DreamWorks Pictures, 2007, disc 2. DVD.

50. Online video If you watched the video on a video-sharing site such as *YouTube* or *Vimeo*, put the name of the uploader after the name of the website. If the video emphasizes a single speaker or presenter, list that person as the author.

> "The Art of Single Stroke Painting in Japan." *YouTube*, uploaded by National Geographic, 13 July 2018, www.youtube.com /watch?v=g7H8IhGZnpM.

> Kundu, Anindya. "The 'Opportunity Gap' in US Public Education—and How to Close It." *TED*, May 2019, www.ted.com/talks/anindya_kundu _the_opportunity_gap_in_us_public_education_and_how_to_close_it.

51. Television, radio, or podcast episode or series If you are citing a particular episode or segment, begin with the title in quotation marks. Otherwise, begin with the program title in italics. List important contributors (narrator, writer, director, actors) if relevant to your writing; the network, distributor, or production company; and the date of broadcast or publication. Unless you viewed or listened to the program on a live broadcast, end with the site or service on which you accessed it. If you're referencing the show in a general way, mention it in your research project, but don't include it in your list of works cited.

> *Dolly Parton's America.* Hosted by Jad Abumrad, produced and reported by Shima Oliaee, WNYC Studios, 2019, www.wnycstudios.org/podcasts /dolly-partons-america.

> *Hillary.* Directed by Nanette Burstein, Propagate Content / Hulu, 2020. *Hulu* app.

> "Umbrellas Down." *This American Life*, episode 710, hosted by Ira Glass, WBEZ, 10 July 2020.

> "Shock and Delight." *Bridgerton*, season 1, episode 2, Shondaland / Netflix, 2020. *Netflix*, www.netflix.com.

52. Television, radio, or podcast interview   Begin with the name of the person interviewed, followed by the words *Interview by* and the interviewer's name, if relevant. End with information about the program as in item 51.

> Kendi, Ibram X. Interview by Eric Deggans. *Life Kit*, NPR, 24 Oct. 2020.

53. Standalone audio segment

> "The Past Returns to Gdańsk." Written and narrated by Michael Segalov,
> *BBC*, 26 Apr. 2021, www.bbc.co.uk/sounds/play/m000vh4f.

54. Live performance   Begin with either the title of the work performed or the author, composer, or main performer, if relevant. After the title, include relevant contributors (director, choreographer, conductor, major performers). End with the theater, ballet, or opera company, if any; the date of the performance; and the location.

> Beethoven, Ludwig van. *Piano Concerto No. 3*. Conducted by Andris
> Nelsons, performed by Paul Lewis and Boston Symphony Orchestra,
> 9 Oct. 2015, Symphony Hall, Boston.

> Nwandu, Antoinette Chinonye. *Pass Over*. Directed by Danya Taymor,
> 10 Sept. 2021, August Wilson Theater, New York City.

55. Lecture or public address   Cite the speaker's name, followed by the title of the lecture (if any) in quotation marks; the organization sponsoring the lecture; the date; and the location. If the lecture or address has no title, use the label "Lecture" or "Address" after the speaker's name.

> Gay, Roxane. "Difficult Women, Bad Feminists and Unruly Bodies." Beatty
> Lecture Series, 18 Oct. 2018, McGill University.

56. Personal interview   Begin with the name of the person interviewed. Then include the format of the interview (if not in person), followed by the date of the interview.

> Freedman, Sasha. Video interview with the author. 10 Nov. 2020.

57. Personal communication

> Primak, Shoshana. Text message to the author. 6 May 2021.

> Lewis-Truth, Antoine. E-mail to the Office of Student Financial Assistance.
> 30 Aug. 2020.

Other Sources

58. Government publication   Treat authors either exactly as listed in the source or, if citing multiple government sources, treat them in a standardized way, starting with the name of the government (spelled out), followed by the name of any agencies and subagencies.

> U.S. Bureau of Labor Statistics. "Consumer Expenditures Report 2019."
> *BLS Reports,* Dec. 2020, www.bls.gov/opub/reports/consumer
> -expenditures/2019/home.htm.

> United States, Department of Labor, Bureau of Labor Statistics. "Consumer
> Expenditures Report 2019." *BLS Reports*, Dec. 2020, www.bls.gov
> /opub/reports/consumer-expenditures/2019/home.htm.

59. Legal source   For a legislative act (law), give the government body, the Public Law number, and the publication information.

> United States, Congress. Public Law 116-136. *United States Statutes at
> Large,* vol. 134, 2019, pp. 281–615. *U.S. Government Publishing Office,*
> www.govinfo.gov/content/pkg/PLAW-116publ136/uslm/PLAW
> -116publ136.xml.

For a court case, name the court and then name the case (in italics). Give the date of the decision and publication information.

> United States, Supreme Court. *Miller v. Alabama.* 25 June 2012. *Legal
> Information Institute,* Cornell Law School, www.law.cornell.edu
> /supremecourt/text/10-9646.

D2.4 Advice
MLA-Style Formatting

The following guidelines are consistent with advice given in the *MLA Handbook*, 9th edition (2021), and with typical requirements for student projects. If you are creating a digital or multimedia project or have formatting questions, check with your instructor before preparing your final draft.

Formatting an MLA Project

Margins and spacing.   Leave one-inch margins at the top and bottom and on both sides of each page. Double-space the entire text, including set-off quotations, notes, tables, and the list of works cited. Indent the first line of a paragraph half an inch.

First page and title page.   For a project authored by an individual writer, a title page is not needed. Type each of the following items on a separate double-spaced line on the first page of your essay, beginning one inch from the top and aligned with the left margin: your name, the instructor's name, the course name and number, and the date. On the next line, place your title, centered, with no additional spacing above or below it. (See p. 355 for an example showing the first text page of a student paper.)

For a group project, create a title page with all members' names, the instructor's name, the course, and the date, all left-aligned on separate double-spaced lines. Center the title on a new line a few spaces down. (See p. 358 for an example of a title page for a group project.)

Page numbers.   Include your last name and the page number on each page, half an inch below the top of the page and aligned with the right margin. For a group project, include all members' last names and the page number; if the names will not all fit on a single line, include only the page number on each page.

Long quotations.   Set off a long quotation (one with more than four typed lines) in block format by starting it on a new line and indenting each line half an inch from the left margin. Do not enclose the passage in quotation marks. (See p. 361 for an example of a quotation indented as a block.)

Headings.   While headings are generally not needed for brief essays, readers may find them helpful for long or complex essays. Set each heading in the same style and size. If you need subheadings, be consistent in styling them. Place headings at the left margin without any indent. Capitalize headings as you would titles.

Visuals.   Place tables, photographs, drawings, charts, graphs, and other visuals as near as possible to the relevant text. A table should have a label and number (*Table 1*) and a clear title, each on its own line above the table and aligned with the left margin. For a table that you have borrowed or adapted, give the source below the table in a note like the following:

Source: Boris Groysberg and Michael Slind. "Leadership Is a Conversation." *Harvard Business Review*, June 2012, p. 83.

All other visuals should be labeled *Figure* (usually abbreviated *Fig.*), numbered, and captioned below the visual. The label and caption should appear on the same line. If your caption includes full source information and you don't cite the source anywhere else in your text, you don't need to include an entry in your works cited list. Be sure to refer to each visual in your text—*see table 1*; *as shown in figure 2*—and explain how it contributes to the point you are making. (See p. 356 for an example of a table in a student paper; see p. 357 for an example of a figure in a student paper.)

Formatting an MLA Works Cited List

Begin the list of works cited on a new page at the end of the project. Center the title *Works Cited* one inch from the top of the page. Double-space throughout.

Alphabetizing the list.   Alphabetize the list by the last names of the authors (or the names of corporate or government authors); if a work has no author, alphabetize by the first word of the title other than *A*, *An*, or *The*.

Indenting the entries.   Set entries with a *hanging indent*: don't indent the first line of each works cited entry, but indent any additional lines half an inch.

Including URLs.   If you include a URL in a works cited entry, copy the URL directly from your browser. If the entire URL moves to another line, creating a short line, leave it that way. Never add hyphens or spaces to break a URL across lines.

> Kundu, Anindya. "The 'Opportunity Gap' in US Public Education—and How
>   to Close It." *TED*, May 2019, https://www.ted.com/talks/anindya
>   _kundu_the_opportunity_gap_in_us_public_education_and_how_to
>   _close_it.

Professionally typeset works (like this one) may introduce line breaks to avoid uneven line displays, but student writing should not.

If a URL is longer than three lines in the list of works cited, you may shorten it, leaving at least the website host (for example, *cnn.com* or *www.usda.gov*) in the entry. If you will post your project online or submit it electronically and you want your readers to click on your URLs, do not shorten the URL or delete the protocol (*https://* or *http://*).

Sample Pages from Student Writing in MLA Style

Pages from a variety of student essays are included to show the following elements in MLA style:

- formatting the first page of a student essay (pp. 355, 359)
- placing and labeling tables and figures (pp. 356, 357)
- formatting long quotations (p. 361)
- composing a list of works cited (p. 364) and citing sources (throughout)

A complete student essay appears on pp. 359–64.

First Text Page of a Student Essay

1″

½″
Sakowitz 1

Julia Sakowitz

Professor Yamboliev

PWR 1

6 May 2022

Name, instructor, course, and date aligned at left

Writer's last name and page number in upper right corner of each page

"We're a Lot More Than Gospel Singing":

Tourism in Harlem

Title centered

½″
As a New York City resident of the new millennium, I grew up

barely aware that Harlem had ever been a *no-go* zone and couldn't

understand why people of the older generation, my parents included,

were afraid to venture uptown. I knew nothing about the heroin

and crack epidemics of the 1960s, 70s, and 80s and in general was

accustomed to a New York City that was safer than it had been

in years.

1″

Double-spacing throughout

Harlem has changed rapidly over the past several decades.

As problems with crime and drug abuse in the storied New York

neighborhood decreased in the 1980s and 1990s, new government-

sponsored and privately funded economic initiatives like the

Upper Manhattan Empowerment Zone (UMEZ) pushed for outside

investment and economic development (Hoffman 288; Zukin et al.

50). In a recent interview, Carolyn Johnson, owner of "Welcome to

Harlem," a boutique tour company, recalled that "[Harlem] went

from 0 to 100 in a short period of time," to the point that even Harlem

residents themselves weren't aware of new businesses in their

neighborhood. Tourism in Harlem clearly played a central role in this

process, both responding to and creating social and economic change.

By 2000, more than 800,000 people were visiting Harlem each year

(Hoffman 288).

Multiple sources in parenthetical citation separated by semicolon

1″

Author's last name and page number in parentheses for paraphrase of source

1″

Table in Text

Table number and title given on separate lines above table

Table 1

Comparison of Two Approaches to Teaching and Learning

Period	Instructor Centered	Student Centered
Before Class	• Instructor prepares lesson. • Students do HW on previous topic.	• Students read new material. • Instructor views student work.
During Class	• Instructor delivers new lesson. • Students—unprepared—try to follow along.	• Students lead discussions of new material. • Instructor gives feedback.
After Class	• Instructor grades HW. • Students practice concepts alone.	• Students apply concepts alone / in groups. • Instructor posts resources for help.

Double-spacing throughout

Source information provided in caption

Adapted from: "The Flipped Class Demystified." *NYU*, www.nyu.edu. Accessed 6 Mar. 2018.

Reference to table in text

Student-centered and instructor-centered learning are contrasted in table 1 (above). In a Stanford study researchers examined four schools that had moved from teacher-driven instruction to student-centered learning (Friedlaender et al.). The study focused on

Visual in Text

elderly, people of color, and people with low incomes" ("Voter ID").
Many continue to advocate for voter ID laws, citing how easily
the abolition of voter ID requirements could lead to voter fraud.
However, one study found only thirty-one credible incidents of voter
impersonation out of more than one billion ballots cast between 2000
to 2014, and another found that in only four states during this same
time period "more than 3,000 votes (in general elections alone) have
reportedly been affirmatively rejected for lack of ID" (Levitt). Studies
like these highlight both the uselessness and the harm of voter ID laws.

In addition to voter ID laws, some voters are held up by prohibitively
long lines, seen in figure 1, and mishandling of polling procedures. The

Shortened title used for source with no author; full title is "Voter ID 101: The Right to Vote Shouldn't Come with Barriers"

Only author name appears in parentheses for unpaginated online source

Reference to figure in text

Ethan Miller/Getty Images

Figure number and caption providing source information

Fig. 1. In a primary election in North Las Vegas, people waited in a
long line to register to vote and drop off ballots. (Ethan Miller. "Five
States Hold Primaries as Pandemic Continues in North America."
9 June 2020. Getty Images, www.gettyimages.com.)

When full publication information is given in caption, no entry needed in list of works cited

Title Page for Group Project

Title page created for group project; all authors' names, instructor's name, course title, and date listed and aligned left

Running head starts on first text page, not title page; for group project, all author last names and page number appear in running head; if all names do not fit, include only page number

Nikole Carter

Andrea Hidalgo-Vásquez

Jaylen Johnson

Sujan Kapoor

Professor Hamada

English 102

29 April 2022

Title centered a few lines down from heading

Still Alice and Representations of Aging in America

Complete Student Research Project

Writer's name and page number in upper right corner of each page

Benjy Mercer-Golden

Ms. Tavani

ENG 120

18 November 2022

Name, instructor, course, and date aligned at left

Lessons from Tree-Huggers and Corporate Mercenaries:

A New Model of Sustainable Capitalism

Title centered

Televised images of environmental degradation—seagulls with oil coating their feathers, smokestacks belching gray fumes—often seem designed to shock, but these images also represent very real issues: climate change, dwindling energy resources like coal and oil, a scarcity of clean drinking water. In response, businesspeople around the world are thinking about how they can make their companies greener or more socially beneficial to ensure a brighter future for humanity. But progress in the private sector has been slow and inconsistent. To accelerate the move to sustainability, for-profit businesses need to learn from the hybrid model of social entrepreneurship to ensure that the company is efficient and profitable while still working for social change, and more investors need to support companies with long-term, revolutionary visions for improving the world.

In fact, both for-profit corporations and "social good" businesses could take steps to reshape their strategies. First, for-profit corporations need to operate sustainably and be evaluated for their performance with long-term measurements and incentives. The conventional argument against for-profit companies deeply embedding environmental and social goals into their corporate strategies is that caring about the world does not go hand in hand with lining pockets. This morally toxic case is also problematic from a business standpoint. A 2012 study of 180 high-profile companies by Harvard Business

School professors Robert G. Eccles and colleagues shows that "high sustainability companies," as defined by environmental and social variables, "significantly outperform their counterparts over the long term, both in terms of stock market and accounting performance." The study argues that the better financial returns of these companies are especially evident in sectors where "companies' products significantly depend upon extracting large amounts of natural resources."

Such empirical financial evidence to support a shift toward using energy from renewable sources to run manufacturing plants argues that executives should think more sustainably, but other underlying incentives need to evolve in order to bring about tangible change. David Blood and Al Gore of Generation Foundation, an investment firm focused on "sustainable investing for the long term" ("About Us"), wrote a groundbreaking white paper that outlined the perverse incentives company managers face. For public companies, the default practice is to issue earnings guidance announcements of projected future earnings every quarter. This practice encourages executives to manage for the short term instead of adding long-term value to their company and the earth (Gore and Blood). Only the most uncompromisingly green CEOs would still advocate for stricter carbon emissions standards at the company's factories if a few mediocre quarters left investors demanding that they be fired. Gore and Blood make a powerful case against subjecting companies to this "What have you done for me lately?" philosophy, arguing that quarterly earnings guidances should be abolished in favor of companies releasing information when they consider it appropriate. Companies also need to change the way the managers get paid. Currently, the CEO of ExxonMobil is rewarded for a highly profitable year but is not held accountable for depleting nonrenewable oil reserves. A new model should incentivize thinking for the long run. Multiyear milestones for

First author's name plus *and colleagues* for an in-text reference to a source with three or more authors

Shortened title for source with no author

Double-spaced throughout

performance evaluation, as Gore and Blood suggest, are essential to pushing executives to manage sustainably.

But it's not just for-profit companies that need to rethink strategies. Social good-oriented leaders also stand to learn from the people often vilified in environmental circles: corporate CEOs. To survive in today's economy, companies building sustainable products must operate under the same strict business standards as profit-driven companies. Two social enterprises, Nika Water and Belu, provide perfect examples. Both sell bottled water in the developed world with the mission of providing clean water to impoverished communities through their profits. Both have visionary leaders who define a critical lesson: financial pragmatism will add far more value to the world than idealistic dreams. Nika Water founder Jeff Church explained this in a speech at Stanford University:

> Social entrepreneurs look at their businesses as nine parts cause, one part business. In the beginning, it needs to be nine parts business, one part cause, because if the business doesn't stay around long enough because it can't make it, you can't do anything about the cause.

When UK-based Belu lost £600,000 ($940,000) in 2007, it could only give around £30,000 ($47,000) to charity. Karen Lynch took over as CEO, cutting costs, outsourcing significant parts of the company's operations, and redesigning the entire business model; the company now donates four times as much to charity (Hurley). The conventional portrayal of do-gooders is that they tend to be terrible businesspeople, an argument often grounded in reality. It is easy to criticize the Walmarts of the world for caring little about sustainability or social good, but the idealists with big visions who do not follow through on their promises because their businesses cannot survive are no more praiseworthy. Walmart should learn from nonprofits and social

Long quotation indented as a block by ½"

enterprises about the benefits of advancing a positive environmental and social agenda, but idealist entrepreneurs should also learn from corporations about building successful businesses.

      The final piece of the sustainable business ecosystem is the investors who help get potentially world-changing companies off the ground. Industries that require a large amount of money to build complex products with expensive materials, such as solar power companies, rely heavily on investors—often venture capitalists based in California's Silicon Valley (Knight). The problem is that venture capitalists are not doing enough to fund truly groundbreaking companies. In an oft-cited blog post entitled "Why Facebook Is Killing Silicon Valley," entrepreneur Steve Blank argues that the financial returns on social media companies have been so quick and so outsized that the companies with the *really* big ideas—like providing efficient, cheap, scalable solar power—are not being backed: "In the past, if you were a great [venture capitalist], you could make $100 million on an investment in 5-7 years. Today, social media startups can return hundreds of millions or even billions in less than 3 years." The point Blank makes is that what is earning investors lots of money right now is not what is best for the United States or the world.

      There are, however, signs of hope. Paypal founder Peter Thiel runs his venture capital firm, the Founders Fund, on the philosophy that investors should support "flying cars" instead of new social media ventures (Packer). While the next company with the next great social media idea might be both profitable and valuable, Thiel and a select few others fund technology that has the potential to solve the huge problems essential to human survival.

      The world's need for sustainable companies that can build products from renewable energy or make nonpolluting cars will inevitably create opportunities for smart companies to make money.

No page number for unpaginated online source

In fact, significant opportunities already exist for venture capitalists willing to step away from what is easy today and shift their investment strategies toward what will help us continue to live on this planet tomorrow—even if seeing strong returns may take a few more years. Visionaries like Blank and Thiel need more allies (and dollars) in their fight to help produce more pioneering, sustainable companies. And global warming won't abate before investors wise up. It is vital that this shift happen now.

When we think about organizations today, we think about nonprofits, which have long-term social missions, and corporations, which we judge by their immediate financial returns like quarterly earnings. That is a treacherous dichotomy. Instead, we need to see the three major players in the business ecosystem—corporations, social enterprises, and investors—moving toward a *single* model of long-term, sustainable capitalism. We need visionary companies that not only set out to solve humankind's biggest problems but also have the business intelligence to accomplish these goals, and we need investors willing to fund these companies. Gore and Blood argue that "the imperative for change has never been greater." We will see this change when the world realizes that sustainable capitalism shares the same goals as creating a sustainable environment. Let us hope that this realization comes soon.

Works Cited

"About Us." *Generation Foundation,* 2012, www.genfound.org.

Blank, Steve. "Why Facebook Is Killing Silicon Valley." *Steveblank
.com,* 21 May 2012, steveblank.com/2012/05/21/why-facebook-is
-killing-silicon-valley/.

Church, Jeff. "The Wave of Social Entrepreneurship."
Entrepreneurial Thought Leaders Seminar, 11 Apr. 2012,
Stanford University.

Eccles, Robert G., et al. "The Impact of a Corporate Culture of
Sustainability on Corporate Behavior and Performance." *Working
Knowledge*, Harvard Business School, 14 Nov. 2011, hbswk
.hbs.edu/item/the-impact-of-corporate-sustainability-on
-organizational-process-and-performance.

Gore, Al, and David Blood. "Sustainable Capitalism." *Generation
Foundation*, 15 Feb. 2012, www.genfound.org/media/1375/pdf
-generation-sustainable-capitalism-v1.pdf.

Hurley, James. "Belu Boss Shows Bottle for a Turnaround." *The Daily
Telegraph*, 28 Feb. 2007, www.telegraph.co.uk/finance
/businessclub/9109449/Belu-boss-shows-bottle-for-a-turnaround
.html.

Knight, Eric R. W. "The Economic Geography of Clean Tech Venture
Capital." *Oxford U Working Paper Series in Employment, Work,
and Finance*, 13 Apr. 2010. *Social Science Research Network*,
https://doi.org/10.2139/ssrn1588806.

Packer, George. "No Death, No Taxes: The Libertarian Futurism of a
Silicon Valley Billionaire." *The New Yorker*, 28 Nov. 2011, www
.newyorker.com/magazine/2011/11/28/no-death-no-taxes.

Works cited list starts on new page; title centered

Sources arranged alphabetically by authors' last names or by title for sources with no author

Source with three or more authors listed by first author's name followed by *et al.*

Full name of publication given, including article *The*

DOI used if source has one

First line of each entry at left margin, subsequent lines indented ½"

D3 ▸ APA Documentation

In psychology and other social science classes (and even some English classes), you might be asked to use the APA (American Psychological Association) system for documenting sources. The guidelines below follow those set forth in the *Publication Manual of the American Psychological Association*, 7th ed. (APA, 2020).

Rather than thinking of the APA guidelines simply as rules to be followed, think of them as guidelines for participating in an academic community—a community in which the exchange and extension of ideas require a system. Even though the guidelines present a system for citing many different kinds of sources, they don't cover everything, and at times you will have to adapt the guidelines to the source you are using.

Introduction to APA Style

D3.1 Advice

Documenting Sources in APA Style

To cite and document sources in APA style, you will need to use four main categories of information:

- **Author's (or authors') names.** The author's last name is used in in-text citations, and the last name with first and any middle initials is used in reference list entries.
- **Date of publication.** The year appears in in-text citations. The full date is used in reference list entries.
- **Title of the work.** The work you cite may be a standalone work such as a book, a report, or a film, or it might be part of a larger whole such as an article in a journal, a page on a website, or a chapter in an edited book.
- **Source of the work (retrieval information).** Retrieval information might include the publisher of a book; the volume, issue, and page numbers of a journal article; or a DOI (digital object identifier, a permanent code) or URL (if no DOI is available) for an article from an online journal.

The APA recommends in-text citations that refer readers to a list of references.

An in-text citation gives the author of the source (often in a signal phrase incorporated into the text of the research project), the year of publication, and at times a page number in parentheses for words borrowed from a source. At the end of the paper, a list of references provides full publication information for the source.

In-Text Citation

Bruns (2017) argued that by imprisoning men—"which discourages shared responsibility for children, the home, and the household economy—prisons, jails, and justice system processes reproduce gender inequality" (p. 1332).

Entry in the List of References

Bruns, A. (2017). Consequences of partner incarceration for women's employment. *Journal of Marriage and Family, 79*(5), 1331–1352. https://doi.org/10.1111/jomf.12412

D3.2 Advice

APA In-Text Citations

APA's in-text citations provide at least the author's last name and the year of publication. For direct quotations and some paraphrases, a page number is given as well.

Sample Quotation

Ordinarily, introduce the quotation with a signal phrase that includes the author's last name followed by the year of publication in parentheses and a verb in the past tense or the present perfect tense: *Smith (2005) reported; Smith (2005) has argued.* Put the page number (preceded by "p." or "pp.") in parentheses after the quotation.

Mischel (2014) revisited his groundbreaking research on self-control, arguing that those who resisted temptation as preschoolers "yielded less to temptation . . . and trusted their own judgment" more as teenagers (p. 23).

If the author is not named in the signal phrase, place the author's name, the year, and the page number in parentheses after the quotation: (*Mischel, 2014, p. 23*).

APA style requires only the year of publication in an in-text citation. Do not include a month, even if the entry in the reference list includes one.

Sample Summary or Paraphrase

Include the author's last name and the year either in a signal phrase introducing the material or in parentheses following it. A page number is not required for a summary or a paraphrase, but include one if it would help readers find the passage in a long work.

Instructors' positive feelings about teaching carry over into their feelings about the schools at which they teach (Zhang, 2019, p. 211).

Guidelines for In-Text Citations

Directory to APA In-Text Citation Models

1. One author   367
2. Two authors   367
3. Three or more authors   367
4. Organization as author   368
5. Unknown author   368
6. Authors with the same last name   368
7. Two or more works by the same author in the same year   368

8. Two or more works in the same parentheses   369
9. Personal communication   369
10. Indirect source   369
11. Sacred or classical text   369
12. Online or digital source   369
13. Audiovisual or multimedia work   370

1. One author   Name the author in a signal phrase at first mention. Later mentions can be in a parenthetical citation.

> **Signal Phrase**   Critser (2003) has argued. . . .
>
> **Parenthetical Citation**   . . . (Critser, 2003).

2. Two authors   Name both authors in the signal phrase or the parentheses each time you cite the work. In the parenthetical citation, use the ampersand symbol (&) between the authors' names; in the signal phrase, use the word *and* spelled out.

> Bloomberg and Pope (2017) have argued that with global warming we are facing a "kairos: a supreme moment at which one simply must act, however implausible or inconvenient" (p. 12).

> Some have argued that we are facing a watershed moment, or "kairos," in the fight against global warming (Bloomberg & Pope, 2017, p. 12).

3. Three or more authors   Use the first author's name followed by the abbreviation *et al.* (Latin for "and others").

> Similarly, as Belenky et al. (1986) showed, examining the lives of women expands our understanding of human development.

> Examining the lives of women expands our understanding of human development (Belenky et al., 1986).

4. Organization as author   Give the organization's or government agency's full name in the signal phrase or in the parenthetical citation the first time you cite the source.

> The Kaiser Family Foundation (2018) found that 11% of children living in Texas were uninsured in 2017.

> In 2017, 11% of children living in Texas were uninsured (Kaiser Family Foundation, 2018).

If the organization's name is lengthy, you can abbreviate it; include the abbreviation in parentheses (in the signal phrase) or in brackets (in the parenthetical citation) the first time you cite the organization.

> **First Citation**   (Centers for Disease Control and Prevention [CDC], 2021)

> **Later Citations**   (CDC, 2021)

5. Unknown author   If the author is unknown, include the work's title (shortened if lengthy) in the in-text citation. Capitalize important words and words of four or more letters. Titles of articles and chapters are put in quotation marks; titles of books and reports are italicized. (For online sources with no author, see item 12.)

> As a result of changes in the city's eviction laws, New York's eviction rate dropped by over a third from 2013 to 2018 ("Pushed Out," 2019).

In the rare case when *Anonymous* is specified as the author, treat it as if it were a real name: (*Anonymous, 2001*). Also use the word *Anonymous* in the reference list entry.

6. Authors with the same last name   To avoid confusion, use initials with the last names if your reference list includes two or more authors with the same last name.

> K. Yi (2022) has demonstrated . . .

If the authors share the same initials, spell out each author's first name: (*Kim Yi*, *2022*), (*Kenneth Yi, 2022*).

7. Two or more works by the same author in the same year   When your list of references includes more than one work by the same author in the same year, use lowercase letters (*a*, *b*, and so on) with the year to order the entries in the reference list. (See item 7, p. 371, in the reference list section below.) Use those same letters with the year in the in-text citation.

> Soot-free flames can be produced by stripping the air of nitrogen and then adding that nitrogen to the fuel (Conover, 2019b).

8. Two or more works in the same parentheses   When your parenthetical citation names two or more works, put them in alphabetical order, separated with semicolons.

> Two clear types of social relationships have been theorized several times by different researchers (Dumont, 1977; Mead, 1934; Triandis, 1995).

9. Personal communication   Personal interviews, memos, letters, email, and similar unpublished communications should be cited in the text only, not in the reference list. (Use the first initial with the last name in parentheses.)

> One of Atkinson's colleagues, who has studied the effect of the media on children's eating habits, has contended that advertisers for snack foods will need to design ads responsibly for their younger viewers (F. Johnson, personal communication, October 20, 2022).

10. Indirect source   Ideally, find and use the original source. If you can't (for example, if the source hasn't been translated), name the original source in your in-text citation and then include *as cited in* plus the author's name and the date of the secondary source. In the following example, Brailsford is the original source, and Chow is the secondary source, given in the reference list.

> One reviewer commended the author's "sure understanding of the thoughts of young people" (Brailsford, 1990, as cited in Chow, 2019, para. 9).

11. Sacred or classical text   Identify the title of the version or edition you used, the year of that version's publication, and the relevant part (chapter, verse, line).

> Peace activists have long cited the biblical prophet's vision of a world without war: "And they shall beat their swords into plowshares, and their spears into pruning hooks; nation shall not lift up sword against nation, neither shall they learn war any more" (*Revised Standard Version Bible*, 1952, Isaiah 2:4).

12. Online or digital source   Most references to online or digital sources can be cited using one of the models supplied earlier in this section.

- If author and publication date are supplied, use the usual author-date format: (*Young, 2022*).
- If no publication date is given, use "n.d." (*no date*): (*Young, n.d.*) (See items 19, 39, 40, and 44 in D3.3, APA Reference List.)

- If the organization's name is given in place of a specific author, use the organization's name in your citation: (*Greenpeace, 2022*). (See item 4 in this section.)
- If no author is given at all, use the title in your signal phrase or include an abbreviated title in a parenthetical citation: (*"Pushed Out," 2019*). (See item 5 in this section.)

Whichever format you use, be sure that your in-text citation matches the first part of your reference list entry. If you merely refer to a website, a type of software, or an app in your text without citing specific information from that work, though, no formal in-text citation (or reference list entry) is needed. Just mention the work, and include the URL.

13. Audiovisual or multimedia work   In the "author" position, include the name of the person (or people) primarily responsible for producing the work, along with the date the work was created or released.

- To cite a work of art, include the artist's name and the date the work was created: (*Basquiat, 1980*).
- To cite a film, include the director's name and the date the film was released: (*DuVernay, 2018*).
- To cite a podcast or episode from a podcast, list the host: (*Longoria, 2019*).
- To cite an online video or audio, list the person or organization that posted the file: (*TED, 2019*).

See Guidelines for Listing Authors in D3.3, APA Reference List (p. 370).

D3.3   Advice
APA Reference List

In APA style, the alphabetical list of works cited, which appears at the end of the paper, is titled *References*. For advice on preparing the list of references, see Preparing the Reference List in D3.4, APA-Style Formatting (p. 394). For a sample reference list, see the student research project at the end of this chapter (p. 395).

   Alphabetize entries in the list of references by authors' (or editors') last names; if a work has no author or editor, alphabetize it by its title. The first element of each entry is important because citations in the text of the paper refer to it and readers will be looking for it in the alphabetized list. The date of publication appears immediately after the first element of the citation.

   In APA style, titles of standalone works, like books and periodicals, are italicized; titles of articles and names of websites are neither italicized nor put in quotation marks. (For rules on capitalizing titles, see D3.4, APA-Style Formatting, p. 391.)

Directory of APA Reference List Models

Guidelines for Listing Authors

In APA style, all authors' names are inverted (the last name comes first), and initials only are used for all first and middle names.

Name and Date Cited in Text

Zhang (2022) showed that . . .

Beginning of Entry in the List of References

Zhang, X. (2022).

If the first name is hyphenated, include a hyphen with no spaces between the initials.

Kang, D.-W.

If an author's name has a suffix, such as *Jr.*, include it after the initials.

Foreman, G., Jr.

1. One author

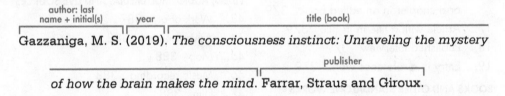

Gazzaniga, M. S. (2019). *The consciousness instinct: Unraveling the mystery of how the brain makes the mind*. Farrar, Straus and Giroux.

2. Multiple authors

List up to twenty authors by last names followed by initials. Use an ampersand (&) before the name of the last author. If there are more than twenty authors, list the first nineteen followed by three ellipsis dots and the last author's name.

Up to Twenty Authors

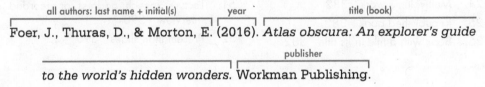

Foer, J., Thuras, D., & Morton, E. (2016). *Atlas obscura: An explorer's guide to the world's hidden wonders*. Workman Publishing.

Twenty-one or More Authors

first nineteen authors: last name + initial(s)

Sharon, G., Cruz, N. J., Kang, D.-W., Gandal, M. J., Wang, B., Kim, Y.-M., Zink, E. M.,

Casey, C. P., Taylor, B. C., Lane, C. J., Bramer, L. M., Isern, N. G.,

Hoyt, D. W., Noecker, C., Sweredoski, M. J., Moradian, A., Borenstein, E.,

ellipsis + last author   *year*   *title (article)*

Jansson, J. K., Knight, R., . . . Mazmanian, S. K. (2019). *Human gut*

microbiota from autism spectrum disorder promote behavioral

journal title   *volume, issue*   *page range*

symptoms in mice. Cell, 177(6), 1600–1618.

3. Organization as author   If the publisher is the same as the author, omit the publisher's name.

author: organization name   *year*   *title (book)*

American Psychiatric Association. (1994). *Diagnostic and statistical manual*

edition number

of mental disorders (4th ed.).

4. Unknown author   Begin the entry with the work's title.

Atlas of the world. (2019). Oxford University Press.

Pushed out. (2019, August 24). *The Economist, 432* (9157), 19–20.

5. Author using a pseudonym or screen name   If you know the writer's actual name, provide it (last name first), with the screen name, or "handle," following in square brackets.

Abdurraqib, Hanif [@NifMuhammad]. (2021, March 30). Tracy Chapman really one of the greatest Ohio writers. [Tweet]. Twitter. http://twitter.com/NifMuhammad/status/1377086355667320836.

If you do not know the writer's actual name, just provide the full screen name, not inverted.

Trinity Resists.

6. Multiple works by the same author Use the author's name for all entries. List the entries by year, the earliest first.

> Barry, P. (2007, December 8). Putting tumors on pause. *Science News,*
> *172*(23), 365.

> Barry, P. (2008, August 2). Finding the golden genes. *Science News,*
> *174*(3), 16–21.

7. Multiple works by the same author in the same year List the works chronologically or, if they have the same date, alphabetize them by title. Following the year, add *a, b,* and so on. Use these same letters in the in-text citation.

> Gladwell, M. (2019a, January 14). Is marijuana as safe as we think? *The*
> *New Yorker.* https://www.newyorker.com/magazine/2019/01/14/
> is-marijuana-as-safe-as-we-think

> Gladwell, M. (2019b). *Talking to strangers: What we should know about the*
> *people we don't know.* Little, Brown.

Articles and Other Parts of Longer Works

Periodicals, works published at regular intervals (daily, monthly, or seasonally), include scholarly journals, magazines, newspapers, even blogs. Most journals and some magazines are published with volume and issue numbers. If available, give the volume and issue numbers after the title of the periodical. Italicize the volume number and put the issue number, not italicized, in parentheses.

For all print periodicals, when an article appears on consecutive pages, provide the range of pages. When an article does not appear on consecutive pages, give all page numbers: *A1, A17.* For online periodicals, include print publication information (including page numbers) if available in your source. Add the DOI (digital object identifier, a permanent code) at the end of the citation, in link format (with *https://doi.org/*). If no DOI is provided, include a direct-link URL (preferably a permalink). If you don't have a direct-link URL (which will probably be the case if you accessed the article through an academic research database), omit the URL. (For an illustration showing where to find the information you need to cite an article in a periodical, see APA Citation at a Glance: Article in a Journal, p. 338.)

8. Journal article

author: last name + initial(s) — year — article title

Zhang, L. F. (2008). Teachers' styles of thinking: An exploratory study.

journal title — volume, issue — page range

The Journal of Psychology, 142(1), 37–55.

Ganegoda, D. B., & Bordia, P. (2019). I can be happy for you, but not all
the time: A contingency model of envy and positive empathy in
the workplace. *Journal of Applied Psychology, 104*(6), 776–795.
https://doi.org/10.1037/apl0000377

Hung, J. (2018). Educational investment and sociopsychological
wellbeing among rural Chinese women. *Inquiries Journal, 10*(05).
http://www.inquiriesjournal.com/a?id=1736

9. Magazine article   Cite as a journal article, but give the year and the month for monthly magazines; add the day for weekly magazines.

McKibben, B. (2021, November 4). The future is electric. *The New York
Review of Books, 68*(17), 39–40.

Vlahos, J. (2019, March). Alexa, I want answers. *Wired*, 58–65. https://www.
wired.com/story/amazon-alexa-search-for-the-one-perfect-answer/

10. Newspaper article

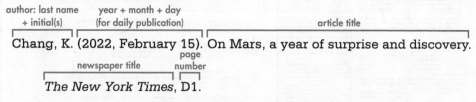

author: last name + initial(s) — year + month + day (for daily publication) — article title

Chang, K. (2022, February 15). On Mars, a year of surprise and discovery.

newspaper title — page number

The New York Times, D1.

Finucane, M. (2019, September 25). Americans still eating too many
low-quality carbs. *The Boston Globe*, B2.

Daly, J. (2019, August 2). Duquesne's med school plan part of national
trend to train more doctors. *Pittsburgh Post-Gazette.* https://
www.post-gazette.com/news/health/2019/08/02/Duquesne-med-
school-national-trend-doctorsosteopathic-medicine-pittsburgh/
stories/201908010181

For news from a website such as BBC News, cite the article as you would a web
page. (See item 35, p. 385, in this section.)

APA Citation at a Glance Article in a Journal

To cite an article in a scholarly journal in APA style, include the following elements:

1 Author

2 Year of publication

3 Title of article

4 Name of journal

5 Volume number; issue number, if available

6 Page numbers of article

7 DOI (digital object identifier)

First Page of Article

Journal Table of Contents

Database Record

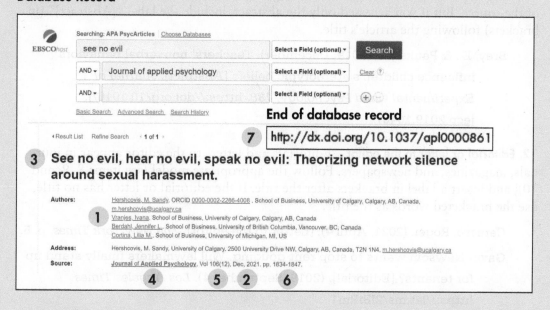

End of database record

⑦ http://dx.doi.org/10.1037/apl0000861

③ **See no evil, hear no evil, speak no evil: Theorizing network silence around sexual harassment.**

Authors: Hershcovis, M. Sandy, ORCID 0000-0002-2286-4008 . School of Business, University of Calgary, Calgary, AB, Canada, m.hershcovis@ucalgary.ca
① Vranjes, Ivana. School of Business, University of Calgary, Calgary, AB, Canada
Berdahl, Jennifer L. School of Business, University of British Columbia, Vancouver, BC, Canada
Cortina, Lilia M. School of Business, University of Michigan, MI, US

Address: Hershcovis, M. Sandy, University of Calgary, 2500 University Drive NW, Calgary, AB, Canada, T2N 1N4, m.hershcovis@ucalgary.ca

Source: Journal of Applied Psychology, Vol 106(12), Dec, 2021. pp. 1834-1847.

④ ⑤ ② ⑥

Reference List Entry for an Article from a Journal

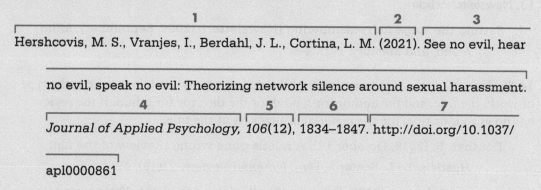

Hershcovis, M. S., Vranjes, I., Berdahl, J. L., Cortina, L. M. (2021). See no evil, hear no evil, speak no evil: Theorizing network silence around sexual harassment. *Journal of Applied Psychology, 106*(12), 1834–1847. http://doi.org/10.1037/apl0000861

Adapted from Hacker Handbooks (Bedford/St. Martin's).

11. Abstract   Best practice is to cite the original source, rather than just the abstract of the source. But if you accessed only the abstract, include the label "[Abstract]" (in brackets) following the article's title.

> Brey, E., & Pauker, K. (2019, December). Teachers' nonverbal behaviors influence children's stereotypic beliefs [Abstract]. *Journal of Experimental Child Psychology, 188.* https://doi.org/10.1016/j.jecp.2019.104671

12. Editorial or letter to the editor   Editorials and letters to the editor appear in journals, magazines, and newspapers. Follow the appropriate model (see items 8, 9, and 10), and insert a label in brackets after the title. If the editorial or letter has no title, use the bracketed words as the title.

> Carasso, Roger. (2021, April 4). [Letter to the editor]. *The New York Times*, p. 5.

> Gavin Newsom wants to stop rent gouging. Will lawmakers finally stand up for tenants? [Editorial]. (2019, September 4). *Los Angeles Times.* https://lat.ms/2lBlRm1

> Park, T. (2008, August). Defining the line [Letter to the editor]. *Scientific American, 299*(2), 10.

13. Newsletter article

> Setting the stage for remembering [Newsletter]. (2006, September). *Mind, Mood, and Memory, 2*(9), 4–5.

14. Review   Give the author and title of the review (if any) and, in brackets, the type of work, the title, and the author for a book or the director for a film. If the review has no author or title, use the material in brackets as the title.

> Douthat, R. (2019, October 14). A hustle gone wrong [Review of the film *Hustlers*, by L. Scafaria, Dir.]. *National Review, 71*(18), 47.

> Agents of change. (2008, February 2). [Review of the book *The power of unreasonable people: How social entrepreneurs create markets that change the world*, by J. Elkington & P. Hartigan]. *The Economist, 386*(8565), 94.

15. Comment on an online article   List the name or screen name of the commenter, the comment title or up to the comment's first twenty words, and (in brackets) the label "Comment on" plus the article's title. Include a link to the comment if possible.

> punkTaoist. (2021, October 14). Working on a film crew has *always* been an intense job with long hours. That 99% of the IATSE members [Comment on the article "How the streaming boom is driving the push for an unprecedented Hollywood strike"]. *Slate.* https://slate.com/comments/culture/2021/10/iatse-strike-streaming-tv-film-crews-shutdown.html

16. Selection in a collection or anthology, or a chapter in an edited book   Include the author, title, and page numbers for the section you are using and the publication information for the collection or anthology as a whole.

> Pettigrew, D. (2018). The suppression of cultural memory and identity in Bosnia and Herzegovina. In J. Lindert & A. T. Marsoobian (Eds.), *Multidisciplinary perspectives on genocide and memory* (pp. 187–198). Springer.

17. Article with a title in its title   If the internal title is for a standalone work, like a book or a film, keep the italics for the internal title and set the whole article title in sentence case: Capitalize only the first word of the title and subtitle and any proper nouns.

> Fernandez, M. E. (2019, July 30). How *Orange is the new black* said goodbye to the Litchfield inmates. *Vulture.* https://www.vulture.com/2019/07/orange-is-the-new-black-character-endings.html

18. Published interview   The format of the citation depends on the source type in which the interview appears. For a published interview, include the interviewer in the "author" position. To cite a recorded interview, see item 51.

> Remnick, D. (2019, July 1). Robert Caro reflects on Robert Moses, L.B.J., and his own career in nonfiction. *The New Yorker.* https://bit.ly/2Lukm3X

19. Entry in a reference work   Treat an entry in a reference work like a selection in a collection or anthology, or a chapter in an edited book. (See item 16 in this section.)

> Brue, A. W., & Wilmshurst, L. (2018). Adaptive behavior assessments. In B. B. Frey (Ed.), *The SAGE encyclopedia of educational research, measurement, and evaluation* (pp. 40–44). SAGE Publications. https://doi.org/10.4135/9781506326139.n21

If a source is intended to be updated regularly, include a retrieval date.

Merriam-Webster. (n.d.). Adscititious. In *Merriam-Webster.com dictionary*.
Retrieved October 14, 2022, from https://www.merriam-webster.com/
dictionary/adscititious

Since Wikipedia makes archived versions available, you need not include a retrieval date. Instead, include the URL from the "View history" tab for the version of the page you used.

Behaviorism. (2019, October 11). In *Wikipedia*. https://en.wikipedia.org/w/
index.php?title=Behaviorism&oldid=915544724

Books and Other Standalone Works

For most books, include the author's name, the year of publication, the title (in sentence case and italics), the name of the publisher (no location needed), and, if accessed online, the book's DOI or direct-link URL. Give the publisher's name as it appears in the book, but don't include business terms such as *Inc.*, *Company*, or *Ltd.*

20. Basic format for a book

author: last name + initials   year of publication   book title

Treuer, D. (2019). *The heartbeat of Wounded Knee: Native America from 1890*

publisher

to the present. Riverhead Books.

Kilby, P. (2019). *The green revolution: Narratives of politics, technology and
gender*. Routledge. https://doi.org/10.4324/9780429200823

21. Book with an editor

For an edited work, put the editor's name in the author position, followed by the label "Ed." for *Editor* or "Eds." for *Editors*.

Yeh, K.-H. (Ed.). (2019). *Asian indigenous psychologies in the global context*.
Palgrave Macmillan.

22. Book with an author and editor or translator

Include the editor's or translator's name, in parentheses, following the title, plus the label "Ed." (for *Editor*) or "Trans." (for *Translator*).

Sontag, S. (2018). *Debriefing: Collected stories* (B. Taylor, Ed.). Picador.

Calasso, R. (2019). *The unnamable present* (R. Dixon, Trans.). Farrar, Straus
and Giroux. (Original work published 2017)

APA Citation at a Glance Book

To cite a book in APA style, include the following elements:

1 Author

2 Year of publication

3 Title and subtitle

4 Publisher

5 DOI or URL (at end of citation for online books)

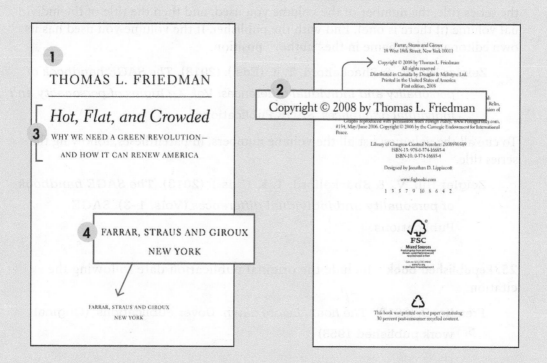

Reference List Entry for a Print Book

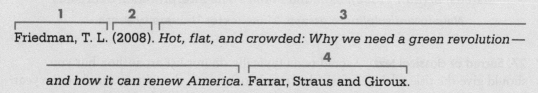

Friedman, T. L. (2008). *Hot, flat, and crowded: Why we need a green revolution—and how it can renew America.* Farrar, Straus and Giroux.

For more on citing books in APA style, see items 20–28.

Adapted from Hacker Handbooks (Bedford/St. Martin's).

23. Edition other than the first Include the edition number, in parentheses, following the book's title; the period follows the edition number.

> Dessler, A. E., & Parson, E. A. (2019). *The science and politics of global climate change: A guide to the debate* (3rd ed.). Cambridge University Press.

24. Multivolume work If you use a single volume from a multivolume work, include the series title, the number of the volume you used, and then the title of the individual volume (if there is one). End with the publisher. If the volume you used has its own editor, use that name in the "author" position.

> Zeigler-Hill, V., & Shackelford, T. K. (Eds.). (2018). *The SAGE handbook of personality and individual differences: Vol. 2. Origins of personality and individual differences.* SAGE Publications.

To cite all the volumes, list all the volume numbers, in parentheses, following the series title.

> Zeigler-Hill, V., & Shackelford, T. K. (Eds.). (2018). *The SAGE handbook of personality and individual differences* (Vols. 1–3). SAGE Publications.

25. Republished book Include the original publication date following the citation.

> Fremlin, C. (2017). *The hours before dawn.* Dover Publications. (Original work published 1958)

26. Book with a title in its title If the book title contains another book title, omit the italics from the internal book title.

> Marcus, L. (Ed.). (1999). *Sigmund Freud's* The interpretation of dreams: *New interdisciplinary essays.* Manchester University Press.

27. Sacred or classical text Sacred texts typically do not list an author, but you should give the title of the edition, the translator's name, the edition number, the year it was published, and any other source information available for the version you used. For an annotated version, include the editor's name in the author position.

If an original date is known, include it at the end of the citation; if the date is approximate, include "ca." (for *circa*). Include "B.C.E." (for *before the Christian era*) for ancient texts.

> *New International Version Bible.* (2011). Biblica. https://www.biblica.com/bible/ (Original work published 1978)

> Homer. (2018). *The odyssey* (E. Wilson, Trans.). W. W. Norton. (Original work published ca. 675–725 B.C.E.)

> Aurelius, M. (1994). *The meditations* (G. Long, Trans.). The Internet Classics Archive. http://classics.mit.edu/Antoninus/meditations.html (Original work published ca. 167)

28. Book in a language other than English   If you consulted the book in its original language, put the title, translated into English, in brackets following the title in its original language.

> Díaz de Villegas, N. (2019). *De donde son los gusanos: Crónica de un regreso a Cuba después de 37 años de exilio* [Where the worms are: Chronicle of a return to Cuba after 37 years of exile]. Vintage Español.

29. Government document   If no author is listed, include the department that produced the document in the author position. Any broader organization can be included as the publisher of the document. If a specific report number is provided, include it in parentheses after the title.

> National Park Service. (2019, April 11). *Travel where women made history: Ordinary and extraordinary places of American women.* U.S. Department of the Interior. https://www.nps.gov/subjects/travelwomenshistory/index.htm

> Berchick, E. R., Barnett, J. C., & Upton, R. D. (2019, September 10). *Health insurance coverage in the United States: 2018* (Report No. P60-267). U.S. Census Bureau. https://www.census.gov/library/publications/2019/demo/p60-267.html

30. Report from a private organization

Ford Foundation International Fellowships Program. (2019). *Leveraging higher education to promote social justice: Evidence from the IFP alumni tracking study.* https://p.widencdn.net/kei61u/IFP-Alumni-Tracking-Study-Report-5

31. Brochure or fact sheet

National Council of State Boards of Nursing. (2018). *A nurse manager's guide to substance use disorder in nursing* [Brochure].

World Health Organization. (2019, July 15). *Immunization coverage* [Fact sheet]. https://www.who.int/news-room/fact-sheets/detail/immunization-coverage

32. Press release

New York University. (2019, September 5). *NYU Oral Cancer Center awarded $2.5 million NIH grant to study cancer pain* [Press release]. https://www.nyu.edu/about/news-publications/news/2019/september/nyu-oral-cancer-centerawarded-2-5-million-nih-grant-to-study-c.html

33. Dissertation

Bacaksizlar, N. G. (2019). *Understanding social movements through simulations of anger contagion in social media* (Publication No. 13805848) [Doctoral dissertation, University of North Carolina at Charlotte]. ProQuest Dissertations and Theses.

Online and Social Media Sources

34. Website   Cite an entire website only if you borrow ideas or information from its home page. (If you merely refer to a website in your paper, without discussing any specific information or ideas, mention and include a link to the site in the body of your paper.) If you retrieved information that is subject to change, also include the date you accessed the source.

U.S. debt clock. Retrieved December 21, 2021, from https://www.usdebtclock.org/

35. Web page or document on a website Many documents published on websites fall into other categories included in this guide and can be cited using models in other sections. For articles in an online newspaper, for example, follow item 10, "Newspaper article" (p. 375), and for an entry in an online dictionary, follow item 19, "Entry in a reference work" (p. 379). Use one of the models below only when your source doesn't fit in any other category. In these items, the website name follows the web page title unless author and website name are the same.

> Milstein, E., & Wessel, W. (2021, December 17). *What did the Fed do in response to the COVID-19 crisis?* The Brookings Institution. https://www.brookings.edu/research/fed-response-to-covid19/

> National Institute of Mental Health. (2016, March). *Seasonal affective disorder*. National Institutes of Health. https://www.nimh.nih.gov/health/topics/seasonal-affective-disorder/index.shtml

> BBC News. (2019, October 31). Goats help save Ronald Reagan Presidential Library. https://www.bbc.com/news/world-us-canada-50248549

36. Blog Do not include a citation in your reference list if you merely mention the blog. If you discuss characteristics of the blog as a whole, however, include an entry.

> Fister, B. (July 20, 2010–December 18, 2019). *Library Babel Fish*. Inside Higher Ed. https://www.insidehighered.com/blogs/library-babel-fish

37. Blog post Treat a blog post as you would a magazine article (item 9) or a newspaper article (item 10).

> Fister, B. (2019, February 14). Information literacy's third wave. *Library Babel Fish*. https://www.insidehighered.com/blogs/library-babel-fish/information-literacy%E2%80%99s-third-wave

38. Comment on a blog post Treat a comment on a blog post like a comment on an online article (item 15).

> Mollie F. (2019, February 14). It's a daunting task, isn't it? Last year, I got a course on Scholarly Communication and Information Literacy approved for [Comment on the blog post "Information literacy's third wave"]. *Library Babel Fish*. https://disq.us/p/1zr92uc

39. Tweet or Twitter profile

Schiller, Caitlin [@caitlinschiller]. (2019, September 26). *Season 6 of* Simplify *is here! Today we launch with the one and only @susancain, author of* Quiet [Thumbnail with link attached] [Tweet]. Twitter. http://twitter.com/caitlinschiller/status/1177214094191026176

National Science Foundation [@NSF]. (n.d.). *Tweets* [Twitter profile]. Twitter. Retrieved October 15, 2022, from https://twitter.com/NSF

40. Other social media posts

Georgia Aquarium. (2019, October 10). *Meet the bigfin reef squid* [Video]. Facebook. https://www.facebook.com/GeorgiaAquarium/videos/2471961729567512/

Georgia Aquarium. (2019, June 25). *True love* ❦ *Charlie and Lizzy are a bonded pair of African penguins who have been together for more than* [Image attached] [Status update]. Facebook. https://www.facebook.com/GeorgiaAquarium/photos/a.163898398123/10156900637543124/?type=3&theater

Smithsonian [@smithsonian]. (2019, October 7). *You're looking at a ureilite meteorite under a microscope. When illuminated with polarized light, they appear in dazzling colors, influenced* [Photograph]. Instagram. https://www.instagram.com/p/B3VI27yHLQG/

Smithsonian [@smithsonian]. (n.d.). *#Apollo50* [Highlight]. Instagram. Retrieved October 15, 2022, from https://www.instagram.com/stories/highlights/17902787752343364/

ScienceModerator. (2018, November 16). *Science discussion: We are researchers working with some of the largest and most innovative companies using DNA to help people* [Online forum post]. Reddit. https://www.reddit.com/r/science/comments/9xlnm2/science_discussion_we_are_researchers_working/

41. Video game

ConcernedApe. (2016). *Stardew Valley* [Video game]. Chucklefish.

42. Mobile app   Only include a reference list entry if you discuss the app in a significant way.

> Google LLC. (2019). *Google earth* (Version 9.3.3) [Mobile app]. App Store.
> https://apps.apple.com/us/app/google-earth/id293622097

Video, Audio, Multimedia, and Live Sources

List the person or people most responsible for an audiovisual or multimedia work in the author position, with a label (in parentheses) to clarify their role. Who is "most responsible" depends in large part on the source type: for movies, include the director; for a streaming video, include the person who uploaded it; for a photograph or work of art, include the photographer or artist; for TV or podcast episodes, include the writer and director or the episode host.

Do not include information about how you experienced the material—in a movie theater, on broadcast television, or on a streaming service—unless you watched or listened to a special version, such as a director's cut. This information can be included in square brackets following the title or combined with other bracketed information already included after the title.

43. Work of art   If the work of art appears in a museum, include information about the museum following the artwork's title. If a photograph of the work appears on a website, include the direct-link URL.

> O'Keeffe, G. (1931). *Cow's skull: Red, white, and blue* [Painting].
> Metropolitan Museum of Art, New York, NY, United States. https://
> www.metmuseum.org/art/collection/search/488694

> *Helmet mask (kakaparaga)* [Artifact]. (ca. late 19th century). Museum of Fine
> Arts, Boston, MA, United States.

For a photograph that is available outside of a museum's collection, include the title of the photograph (if any), followed by the label "Photograph" in brackets. If the photograph is untitled, include a bracketed description that includes the word "photograph" in the title position. In the source position, include the name of the site you used to access the photograph.

> Browne, M. (1963). *The burning monk* [Photograph]. Time. http://100photos.
> time.com/photos/malcolm-browne-burning-monk

> Liittschwager, D. (2019). [Photograph series of octopuses]. National
> Geographic. https://www.nationalgeographic.com/animals/2019/
> 10/pet-octopuses-are-a-problem/#/01-pet-octopus-trade-
> nationalgeographic_2474095.jpg

44. Advertisement   Use the model for the source in which the advertisement appears.

America's Biopharmaceutical Companies [Advertisement]. (2018, September). *The Atlantic, 322*(2), 2.

Centers for Disease Control and Prevention. (n.d.). *A tip from a former smoker: Beatrice* [Advertisement]. U.S. Department of Health and Human Services. https://www.cdc.gov/tobacco/campaign/tips/ resources/ads/pdf-print-ads/beatrices-tip-print-ad-7x10.pdf

45. Map

Desjardins, J. (2017, November 17). *Walmart nation: Mapping the largest employers in the U.S.* [Map]. Visual Capitalist. https://www. visualcapitalist.com/walmart-nation-mapping-largest-employers-u-s/

46. Music recording   For classical works, put the composer in the author position, and provide information about the performer in brackets after the title. For popular works, put the performer in the author position. Include multiple record labels separated by semicolons.

Nielsen, C. (2014). *Carl Nielsen: Symphonies 1 & 4* [Album recorded by New York Philharmonic Orchestra]. Dacapo Records. (Original work published 1892–1916)

Carlile, B. (2018). *By the way, I forgive you* [Album]. Low Country Sound; Elektra.

Carlile, B. (2018). The mother [Song]. On *By the way, I forgive you*. Low Country Sound; Elektra.

47. Film   Include the production company after the title. Separate multiple production companies with semicolons.

Chung, L. I. (Director). (2021). *Minari* [Film]. Plan B Entertainment.

Hitchcock, A. (Director). (1959). *The essentials collection: North by northwest* [Film; five-disc special ed. on DVD]. Metro-Goldwyn-Mayer; Universal Pictures Home Entertainment.

48. Online video or audio   Think of the author of an online video or audio file as the person or organization that posted it. For a TED Talk, for example, the presenter is the author if the video was accessed on the TED site. However, if the TED Talk was accessed on YouTube, then TED becomes the author because the TED organization posted the video.

> Wray, B. (2019, May). *How climate change affects your mental health* [Video]. TED Conferences. https://www.ted.com/talks/britt_wray_how_ climate_change_affects_your_mental_health

> TED. (2019, September 20). *Britt Wray: How climate change affects your mental health* [Video]. YouTube. https://www.youtube.com/ watch?v=IlDkCEvsYw

When deciding whether to italicize the title of the video or audio file, consider whether it is part of a series (regular font) or a standalone item (italics).

> BBC. (2018, November 19). Why do bad managers flourish? [Audio]. In *Business Matters*. https://www.bbc.co.uk/programmes/p06s8752

> The New York Times. (2018, January 9). *Taking a knee and taking down a monument* [Video]. YouTube. https://www.youtube.com/ watch?v=qY34DQCdUvQ

49. Television, radio, or podcast series or episode   If you merely mention the series in your text, you need not cite it in your reference list. If you discuss characteristics of the series as a whole, however, include an entry.

> Waller-Bridge, P., Williams, H., & Williams, J. (Executive Producers). (2016– 2019). *Fleabag* [TV series]. Two Brothers Pictures; BBC.

> Abumrad, J., & Krulwich, R. (Hosts). (2002–present). *Radiolab* [Audio podcast]. WNYC Studios. https://www.wnycstudios.org/podcasts/ radiolab/podcasts

If the person or people most responsible for an individual episode differ from those of the series in general, put the episode's personnel in the author position, and include the series personnel in the source information.

> Waller-Bridge, P. (Writer), & Bradbeer, H. (Director). (2019, March 18). The provocative request (Season 2, Episode 3) [TV series episode]. In P. Waller-Bridge, H. Williams, & J. Williams (Executive Producers), *Fleabag*. Two Brothers Pictures; BBC.

West, S. (Host). (2018, July 27). Logical positivism (No. 120) [Audio podcast episode]. In *Philosophize this!* https://philosophizethis.org/logical-positivists/

Longoria, J. (Host & Producer). (2019, April 19). Americanish [Audio podcast episode]. In J. Abumrad & R. Krulwich (Hosts), *Radiolab*. WNYC Studios. https://www.wnycstudios.org/podcasts/radiolab/articles/americanish

50. Transcript of an online video or audio file

Gopnik, A. (2019, July 10). *A separate kind of intelligence* [Video transcript]. Edge. https://www.edge.org/conversation/alison_gopnik-a-separate-kind-of-intelligence

Glass, I. (2019, August 23). Ten sessions (No. 682) [Audio podcast episode transcript]. In *This American life*. WBEZ. https://www.thisamericanlife.org/682/transcript

51. Lecture, speech, address, or recorded interview   Include an entry only if the source is accessible to readers.

Grigas, A. (2019, October 8). *The new geopolitics of energy* [Address]. Freeman Spogli Institute for International Studies, Stanford University, Stanford, CA, United States.

For an interview in an archive, put the person interviewed in the author position.

Parrado, N. (2011, March 27). *Nando Parrado, plane crash survivor* [Interview with C. Gracie; audio file]. The Interview Archive; BBC World Service. https://www.bbc.co.uk/programmes/p00fhjnb

52. Presentation slides

Centers for Disease Control and Prevention. (2019, April 16). *Building local response capacity to protect families from emerging health threats* [Presentation slides]. CDC Stacks. https://stacks.cdc.gov/view/cdc/77687

Include an entry only if the presentation slides are accessible to readers.

Other Sources

53. Data set or graphic representation of data (graph, chart, table)

> Reid, L. (2019). *Smarter homes: Experiences of living in low carbon homes 2013–2018* [Data set]. UK Data Service. http://doi.org/10.5255/UKDASN-853485

> Pew Research Center. (2018, November 15). *U.S. public is closely divided about overall health risk from food additives* [Chart]. https://www.pewinternet.org/2018/11/15/public-perspectives-on-food-risks/ps_2018-11-15_food_0-01/

54. Legal source   The title of a court case is not italicized in the reference list, though it is italicized in the in-text citation.

> Sweatt v. Painter, 339 U.S. 629 (1950). http://www.law.cornell.edu/supct/html/historics/USSC_CR_0339_0629_ZS.html

55. Personal communications   Omit unpublished communications—letters, text messages, or email messages you have received, lecture notes that you took or that are posted only on a server your readers cannot access, and so on—from your reference list. Describe them only in the text of your paper. (See item 9 in the section on in-text citations.)

D3.4   Advice

APA-Style Formatting

Many instructors in the social sciences (and sometimes in other disciplines) require students to follow the guidelines spelled out in the *Publication Manual of the American Psychological Association*, 7th ed. (2020). (Ask your instructor if you're in doubt about the formatting required for research projects in your course.)

Formatting Student Papers in APA Style

The *Publication Manual* of the APA provides two sets of instructions: one for students and another for scholars who are preparing their papers for publication in APA journals. The guidelines in this section are for formatting student papers. The excerpts from a sample student paper (pp. 395–400) provide examples.

Margins and fonts.   Use one-inch margins on all sides (the default setting in most word-processing programs). If your instructor doesn't specify a font or size, use a 10- to 12-point font that is accessible to readers, such as Arial, Times New Roman, or Calibri. With the exception of footnotes, which should be set in 10-point type, set the whole paper in the same font size.

Indents.   For the text of the paper, use paragraph indents of half an inch. Indent quotations of forty or more words as a block, half an inch from the left margin but don't use a paragraph indent unless the quotation is more than a paragraph long. (A sample block quotation appears on p. 399.)

Line spacing.   Except for footnotes or tables, double-space your whole paper, including the title page and reference list. Set footnotes single-spaced, and set tables single-, one-and-a-half-, or double-spaced, depending on what's easiest to read and understand.

Page numbering.   Number all pages in the upper-right corner, half an inch from the top of the page and an inch from the right margin. The title page is page 1. Unless your instructor requires it, do not include your name or the title of your paper at the top of each page.

Headings.   Most student research projects will not need headings, but if you are writing a long or complex paper and headings would help guide your reader, insert them. All headings use *title case*: that means you should capitalize the first and last words, all other significant words, and any other words of four or more letters (including prepositions such as *between*, *underneath*, or *without*). (In MLA and other styles, prepositions—no matter how long—are set lower case.)

First-Level Heading (centered, boldface)

Second-Level Heading (left-aligned, boldface)

Third-Level Heading (left-aligned, boldface, italics)

Title page.   Unless your instructor tells you otherwise, your title page should include the following information, centered on the page:

- The title of the paper in boldface type, three or four double-spaced lines from the top margin
- Your name and the names of any coauthors, one blank double-spaced line below the title
- The department and college or university in which the course is offered

- The course number and name of the course (using the format shown in the course catalog or on other school sites)
- Your instructor's name (Check to see how your instructor would like to be addressed: for example, as *Professor* or *Dr.*)
- The assignment due date in the date format of the country you're in (In the United States, that would be *month day, year—April 24, 2023*—unless your instructor requests a different format.)

(A sample title page appears on p. 395.)

Visuals.   Visuals include tables and figures (such as graphs, charts, drawings, and photographs). In the body of your text, include a callout (such as *The data are summarized in Table 1* or *See Figure 1*) for any visuals you plan to include, and place them as close as possible following the paragraph in which the callout appears. (Some instructors may ask that you group all visuals in an appendix.)

Readers should be able to understand all visuals on their own, without reference to the text. When creating tables and figures, keep your readers' needs in mind.

- Label all the elements of the table or figure (columns in tables, axes in graphs).
- Set labels in a large enough font that readers can actually read them.
- Avoid distracting ornamentation (for example, avoid selecting 3-D versions of pie charts or bar charts).
- If you did not create the visual or if it is based on data collected by another researcher, include source information in a note below the visual.
- If any data in a table require explanation, include footnote callouts (using lowercase letters) in the body of the table and footnotes following the table's source note.
- Number all tables and figures using Arabic numerals in boldface type: *Table 1, Table 2, Figure 1, Figure 2* (and so on).
- Give each table or figure a brief but explanatory title, set the title in italics, and place it one line space below the table or figure number.
- Use single-, one-and-a-half-, or double-spacing for tables, depending on what will be easiest to read.

(A sample table appears on p. 398.)

Abstract.   An abstract is a one-paragraph summary (fewer than 250 words) of the main points of the paper. APA style does not require students to include an abstract, but if your instructor requests one, use the following format:

- Place the abstract on its own page, after the title page.
- Center the heading *Abstract* (in boldface type) at the top of the page.
- Start the abstract itself one double-spaced line below the heading.
- Do not indent the first line of the paragraph.

Preparing the Reference List

Your reference list should start on a new page at the end of the research project. Center the heading *References* in boldface, an inch from the top of the page. Double-space the whole list. (A sample reference list appears on p. 400.)

Alphabetizing the list.   Alphabetize the reference list by the authors' (or editors') last names; when a work has no author or editor, alphabetize it by the first word of the title other than *A, An,* or *The.*

If you used more than one work by the same author, order those works by date from earliest to latest. If your list includes two or more works by the same author in the same year, arrange those works alphabetically by title, and then add a lowercase letter (*a* for the first source, *b* for the second source, and so on) following each year: *(2023a).* Use the same letters with the years in the in-text citations. (For models, see item 7, D3.2, APA In-Text Citations, p. 366, and item 7, D3.3, APA Reference List, p. 370.)

Formatting the entries.   Use a *hanging indent*: Start the first line of each entry at the left margin and indent lines after the first by half an inch. You can use your word processor's ruler settings to create a reference list using a hanging indent.

DOIs and URLs.   DOIs and especially URLs can be quite lengthy. To avoid making an error, copy and paste DOIs and URLs into your paper. Never manually break a DOI or URL by adding a space or a hyphen. If your word processor inserts a line break automatically or moves a DOI or URL to its own line, you can accept that formatting. (Professionally published texts like this one may break DOIs or URLs to avoid uneven lines, but writers should not.) You can also shorten lengthy DOIs or URLs using a site like shortdoi.org or bit.ly.com. Some publications may also provide permalinks; use these if available.

Excerpts from a Sample Student Research Project

**Technology and the Shift From Teacher-Delivered to
Student-Centered Learning: A Review of the Literature**

Title centered, boldface, 3–4 lines below top margin, followed by blank line

April Bo Wang
Department of Education, Glen County Community College
EDU 107: Education, Technology, and Media
Dr. Julien Gomez
October 29, 2022

Author's name, department & school, course number & name, instructor's name, and assignment due date, centered

Example of a Sample Student Research Paper

Technology and the Shift From Teacher-Delivered to
Student-Centered Learning: A Review of the Literature

Technology and the Shift From Teacher-Delivered to

Student-Centered Learning: A Review of the Literature

In the United States, most public school systems are struggling

with teacher shortages, which are projected to worsen as the number

of applicants to education schools decreases (Donitsa-Schmidt &

Zuzovsky, 2014, p. 420). Citing federal data, *The New York Times*

reported a 30% drop in "people entering teacher preparation

programs" between 2010 and 2014 (Rich, 2015, para. 10). Especially in

science and math fields, the teacher shortage is projected to escalate

in the next 10 years (Hutchison, 2012). In recent decades, instructors

and administrators have viewed the practice of student-centered

learning as one promising solution. Unlike traditional teacher-delivered

(also called "transmissive") instruction, student-centered learning

allows students to help direct their own education by setting their own

goals and selecting appropriate resources for achieving those goals.

Though student-centered learning might once have been viewed as an

experimental solution in understaffed schools, it is gaining credibility

as an effective pedagogical practice. What is also gaining momentum

is the idea that technology might play a significant role in fostering

student-centered learning. This literature review will examine three

key questions:

1. In what ways is student-centered learning effective?
2. Can educational technology help students drive their own
   learning?
3. How can public schools effectively combine teacher talent and
   educational technology?

In the face of mounting teacher shortages, public schools should

embrace educational technology that promotes student-centered learning

in order to help all students become engaged and successful learners.

Both names of
two-author source
in parenthetical
citation;
page number
optional when
paraphrasing
from a paginated
source

Parenthetical
citation following
quotation;
paragraph
number provided
for unpaginated
source

All text double-
spaced

½"

2

1"

1"

1"

1"

In What Ways Is Student-Centered Learning Effective?

According to the International Society for Technology in Education (2016), "Student-centered learning moves students from passive receivers of information to active participants in their own discovery process. What students learn, how they learn it, and how their learning is assessed are all driven by each individual student's needs and abilities" ("What Is It" section). The results of student-centered learning have been positive, not only for academic achievement but also for student self-esteem. In this model of instruction, the teacher acts as a facilitator, and the students actively participate in the process of learning and teaching. With guidance, students decide on the learning goals most pertinent to themselves, they devise a learning plan that will most likely help them achieve those goals, they direct themselves in carrying out that learning plan, and they assess how much they learned (Çubukçu, 2012). The major differences between student-centered learning and instructor-centered learning are summarized in Table 1.

Bell (2010) has argued that the chief benefit of student-centered learning is that it can connect students with "real-world tasks" (p. 42), thus making learning more engaging as well as more comprehensive. For example, Bell observed a group of middle-school students who wanted to build a social justice monument for their school. They researched social justice issues, selected several to focus on, and then designed a three-dimensional playground to represent those issues. In doing so, they achieved learning goals in the areas of social studies, physics, and mathematics and practiced research and teamwork.

Heading centered and boldface

Signal phrase followed by year in parentheses

Shortened section heading (in quotation marks) for direct quotation from unpaginated source

Callout for table that appears on next page

Page number provided for quotation from paginated source

Table left-aligned, number boldface, title italic

Table 1

Comparison of Two Approaches to Teaching and Learning

Column heads centered

Teaching and learning period	Instructor-centered approach	Student-centered approach
Before class	• Instructor prepares a lecture/instruction on a new topic. • Students complete homework on the previous topic.	• Students read and practice new concepts, and prepare questions ahead of class. • Instructor views student questions and practice and identifies learning opportunities.
During class	• Instructor delivers new material in a lecture or prepared discussion. • Students—unprepared—listen, watch, take notes, and try to follow along with the new material.	• Students lead discussions or practice applying the concepts or skills in an active environment. • Instructor answers student questions and provides immediate feedback.
After class	• Instructor grades homework and gives feedback about the previous lesson. • Students work independently to practice or apply the new concepts.	• Students apply the concepts/skills to more complex tasks, individually and in groups. • Instructor posts additional resources to help students.

Note providing source of information in table

Note. Adapted from *The Flipped Class Demystified*, by New York University, n.d. (https://www.nyu.edu/faculty/teaching-and-learning-resources/instructional-technology-support/instructional-design-assessment/flipped-classes/the-flipped-class-demystified.html).

As the teacher shortage has intensified, educational technology has become tailored to student needs and more affordable. Backpacks that charge electronic devices and apps that create audiovisual flash cards are just two of the more recent innovations. According to Svokos (2015), College and Education Fellow for *The Huffington Post*, some educational technology entertains students while supporting student-centered learning:

> GlassLab, a nonprofit that was launched with grants from the Bill & Melinda Gates and MacArthur Foundations, creates educational games that are now being used in more than 6,000 classrooms across the country. Some of the company's games are education versions of existing ones—for example, its first release was SimCity EDU—while others are originals. Teachers get realtime updates on students' progress as well as suggestions on what subjects they need to spend more time perfecting.
>
> (5. Educational Games section)

Many of the companies behind these products offer discounts to schools where such devices are widely used.

Conclusion

Not only has student-centered learning proved effective in improving student academic and developmental outcomes, but it can also synchronize with technological learning for widespread adaptability across schools. Because it relies on student direction rather than an established curriculum, student-centered learning supported by educational technology can adapt to the different needs of individual students and a variety of learning environments—urban and rural, well funded and underfunded. Similarly, when student-centered learning relies on technology rather than a corps of uniformly trained teachers, it holds promise for schools that would otherwise suffer from a lack of human or financial resources.

Side notes:

Block quotation (forty or more words) set off with ½" indent; no quotation marks

Quotation location provided after period

Conclusion, with heading centered, boldface

References

Bell, S. (2010). Project-based learning for the 21st century: Skills for the future. *The Clearing House, 83*(2), 39–43.

Çubukçu, Z. (2012). Teachers' evaluation of student-centered learning environments. *Education, 133*(1), 49–66.

Donitsa-Schmidt, S., & Zuzovsky, R. (2014). Teacher supply and demand: The school level perspective. *American Journal of Educational Research, 2*(6), 420–429. https://doi.org/10.12691/education-2-6-14

Friedlaender, D., Burns, D., Lewis-Charp, H., Cook-Harvey, C. M., & Darling-Hammond, L. (2014). *Student-centered schools: Closing the opportunity gap* [Research brief]. Stanford Center for Opportunity Policy in Education. https://edpolicy.stanford.edu/sites/default/files/scope-pub-student-centered-research-brief.pdf

Hutchison, L. F. (2012). Addressing the STEM teacher shortage in American schools: Ways to recruit and retain effective STEM teachers. *Action in Teacher Education, 34*(5/6), 541–550. https://doi.org/10.1080/01626620.2012.729483

International Society for Technology in Education. (2016). *Student-centered learning.* https://id.iste.org/connected/standards/essential-conditions/

Rich, M. (2015, August 9). Teacher shortages spur a nationwide hiring scramble (credentials optional). *The New York Times.* https://nyti.ms/1WaaV7a

Svokos, A. (2015, May 7). Five innovations from the past decade that aim to change the American classroom. *The Huffington Post.* https://bit.ly/33FjRcW

References heading centered, boldface

First line of each entry at left margin; all other lines indented ½"

DOI included when available

All authors' names listed, up to twenty authors

References ordered alphabetically by author or editor or by title if no author or editor listed

Organization as author

Shortened URL created and provided for complex URL

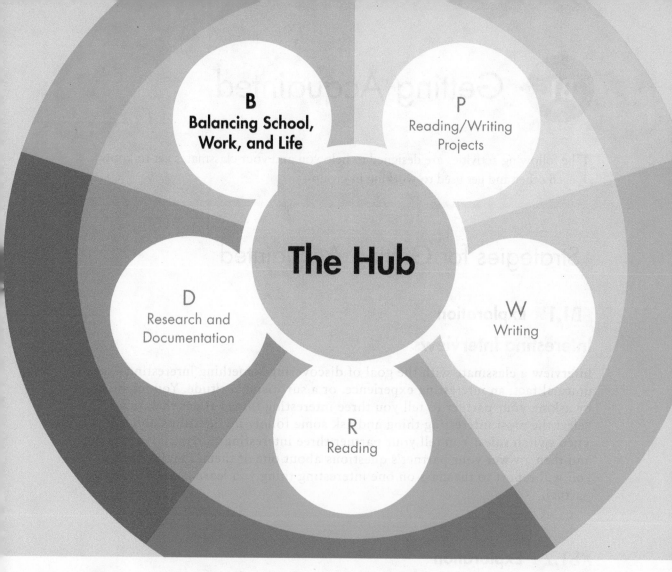

B Balancing School, Work, and Life

B1 ▸ Getting Acquainted

The following activities are designed to help you and your classmates get to know each other and get used to working in groups.

Strategies for Getting Acquainted

B1.1 Exploration
Interesting Interviews

Interview a classmate with the goal of discovering something interesting—an unusual fact, an interesting experience, or a surprising attitude. You might start by asking your partner to tell you three interesting things about themselves. Select the most interesting thing and ask some follow-up questions about it. Then switch roles: You tell your partner three interesting things about yourself and then answer your partner's questions about one of them. Finally, each of you will report to the class on one interesting thing you learned about your partner.

B1.2 Exploration
Meet and Greet Bingo

For each of the boxes in the chart below (also available as a downloadable PDF in Achieve with *The Hub*), write the name of a classmate who fits the description in the box. Let your instructor know when you've filled in five boxes in a row or in a column or diagonally.

Loves to read	Speaks a language other than English	Is good at grammar	Owns a bicycle	Ate breakfast this morning
Plays Sudoku	Has been out of high school at least five years	Hated English in high school	Is a vegan	Keeps a diary
Is wearing something purple	Has a parent who has served in the military	Loves to write	Reads science fiction	Writes poetry
Has posted at least one TikTok video	Knows where the next Summer Olympics will be held	Knows what haiku is	Has a full-time job	Knows what it means to "86" something
Tweets regularly	Has eaten dim sum	Works in a restaurant	Owns a dictionary	Has done yoga

B1.3 Exploration

Getting to Know You

This activity is designed to help you get to know some of the other members of this class. Working with the members of your group, figure out the answer to each of the following questions.

1. Who was born in the most interesting place? Where?

2. Who has the most interesting nickname? What is it?

3. Who has the worst boss? What's so terrible about that boss?

4. Who is the best cook? What is their best dish?

5. Who speaks the most languages? What are they?

Be prepared to share your group's answers with the rest of the class.

B1.4 Exploration

Two Truths and a Lie

To start, take a few minutes to think of three statements about yourself, two that are true and one that is a lie. Next, tell two or more classmates (your instructor will tell you how many) your three statements, and have the others guess which statement is the lie. Continue the process until everyone has told their three statements.

Attending college and trying to cope with the rest of life can sometimes be a challenge. The activities that follow are designed to help you develop strategies for balancing school, work, and the rest of your life.

Managing Your Life

B2.1 **Writing**

Money Matters

At the same time that they struggle to become more effective writers, many students also struggle to pay their bills and put food on the table. Financial pressures are one of the biggest sources of stress for many students.

For this short writing assignment, you will do a little research, a little thinking, and a little writing about one of the financial topics listed below. The plan is that, as the class researches, discusses, and writes about these topics, many of you will learn things that will help ease your financial pressures. At the same time, you should also begin to understand a little about doing research and incorporating the results into your writing.

Researching a Financial Topic

You will need to find some information about your topic. You can do this on the internet, using Google or a similar search engine, or you can look in the library for a book or an article in a magazine, newspaper, or journal that discusses your topic. For more detailed information, see D1, Research (p. 294).

You are not being asked to do a really thorough research project, just to find one piece of information that will be helpful as you write a short essay on one of the financial topics below. At this point in the course, you have probably not had any formal instruction in how to do research, so you're not being asked to give formal citations and lists of references. All you need to do is quote one brief passage—a sentence or more—that you found in your research and that helps to support the argument you are making in your essay. Of course, more than one quotation is fine, but only one is required. (You may want to consult D1.10, Quoting and Paraphrasing, p. 309, for advice on how to integrate quotations into your text. Because you aren't asked to paraphrase, you can ignore the section there on paraphrasing for now.)

Writing about Money

Select one of the questions below and search online or in your college library for credible information to help you answer it. Then write a short paper—about a page—in which you answer the question. In your paper, quote at least one sentence or phrase that you found in your research that supports your argument.

1. Is a "payday loan" ever a good idea? What are some reasons for or against taking one out?
2. What are some arguments for and against taking out a student loan?
3. What are the most important rules associated with a Pell Grant?
4. What rights do consumers have if they are behind in making payments on their credit card?
5. What should renters know if they are threatened with eviction?

B2.2 Exploration

Renting

On your own or in a group (your instructor will tell you which), brainstorm a list of ideas for how you could lower the amount you are currently paying for rent. Be prepared to report out on your list.

B2.3 Exploration

Health Care

If you or someone you care for became ill, what are your options for getting medical care? Working on your own or in a group, brainstorm a list of options for getting medical care. Be prepared to report out on your list.

B2.4 Exploration

Child Care

Working on your own or in a group, brainstorm a list of options for child care. List not only what you do but also options that other people you know have done. Be prepared to report out on your list.

Managing Your Time

B2.5 Exploration

Time Management: Keeping a Log

Use the blank chart later on in this section (also available as a downloadable PDF in Achieve with *The Hub*) to keep track of how you use your time for one week. If you've been asked to complete an activity log in another course, you don't need to do a second one; just use the one you compiled for that course.

Advice for the Specific Columns

1st Column	Enter a three-letter abbreviation for the day of the week.
2nd Column	Enter the time you spent on the activity. Example: 9:00–9:45
3rd Column	Enter a brief description of the activity.
4th Column	Enter a number indicating how important this activity is to you—4 is most important; 1 is least important.

Keep the log for one week.

Sample Time Management Log   Name: _____

Day	Time	Activity	Priority
Mon.	11:10–12:00	English class	4
Mon.	12:00–1:15	bus home	4
Mon.	1:15–2:30	lunch and video games	1
Mon.	2:30–3:00	walk to Romano's	4
Mon.	3:00–9:00	wait tables	4
Mon.	9:00–10:00	have a beer with friends	1
Mon.	10:00–11:00	work on English paper	4

Time Management Log

Name: _____

Day	Time	Activity	Priority

B2.6 Exploration

Time Management: Analyzing Your Log

At the end of a week, take a look at your activity log, and then answer the following questions.

1. Are there any surprises in your log? Are you spending more time than you thought you were on some tasks? Less time on others?
2. Are there times of the day when you are most productive? Are you working on low-priority activities in these high-productivity times?
3. Are there little stretches of time that you could use to squeeze in small tasks?
4. Are you spending lots of time on low-priority tasks? Doing so can be a sign that you are procrastinating.
5. Are there things you are doing that don't need to be done, things that can be delayed or cancelled or even done by someone else?
6. Is it possible to do everything you have committed to doing? If so, great. If not, what can you change to make it possible to accomplish everything you need to do?

B2.7 Exploration

Time Management: Strategies

In a group or on your own (your instructor will tell you which), make a list of time-management strategies. To get you started, here's one strategy:

Do the hardest task first. Sometimes a difficult task gets pushed to later in the day or even later in the week. Then you spend time dreading it, which makes you less effective at completing other tasks. There's nothing more satisfying than taking on that hard task first, preferably earlier in the day when you are at your most alert, and getting it done.

B2.8 Exploration

Time Management: Creating a Calendar

Most busy people find that they cannot keep themselves organized, meet deadlines, and show up on time at events they need to attend without keeping a calendar.

Many versions of online calendars are available, although some people still prefer the old-fashioned wall calendar or a weekly planner in spiral notebook form. Print and online forms both have their advantages, so choose whatever works best for you, but using a calendar is something that will definitely help with organizing your time.

Print and online calendars can be arranged to display a day at a time, a week at a time, a month at a time, or even a year at a glance. Most students find a week-at-a-time format works best for them. Here are some suggestions for how to create an effective calendar:

- Set aside time to work on your calendar before the week begins—Sunday evenings work well.

- Start by filling in the times that are fixed: the times you are scheduled to be in class, the times you are scheduled to work, and the hours you will be sleeping.

- Then add any one-time events you know about that are coming up during the week: your mother's 50th birthday party on Saturday night, the time you've volunteered to babysit your sister's daughter, a party you plan to attend.

- Be sure to build in time for studying. Don't just write "9:00–11:00 study." Make a specific plan: "9:00–11:00 Revise essay for English class."

- Don't forget to include travel time and time for household tasks like grocery shopping or doing laundry.

- Schedule breaks—time to relax, have a coffee, or text with a friend.

Below, you will find a blank calendar for a week. Working with this form (also available as a downloadable PDF in Achieve with *The Hub*), plan out the next week for yourself. While you might normally do this planning on a Sunday, if you start working on some other day—say, Thursday—then just start with Thursday and plan for the next seven days. You should find the Time Management Log you created (B2.5, p. 407), the analysis of your Time Management Log (B2.6, p. 409), and the strategies you established (B2.7, p. 409) to be helpful as you work on this calendar.

	Monday	Tuesday	Wednesday	Thursday	Friday	Saturday	Sunday
7:00–7:30							
7:30–8:00							
8:00–8:30							
8:30–9:00							
9:00–9:30							
9:30–10:00							
10:00–10:30							
10:30–11:00							
11:00–11:30							
11:30–12:00							
12:00–12:30							
12:30–1:00							
1:00–1:30							
1:30–2:00							
2:00–2:30							
2:30–3:00							
3:00–3:30							
3:30–4:00							
4:00–4:30							
4:30–5:00							
5:00–5:30							
5:30–6:00							
6:00–6:30							
6:30–7:00							
7:00–7:30							
7:30–8:00							
8:00–8:30							
8:30–9:00							
9:00–9:30							
9:30–10:00							
10:00–10:30							
10:30–11:00							

B3 Staying the Course

Going to college creates stress and anxiety for some students. The activities in this section provide suggestions for how to deal with these kinds of issues.

Coping in College

B3.1 Exploration
What Worries You?

Write down one thing you are worried about and give it to your instructor. Don't put your name on it. Anything you are worried about is okay—something about school or work or your relationships or your family or the country or the world. Your instructor will share as many of these as possible with the class so the class can discuss them.

B3.2 Writing
Who Is "College Material"?

Many students arrive in college with insecurities, doubts about whether they belong, doubts about whether they can succeed. In some cases, they express these doubts by saying something like this: "I'm just not sure I'm 'college material.'"

For this assignment, write a short essay—about a page—in which you discuss the term *college material*. You don't have to answer all of the following questions, or any of them, but they're here to help you think about the term.

1. What does *college material* mean?
2. Where do you suppose that students who wonder about whether they are *college material* learned the term? Who told them there was such a thing as students who are not "college material"?
3. Are you sure you are "college material"? If so, how did you avoid the doubt that comes from wondering whether you are?

4. Do you think anyone is not "college material"? What would put someone into that category? What keeps someone from being "college material"?

5. Do you know anyone who has these kinds of doubts about themselves? Are they "college material," in your opinion? Why do they have these doubts about whether they belong in college?

6. Do people get the idea they may not be "college material" in high school or does that doubt occur once they get to college?

B3.3 Writing
Responding to Setbacks

Think about a setback you have experienced—a time you got a low grade in school, a time when you weren't hired for a job you wanted, a time your performance in a sport was publicly bad, or even a time when you learned that someone you loved did not return your affection. Write a short paper—about a page—in which you describe what you learned from that experience.

Getting Where You Want to Go

B3.4 Writing
Goal Setting and Planning

Where do you want to be in five years? What do you want to be doing? Where do you want to be living? What kind of car do you want to be driving? How many children would you like to have (if any)? How much education do you want? Write a paragraph in which you answer at least some of these questions.

Now think about what you need to do in the next twelve months to make those goals possible. Make a list of your twelve-month goals.

B3.5 Exploration
Writing and Your Goals

Working individually or in your group (your instructor will tell you which), make a list of the ways that writing effectively will be important to the goals you set in B3.4.

Plan B

Most students find going to college stressful. There's the pressure to do all the reading and all the homework, and to prepare for all the quizzes and tests. But for many students, there are also life stresses: financial pressures, family problems, health issues, legal problems.

Much of the time, the stress is manageable if distressing. Most students deal with stress by digging down a little deeper, working a little harder, sleeping a little less, and remembering that the semester lasts just fifteen weeks or so. But for some students the stress can become unbearable, efforts grind to a halt, and they end up dropping out of school.

If digging a little deeper and working a little harder is Plan A for dealing with stress, in this activity think about Plan B. If you felt that all the pressures of school, family, work, and life were approaching the point where you might have to give up on school, what could you do? What changes could you make *before* the stress overwhelmed you?

1. Working on your own or in a group, make a list of possible strategies that could help you avoid dropping out of school because of stress.

2. Share these strategies with the whole class.

B4 ▸ College Knowledge

The world of college can be quite different from the world outside. It has its own terminology, procedures, and expectations. The activities in this section are designed to help you understand and thrive in this specialized world.

Learning College Lingo

B4.1 Exploration

College Terminology

Colleges and universities have a language of their own. Sometimes students new to college run into difficulty because of terms they don't know. The following is a list of such terms.

AA degree	dean	incomplete	registrar
advisor	department	late start classes	registration
appeal	discipline	major	rubric
bachelor's degree	dismissal	matriculation	school
books on reserve	doctor (PhD)	office hours	syllabus
bursar	drop/add	Pell Grant	transcript
certificate	elective	plagiarism	transfer
composition	essay	prerequisite	tutoring
corequisite	FAFSA	probation	withdrawal
course load	GPA	professor	writing center
credit hour	honors program	program	

Your instructor may assign each student a few of these terms or may divide the class into groups that will work on a set of terms together. Whether working on your own or in a group, write a paragraph explaining the terms you were assigned. Because this activity asks you to define terms, you may want to take a look at W11.22, Strategies for Writing Simple Definitions (p. 226). It's okay to Google a term, but be sure to rewrite the definition in student-friendly language. The audience for this writing is next year's new college students.

B4.2 Writing

Defining Terms for Writing Assignments

Writing assignments in college frequently use terms like those listed below. In order to complete an assignment effectively, you will need to understand each of these terms and the differences in what they ask you to do.

For this short writing assignment, you and your classmates will compile a list of definitions; your audience is next year's new students. Your instructor will assign you (or your group) some of the terms to work on. Because this activity asks you to define terms, you may want to take a look at W11.22, Strategies for Writing Simple Definitions (p. 226). You may not know all these terms, but try first to figure out their meaning on your own. R2.11, Dealing with Difficult Language (p. 271), may help. It's okay to Google a term you can't figure out; just rewrite it in student-friendly language.

agree or disagree	create	evaluate	state
analyze	defend	explain	summarize
argue	define	identify	support
classify	demonstrate	interpret	synthesize
compare	describe	list	
construct	develop	paraphrase	
contrast	discuss	solve	

Getting Help

B4.3 Advice

Advocating for Your Rights

Colleges and universities are required by law—the Americans with Disabilities Act—to provide reasonable accommodations for students with disabilities. If the design of the course is creating a barrier to your education, you may decide you want to advocate for an accommodation.

On every campus, there is an accessibility office for students with disabilities. You should consider visiting that office early in the term to discuss your disability and the accommodations that would help you succeed in college. When you reveal your disability to this office, you may indicate that you want the information kept confidential, or you may ask the office to notify your instructors about your disability or to notify instructors only that you need an accommodation.

Accessibility office staff can suggest reasonable accommodations and provide you with services and support, from note takers, text-to-speech applications for computers, and braille translations of textbooks to extended time for taking tests, sign language interpreters, and much more.

Start the conversation with accessibility services and then bring your professor(s) in. The partnership between all three of you is important to addressing your needs. Most faculty and staff are highly supportive of your right to accommodations. If, however, your college or an individual faculty member does not provide accommodations that meet your needs, you may file a grievance, on your own or in conjunction with other advocates. (Every college has a grievance process to follow; ask about yours.)

B4.4 Exploration

Asking for Help

A website called Academic Tips (search for "academic tips ask help" to locate the site) contains great advice about asking for help when you're in college. Working on your own or in a group (your instructor will tell you which), discuss the tips on asking for help that you find on the Academic Tips website and list some additional tips you would add.

B4.5 Exploration

Locating Resources

Working on your own or in a group, your job for this activity will be to find out where to go on campus for each of the items listed in the chart below (also available as a downloadable PDF in Achieve with *The Hub*). For each resource on campus, be sure to provide the following information:

- Location
- Phone number
- Email
- Hours
- Additional services available

Of course, you may learn that your college doesn't have an office where you can go for several of these items. If that's the case, just write "Not available" next to those items.

		Location	Phone number	Email	Hours	Additional services available
1	Help with financial aid					
2	Assistance with a disability					
3	Help with doing research for a term paper					
4	Advice about a career					
5	Assistance with writing					
6	Assistance with technology					
7	The place to appeal a grade					
8	A place to safely complain about harassment					
9	Advice about transferring to a four-year school					
10	Advice about getting into the Nursing Program					
11	Help with child care					
12	A copy of your transcript					
13	To withdraw from a course					
14	To look at a book that your instructor has placed on reserve					
15	To pay your tuition bill					

Working with Others

B4.6   Advice

What Is Group Work, and Why Do It?

Your instructors may divide classes into small groups to work on some tasks together. Groups will probably be asked to report out on their conclusions or produce a written document to be turned in or shared with the class. If you're not sure why instructors include group work in the course, here are four important reasons why they do:

1. **Group work almost always involves a process known as *active learning* or *discovery learning*.**   In more traditional classrooms, students learn by listening to instructors as they deliver information by means of lectures. In active learning, students learn information by solving a problem or studying examples. They *actively* discover information for themselves, and there is considerable research to support the idea that what students learn through active learning stays with them longer that what they learn through lectures.

2. **Group work creates more of a community in the classroom.**   Students get to know each other and develop a network of other students whom they can ask for advice or assistance. As a result, they feel more connected to the college and have a greater sense of belonging to a community of peers.

3. **Being able to work well in a group is a skill for which many employers are looking.**   Many companies now have staff working together in groups on a wide variety of tasks, such as problem-solving design issues, creating new products, coming up with marketing campaigns, or troubleshooting bad media coverage. Being able to work well with others, share and delegate responsibilities, brainstorm as a team member, and write joint responses to specific prompts or questions are all skills that prove very useful to students when they look for jobs.

4. **Group work can be fun.**   Once students get over any initial anxiety, most find participating in group work much more enjoyable than listening to a lecture.

Tips for Successful Group Participation

Here are some tips to help you participate successfully in group work:

1. **Come to class prepared.**   If a reading was assigned, make sure you have read it. If you were supposed to bring a draft of an essay, make sure you bring it. If you

were supposed to do anything else in preparation for the class, make sure you have done it.

2. **Participate.** Everyone feels a little anxiety about expressing their ideas in a group at first, but once you join in, you will find it's easier than you expected. It's certainly more fun and more helpful if you are actively involved.

3. **Avoid dominating the conversation.** Talking too much can be as harmful to the group as not participating. Take the time to listen to and understand the ideas expressed by other members of your group in addition to sharing your own thoughts and opinions.

4. **Perform any assigned role diligently.** Sometimes it's easy to get so caught up in the discussion that you forget to take notes, keep track of time, or perform some other assigned task. But for a group to work well, you need to fulfill your responsibilities.

5. **Listen carefully to what your classmates are saying.** Responding appropriately and politely is crucial to good group dynamics.

6. **Be respectful of everyone's opinions.** Avoid being judgmental.

7. **Take on your share of the responsibilities.** Make sure you come to class prepared to participate, that you make your share of contributions to the group's efforts, and that you follow through on any tasks assigned.

Tips for Group Success

Here are some tips to help groups be more successful.

1. **Understand the assignment.** Make sure every member shares the same understanding of the task the group is asked to perform.

2. **Make a plan.** Plan how you are going to use the allocated time.

3. **Manage time.** Keep an eye on the clock. If you've used half your time and are still discussing the first task of three, you need to move on.

4. **Assign roles.** If the instructor hasn't assigned roles, the group should decide who will take on which roles themselves. If there is to be a written project, who is going to do the actual writing? If the group will be asked to report out at the end of their work, who will do this reporting?

5. **Be flexible about settling disagreements.** Sometimes a compromise can be reached. Sometimes, a group has to recognize that they cannot agree and, therefore, submit two reports or a primary report and a minority report in response to the assigned task. Be polite with other group members, even if you disagree.

6. **Address "slacking."** The most common problem groups have happens when a member or two don't do their share of the work. Groups need to confront this problem directly. It is not an acceptable solution for the other members of the group to do most of the work. The group needs to confront the "slacker(s)" directly and discuss the problem. If it cannot be resolved within the group, then the instructor should be consulted. Learning how to handle slackers is an important skill that will be beneficial in the workplace.

B4.7 Exploration

Planning for Next Semester

Discuss with your group or with the class what courses you plan to take next semester and why.

Acknowledgments

Brenda Álvarez. "Teaching with an Anti-Racist Lens." From *National Education Association/ NEA Today*, September 21, 2021. Copyright © 2021 by National Education Association. Used with permission.

American Immigration Council. "How the US Immigration System Works." October 10, 2019. Copyright © 2019 by American Immigration Council. All rights reserved. Used with permission.

Gloria Anzaldúa. "The Strength of My Rebellion." Excerpt from *Borderlands/La Frontera: The New Mestiza*. Copyright © 1987, 1999, 2007, 2012 by Gloria Anzaldúa. Reprinted by permission of Aunt Lute Books. www.auntlute.com.

Julian Baggini. "The Nature of Truth." From *A Short History of Truth*. Copyright © 2017 by Julian Baggini. Reprinted with permission of David Higham Associates.

James Baldwin. "On Being 'White' . . . and Other Lies." Copyright © 1984 by James Baldwin. Originally published in *Essence Magazine*, Collected in *Cross of Redemption* by James Baldwin, published by Pantheon/Vintage. Used by arrangement with the James Baldwin Estate.

Imani Barbarin. "Disabled People Have an Ally Problem: They Need to Stop Talking for Us." From *Crutches and Spice*, May 15, 2018. Copyright © 2018 by Imani Barbarin. Used with permission.

William Burnett and David J. Evans. Introduction from *Designing Your Life: How to Build a Well-Lived, Joyful Life*, published by Vintage. Copyright © 2016 by William Burnett and David J. Evans. Used by permission of Alfred A. Knopf, an imprint of the Knopf Doubleday Publishing Group, a division of Penguin Random House LLC, and by permission of The Random House Group Ltd. All rights reserved.

Lan Cao and Harlan Margaret Van Cao. Excerpt(s) from *Family in Six Tones: A Refugee Mother, an American Daughter* by Lan Cao and Harlan Margaret Van Cao. Copyright © 2020 by Lan Cao and Harlan Margaret Van Cao. Used by permission of Viking Books, an imprint of Penguin Publishing Group, a division of Penguin Random House LLC. All rights reserved.

Mark Carman. "Gun Control. Now." https://petitions.moveon.org/sign/gun-control -now-1. Reprinted by permission of MoveOn.org.

Ta-Nehisi Coates. "Countries Have Borders: Deal with It." From *The Atlantic*, August 11, 2011. Copyright © 2011 by The Atlantic Monthly Group, Inc. All rights reserved. Distributed by Tribune Content Agency, LLC.

D'Vera Cohn. "How U.S. Immigration Laws and Rules Have Changed through History." From *Pew Research Center*, Washington, D.C. (September 30, 2015). https://www.pewresearch .org/fact-tank/2015/09/30/how-u-s-immigration -laws-and-rules-have-changed-through-history/

Luticha Doucette. "If You're in a Wheelchair, Segregation Lives." From *The New York Times*, May 17, 2017. Copyright © 2017 by The New York Times. All rights reserved. Used under license. https://nytimes.com

Daniel Goleman. Editorial review from the cover of *The Marshmallow Test: Mastering Self-Control* by Walter Mischel. Used with permission.

Mike Gonzalez. "Institutionalizing Racial Fanaticism across American Society." From *The Heritage Foundation*, May 12, 2021. Copyright © 2021 by The Heritage Foundation. Used with permission.

Anemona Hartocollis and Jacey Fortin. "Should Teachers Carry Guns? Are Metal Detectors Safe? What Experts Say." From *The New York Times*, February 24, 2018. Copyright © 2018 by The New York Times. All rights reserved. Used under license. https://nytmes.com

Dr. Kristian Henderson. "Black Girl Happiness." From *21N1nety*, February 1, 2021. Copyright © 2022 by Kristian Henderson. Used with permission.

Daniel Kahneman. Editorial review from the cover of *The Marshmallow Test: Mastering Self-Control* by Walter Mischel. Reprinted by permission.

Eric R. Kandel, MD. Quote from editorial review. Reprinted by permission of Eric R. Kandel.

Roo Kavathekar. "Educated & Independent." Used with permission.

Ibram X. Kendi. "We're Still Living and Dying in the Slaveholders' Republic." From *The Atlantic*, May 4, 2020. Copyright © 2020 by The Atlantic Monthly Group, Inc. All rights reserved. Distributed by Tribune Content Agency, LLC.

Eugene Kiely and Lori Robertson. "How to Spot Fake News." From *FactCheck.org*, November 18, 2016. Copyright © 2016. Reprinted by permission of FactCheck.org, a project of the Annenberg Public Policy Center.

Danielle Kilgo. "Unraveling the Protest Paradigm." From *Columbia Journalism Review*, April 30, 2021. Copyright © 2021 by Columbia Journalism Review. cjr.org. Used with permission.

Elizabeth Kolbert. "Why Facts Don't Change Our Minds." From *The New Yorker*, February 27, 2017. Copyright © 2017 by Conde Nast. Used with permission.

Lalit Kumar. "Models of Disability: Medical, Social, Religious, Affirmative and More. . . ." From *Wecapable.com*. Web. March 11, 2022. Copyright © 2022 by Lalit Kumar. Used with permission. https://wecapable.com/disability-models-medical-social-religious-affirmative/

Daniel J. Levitin. "Plausibility." From *A Field Guide to Lies: Critical Thinking in the Information Age* by Daniel J. Levitin, published by Viking, copyright © 2016 by Daniel J. Levitin. Used by permission of Dutton, an imprint of Penguin Publishing Group, a division of Penguin Random House LLC, and by permission of Penguin Books Limited. All rights reserved.

Hazel Rose Markus and Shinobu Kitayama. "What Is Independence and Interdependence?" (Excerpt from the article "Cultures and Selves: A Cycle of Mutual Constitution," *Perspectives on Psychological Science*, vol. 5, no. 4, pp. 420–30), 2 Aug 2010. https://doi.org/10.1177/1745691610375557. Copyright © 2010 Sage Publications. Republished with permission of Sage Publications, permission conveyed through Copyright Clearance Center, Inc.

Ben Mattlin. "'Cure' Me? No, Thanks." From *The New York Times*, March 22, 2017. Copyright © 2017 by The New York Times. All rights reserved. Used under license. https://nytimes.com

Walter Mischel. From *The Marshmallow Test: Why Self-Control Is the Engine of Success* by Walter Mischel. Copyright © 2014 by Walter Mischel. Reprinted by permission of Little, Brown Spark, an imprint of Hachette Book Group, Inc., and Penguin Books Limited.

Walter Mischel, Yuichi Shoda, and Monica L. Rodriguez. "Delay of Gratification in Children." Vol. 244, Issue 4907, May 26, 1989. Copyright © 1989 by the American Association for the Advancement of Science. Republished with permission of the American Association for the Advancement of Science, permission conveyed through Copyright Clearance Center, Inc.

Jonathan Mooney. "You Are Special! Now Stop Being Different." From *The New York Times*, February 23, 2021. Copyright © 2021 by The New York Times. All rights reserved. Used under license. https://nytimes.com

Wayétu Moore. "How the Africans Became Black." From *The Atlantic*, December 13, 2012. Copyright © 2012 by The Atlantic Monthly Group, Inc. All rights reserved. Distributed by Tribune Content Agency, LLC.

Viet Thanh Nguyen. "Advice for Artists Whose Parents Want Them to Be Engineers." From *The New York Times*, July 8, 2021. Copyright © 2021 by The New York Times. All rights reserved. Used under license. https://nytimes.com

Robert Nisbet. "The Quest for Community" (excerpt). Copyright © 2010 by Intercollegiate Studies Institute. Used with permission.

Timothy Noah. "The Great Divergence: America's Growing Inequality Crisis and What We Can Do About It." Copyright © 2012 by Timothy Noah. Reprinted by permission of Bloomsbury Publishing Inc.

Our Revolution. "Medicare for All." https://ourrevolution.com/2021/06/05/m4a/. Reprinted by permission.

Danielle Paquette. "What It's Like to Graduate from College with the Lowest-Paying Major." From *The Washington Post*, September 29, 2014. Copyright © 2014 by The Washington Post. All rights reserved. Used under license. https://washingtonpost.com

PETA. "The Issues." From *PETA.org/issues*. Reprinted with permission of People for the Ethical Treatment of Animals (PETA). All rights reserved.

Steven Pinker. "Preface" and "Words and Worlds." From *The Stuff of Thought: Language as a Window into Human Nature* by Steven Pinker, published by Allen Lane, copyright © 2007, 2008 by Steven Pinker. Used by permission of Viking Books, an imprint of Penguin Publishing Group, a division of Penguin Random House LLC, and by permission of Penguin Books Ltd. All rights reserved.